Fast Vegetarian Feasts

Also By Martha Rose Shulman

THE VEGETARIAN FEAST

FAST VEGETARIAN FEASTS

THE REVISED EDITION
WITH FISH

MARTHA ROSE SHULMAN

MAIN STREET BOOKS

DOUBLEDAY

NEW YORK LONDON TORONTO SYDNEY AUCKLAND

A MAIN STREET BOOK
PUBLISHED BY DOUBLEDAY
a division of Bantam Doubleday Dell Publishing Group, Inc.
1540 Broadway, New York, New York 10036

MAIN STREET BOOKS, DOUBLEDAY and the portrayal of a
building with a tree are trademarks of Doubleday, a
division of Bantam Doubleday Dell Publishing Group, Inc.

The recipes for tofu "Dipping Sauces" on pages 132–33 and for "Guacamole" on page 243 are from *The Vegetarian Feast* copyright © 1979 by Martha Rose Shulman, published by Harper & Row, Publishers, Inc., and reprinted with their permission.

Illustrations from *Food and Drink, A Pictorial Archive from Nineteenth-Century Sources* selected by Jim Harter used with permission of Dover Publications, Inc.

DESIGN BY GINGER LEGATO

Library of Congress Cataloging-in-Publication Data
Shulman, Martha Rose.
  Fast vegetarian feasts.
  Includes index.
  ISBN 0-385-23330-2
  1. Vegetarian cookery. I. Title.
TX837.S4678   1986   641.5'636   86-8838

FOR MY SISTER

ACKNOWLEDGMENTS

As ALWAYS, I am indebted to all my eaters, but especially to Jackie and Steve Van Erp, both for having faithful appetites and for being helpful critics. I am also grateful to Irene Goss, who did the metric equivalencies.

My thanks to my editors, Frances McCullough and Rick Kot, not only for their invaluable editorial assistance, but also for their unfailing good humor and good company.

I could not have brought this book to completion without the help of my friends Mary Collins and Maggie Megaw, who shut themselves up with me in our Paris apartment for a week to read and correct galleys, double-check page references, and lend their moral support.

And finally, again, thanks to my mother, Mary, for her constant support and enthusiasm.

M.R.S.
August 1981

CONTENTS

PREFACE TO THE NEW EDITION

IN SEPTEMBER 1981, I left Austin, Texas, my home of ten years; drove to Montreal with as much cooking equipment, cookbooks, and clothes as I could fit into my car; and sailed to Europe. Paris was my final destination; I was coming here for an "open-ended year." If things worked out, I'd stay. Things worked out.

I delivered my manuscript for the first edition of this book, then called *Fast Vegetarian Feasts,* to my editor, Frances McCullough, at her house in Hastings-on-Hudson on my way to Montreal, finishing up the last pages in Holiday Inns along the way. But during my first week in Paris I decided to add one last recipe, the Fruit and Cheese Platter in the desserts chapter (page 322); this seemed the fitting place to research such a listing, especially when I found out that one of the best cheese stores in Paris is a five-minute walk from my apartment.

The French approach to vegetarianism is a little different from the American approach. In the United States most people assume that vegetarian cuisine involves no flesh of any kind—no meat, fish, or poultry. Here, when I tell people I write vegetarian cookbooks, first they ask me if I'm a vegetarian, then, a little disbelieving and perhaps uncomprehending, they say: "*Mais vous mangez un peu de viande quand même* [But you do eat some meat, don't you?]"; then they assume I eat chicken and fish. They are always a little relieved when I tell them I eat fish, and how much I love it.

The essential nature of my diet hasn't changed too much since my arrival here, except that there is more variety to it, because every day I walk through beautiful markets where the seasonal choice of vegetables and fruits is outstanding. I can get all the grains, beans, tofu, and flours that I worked with in the United States, and have had no trouble preparing the recipes in the first edition of this book. My copy is now dog-eared and frayed after three years of constant use.

But in one respect my diet has changed: I eat a great deal more fish than I ate in the States. I've discovered that I adore oysters, fresh and briny without even any lemon juice to interfere with their purity of flavor, and mussels, simply steamed in wine. During their "season" (the late fall and winter), I get cravings for these mollusks. I've tried all kinds of fish and know what kinds I prefer. Before coming here I ate fish, mostly sole and redfish, at restaurants, but rarely did I prepare it at home. In France all the different varieties of fish are as tempting as the produce, and my responsibilities as a caterer, private cook, and director of my own private "supper club" have led me into more and more fish cookery.

I've been strongly influenced by and have learned a lot from my friend Lulu Peyraud, the wife of a winemaker at Domaine Tempier, a vineyard in Bandol, on the Mediterranean coast of France. Lulu is a fabulous cook; her bouillabaisse was the first one I ever ate, and it's still the best. I spent three weeks cooking with her during the harvest in 1981, after I'd been in France only a few weeks. She always made fish for me, even if she was preparing meat for the other workers. She is from Marseille, which is a great port, known for its bouillabaisse, and she knows everything there is to know about seafood. I would go with her to the docks when the fishing boats came in and watch her pick the most beautiful of the day's catch. I learned about grilling fish from Lulu, and it was in her lovely Provençal kitchen that I was introduced to many of the dishes that you will find in the new fish chapter in this book. I still call her when I have a question about some kind of seafood preparation.

As I became a more serious fish cook, I grew curious about the availability of fish in the United States. Every time I go home I wander into fish markets, where I'm impressed by the variety. Even many health-food stores, like the beautiful Whole Foods Markets in Austin, San Antonio, and Houston, have fish counters, where you can count on getting the freshest fish possible. Clearly, Americans are eating more fish, probably because they're eating less meat.

As I've never been a vegetarian for moral or ideological reasons, I do not feel that my increasing involvement with these sea creatures is contradictory to the principles of my cuisine, which I define simply as eclectic, low-fat, and delicious. Fish is light, high in protein, low in fat and calories, and high in minerals, especially calcium, phosphorus, and potassium. It is easy to digest and has a simple, fresh, satisfying taste. For the busy cook fish is a godsend, because it can be so easy and quick to prepare.

That is why I and my editors have decided to do a new edition of *Fast Vegetarian Feasts*. So many of the fish recipes I've developed over the last four years fit perfectly into the format of the book. They are not intended to replace existing material, but by adding the chapter I hope to help you expand your repertoire, just as mine has filled out over the years. As I've often said, many if not most of my readers are not strict vegetarians (nor, for that matter, am I), and the more material I can provide in one book, the better. I hope you will enjoy the new recipes as much as I do.

MARTHA ROSE SHULMAN
Paris, May 1985

INTRODUCTION

FOR THE PAST FEW years, people have not been running in the opposite direction as often when I tell them that my special food area is vegetarian. One out of two responds with "I'm not a vegetarian, but I don't eat meat every night." Many tell me they've cut red meat out of their diets altogether. For some the reasons are economical, while others want to eat less fat or just want a lighter diet. Whatever the motives, it's clear that the American diet is changing.

But the word "vegetarian" still does have its stigma, and I continue to search for a better term. I feel, however, that I must use it, if only to clarify the point that I don't use meat in my cooking. But it's almost beside the point, since my food is delicious, festive and healthy, and not based on a cult, but on cuisines from many countries, including our own. I have never been "against" eating meat, and am thankful that old friends know and new acquaintances quickly understand that I'm not "that" kind of vegetarian. Just the other night a friend who is a great cook invited me for dinner, and she served a beautiful roast leg of lamb. Though I skipped the main course, with the luscious hors d'oeuvres, puree of artichoke, and hazelnut soup, Caesar salad, goat cheese, and strawberry sorbet I had plenty to eat, and I especially appreciated the fact that my hostess felt no qualms about serving lamb in my presence.

I am a vegetarian for the same reasons that most people choose not to eat meat every night. I enjoy a diet that is low in fat, light on the stomach, and economical. I ate vast quantities of meat as a child, but as it is now I've lost my desire for it (though I do occasionally eat fish).

As far as my cooking goes, I've hardly made a dent in vegetables and whole foods. My diet is both sensuous and sensible; there is much more protein available from vegetable sources than from animals. Most of the world has always lived eating meat only when it was around, or eaten it in moderation. Our culture has somehow established it as a given that we must eat pound after pound of animal protein to survive. But we are just beginning, as a country, to see that this isn't the case. Indeed, if we continue to consume such vast, fat-laden amounts of meat, we *won't* survive; our hearts will stop pumping well before their times.

I have spent almost nine years drawing on many cultures to develop a cuisine that is healthy and enticing. When I first decided to make a career out of this passion of mine, I ran a once-a-week "supper club," which eventually turned into a catering service. I developed dishes that proved once and for all that vegetarian dining need not be dull or ascetic.

I succeeded with this fare, but there was one problem with many of the meals. Not a problem for the eater, but for the cook: the preparation of the food took too much time. I had always insisted that vegetarian cooking was not time consuming, that this was one of the "myths of vegetarianism." But some of my favorite specialties really did take a lot of effort. I came to realize that my perspective was different because while I was a working person, my office was my kitchen. Spending hours in it was something I was used to doing; I did not come home at night faced with the problem of turning out a meal; they were always there for me, the product of a day's work.

I then began to listen to friends who were trying in earnest to change their diets but were having trouble because of the time involved. A good example was my friend Rachelle, a second-year medical student who had eaten my food for a month and had felt so good that she and her husband Terry had decided to stop eating meat. Being a medical student is synonymous with having no free time, and Rachelle was distressed by the fact that she was spending weekends, when she should have been studying, preparing food for the week. It upset me too; I was sure that a vegetarian diet needn't take up so much time. I decided to look into the matter of helping people assemble fast meatless dinners that were healthy and delicious.

I got to work at once, and was soon immersed in the project that became this book. The challenge was always to simplify while retaining enough ingredients to make the dish tasty and special. Beyond a certain point the food would have fallen into that hair-shirt vegetarian bracket, and I decided it was worth it to take those few extra minutes to grate fresh ginger or measure out herbs. What I did do away with were dishes that involved several steps, like casseroles whose components must first be cooked, then assembled and baked. The recipes in this book are straightforward, involving two to three steps: the first step is ingredient preparation—the chopping and measuring (anywhere from 5 to 20 minutes)—the second is supervised cooking, and the third unsupervised. Unsupervised cooking requires no work on your part. It is the time when the grains, beans, or vegetables are cooking. During that period you can relax, take a bath, have a drink, or prepare the rest of the meal.

As I explored my files and cookbooks, I found a wealth of material that would meet my needs. I tested recipes feverishly, sometimes as many as ten a day. (If these were to be "fast vegetarian feasts" I ought to be able to cook ten in five hours; and indeed I could.) I worked first with soups, which are such simple, delightful dishes to base meals on, and with the grain, legume, tofu, and vegetable dishes that appear here on pages 91–173. Then it occurred to me that tacos would be a perfect quick dinner, because you serve them up as you make them, or let people assemble their own. I had a few taco dinner parties, and suddenly there was another chapter for the book. I'd always known how important pasta was for easy vegetarian meals; I'd used pasta dishes for years to prove my point that vegetarianism need not take a great deal of time. I also knew I could come up with enough cheese and egg dishes to fill a chapter, and I never worried about salads and desserts.

In addition to ease and speed in preparation, I concerned myself with balancing protein and keeping fats low. Having cooked for heart patients for a month, I knew how necessary it is for us to have on hand a number of delicious low-fat recipes that will also supply adequate protein.

The problem, as it turned out, was deciding when to stop. Even as I write this introduction there are recipes waiting to be typed, discoveries I decided at the last minute that I couldn't leave out. But my friends, and many people I've only recently met, are impatient for this collection. For we are a nation of busy people with little time, but we want to live and eat well. So for all of you, here it is, *Fast Vegetarian Feasts*.

KEEPING PROTEIN UP AND FATS DOWN

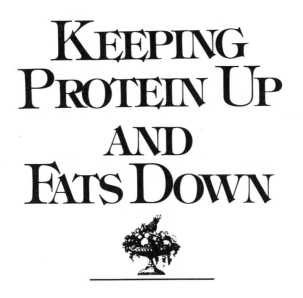

PROTEIN COMPLEMENTARITY

For most people, the big mystery in vegetarian eating remains how to obtain enough protein. It is an easy problem to solve. In order to obtain complete protein at a meal you must do one of the following:

1. Combine beans and grains in relatively equal amounts.
2. Combine beans and dairy products (you need less dairy than beans).
3. Combine grains and dairy products (you need less dairy than grains).
4. Include dairy products or eggs somewhere in your meal (this could be in the dessert, as a soufflé or pudding).
5. Include tofu or other soy products somewhere in your meal (as with eggs and dairy products, this could be in the dessert).

All of the above are high-protein foods or combinations. A protein is a long chain of molecules called amino acids. When we refer to the protein we obtain from food we're talking specifically about eight of these amino acids. They all exist in an equal proportion in meat, fish, dairy products, eggs, tofu, and soybeans. That's why we can eat these foods alone and obtain "complete protein." Grains and legumes, however, are high in some amino acids and low in others. Taken together, though, their protein quality is high, because grains have those amino acids which beans lack, and vice versa. Beans and grains can therefore be said to "complement" each other. Dairy products, tofu, soy, and eggs are high in all the amino acids, and so will complement both beans *and* grains. Foods of different amino acid patterns that when combined form complete protein are said to contain "complementary proteins." The complementarity of protein is really a simple concept, one I always work with when I compose dishes and menus. Thus I include soy flakes in brown rice risotto, tofu in my Spicy Eggplant-Miso Sauté with Bulgur (page 122), soy grits with fried rice. Beans and cornbread were made for each other, and lentils complement rice. If, in a given menu, a dish does not contain complete protein on its own, I will recommend another course in which you can obtain it. This may even be dessert, in the form of a puffed omelet. Why not?

FATS

People are always asking me how I manage to stay so thin if I'm a cook. It's an easy question to answer: because my diet is grain-oriented, it's naturally low in fats. I eat as much whole-grain bread as I please, but because I don't put butter on it, the pounds stay off. When I make a dish that involves stir-frying or sautéing I keep the butter or oil at a minimum. In fact, I've found that I can take almost any given recipe that lists butter or oil for frying and cut the amount by half. You usually just don't need 3 tablespoons of butter to sauté a single onion. The flavor may be important, but a little goes a long way. If you don't cook foods at very high heat, or if you use good-quality nonstick cookware like Silverstone, you can keep the quantity of oils you use low. As long as you are there to stir, foods will not stick.

In fact, in the same way that I've lost my appetite for meat, large amounts of butter and oil no longer appeal to me. I appreciate their flavor and the way they enhance food, but when there is a surfeit, I feel that my system has been coated, "oiled" with something I don't want. I suffer after too rich a meal with a "food hangover" every bit as debilitating as an alcoholic one, for it's the liver that must work overtime to metabolize these fatty foods.

Salad dressings and sauces are another group of foods that traditionally depend on a great deal of fat, but needn't. In my never-ending quest to keep fats low but quality high I've developed salad dressings and sauces whose creamy qualities come from blended-up vegetables, tofu, or yogurt. My heady sauce for braised artichokes is thickened with arrowroot, my "cream" soups with pureed potatoes.

While I do include several cheese- and egg-based dishes in this book, they are outnumbered about three to one by the grain, legume, tofu, and vegetable recipes. To my mind, a rich dish is one that lingers on the palate and excites the senses. Fortunately, many foods that are naturally low in fat can achieve this, for butter is not the only thing that can melt in your mouth.

COOKING FOR THE HEART

FOR THOSE OF YOU with heart conditions, cutting down on fats and eliminating salt is really a matter of life and death. Many of these recipes will be fine for you; indeed, you'll be pleased to see that most of the dishes in this book, including the desserts, can be eaten with safety, or can be adapted. Wherever a heart symbol (♥) appears next to a recipe, that dish is acceptable for low-salt and low-fat dishes; but you *must check* the note following the text of the recipe to see how you should alter it. For example, a grain and vegetable dish will be fine if you omit the tamari called for and reduce the amount of oil, say from 1 tablespoon to 2 teaspoons (15–10 ml). If there are no modifications following the recipes, then proceed with them as they are written, as long as they are marked with the (♥) symbol. If they are not, find another dish. If you have questions about recipes, you should consult your physician.

Cheese and egg dishes, of course, and many of the soups cannot be adapted. There is just no way to make a tamari-bouillon broth without salt, as salt is its principal ingredient. The soups that are light and brothy, like the Simple Garlic Soup Provençal on page 64 may be disappointingly bland without salt. However, thicker bean-based soups like the Lentil and Tomato Soup with Pasta (page 84) or the Thick Split Pea and Rice Soup (page 83) have enough flavor, as do some of the purees and cold soups.

INGREDIENTS: STOCKING THE LARDER

A FRIEND RECENTLY told me that she loves to read my weekly recipe column in the newspaper but never has any of the ingredients for the dishes. My response: Go out and get them. All you have to do to stock up your kitchen is make one trip to a whole-foods store armed with the list on the following pages. Once you have filled the larder, you will find that vegetarian meals are, in fact, remarkably convenient. You will only have to shop for produce, tofu, and dairy products, because, stored in well-sealed jars, dry goods will keep for months.

During the month of September 1980, I was the menu planner and cook for a cardiology study which took place at an isolated resort on a lake, fifty miles from the nearest natural foods stores. I cooked three meals a day for thirty-five people and certainly had no time for marketing trips. Before I began, I loaded a station wagon with big bags of grains, beans, and other dry goods and brought them out to my makeshift kitchen, where I set up a beautiful pantry. People loved to come and look at all the different dry foods, so many of which they were just learning to eat. We ordered produce every other day, but our staples were always on hand. And because the staples were so economical, my food budget was impressively low: I served large, healthful meals and still spent little more than a dollar per person per meal.

A natural foods store can be intimidating if you're unfamiliar with its stock. But shopping at these stores can be a very pleasant experience, because the people who work there usually live on a vegetarian diet and are very willing to take the time to explain things to you. So don't be afraid to ask questions. Well-informed retailers are one of the great assets of the health food industry.

If you are a novice, there are two ways you can go about stocking up. You can shop recipe by recipe, building up your collection of grains, legumes, and so on, as you go along. Then, if you find that you don't like a particular food, you won't be left with a large quantity to use up. Or, you can plunge and buy a number of basic ingredients. This may leave you with an overwhelming supply; on the other hand, it may encourage you to try some unfamiliar foods.

Whichever method you choose, arrive at your natural foods store with a list of supplies you need. Although dry goods are all sold packaged as well as in bulk, it is more economical to buy in bulk whenever possible. Ingredients are often sold from large bins or barrels; just scoop out the amount that you need. If the foods you are buying this way are completely new to you, *label your bags,* because by the time you get home you might not be able to identify what you've bought.

Before you buy your dry goods, purchase a case or two of mason jars and label them. Rather than placing a pile of bags on your shelf, you can line it with jars full of colorful beans and grains. You'll feel that your larder could sustain you forever.

The list that follows is by no means an exhaustive inventory of natural foods. It will, however, describe the staples you need for the recipes in this book.

GRAINS
Store in well-sealed jars in a cool, dry place.

Barley: Similar in appearance to brown rice. Barley swells when you cook it and has a wonderful, nutty flavor. It's chewy and delicious in soups (especially with mushrooms; see page 73) and pilaffs (see page 127), and also makes a great stuffing.

Brown rice: Probably the most familiar of the whole grains. Both long and short grains are available in supermarkets and whole-foods stores.

Buckwheat groats: Brown, pyramid-shaped grains (actually buckwheat is not a grain but a member of the rhubarb family) that are also called "kasha" (a name used as well for cooked buckwheat groats). Buckwheat groats have the most distinctive flavor of any of the grains and make delicious pilaffs and stuffings. They are a good source of protein and B-vitamins, and are lower in calories than rice and corn.

Both light (untoasted) and dark (toasted) buckwheat groats are available; the dark groats have an earthier, richer flavor. Some stores also sell unhulled groats for sprouting. Don't buy these for cooking, as the hulls will float to the surface of your pilaff or soup.

Bulgur: Cracked wheat that has been precooked and dried. Bulgur is one of the fastest grains to prepare. All you have to do is cover it with hot water and let it stand for half an hour. You can also marinate it in a salad dressing for about an hour or two and not even bother with the hot water. Bulgur has a nutty taste and fluffy texture.

Couscous: Another precooked cracked-wheat product, made from hard white semolina wheat. The most elegant grain, it has a satiny texture and is very light. To prepare, pour on water (right from the tap is fine), wait 15 minutes, and fluff with a fork. Couscous is available in imported foods stores and fancy foods sections of supermarkets if you can't find it in whole-foods stores.

Cracked wheat: A cracked-wheat product that differs from bulgur in that it hasn't been precooked. It resembles bulgur, which can be substituted for it (though not vice versa). Cracked wheat is good in breads and cooked for breakfast like oatmeal.

Millet: A pretty, delicate round grain, yellow in color. It cooks like rice but is lighter, and has a nutty, subtle flavor. With honey, it is as tasty for breakfast as it is as a side dish, plain, for dinner.

Oats (rolled and flaked): Oat flakes and rolled oats are synonymous with oatmeal (but not the instant variety). Use them in breads, cookies, casseroles, and soups as well as for breakfast.

Rye (whole and flaked): Whole rye resembles dark long-grain brown rice. It can be used like rice, but it takes longer to cook and has a harder hull. Whole rye is especially good in soups. Flaked rye looks like dark oatmeal and can be used in the same ways. Rye has a distinctive, somewhat salty, earthy taste.

Triticale (pronounced *tri-ti-kay-lee*): A hybrid of wheat and rye, it can be substituted for either, and also for rice. It resembles whole rye, is very tasty, and is higher in protein than either of its parent grains.

Wheat germ: Wheat germ is the embryo of the wheat kernel, as flakes are high in oil, protein, and vitamins (especially E and B). They should be kept refrigerated. Raw wheat germ can be toasted in a slow oven (20 to 30 minutes at 250 degrees; 120°C) and sprinkled over yogurt, salads, and fruits. It's frequently eaten as a cereal, or added to granola; it also makes a nutritious addition to breads and other baked goods.

Whole wheat berries and flaked wheat: The whole grains from which wheat flour is ground. They are a rich brown color, and are similar in appearance to rice, but the grains are larger. You can use them in place of rice, but like rye, they take longer to cook and require more water. Wheat berries have a marvelous sweet taste and make nice sprouts. The flakes make a chewy, filling cereal with a texture like that of oatmeal.

FLOURS
These are made from the grains listed above and from some of the beans listed below. Although this book does not include many bread recipes, I am listing the flours to familiarize you with them. Because the flours that are not derived from wheat have an insufficient gluten content, they must be used in conjunction with wheat flour to achieve good loaves of yeasted bread.

Store in well-sealed jars in the refrigerator or freezer.

Buckwheat
Cornmeal (A staple—have this on hand.)
Garbanzo or chick-pea flour
Millet meal
Oat flour
Rice flour
Rye flour
Soy flour
Triticale flour
Whole-wheat and whole-wheat pastry flour (Have these on hand.)
Unbleached white flour

PASTAS
There is an unbelievable variety of whole-grain pastas on the market, formed in different shapes and made from different mixtures of flours. Compared to enriched white pasta, they may seem heavy, but I find them much tastier. Pasta is a true convenience food, taking only minutes to cook, so have several kinds on hand.

Store in well-sealed jars in a cool, dry place.

Buckwheat noodles: Often called *soba,* these noodles have a distinctive, nutty taste and are used in a number of the recipes in this collection.

LEGUMES

Each kind of bean has its own distinctive flavor. Try them all and choose your favorites, to have on hand whenever you have a taste for them.

Store in well-sealed jars in a cool, dry place.

Aduki beans: Small red Japanese beans, not as large as red beans. Delicate in flavor, they go nicely with grains.

Black beans: Very black (well, some would say deep purple) medium-sized beans that make a rich soup and a delicious enchilada or taco filling. Excellent refried.

Black-eyed peas (or cowpeas): Medium-sized, oval-shaped, creamy white with a black spot on one side. These have a savory flavor all their own and have always been a favorite of mine. Good as a main dish or side dish, especially with cornbread. Serve them on New Year's Day for good luck.

Cannelini: White beans, slightly larger than navies and a little fluffier in texture.

Chick-peas or garbanzos: Large and round with a nutty, distinctive flavor. Canned chick-peas don't compare. Wonderful in salads and spreads.

Kidney beans: Large, red, and kidney shaped. Good in salads, soups, and chili.

Lentils: Both red and yellow lentils are available in addition to the familiar brown variety. Lentils make marvelous, peppery sprouts, great soups, and combine nicely with rice.

Limas: Broad, flat and white. I prefer dried limas to fresh ones for textural reasons (fresh, they are more mealy). Best in soups and casseroles.

Navy or Great Northern beans: Medium-sized white beans. Along with small white beans, these are, in my opinion, the most elegant of the legumes. A must in minestrone and other vegetable soups; they also make a superb pureed soup (page 74), a delicious pâté (page 55), and one of my favorite salads (page 294).

Small white beans (or Boston or pea beans): Just like navies except smaller, and just as good. They can cook a long time and still retain their shape.

Peanuts: Also considered a legume, though we eat them like nuts. Like all dried legumes, they have to be cooked or roasted to be digestible.

Pintos: Medium-sized, beige-colored speckled beans, most often used in Tex-Mex food. They have a more delicate flavor than kidney beans and are not as rich as black beans.

Mung beans: Very small round green beans that make excellent sprouts. Mung beans are quite high in protein.

Split peas: You'll see yellow ones as well as the common green variety. Wonderful for soups (see page 83).

Soybeans: The king of the beans, as far as nutrients are concerned. They are the richest in protein and B vitamins of all the legumes, and the lowest in carbohydrates. From soybeans we get tofu (high-protein bean curd), soy milk, soy flour, and tempeh (a fermented soy product with high protein and B_{12} content). Unfortunately, cooked soybeans are not too palatable alone, but they are a fine component in casseroles and soups, and a good base for pâté. For a tasty soy pâté, refer to my first cookbook, *The Vegetarian Feast* (Harper & Row, 1979).

Soy flakes: Soybeans that have been cooked, split, and dehydrated. Because they take only 30 minutes to cook and are as high in nutrients as soybeans, they are a perfect high-protein convenience food. Soy flakes can always be substituted in recipes for soybeans.

Soy grits: Cracked soybeans. These are a nutritious addition to grain dishes (you can cook them along with the grains), have a nutty texture and taste, and take only 40 minutes to cook—another good convenience food.

NUTS AND SEEDS
Store in jars in the freezer or refrigerator.

Almonds
Pecans
Sesame seeds
Sunflower seeds
Walnuts

OILS

Most of the oils sold in health food stores are cold-pressed oils, which means that the oil is extracted without using heating and chemical processes that cause a loss of nutrients. Because they are not refined, their colors are darker and their flavors stronger than the oils you may be accustomed to. Some are more subtle than others. It's important to refrigerate all these oils once you open them to avoid rancidity, *even if it doesn't say so on the bottle.*

Olive oil: Try to find virgin olive oil. Some of these are sweet, some very strong. I like Provençal oil, and a California brand called Sciabacus. Use in salad dressings and garlicky dishes, especially Italian ones.

Peanut oil: Has a nutty, earthy flavor and an amber color. It is high in saturated fats, and becomes solid when refrigerated. Peanut oil is good for stir-fried dishes and curries, but too strong-flavored for salad dressings and baking. Safflower oil may be substituted.

Safflower oil: The most versatile. Safflower has a mild, slightly nutty flavor, is low in saturated fats, and is economical.

Sesame oil: Has the rich, strong flavor of sesame seeds. Sesame oil is wonderful as a flavoring in Oriental dishes, but it is not good as an all-purpose oil. It's expensive.

SWEETENERS

Honey: There are many different kinds and grades of honey, produced from a variety of flowers. The lighter the color, the milder the taste, and that's what you're looking for; otherwise, the flavor of honey will dominate. Honey tends to crystalize after it has been stored awhile. To remedy this, simply place it (in a jar) in a pot of water over a medium flame. Bring the water to a simmer and heat the jar until the honey melts down.

Malt syrup: A sweet, viscous syrup made from sprouted barley. It has a subtle taste and is excellent for baking. Not quite as sweet as honey, malt syrup is economical and higher in trace nutrients.

Maple syrup: Make sure it's pure and not the sugar water that many commercial brands actually are.

Molasses: A syrup separated from raw sugar during the sugar-making process. Molasses is high in minerals, especially iron. Its quality varies with the grade. Blackstrap molasses is dark, thick, and strong, but there are lighter, more subtle varieties. Don't substitute molasses for honey or malt syrup, as its flavor is so strong. High in sodium, so people on a low sodium diet should avoid it.

Sorghum syrup: This is high in minerals, like molasses, but has a much milder flavor. I often use it in baking.

MISCELLANEOUS

Alfalfa seeds: Very small seeds that make excellent sprouts. They can be found in natural foods stores, and will keep several months in a covered jar.

Arrowroot: A powdery thickener, like cornstarch. Because it tends to lump, arrowroot must be dissolved in a little water before using.

Miso: A thick paste made from fermented soybeans and grains. It's very versatile, and can be used to flavor sauces, dressings, spreads, and soups. Miso is high in protein and, like yogurt, full of lactobacilli. There are several varieties available, some quite salty, others rather sweet. For the recipes in this book, get the saltier varieties, such as hatcho miso and red miso. I store my miso in the refrigerator.

Savorex, Marmite, and Vegex: Three different brand names for the same product, a yeast extract that comes in the form of a dark, viscous paste. It adds a savory, almost meaty taste to soups, pâtés, and sauces. These products are very salty, and do not need refrigeration.

Seaweeds: *Hiziki, kombu,* and *nori* are the most common varieties. They are all different, and are used in soups and other dishes. Seaweed is sold dried and must be rehydrated. All are strong in flavor; a little goes a long way.

Spray-dried milk: A highly concentrated powdered milk, about twice as concentrated as regular instant milk. A few commercial brands, like Sanalac, contain no fat at all. Instead of using cream, use spray-dried milk to enrich milk. It keeps for several months in a covered container.

Tahini: A raw nut butter made from sesame seeds. Tahini is delicious plain, on bread, or as a component in dips, spreads, and sauces.

Tamari-shoyu (or shoyu, or tamari): Rich, dark soy sauce made by a long, natural fermentation process. In these recipes, tamari can always be substituted for shoyu and vice versa. Different from regular soy sauce because it's naturally fermented, with no flavoring or caramel added, and aged longer.

Vegetable bouillon cubes and powders: Very important for the soups in this collection, as they free you from having to make stocks. But buy only the products sold in whole-foods stores, as many commercial brands are full of additives. Most are high in salt, but you can find lower-sodium brands. Whenever a recipe in this book calls for "vegetable bouillon," simply dissolve the cubes in boiling water according to the directions on the package. I sometimes double the amount of water for a milder, less salty broth.

A WORD ABOUT TOFU

Tofu isn't a larder staple—you have to buy it fresh either from the produce section of your supermarket or the dairy case in your natural foods store, or from Oriental markets and produce stands, and keep it refrigerated. But it's an ingredient you should always have on hand and learn to work with, because you can make a meal in minutes with it, as well as delicious sauces, dressings, and desserts.

Tofu is bean curd made from soy milk. Soy milk is heated to the boiling point, a curdling agent is added, and the curds are separated from the whey. These curds are pressed together to make tofu. It is the equivalent of cheese made from soy, but is very low in fat compared to regular cheese. Tofu is my mainstay. It's a miracle food, high in protein, economical and versatile. A 4-ounce (100 gm) serving, which yields roughly 8 grams of usable protein (the same as many varieties of fish), costs about $1.15 per pound (450 gm). It's also very low in calories—4 ounces (100 gm) have about 72. Tofu keeps well, although the fresher it is, the better. (I have kept it in my refrigerator for as long as a week.) The white cakes come water packed, and you must change the water every day or two. If you forget for a day, don't worry. If your refrigerator is good, your tofu shouldn't spoil.

By itself tofu is bland and, unless you're a fanatic like me (I eat it plain, and sometimes season it only with soy sauce, on whole-wheat bread), it's not especially appetizing. But because of its porosity it absorbs the flavors of the foods it's cooked or blended with, creating a wide range of possibilities for its use, as you can see in the recipes that follow. See, among others, Chinese-style Tofu and Vegetables with Grains (page 138), Spicy Eggplant-Miso Sauté with Bulgur (page 122), and Tofu Vegetable Curry (page 136).

Tofu can also be cooked in a number of different forms. It can be broiled like a cutlet, pressed to take on a firm consistency so it has the texture of chicken, deep-fried in batter, or sautéed. It can be marinated and eaten as a simple meal or an hors d'oeuvre with dipping sauces (see page 132). It can be slivered into soups, or crumbled into salads. It can be mashed with vegetables and seasonings for a sandwich spread or blended to make a marvelous sauce or dressing. I make a cheese substitute and cream sauce with tofu and use it in delicious low-fat gratins (see pages 142 and 143), and on pasta and other sauced dishes. Not only does this sauce taste wonderful, but it's a perfect way to cut down on fat and cholesterol at no expense to the palate. If you are as delighted with this food as I am, cheese will slowly disappear from your everyday diet and your pocketbook will expand in inverse proportion to your waistline.

HERBS AND SPICES

Good-quality herbs and spices make all the difference in many of the recipes in this book. Designate an area away from your stove (heat dries them out) and store your herbs and spices in alphabetical order. That way, you can locate them easily and won't knock half of them over when you're reaching for those called for in specific recipes. This will cut down on time.

The best way to learn about herbs and spices is to use them. The following lists are only partial, but they will cover what is called for in these recipes.

Herbs (dried):
Basil
Bay leaves
Cumin
Dillweed
Marjoram
Oregano
Rosemary
Sage
Tarragon
Thyme

Herbs (fresh): Store these in a jar in a little water, covered with a lid or plastic bag fastened to the jar with a rubber band. Or grow them and pick them when you need them.

Basil
Cilantro (fresh coriander, or Chinese parsley)

Dill
Marjoram (if at all possible)
Mints
Parsley

Spices:
Allspice (whole and ground)
Anise seeds
Caraway seeds
Cardamom
Chili powder
Cinnamon (stick and ground)
Cloves (whole and ground)
Coriander seeds
Cumin seed (whole and ground)
Curry powder
Dillseed
Ginger (dried and fresh; keep fresh, cut ginger immersed in a jar of sherry in the refrigerator)
Ground red (cayenne) pepper
Nutmeg (use whole, freshly grated whenever possible)
Black peppercorns
Red pepper flakes, or dried red peppers
Turmeric

USEFUL EQUIPMENT AND RELATED MAXIMS

CONTRARY TO POPULAR belief, "time-saving gadgets" do not always save time. I once spent an hour washing the parts to an electric pasta maker, seething all the while because I could have made the pasta by hand and rolled it out in the time it took me to clean the machine.

But there are a few items that can aid you in preparing the recipes in this book. I tested all the recipes—over two hundred of them—with the cook without-a-food-processor in mind, and kept note of what equipment eased the tasks. What is listed below is not a *batterie de cuisine,* but just a sampling of equipment that will speed up your time in the kitchen.

GOOD, SHARP KNIVES

These are the most important tools of the trade. You should have an 8-inch (20 cm) knife and a paring knife, and, if you like handling a longer one, a 10-inch (25 cm) knife. Use a good stainless brand such as J. A. Henckels-Solingen or Forschner if you are not in the habit of wiping wet knives dry. Their other advantage is that they will not discolor or react with fruit. The disadvantage of stainless is that it cannot hold as sharp an edge as carbon steel for as long a time. However, stainless knives seem to be getting better every day, and mine accompany me wherever I go.

Maxim: Hone your knives before and after every use, and sharpen them regularly. Equipment for honing and sharpening is described below. If you make this a habit, chopping will go very quickly. I often find that friends who complain about the amount of time involved in vegetarian cooking don't have sharp knives. It's also been my experience that dull knives tend to slip off vegetables and cut fingers more often than sharp ones.

A GOOD OILSTONE OR WHETSTONE AND
A SHARPENING STEEL

The stone is for sharpening the blade, the steel just for honing. You really need the stone to get a good edge, but once you achieve it you can keep it for a long time by honing your knife (sliding it toward you along the steel) on both sides after each use. I suggest you find a friend who knows how to sharpen and hone knives to give you a lesson, as there is a right way to do this.

PRESSURE COOKER

This device will change your life considerably. I didn't really use mine very often until I had to cook three meals a day for thirty-five to fifty people for a month. I then found it a great convenience for beans, which will cook in 45 to 50 minutes with no soaking at 15 pounds (7 kg) pressure. I never pressure-cook delicate, quick-cooking vegetables, but often prepare potatoes, beets, and artichokes this way all of which take 15 minutes at 15 pounds (7 kg) pressure. Your pressure cooker will come with a booklet that gives you specific times for different foods.

I do understand the fear some of you may have of this gadget. It rattles loudly and you may have heard horror stories about explosions. But pressure cookers are actually quite simple to operate if you follow these rules:

1. *Never* cook split peas, lentils, or soybeans in a pressure cooker. These legumes tend to foam and clog the safety valve, which is what causes explosions (I know all too well, as did my splattered ceiling). I also rarely cook grains in my pressure cooker because I'm afraid they'll either clog the cooker or get too mushy.

2. *Never* remove the lid before all the steam has escaped. As soon as the cooking time is up, remove the pot from the heat and transfer it immediately to the sink. Run a steady stream of cold water over the lid. The pressure cooker will soon heave a great sigh; when that subsides, remove the gauge. In a few seconds all the steam will have escaped, and the pressure cooker will be silent. *Now* you may remove the lid.

3. *Always* make certain you have enough water in your cooker so it doesn't evaporate before the end of the cooking time. Your instruction book will tell you how much water to add. If the hissing sound of steam suddenly stops while your cooker is still on the heat, that's an indication that the water has dried up. Remove from

the heat at once and run under cold water until the pressure has escaped, then remove lid and add more water.

Should you find that what you're cooking isn't ready, add some water, if necessary, return the cooker to heat, and bring again to 15 pounds (7 kg) pressure. Five additional minutes after the gauge begins to rattle should be sufficient.

General Directions for Use of the Pressure Cooker: Place ingredients with a sufficient amount of water in the cooker. Cover and place the gauge on at 15 pounds (7 kg) pressure. Turn heat on high. When the pot begins to make a hissing sound and the gauge begins to rattle, reduce heat to medium and set timer. When the time is up, remove from the heat and place in the sink. Follow directions in Rule 2.

SLOW COOKER OR CROCKPOT
These are particularly good for cooking beans. Just put in all the ingredients before you go to work and set the machine on low. When you get home they're done.

BLENDER
Essential for pureed soups, yogurt, smooth tofu sauces and other dressings and sauces. The best are the standard brands like Waring and Osterizer.

FOOD PROCESSOR
You certainly don't *need* one—sharp knives and a blender can do the same work. But I must admit, they are marvelous to have around, especially for tasks like grating cheeses and making pestos and frozen fruit ices. They don't work as well as blenders for pureeing soups, because they often leave chunks and sometimes potatoes become gummy.

Maxim: I think I appreciate mine most for grating Parmesan. Don't use the grater blade for this. Cut the Parmesan into small (1-inch; 2.5 cm) squares and place in the bowl with the steel blade. The machine will make a horrible racket when you turn it on, and will jump around for about 30 seconds, then it will run smoothly. You have to process the cheese for a while, because first the blades cut it into little specks or balls, and it will be a few more minutes before it's finely grated.

SORBETTIER
An electric ice-cream aerator which you fill with sherbet mixture

(sometimes simply pureed fruit) and set in a freezer. Then you plug it into the nearest wall socket and its blades will turn like the paddles in an ice cream freezer until your sherbet is ready. This usually takes about an hour. These don't cost much and will allow you to make any number of fruit ices simply by pureeing the fruit.

LETTUCE SPINNER

This wonderful tool will speed up the process of drying lettuce, spinach, and other greens considerably.

Maxim: Always wash spinach and lettuce all at once, ideally right after you get home from the store. Dry it, wrap it in a dish towel or tea towel and seal it (in the towel) in a plastic bag. This takes about ten minutes and will cut that time off the preparation of your meal. Wrapped in the towel and sealed in plastic, the lettuce will stay crisp for several days.

OMELET PAN

Since the omelet is the Fast Vegetarian Feast par excellence, I suggest you invest in a good omelet pan. Calphalon or Silverstone—both nonstick varieties—are my preference. They're easy to clean, you don't have to use as much butter, and you don't have to be as finicky about drying and reseasoning them as you do with other cookware.

A HEAVY 12- OR 14-INCH (30–35 CM) NONSTICK FRYING PAN

Before Silverstone, you would never have found me recommending nonstick cookware. But the substance used in this product is shot through the metal and, so, won't peel. It will, however, scratch, and you must use wooden spoons and spatulas for cooking. The reason I recommend them is that if you have a good *heavy* one, you can cook quickly with very little oil and less chance of burning than usual. When I was testing recipes I found that it was my Silverstone pan that I kept using. Shop around for these (restaurant supply houses are good places to locate them), and make sure you get one with a welded metal handle, not a plastic one, which will eventually begin to wobble.

Calphalon, a metal blend, is also good, but quite expensive.

GADGETS

A few things which will speed up tasks:

> A good potato peeler
> A citrus juicer (a hand one is fine)
> A kitchen scale

Several bowls or plastic food containers (for neatness while preparing vegetables, etc.)
A hand egg-beater or large whip for egg whites
A timer

SPROUTING LIDS OR A SPROUTING BOX

Sprouting lids are meshed caps that fit over mason jars for easy draining when making your own sprouts. Sprouting boxes are wooden frames whose plastic bottoms are perforated with small holes for draining. Both are available in natural food stores.

A Note on Skillet and Saucepan Sizes: Whenever a recipe in this book instructs you to sauté something, you should use a 10-inch (25 cm) or larger skillet. Otherwise you won't have a large enough heat surface. You can also use a wok or Dutch oven for some of these recipes.

For cooking grains, your saucepans will need to have at least a 1-quart (1 L) capacity, and preferably more.

MENUS AND SHOPPING BY THE WEEK

MY MOTHER WAS a very organized woman, and I have early memories of sitting at her desk in the kitchen and looking at her menu book, where she would have outlined two weeks' worth of meals, with extensive shopping lists. She was definitely the source of my caterer's sense of organization.

Most people, however, are not as orderly as my mother, nor do they have an interest in planning out meals in advance. So meals become a chore, especially if the kind of food you're dealing with is new to you. You might find yourself cooking rice and vegetables night after night, and finally throw up your hands.

Another problem you might run into when you do go to the grocery store, even if you have planned carefully, is impulse buying. You arrive home having spent more money than you had intended, stocked with a number of items you may never get around to cooking because you don't really know what to do with them. I myself can rarely resist a pretty artichoke at a good price, even if it's not on my shopping list. Unfortunately, I've watched more than one of those artichokes shrivel up in my refrigerator before I got around to cooking it.

I've tried to take both extremes of shopping patterns into consideration in this book. Being a busy, single woman who often eats at odd hours myself, I understand the "What am I going to have for dinner?" syndrome. My safeguard is always to have enough staples on hand (see Staples: Master List, this section, pages 28–29) around which to build a meal. For instance, if I have rice, soy flakes, and a

25

bottle of white wine, I can poach that troubling artichoke in wine and stuff it with cooked rice and soyflakes (see Stuffed Artichokes, Braised and Sauced in Wine, page 116). Along with a salad, it makes an impressive meal and the effort involved is minimal. There is a sufficient variety of recipes in this book to enable you to find a satisfactory dish for whatever you may bring home from the store.

If you are a nonplanner, turn to the index for recipe ideas. For menus you can either check this section, the Appendix (page 326), or the suggestions following the recipes themselves.

If you *are* an organizer, or would like to be, then you can make full use of the pages that follow. I have compiled four weeks' worth of menus, one week for each season, all designed with protein balance, economy, ease, and, of course, delightful eating in mind. Each week you should begin by making certain that you have each of the items on the "Staples: Master List." Then check the staple amounts to the right of the menus and note those you need to buy. Following the menus will be a list of all the fresh ingredients called for in the recipes. The list looks so long because it is designed for people who shop *by the week*. Keep in mind also that the recipes are written for four to six people; that way, you'll understand why you might need nine pounds of tomatoes for a week in which you'll make Pasta with Uncooked Tomatoes and Cheese, Gazpacho, Green Beans à la Provençale, and Tacos with Salsa Fresca. You may be used to such long shopping lists, but if not, don't be overwhelmed.

If you market a few times a week and want to use these menus, it's best to buy all the staples on one trip and turn to the individual recipes to determine when you'll need fresh ingredients.

Because my menus are meant to serve only as guides they are easily alterable. You can lighten your meals and still get enough protein and nutrients by deleting one of the vegetable side dishes. If you are not a strict vegetarian you could easily add or substitute a meat or fish dish. You can simplify menus and cut costs by serving a plain steamed vegetable instead of a more complex vegetable preparation. The same principle applies to salads and desserts: a green salad can always replace a more complicated one, and fresh fruit can always stand alone, without the costly liqueur called for in a recipe.

For example, let's take the third meal in the Spring Menus list:

Mushroom Omelet
Leftover Grains Salad
Green Beans Amandine
Peaches with Marsala

and its more than acceptable modification:

Mushroom Omelet
Tossed Green Salad
Steamed Green Beans
(or the beans could be deleted altogether)
Fresh Peaches

I'd get plenty of protein and nutrients from the omelet and the salad, and I certainly wouldn't miss the Marsala if the peaches were juicy and ripe.

Similarly, a soup and salad, with bread, can stand alone and form a satisfying meal. I have friends who insist that they live on the soups in my first book, *The Vegetarian Feast* (Harper & Row, 1979). Dinner should be a light meal, and if a menu with a soup *and* main dish looks as if it will be too filling, delete one or the other. If the soup is a very thin, light one like Simple Garlic Soup Provençal (page 64), and you want more protein, opt for deleting that course. But if you're tired and not too hungry, a light broth may be just the meal for you. If you do modify the menus, remember that the shopping lists that follow the weekly plans are designed with these specific meals in mind, so, revise your marketing list or you'll end up with too much food.

Several of the dishes in these menus, most notably the stuffed vegetables and the grain and bean salads, call for cooked grains or beans that you already have on hand. I call them "auxiliary recipes" and have asterisked them. For these you can either use leftovers from last night's meal, or cook double quantities one night with tomorrow's dinner in mind. After all, it's as easy to cook 2 cups of rice as it is to cook one, and this will eliminate the time-consuming element of two meals in one.

Use the following guide as a starting point. The Appendix includes three additional weeks' worth of menus for each season (without the shopping lists), and the individual recipes are sometimes followed by menu suggestions. As you can see, I'm determined to prove that one need never experience vegetarian doldrums.

STAPLES: MASTER LIST

These are the staples that will come up again and again in your recipes. You probably won't need nearly as much as you have on hand, but there's nothing more frustrating than having only a tablespoon (15 ml) of an ingredient when the recipe calls for three (45 ml). Check these items every week before you market, even if you're just shopping by individual recipes.

HERBS AND SPICES
Have at least 2 tablespoons (30 ml) of each on hand. (See Ingredients section, page 9.)

OTHER SEASONINGS, FLAVORINGS, SWEETENERS, AND MISCELLANEOUS INGREDIENTS
Tamari (for broths, always have 1 to 2 cups; 250–475 ml)
Vinegar (cider or wine, 1 cup; 250 ml)
Fresh ginger (a 2-inch piece, stored in a jar of sherry and refrigerated)
Mild-flavored honey (1 cup; 250 ml)
Garlic (2 heads)
Onions (2 or 3)
Dijon mustard (¼ to ½ cup; 60–120 ml)
Arrowroot or cornstarch (at least 2 tablespoons; 30 ml)
Salt
Vanilla
Vegetable bouillon cubes (12 will see you through the week, easily)
Miso
Baking soda
Baking powder (Royal is my preference, or use a low-sodium brand)
Cream of tartar
Lemons (2 or 3)

OILS
(have a pint of each on hand, except sesame oil, of which a cup is sufficient):

Olive oil
Safflower oil
Sesame oil

LIQUORS
Dry white wine (1 full bottle)
Dry sherry (1 cup; 250 ml)

NUTS AND NUT BUTTERS
(Don't go below half a cup; check recipes for additional quantities):

Tahini
Walnuts
Sesame seeds
Sunflower seeds
Almonds
Roasted soybeans (see recipe, page 60)

DRIED FRUIT
Raisins (1 cup; 250 ml)
Currants

GRAINS AND LEGUMES
Any grains and legumes in the Ingredients section will keep well. If you have a pound (450 gm) of your favorites on hand at all times, you'll eat quite well without having to run to the whole-foods store every day. In addition to the master list, staples to check specifically will be listed next to the menus on the pages that follow. Note that the liqueurs are optional. They are expensive, and, certainly, fresh fruit is marvelous without them.

SPRING MENUS

MENUS	STAPLES

MENUS

Chilled Tofu with Dipping Sauces
(page 132)
Chinese-Style Vegetables with Couscous
(page 137)
Tossed Green Salad (page 280)
Fresh strawberries

―――――

Iced Tomato Soup (page 72)
Braised Stuffed Artichokes in Wine
(page 116)
Tossed Green Salad (page 280) with
Tofu Mayonnaise (page 277)
Pineapple Banana Mint Sherbet
(page 316)

―――――

Mushroom Omelet (page 179)
Leftover Grains Salad* (page 293)
Green Beans Amandine (page 146)
Peaches with Marsala (page 314)

―――――

Spinach and Whole-Wheat Fettuccine
with Wild Mushrooms and Cheese
(page 210)
Asparagi alla Parmigiana (page 190)
Tomato Salad (page 284)
Orange Ice (page 318)

―――――

Buckwheat Noodle Soup with Green
Beans (page 63)
Warm Potato Salad with Caraway
(page 291)
Carrots with Dill (page 150)
Apricot Soufflé (page 308)

―――――

Tofu Vegetable Curry (page 136)
Millet
Curried Carrot Salad (page 284)
Pineapple with Mint

―――――

Corn Pudding (page 196)
Cauliflower Cooked in Red Wine
(page 152)
Simple Cabbage and Carrot Salad with
Fresh Herbs (page 298)
Oranges with Mint or Fruit and Cheese
Platter (page 322)

STAPLES

Check Master List

Grains and legumes:
Couscous
Soy flakes
Brown rice
Millet

Wine and optional liqueurs:
Red Wine
Marsala
Cognac
Amaretto

Miscellaneous:
6 ounces (175 gm) tomato
paste
2 small cans frozen orange
juice
1 small jar capers
1 to 2 ounces (25–50 gm)
dried mushrooms

Pasta:
1 pound (450 gm) fettuccine
½ pound (225 gm) buckwheat
noodles

Dried fruit:
1 pound (450 gm) pitted dried
apricots

*Auxiliary recipe
**Ingredients doubled for
auxiliary recipes
*See Appendix for additional menus

MARKETING FOR FRESH INGREDIENTS

Vegetables:
Eggplant: 1 medium
Onions: 3½ pounds (1.5 kg)
Zucchini: 1 pound (450 gm)
Asparagus: 3½ pounds (1.5 kg)
Lettuce (choice of Boston, leaf, red tip, romaine): 1½ pounds (700 gm)
Mushrooms: 1 pound (350 gm)
Radishes: 1 large bunch
Green onions: 2 bunches
Cucumber: 1 medium
Alfalfa sprouts: 2 cups (475 ml)
Tomatoes: 4½ pounds (2 kg) (use canned if good fresh ones aren't available)
Artichokes: 2 to 4, or 3 to 6 (for 4 or 6 people, respectively)
Carrots: 3½ pounds (1.5 kg)
Green beans: 1½ pounds (700 gm)
Sweet green or red peppers: 2 medium or large
Red pepper (if available): 1
Celery: 1 bunch
New potatoes: 2 pounds (1 kg)
Corn: 2 ears
Purple cabbage: 1 pound (450 gm)
Cauliflower: 1½ pounds (700 gm)
Potatoes: 2 pounds (1 kg)

Fruit:
Oranges: 3
Lemons: 7
Strawberries: 2 pints (1 L), plus 1 (0.5 L) optional for garnish
Pineapples: 2 ripe
Limes: 1
Bananas: 1
Peaches: 2 to 4, or 3 to 6 (for 4 or 6 people, respectively)

Fresh herbs (if available):
Parsley: 1 large bunch
Cilantro: 1 bunch
Mint: 1 bunch
Italian parsley: 1 bunch
Dill: 1 bunch
Chives (green onion tops may be substituted): 1 bunch

Eggs and dairy products:
Cheese of your choice for Fruit and Cheese Platter

31

Yogurt: 1 quart (1 L)
Eggs: 2¼ dozen
Parmesan: 12 oz. (350 gm)
Mozzarella: 8 oz. (225 gm)
Heavy cream (optional): ½ cup (120 ml)
Butter: 1 stick

Tofu: 2 pounds (1 kg)

SUMMER MENUS

MENUS:

Pasta with Uncooked Tomatoes and
    Cheese (page 207)
Steamed Green Beans
Tossed Green Salad (page 280)
Cantaloupe with Apricot Puree and
    Almonds (page 313)

——

Potato and Egg Tacos (page 265)
Salsa (page 262)
Simple Picante Zucchini (page 168)
Jícama and Orange Salad with Avocados
    (page 295)
Strawberry Freeze (page 317)

——

Black-Eyed Peas (page 104)
Rich Jalapeño Cornbread (page 53)
Okra and Tomatoes (page 159)
Corn on the cob
Coleslaw (page 295)
Sliced Honeydew

——

Cottage Cheese and Tomato Salad with
    Miso Dressing (page 296)
Chinese-Style Snow Peas and Water
    Chestnuts (page 140)
Couscous**
Banana Yogurt Freeze (page 315)

——

STAPLES

Check Master List

Grains and legumes:
Soy flakes: ½ pound (225 gm)
Black-eyed peas: 1 pound (450 gm)
Couscous: 1 pound (450 gm)
Brown rice: 1 pound (450 gm)

Flours:
Cornmeal: 1½ cups (350 ml)
Whole-wheat: 1 cup (250 ml)
Wheat germ: 1 cup (250 ml)

Nuts (check against master list):
Walnuts or pecans: 1 cup (250 ml)
Almonds: ¾ cup (180 ml)
Sunflower seeds: 1 cup (250 ml)
Roasted soybeans: ½ cup (120 ml)

Pasta:
Fettuccine: ¾ to 1 pound (350–450 gm)

*Auxiliary recipe
**Ingredients doubled for auxiliary recipes

MENUS:

Gazpacho (page 87)
Tortillas Españolas (page 181)
*Leftover Grains Salad (page 293)***
Peaches with Marsala (page 314)

———

Eggplant, Potatoes, and Mushrooms
Braised in White Wine (page 157)
Tofu Cutlets (page 131)
Tossed Green Salad (page 280)
Fresh Strawberries

———

*Brown Rice "Risotto" with Soy Flakes****
(page 107)
Peppers, Tomatoes, and Herbs
(page 161)
Tossed Green Salad (page 280)
Pineapple with Mint

STAPLES

Optional Liquors:
Crème de cassis liqueur (black cherry concentrate may be substituted)
Marsala
Pernod

Miscellaneous:
Capers: small jar
Black olives: small can
White wine: 1 cup
Dried mushrooms: 6

*Auxiliary recipe
**Ingredients doubled for auxiliary recipe

MARKETING FOR FRESH INGREDIENTS

Vegetables:
Tomatoes: 10 lbs. (4.5 kg)
Green beans: 1 pound (450 gm)
Leaf lettuce: 1 pound (450 gm)
Other lettuce (Boston, red tip, romaine): 2 pounds (1 kg)
Mushrooms: ½ pound (225 gm)
Radishes: 2 bunches
Green onions: 3 bunches
Onions: 9 medium
Green peppers: 7 medium or large
Avocados: 2
Sprouts (your choice): 4 cups (950 ml)
Serrano or jalapeño peppers: 3
New or boiling potatoes: 2 pounds (1 kg)
Russet potato: 1 medium
Jícama: 1½ pounds (700 gm)
Jalapeño peppers: 2 to 4
Okra: 1 pound (450 gm)
Corn: 4 to 6 ears
Green cabbage: 1½ pounds (700 gm)
Carrots: 4 medium
Cucumbers: 3 medium

Vegetables, con'd.
Snow peas: 1 pound (450 gm)
Red pepper, if available: 1 medium
Celery: 1 bunch
Eggplant: 2 pounds (1 kg)
Zucchini: 1½ pounds (700 gm)
Broccoli or asparagus: 1½ cups (360 ml)

Fresh herbs (if available):
Parsley: 1 large bunch or 2 smaller
Basil: ¾ cup (180 ml)
Cilantro: 1 bunch
Mint: 1 bunch
Mixed herbs: ½ to ¾ cup (thyme, dill, marjoram, oregano, rosemary) (120–180 ml)

Fruit:
Lemons: 10
Cantaloupes: 3 small
Apricots: 1 pound (450 gm)
Oranges: 5
Strawberries: 5 pints (3.5 L)
Honeydew: 1 large
Peaches: 3 to 6
Pineapple: 1 ripe
Bananas: 4 large or 8 small

Tofu: 1¼ pounds (550 gm)

Eggs and dairy products:
Eggs: 1½ dozen
Mozzarella cheese: 8 ounces (225 gm)
Parmesan cheese: 12 ounces (350 gm)
Yogurt: 1 quart (1 L)
Cottage cheese: 2 cups (600 ml) (low fat, small curd)
Buttermilk: 2 cups (475 ml)
Butter: 6 ounces (175 gm)
Farmer cheese or mozzarella cheese: 4 ounces (100 gm)

Miscellaneous:
4-ounce can water chestnuts (100 gm)
12 corn tortillas

FALL MENUS

MENUS

Mushroom and Barley Soup (page 73)
Tossed Green Salad (page 280)
Broiled Tomatoes (page 170)
Grapefruit with Port

———

Southern Spoonbread (page 189)
Steamed Broccoli
Baked Sweet Potatoes (page 169)
Leeks Vinaigrette (page 289)
Red Grapes

———

*Simple Garlic Soup Provençal
(page 64)*
*Pasta with Tofu Cream Sauce
(page 209)*
Tossed Green Salad (page 280)
Apples with Lime Juice (page 312)

———

*Curried Rice with Lentils** (page 118)*
Cooked Curried Cucumbers (page 156)
Lettuce Salad with Oranges (page 281)
Strawberry Sherbet (page 317)

———

*Acorn Squash Stuffed with Curried Rice
(page 120)**
Steamed Broccoli
Tossed Green Salad (page 280)
Gingered Fruit (page 312)

———

*Green Tomato, Corn, and Tofu Tacos
(page 270)*
*Jícama and Orange Salad with Avocados
(page 295)*
Simple Picante Zucchini (page 168)
Banana Yogurt Freeze (page 315)

———

*Thick Split Pea and Rice Soup (page
83)*
Tossed Green Salad (page 280)
*Rye and Corn Muffins with Bran (page
54)*
Fresh Pears

STAPLES

Check Master List

Grains and legumes:
Barley: 1½ cups (350 ml)
Soy flakes: 1 cup (250 ml)
Brown rice: 3 cups (700 ml)
Lentils: 1½ cups (350 ml)
Split peas: 2 cups (475 ml)

Flours:
Cornmeal: 1 cup (250 ml)
Whole-wheat pastry: 1 cup
(250 ml)
Miller's bran: ½ cup (120 ml)
Rye: 1 cup (250 ml)

Nuts and nut butters:
Tahini (1 cup; 250 ml)
Sunflower seeds (1 cup; 250
ml)
Almonds (½ cup; 125 ml)
Pecans (¼ cup; 60 ml)

Pasta:
¾ pound, any shape (350 gm)

Wine and optional liqueurs:
Dry vermouth
Red wine
Crème de cassis (black cherry
concentrate may be
substituted)
Port

Miscellaneous:
Raisins: ½ cup (250 ml)
Chutney: ½ cup (120 ml)
Dried figs: 1 pound (450 gm)

*Auxiliary recipe
**Ingredients doubled for
auxiliary recipes

35

MARKETING FOR FRESH INGREDIENTS

Vegetables:
Onions: 6
Mushrooms: 1½ pounds (700 gm)
Green onions: 3 bunches
Radishes: 2 bunches
Alfalfa sprouts (or others): 4 to 8 ounces (100–225 gm)
Tomatoes: 4½ pounds (canned may be used) (2 kg)
Broccoli: 2 bunches
Sweet potatoes: 4 to 6
Leeks: 1½ pounds (700 gm)
Lettuce (leaf, red tip, or Boston): 3 pounds (1.4 kg)
Green peppers: 1 medium
Acorn squash: 2 to 3
Cucumbers: 5 small or medium
Green tomatoes: ¾ pound (350 gm)
Serrano peppers: 3
Corn on the cob: 2 (frozen, 1½ cups; 350 ml)
Jícama: 1½ pounds (700 gm)
Avocados: 2
Zucchini: 1½ pounds (700 gm)
Carrots: 1
Garlic: 1 head

Fresh herbs (if available):
Parsley: 1 large bunch, or 2 small
Dill: 2 tablespoons (30 ml)
Chives (green onion tops may be substituted)
Cilantro: 1 bunch
Other available herbs (thyme, marjoram, basil, sage, oregano): ¼ cup (60 ml)

Fruit:
Pears: 6
Lemons: 9
Grapefruit: 2 to 3
Limes: 7
Red grapes: 1 pound (450 gm)
Apples: 7 to 9
Oranges: 5
Strawberries (fresh or frozen): 2 pints (1 L)
Additional grapefruit: 2
Bananas: 4

Tofu: 1½ pounds (700 gm)

Eggs and dairy products:
Parmesan cheese: 6 ounces (150 gm)
Milk: 1 pint (0.5 L)
Yogurt: 1 quart (1 L)
Farmer cheese: 4 ounces (100 gm) (mozzarella may be substituted)
Buttermilk: 1 pint (0.5 L)
Eggs: 5
Butter: 4 ounces (100 gm)

Miscellaneous:
½ cup shaved coconut (120 ml)
12 tortillas

WINTER MENUS

MENUS

*Pressure-Cooked Black Beans and
    Triticale** (page 100)*
Simple Picante Zucchini (page 168)
Rich Jalapeño Cornbread (page 53)
*Watercress, Mushroom, and Tofu Salad
    (page 292)*
Orange Ice (page 318)

———

*Green Peppers Stuffed with Beans and
    Grains* (page 103)*
Broiled Tomatoes (page 170)
Tossed Green Salad (page 280)
Figs Poached in Madeira (page 311)

———

Potato Leek Soup (page 65)
*Simple Cheese, Bread, and Mushroom
    Casserole (page 186)*
Steamed broccoli
*Tossed Green Salad (with tomatoes)
    (page 280)*
Apples with Lime Juice (page 312)

———

STAPLES

Check Master List

Grains and legumes:
Black beans: 1 pound (450 gm)
Triticale: ½ pound (225 gm)
Brown rice: 2 pounds (1 kg)
Soy flakes: 1 pound (450 gm)

Flours:
Cornmeal: 1½ cups (350 ml)
Whole-wheat: 1 cup (250 ml)
Whole-wheat pastry: 1 cup
(250 ml)
Wheat germ: 1 cup (250 ml)

Dried fruit:
Figs: 2 pounds (1 kg)
Apricots: 1 pound (450 gm)

*Auxiliary recipe
**Ingredients doubled for auxiliary
recipes

MENUS:

Baked Macaroni with Tofu Cream Sauce (page 211)
Carrots Cooked in Vodka (page 150)
Lettuce Salad with Oranges (page 281)
Apricot Soufflé (page 308)

Tofu Cutlets (page 131)
Potatoes Simmered with Sage, Tomatoes, and Peas (page 162)
Simple Cabbage and Carrot Salad with Fresh Herbs (page 298)
Baked Grapefruit with Tequila or Sherry (page 313)

Simple Garlic Soup Provençal (page 64)
*Brown Rice "Risotto" with Soy Flakes** (page 107)*
Tossed Green Salad (page 280)
Pears Poached in Red Wine (page 309)

Eggplant Stuffed with Rice and Soy "Risotto" or Risi e Bisi (page 110)*
Brussels Sprouts with Lemon-Mustard Butter (page 149)
Fattoush (page 285)
Banana Yogurt Freeze (page 315), or Puffed Dessert Omelet (page 306)

STAPLES

Pasta:
¾ pound (350 gm) flat noodles or elbow macaroni

Wines and optional liqueurs:
Tequila or sherry: ⅓ cup (80 ml)
Madeira: 2 cups (475 ml)
Red wine: 2 cups (475 ml)
Dry white vermouth or sherry
Vodka: ¼ cup (60 ml)
Amaretto:1tablespoon(15ml)
Cognac: 2 tablespoons (30 ml)

Miscellaneous:
1 small can frozen orange juice
Whole-wheat bread for croutons
6 dried mushrooms

Nuts and seeds: All on the Master List

MARKETING FOR FRESH INGREDIENTS

Vegetables:
Onions: 4
Zucchini: 1½ pounds (700 gm)
Tomatoes: 6½ pounds (3 kg) (canned may be used)
Serrano pepper: 1
Jalapeño peppers (optional for cornbread): 2
Mushrooms: 1 pound (450 gm)
Green onions: 4 bunches
Radishes: 2 bunches
Green peppers: 5 to 7
Lettuce: 2 pounds (1 kg)
Sprouts: 1½ cups (350 ml) (any kind)
Potatoes: 4 pounds (1.8 kg)
Leeks: 1 pound (450 gm)

Vegetables, con'd.
Broccoli: 1 bunch
Peas (fresh or frozen): 2 cups (475 ml)
Purple cabbage: 1 pound (450 gm)
Carrots: 1 medium plus ½ pound (225 gm)
Cucumber: 3 medium
Sunflower greens: ½ cup (120 ml) (watercress may be substituted)
Brussels sprouts: 1 pound (450 gm)
Eggplants: 2 small
Watercress: 2 to 2½ bunches

Herbs (if available):
Parsley: 1 large bunch or 2 small
Cilantro: 1 bunch
Fresh sage: 3 tablespoons (45 ml) if available; 1 tablespoon (15 ml) dried leaf, if not
Chives: 3 tablespoons (45 ml) (green onion tops may be substituted)
Dill: 1 bunch
Mint: 1 bunch
Other herbs, if available, such as marjoram, basil, fennel: 2 tablespoons (30 ml)

Fruit:
Lemons: 10
Apples: 4 to 6
Limes: 2
Oranges: 3
Bananas: 4
Pears: 3
Grapefruits: 2 to 3

Tofu: 1½ to 2 pounds (700 gm–1 kg)

Miscellaneous: 1 loaf French bread or 1 package pita

Eggs and dairy products:
Eggs: 2 dozen
Buttermilk: 2 cups (475 ml)
Butter: 6 ounces (175 gm)
Yogurt: 1 quart (1 L)
Whipping cream: 1 pint (0.5 L)
Cheddar cheese: 8 ounces (225 gm)
Milk: 2 cups (475 ml)
Parmesan cheese: 8 ounces (225 gm)

MENUS FOR ENTERTAINING

SOME MONTHS BACK I began to find that I wasn't seeing my friends often enough, because every time I thought about inviting them to dinner I balked at the idea of the amount of time it would involve. A dinner party to me meant at least a day's work. Then I got tired of not having guests; so I pulled out my pressure cooker and began to look through my recipes to see what I had that was fast and easy.

I didn't have to look too long, for certain kinds of dishes lend themselves to easy entertaining. Pasta is the first that comes to mind. You can have a salad and whatever you're tossing the pasta with all prepared before your company comes. As soon as the doorbell rings, start heating the water. You'll be able to visit with your friends until it's time to eat, and then it'll be just a matter of cooking the noodles. I like a little breathing time between dinner and dessert, so depending on the dish I'm serving (a sherbet, for instance, would have to be begun before dinner), I might put it together after the plates are cleared.

Timbales like the ones on pages 192 and 193 are another nice choice. They are always impressive, never temperamental and they go with any number of soups, side vegetable dishes, and salads. Risottos, too, have an inherent elegance. A nice feature of the brown rice versions in this book (pages 107–112) is that you don't have to hover over them with a wooden spoon as they cook, the way you do with classic Italian recipes. While the rice cooks you can be preparing the rest of the meal or sipping wine (or both). And your kitchen will smell heavenly, so your guests' mouths will be watering by the time they get to the table.

Dishes like Chinese-Style Vegetables with Couscous (page 137) cook in minutes on the top of the stove. Here the trick is to have all the ingredients prepared beforehand; the salad, if you're having one, composed; and the grains ready, so that you can just excuse yourself for those few minutes.

With many of the recipes in this book, you can stop at the grocery store on your way home from work, pick up a few things, and throw together an elegant meal. You'll even have time for a bath and a drink before your guests arrive. And don't forget that, with all entertaining, the sooner you can get your table set, the better. No matter how much I'm rushing to get a meal finished, I am always at ease if the table is set and my house *looks* like I'm ready. Remember that this can be taken care of the night before, or before you go to work in the morning.

The meals that follow will make memorable dinner parties. Your friends will be impressed, not by the fact that you worked all day on the dinner but, on the contrary, by the fact that you didn't.

Tomato and Mozzarella Salad (page 282)
Fettuccine with Pesto (page 215)
Asparagi alla Parmigiana (page 190)
Strawberries in Red Wine and Preserves Syrup (page 310)

Potato Leek Soup (page 65)
Broccoli Timbale (page 192)
Broiled Tomatoes (page 170)
Tossed Green Salad (page 280)
Oranges with Mint

Hot and Sour Soup (page 67)
Chinese-Style Vegetables with Couscous (page 137)
Lettuce Salad with Oranges (page 281)
Banana Yogurt Freeze (page 315)

Pressure-Cooked Artichokes with Tofu Mayonnaise (page 237)
Risi e Bisi (page 108)
Tossed Green Salad (page 280)
Puffed Amaretto Omelet (page 306)

Elegant Pressure-Cooked White Bean Soup (page 74) with Bread
Green Beans à la Provençal (page 147)
Oriental Salad (page 297)
Peaches with Marsala (page 304)

Spinach and Whole Wheat Fettuccine with Wild Mushrooms and
Cheese (page 210)
Florentine Tomatoes (page 171)
Tossed Green Salad (page 280)
Orange Ice (page 318)

Hot or Iced Tomato Soup (page 72)
Asparagus Timbale (page 193)
Watercress, Mushroom, and Tofu Salad (page 292)
Pineapple with Mint

RECIPES FOR THE SUNDAY COOK

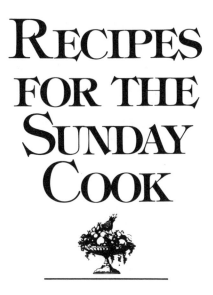

New Mixed Grains Bread
Brown Rice or Leftover Grains Bread
Simple Whole-Wheat Bread with Wheat Germ and Optional
Oats
Herbed Triticale Bread
Rich Jalapeño Cornbread
Rye and Corn Muffins with Bran
White Bean Pâté
Low-Fat Yogurt
Vinaigrette
Tofu Mayonnaise
Tofu Cream Sauce
Tofu Béchamel
Morning Tofu Spread or Evening Pudding
Roasted Soybeans

The recipes in this chapter are not all fast because I can't write a cookbook without including some bread recipes, and whole-grain breads are such an important staple in the vegetarian diet. The weekend is the only practical time for a working person to bake. On a Saturday or Sunday you can easily produce two loaves of any of the breads in this section and be well nourished for the week. The New Mixed Grains, and Whole Wheat and Oatmeal, breads do require four to five hours from start to finish (not all working!), because of all the risings, but when you taste the bread you'll agree that it's been time well spent. The marvelous Herbed Triticale bread, however, takes only three hours. With any of these recipes you can place the dough in the refrigerator if you have to go out. The dough will continue to rise, but very slowly. I sometimes let my bread rise (at any stage) overnight in the refrigerator. Then, first thing in the morning, I preheat the oven and bake my bread. What a wonderful aroma to begin the morning with!

If you're not into baking, or don't want to devote your weekends to it, I urge you to find a local source of good whole-grain bread. It's always the first item I buy (or make) when I find myself with an empty larder. As long as I have bread around, I know I'll survive. And it doesn't have to be a yeast variety; the rich cornbread and the moist, luscious muffins in this chapter satisfy the same needs.

If you have something nutritious to put on that bread, you'll really be in good shape. A pâté like the delicate White Bean Pâté on page 55 is indispensable for easy, delicious, and high-protein lunches or light dinners. With this spread on hand I often go a week without cooking and live quite well on bread, pâté, and salad. Once you have the beans cooked, this pâté is actually quite simple, as the recipe mainly involves blending ingredients and baking the mixture. While it isn't something you can expect to throw together after work and eat that night, making it is no great task.

In the morning I usually eat Morning Tofu Spread (page 59) on my toast. This is a sweet baked cheesecakelike mixture of blended tofu, apples, yogurt, and spices. The only breakfast "dish" I've included in the book, it's such an important staple for me that I couldn't leave it out.

The other items in this section are foods that keep well, are good to have on hand, and will simplify your daily kitchen duties. If you have salad dressings in the refrigerator and lettuce washed, that course is all but done for the week. Tofu Cream Sauce (page 57) and Tofu Béchamel (page 58) keep well and can dress up any meal while increasing the protein content. Yogurt comes up often in the recipes, so I've given you the option of making your own (see page 56).

None of the recipes for fast feasts in the remainder of the book *depend* on those in this chapter. But if you want to get ahead, or have your own wholesome bread around, I think you'll appreciate what follows.

♥ NEW MIXED GRAINS BREAD
2 LOAVES
PREPARATION TIME: 5 hours, start to finish

This bread has long been an important part of my diet. In the last few years I have branched out, and do stock my larder with different kinds of bread. But this one, with its wholesome balance of grains, remains my own favorite. The texture is magnificent. When I made it in the south of France (almost every day, the loaves went so fast), my French neighbors exclaimed that it was like cake. And a Russian friend insists it's the best bread he's eaten since leaving Russia several years ago.

One of the nicest ingredients in this bread is the sesame seeds on the top. They become especially rich and nutty when toasted.

When you make this, don't be alarmed by the density of the dough. Though this is a lighter version than the original model in *The Vegetarian Feast*, it's still a very sturdy loaf. Since this was the first bread I made with any regularity, the weight has never thrown me off. But if you're used to lighter doughs you might fear you are doing something wrong. You're not. As long as you give the bread time to rise, dense as it is, it won't be like a rock.

The instructions for all the steps in this recipe cover the basic techniques in breadmaking. You can refer to them when you make all of the breads in this chapter.

FOR THE SPONGE:
- 1 tablespoon (1 envelope; 15 ml) active dry yeast
- 3 cups (700 ml) lukewarm water
- 2 tablespoons (30 ml) mild honey
- 2 tablespoons (30 ml) molasses (or use ¼ cup honey in all; 60 ml)
- 2 cups (475 ml) unbleached white flour
- 2 cups (475 ml) whole-wheat flour

FOR THE DOUGH:

¼ cup (60 ml) safflower or vegetable oil
1 scant tablespoon (15 ml) salt
¾ cup (180 ml) rolled or flaked oats
¾ cup (180 ml) cracked wheat (you can crack your own by running wheat berries in the blender at high speed, in batches of ½ cup, 120 ml) or bulgur
3 tablespoons (45 ml) chia seeds (optional)
¾ cup (180 ml) soy flour
¾ cup (180 ml) millet meal (can be done in a blender the same way as cracked wheat)
1½ to 2 cups (350–475 ml) whole-wheat flour, more as necessary

FOR THE TOPPING:

1 egg
¼ cup (60 ml) water
Sesame seeds

Step 1: Mixing the sponge: In a large mixing bowl, dissolve the yeast in the water. Add the honey and molasses and stir to dissolve. Use water from the bowl to rinse the measuring spoons.

Add the flour, a cup (250 ml) at a time, stirring with a whisk or wooden spoon to incorporate the flour into the liquid. The mixture will gradually develop a mudlike consistency. Keep stirring in the flour until you have added all 4 cups (950 ml).

Now stir the mudlike mixture a hundred times. This sounds like a lot of work, but it goes very fast. Make sure you are stirring the batter up from the bottom and center of the bowl. There should be no lumps when you are finished. If there are, stir a little while longer.

Cover the bowl with plastic, a damp towel or the lid of a large pot and set aside in a warm place. If the weather is cool, set the bowl over a pilot light, on a heater, in an oven with a pilot light, or in an oven that has been turned on low heat for 10 minutes, then turned off. If your pilot light is very hot, place a baking pan between it and the bread bowl. In summertime almost any place will suffice, and the pilot light will probably be too hot. In Provence I always let my bread rise in the sun.

Let the sponge rise for 50 to 70 minutes. At the end of this time it should be bubbling, and you will actually be able to see the mixture expanding.

Step 2: Adding the remaining ingredients and kneading; second rise: Pour the oil onto the sponge and sprinkle on the salt. Incorporate into the sponge by folding the sponge over with a large wooden spoon, turn-

46

ing a quarter turn, folding again, and so on until you no longer see the oil.

Fold in the ¾ cup (180 ml) oats, then the cracked wheat or bulgur, the chia seeds, soy flour, and millet meal. By the time you have incorporated all of these the dough should be coming away from the sides of the bowl in more or less one piece, though it will be a sticky, formless one. Place a cup (250 ml) of whole-wheat flour on your kneading surface and scrape out the dough. If the dough in the bowl is very wet, fold in ½ cup (120 ml) of whole-wheat flour and place the remaining ½ cup (120 ml) on the kneading surface, then turn out the dough.

Now you are ready to knead. Your working surface should be low, about level with your hips or a little bit lower. The dough will be very sticky initially, so it's a good idea to take off your rings and flour your hands well (a step I rarely seem to remember in time). To knead, carefully take up the far end of the dough and fold it in half toward you; lean into the dough, letting your weight push through the palms of your hands and through your fingertips. Turn the dough a quarter turn, fold toward you, lean into it. Turn, fold, lean; turn, fold, lean. At first you should lean into the dough gingerly, as it will be so sticky, it will cling all over your hands. But it will begin to stiffen up after 4 or 5 turns. Whenever the dough becomes sticky add a handful of whole-wheat flour to the board, and flour your hands. As you continue this process the dough will become stiff and hard to work with, but keep kneading for at least 10 minutes, adding flour—but not too much—whenever it becomes very sticky. After 10 to 15 minutes of kneading, during which time you may have added up to 2 cups (475 ml) of flour, the dough should be stiff, elastic, and heavy. Let it rest for a moment and the surface will become smooth, but not necessarily glossy. If you knead for too long it will keep getting sticky, and you will end up adding too much flour. This will result in a heavy bread. If the dough seems impossibly sticky, even after adding 2 cups (475 ml) whole-wheat flour, continue to dust your board lightly with unbleached white flour.

Now the dough is ready to rise. Fold the edges toward the center and turn over without kneading. Pinch the folds together at the bottom so that the dough is formed into a ball. Oil the bread bowl well; place the dough, round side down, in the bowl. Roll the dough around to coat it with the oil. This will prevent it from getting a dry, crusty shell. Turn the dough over and cover with plastic, a damp towel or a lid. Set in a warm place and let rise 1 hour, until doubled in bulk.

Step 3: Punching down; third rise: Punch down by gently pushing your fists into the puffed-up dough 20 or 30 times. This is the easiest and probably the most delightful part of the whole process; I love the way the dough balloons around my fist. Let rise again for 45 minutes to an hour. The dough should be very puffed up, doubled in bulk but much lighter than after the previous rise.

Step 4: Forming the loaves; fourth and last rise: Remove the dough from the bowl and place it on your kneading surface. If the dough is sticky you will have to flour the surface lightly.

Shape the dough into a ball by folding all the way around in the same manner as in Step 2. Cut this ball into two equal pieces with a sharp knife and shape each of these into a ball. (You can weigh the pieces to make sure they're equal.)

Oil two bread pans generously, making sure you coat the corners of the pans, as well as the sides and bottom. If the pans aren't well oiled the bread will stick, which will be depressing after all that work.

Preheat the oven to 350 degrees (180°C).

To make the loaves, take each ball, beginning with the one you made first, knead a few times for extra spring, then press out into a rectangle and roll up lengthwise into a "log" shape; or fold like a business letter. Pinch together firmly along the lengthwise crease; fold the ends over toward the crease and pinch the folds.

Place the loaves creased side up in the greased pans, and gently push them with the backs of your hands to allow them to be oiled and shaped by the pan. They should be two thirds to three quarters the volume of the pans. Then turn the loaves so that the smooth side is up and gently press into shape again. Set aside to rise, covered with a towel, for 15 to 25 minutes, until the middle of each loaf is a little higher than the edge of the bread pan.

Step 5: Preparation for baking; baking, cooling, and storing: With a very sharp knife or a razor blade, make three $\frac{1}{2}$-inch (1.5 cm) deep slashes across each loaf. This allows air to escape as the bread bakes; otherwise, the loaves will tear.

Make an egg wash by mixing together the egg and $\frac{1}{4}$ cup (60 ml) water. Brush each loaf generously to obtain a rich, shiny brown surface. Sprinkle with sesame seeds and brush again with egg wash to paste on the seeds. Don't press too hard with the brush or you may cause the loaves to deflate.

Bake in the preheated 350-degree (180°C) oven for 50 to 60 minutes. For extra-shiny, rich brown loaves, brush again with the egg wash halfway through baking. The bread is ready when the surface of each loaf is golden brown and it responds with a hollow thumping sound when tapped with the tips of the fingers. Remove from the bread pans at once and cool on racks. (Sometimes the egg wash will run down the sides of the loaf and cause it to stick to the bottom of the pan. Oiling the pan very well will help prevent this.) If you do have trouble removing the bread, run a butter knife around the edges of the loaf several times, turn upside down, and shake the pan or beat on the bottom of it.

Let the loaves cool several hours. When they are completely cool, place them in plastic bags and store in your bread box, or freeze the bread (wrapped first in plastic, tightly, then in plastic bags or foil) and thaw out at a later date. After 2 to 3 days in the bread box, the bread should be stored in the refrigerator to prevent spoilage.

♥ Omit salt.

BROWN RICE OR LEFTOVER GRAINS BREAD
In Step 2 of the preceding recipe, substitute 1 to 3 cups (250–700 ml) cooked brown rice or other cooked grains for the cracked wheat, millet, and chia. Because the cooked grains contain more water than raw grains, the dough will be stickier and you will need more whole-wheat flour. The dough will also be lighter and will rise more than the mixed grains dough. Don't be alarmed if the dough is very sticky when you turn it out onto the board to make the loaves. Just sprinkle the board with a small amount of unbleached white or whole-wheat flour and handle carefully. Proceed as in the previous recipe. This is a good way to use up leftover grains.

♥ SIMPLE WHOLE-WHEAT BREAD WITH WHEAT GERM AND OPTIONAL OATS

2 LOAVES

PREPARATION TIME: 4 hours

This bread is also a dense one, requiring no sponge. The loaves are smaller than mixed grains loaves, but they are a little lighter. The bread has a rich taste due in part to the milk and wheat germ, and a slice toasts nicely.

> 2 cups (475 ml) milk, whole or skim
> 3 tablespoons (45 ml) mild honey
> 3 tablespoons (45 ml) safflower oil
> 1 scant tablespoon (15 ml) salt
> 2 tablespoons (30 ml) active dry yeast
> ⅓ cup (80 ml) lukewarm water
> ¾ cup (180 ml) wheat germ
> 1 cup (250 ml) flaked oats (optional)
> 5 to 6 cups (1.2–1.5 L) whole-wheat flour, depending on whether or not you include oats
> ¼ to ½ cup (60–120 ml) unbleached white flour, for kneading
> 1 egg, mixed with ¼ cup (60 ml) water for the egg wash
> Sesame seeds

Scald the milk and stir in 2 tablespoons (30 ml) of the honey, the oil, and salt. Cool to lukewarm in the freezer. (If you are mixing up dry milk, you can just mix it with lukewarm water and omit the scalding.)

Meanwhile dissolve the yeast in the ⅓ cup (80 ml) of lukewarm water and stir in the remaining tablespoon of honey. Let sit until it begins to foam, about 10 minutes. Put the cooled milk mixture into a large bowl and pour in the yeast mixture, then stir in the wheat germ and the oats. Mix well.

Add the flour, a cup at a time, and fold in. After 3 cups (700 ml) you should be able to turn out the dough in a sticky mass. Place the next cup of flour on your board and turn out the dough. Knead the dough as in Mixed Grains Bread (page 45), and work in the flour. Continue to add flour to your work surface, ½ cup (120 ml) at a time, and knead until you have a stiff, smooth dough, 10 to 15 minutes.

Oil your bowl and form your dough into a ball. Place the dough in the bowl seam side up first, then seam side down. Cover and place in a warm place to rise for 1 hour, or until doubled in size.

Punch down the dough and let rise for another hour.

Oil two bread pans. Lightly flour your work surface, if necessary, with unbleached flour, and turn out the dough. Knead a couple of times and cut into two equal pieces. Form the pieces into balls, then shape loaves.

Place the loaves in the bread pans, seam side up first, then seam side down. Slash and brush with egg wash. Sprinkle with sesame seeds and brush again. Cover and let rise 30 minutes. Meanwhile preheat the oven to 375 degrees (190°C).

Bake the loaves in the preheated oven for 45 minutes, until golden brown. Remove from the pans and cool on a rack.

♥ Use skimmed milk. Omit salt. Use only 2 tablespoons oil. Omit egg wash and sesame seeds.

♥ HERBED TRITICALE BREAD
1 LOAF

This is the easiest, most reliable yeast bread I've ever made, and one of the most popular. It slices beautifully, freezes well, and takes only 3 hours (at most) from start to finish.

If you are on a low-sodium diet, this is the bread for you. You can leave out the salt entirely and you'll never know the difference, because of the savory herbs. I served it to heart patients every day for a month, and they loved it.

 1 tablespoon (15 ml) active dry yeast
 1 cup (250 ml) lukewarm water
 1 tablespoon (15 ml) mild honey
 ½ medium onion, minced
 2 tablespoons plus 1½ teaspoons (scant 40 ml) safflower oil
 1½ teaspoons (7 ml) salt
 1 cup (250 ml) plain low-fat yogurt
 1½ cups (350 ml) triticale flour
 1 tablespoon (15 ml) dillweed
 1 tablespoon (15 ml) dillseed
 1 teaspoon (5 ml) dried sage
 3 cups (700 ml) whole-wheat flour

Dissolve the yeast in the water in a large bowl. Add the honey and let proof (let set until bubbly) 10 minutes. Meanwhile, heat the 1½ teaspoons (7 ml) safflower oil in a skillet and sauté the onion until tender. Remove from the heat and cool.

When the yeast is bubbly, stir in the 2 tablespoons (30 ml) safflower oil, the salt, yogurt, onion, triticale flour, dillweed, dillseed, and sage. Beat well, then begin to fold in the whole-wheat flour, a cup (250 ml) at a time. When you have added all 3 cups (700 ml), knead the dough in the bowl for about 10 minutes (I usually knead this dough right in the bowl, because it's a sticky one). Or you can put the last ⅓ cup (250 ml) of flour on your board and turn the dough out. Don't be alarmed if it is very sticky, which it will be. Just keep your hands well floured and knead quickly. Use a pastry scraper, if you wish, to scrape the dough off the board and fold it over.

Clean out your bowl and oil it. Form the dough into a ball and place in the bowl, seam side up first, then seam side down. Cover the bowl tightly with plastic wrap and let rise in a warm place for 1 hour, until almost doubled in bulk. Flour your fist, because the dough will be sticky, and punch down.

Oil a bread pan or a 2-quart (2 L) soufflé dish. (If using a soufflé dish or pans that aren't well seasoned, you should line them with parchment.) Form the dough into a loaf (or a ball for the soufflé dish) and place in the pan or dish. Make three ½-inch (1.5 cm)-deep slashes across the surface and let the dough rise, covered, for 40 minutes in a warm place.

Ten minutes before the end of the rising time, preheat the oven to 350 degrees (180°C).

Bake in the preheated oven for 50 minutes, or until the loaf is brown and responds to tapping with a hollow thumping sound. Cool on a rack.

Note: This bread can be made with all whole-wheat flour, or rye flour may be substituted for the triticale flour, which is sometimes hard to come by.

♥ Omit salt.

RICH JALAPEÑO CORNBREAD
SERVES 12

PREPARATION TIME: 20 minutes
BAKING TIME: 30–40 minutes

For me nothing goes with a bowl of beans better than a thick piece of jalapeño cornbread. This one is almost like cake. You can, of course, omit the jalapeño and have a delicious regular cornbread.

- 1½ cups (350 ml) yellow cornmeal
- ½ cup (120 ml) whole-wheat flour
- ¼ cup (60 ml) untoasted wheat germ
- ½ teaspoon (2.5 ml) salt
- ½ teaspoon (2.5 ml) baking soda
- 2 teaspoons (10 ml) baking powder
- 3 large eggs
- 2 cups (475 ml) buttermilk or 1 cup (250 ml) plain low-fat yogurt mixed with 1 cup (250 ml) milk
- 1 tablespoon (15 ml) honey
- 2 to 4 jalapeño peppers, seeds removed, chopped
- 2 tablespoons (30 ml) butter

Preheat the oven to 375 degrees (190°C). Place a 9 × 9-inch (25 cm × 25 cm) baking pan or a 9-inch (25 cm) cast-iron skillet in the oven.

Sift together the cornmeal, whole-wheat flour, wheat germ, salt, baking soda, and baking powder. In another bowl, beat together the eggs, buttermilk, and honey. Stir in the jalapeños.

Stir the wet ingredients into the dry. Mix together until blended, but do not beat.

Slide out the oven rack holding the hot baking dish or skillet, put in the butter, and return to the oven for a minute. When the butter begins to sizzle, remove the pan from the oven. Using a pastry brush, brush the pan with the butter and pour off any remaining butter into the batter. Stir to combine, then pour the batter into the hot baking dish and set in the oven. Bake 30 to 40 minutes, until the top begins to brown. Cool in the pan, or cut into squares and serve hot.

RYE AND CORN MUFFINS WITH BRAN
12 TO 14 MUFFINS

PREPARATION TIME: 10 minutes
BAKING TIME: 25 minutes

Because they are so fast and easy, muffin recipes needn't be restricted to the Sunday cook. The return you get on your time and money is extraordinary. With the buttermilk, eggs, and mixed flours, these Rye and Corn Muffins are as nutritious as Mixed Grains Bread. The cornmeal gives them a delightful texture, and the rye and buttermilk a wonderful sour flavor. They are moist and heavenly, good at any meal.

>   2 eggs
>   ¼ cup (60 ml) safflower oil
>   1½ cups (350 ml) buttermilk
>   2 tablespoons (30 ml) mild honey
>   ¾ cup (180 ml) whole-wheat pastry flour or unbleached white
>   ¾ cup (180 ml) rye flour
>   ½ cup (120 ml) yellow cornmeal
> Scant ½ teaspoon (2.5 ml) salt
>   2 teaspoons (10 ml) baking powder, or use 1½ teaspoons (7 ml) cream of tartar and ¾ teaspoon (4 ml) baking soda
>   ¼ cup (60 ml) miller's bran

Preheat oven to 375 degrees (190°C) and butter muffin tins.

Beat together the eggs, oil, buttermilk, and honey. Sift together the flours, cornmeal, salt, and baking powder. Stir into the liquid ingredients along with the bran, with just a few strokes. Batter should be lumpy, not smooth.

Spoon the batter into the prepared muffin tins filling them ⅔ full and bake for 25 minutes, or until the tops begin to brown and a toothpick comes out clean when inserted. Cool the muffins in the tins on a rack.

WHITE BEAN PÂTÉ
4 CUPS (ABOUT 1 L)

PREPARATION TIME: 20 to 30 minutes, not including cooking of beans
UNSUPERVISED COOKING: 50 minutes

This has a subtle, refined flavor, is high in protein, and versatile. I serve it often as an hors d'oeuvre and it is a lunchtime favorite.

     1 cup (250 ml) navy beans or small white beans, washed and picked over
     3 cups (700 ml) water
     2 tablespoons (30 ml) olive oil, safflower oil, or butter
     1 small or medium onion, chopped
     5 large cloves garlic, minced or put through a press
     1 large bay leaf
Up to 2 teaspoons (10 ml) salt, to taste
     ⅔ cup (160 ml) finely grated carrot
     2 eggs
     3 tablespoons (45 ml) beer
     2 tablespoons (30 ml) plus 1 teaspoon (5 ml) lemon juice
    10 twists freshly ground pepper
     ½ cup (120 ml) whole-wheat bread crumbs
     ¼ cup (60 ml) chopped fresh parsley
     ¼ teaspoon (1.25 ml) ground coriander
     ¼ teaspoon (1.25 ml) dried basil
     ¼ teaspoon (1.25 ml) dried thyme

Soak the beans in the water for several hours or overnight, or bring to a boil, boil 2 minutes, cover, and let stand 2 hours.

Heat 1 tablespoon (15 ml) of the oil in a heavy-bottomed saucepan, bean pot, or Dutch oven and gently sauté half the onion and 2 cloves of the garlic until the onion is tender. Add the beans and their liquid, raise the heat, and bring to a boil. Add the bay leaf, then cover, reduce the heat, and simmer 2 hours, or until the beans are tender and aromatic. Add up to 1 teaspoon (5 ml) salt to taste. Drain the beans and retain their cooking liquid.

Preheat the oven to 400 degrees (200°C). Butter a 2-quart (2 L) casserole or pâté tureen.

Heat the remaining 1 tablespoon oil (15 ml) in a heavy-bottomed skillet and gently sauté the remaining onion and garlic, along with the carrot, until the onion is tender. Remove from the pan and place in a mixing bowl.

Put the cooked beans in a blender or food processor fitted with the steel blade. Add the eggs, ⅓ cup (80 ml) stock from the beans (freeze the rest for use in soups), the beer, lemon juice, pepper, and up to 1 teaspoon (5 ml) salt, to taste. Puree until smooth, adding more stock if the blades of your blender stick.

Pour the bean puree into the mixing bowl with the onion, carrot, and garlic. Add the bread crumbs, parsley, coriander, basil, and thyme and mix everything together well. Adjust salt and pepper.

Spoon the pâté mixture into the prepared casserole or tureen and cover tightly with a lid or foil. Bake in the preheated oven for 50 minutes to an hour, until the top begins to brown. Remove from the oven and cool. Serve warm or chilled. The flavors will mature overnight. This dish freezes well.

♥ LOW-FAT YOGURT
1 QUART (1 L)

PREPARATION TIME: 5 minutes
INCUBATION TIME: 3 to 6 hours

Yogurt is quite easy to make at home, and you don't have to have any fancy apparatus to do so. All you need is a place to incubate it; this can be done over a pilot light, a hot-water heater, or a space heater; in an oven with a pilot light; in a cooler filled with warm water; and even wrapped in an electric blanket.

Be sure you use either Dannon plain yogurt or a yogurt recommended by a natural foods store as a starter, since the amount of bacteria in most commercial brands isn't sufficient. If your yogurt fails, it probably will be because you used the wrong kind of yogurt as a starter or because your water bath was either too hot or not warm enough. Once you've made your own yogurt, use that as a starter.

    3½ cups (800 ml) lukewarm water
    2 to 3 tablespoons (30–45 ml) plain yogurt (see note above)
    1 heaping cup (250 ml) spray-dried nonfat dry milk or 1½ envelopes Sanalac commercial spray-dried milk

Place 2 cups (475 ml) of the water in a blender jar along with the plain yogurt. Turn on the blender to low and slowly pour in the spray-dried milk. Blend until the milk is dissolved, about 10 to 15 seconds. Add the remaining water. Pour the mixture into a quart jar and cover tightly.

Place the jar in a pan of lukewarm water. The pan must be high enough so that the water covers the entire jar. Cover and place in a warm spot where the temperature will remain constant, such as over a pilot light, on a heater, or in a cooler full of warm water. If the weather is warm, the yogurt will thicken in about 4 hours; in cold weather it will take at least 6. Check from time to time to make sure the water doesn't become too hot, or cool off, and adjust as necessary by adding hot or cold water. Refrigerate when thick.

VINAIGRETTE

The recipe for Vinaigrette is in the Salads and Dressings chapter (page 274), but I think it's important to mention it here, too. I sometimes find myself deterred from eating a salad just because I feel too lazy or tired to make a dressing. A vinaigrette, though, takes only about 5 minutes to whip up, so I often make a batch in the beginning of the week and keep it on hand in the refrigerator. I realize that it's anathema to many cooks to use anything other than freshly made vinaigrette, but sometimes that just isn't practical. While the fresh dressing is admittedly far tastier, it really keeps very satisfactorily in the refrigerator. After a big catering job, when I have a quantity left over, I'll enjoy it for weeks.

TOFU MAYONNAISE

Like vinaigrette, Tofu Mayonnaise (page 277) will make your life quite simple if you make it once a week and have it on hand for sandwiches, salad dressings, and dips. It's a true convenience food, and doesn't deteriorate in quality for a week; then I think it's best to make a new batch.

TOFU CREAM SAUCE
1½ CUPS (350 ML)
PREPARATION TIME: 5 minutes

This recipe will come up time and again, in dishes like Pasta with Tofu Cream Sauce (page 209) and vegetable gratins like those on pages 142 and 143. It may be the easiest recipe in this book, and the most versatile. It's like the Tofu Béchamel (page 58), but simpler. I make up a batch every week and use it on salads, with pasta and grains, as a sauce for vegetables, even as a spread on bread or tofu.

2 cakes (½ pound; 225 gm) tofu
1 tablespoon (15 ml) sesame tahini
1 tablespoon (15 ml) miso
½ cup (120 ml) plain low-fat yogurt
1 tablespoon (15 ml) lemon juice
  Pinch of freshly grated nutmeg (optional)

In a blender or food processor fitted with the steel blade, blend all the ingredients until completely smooth. Keeps for up to a week in the refrigerator in a covered container.

TOFU BÉCHAMEL
2 CUPS (475 ML)
PREPARATION TIME: 7 minutes

I can't remember exactly when I developed this heavenly sauce, but it's truly remarkable. It's good uncooked, as a sauce with vegetables or as a dip, and as a topping it bakes to a golden brown. You can substitute it for cheese or a cream sauce in pasta dishes, vegetable dishes, and quiches with no loss of protein but quite a loss of fat; it will firm up, when baked, like a custard. This will keep for a week in a covered container in the refrigerator.

3 cakes (¾ pound; 350 gm) tofu
1 tablespoon (15 ml) miso
2 teaspoons (10 ml) tamari
½ cup (120 ml) plain low-fat yogurt
¼ cup (60 ml) water
¾ teaspoon (4 ml) freshly minced or grated ginger
2 tablespoons (30 ml) sesame tahini
2 tablespoons (30 ml) dry sherry
1 tablespoon (15 ml) lemon juice
  Freshly grated nutmeg to taste
  Pinch of cayenne (optional)

In a blender or food processor fitted with the steel blade, blend all the ingredients together until completely smooth.

♥ MORNING TOFU SPREAD OR EVENING PUDDING
2 CUPS (475 ML)

PREPARATION TIME: 10 minutes

BAKING TIME, INCLUDING THE APPLES: ABOUT 1½ HOURS

I always try to have this on hand for toast in the morning. It's much better for you than, say, cream cheese, which is so high in fat. Not only does it make a delicious spread, but it also makes a nice pudding or cheesecake. Note that the recipe calls for 2 baked apples, so you will have to give yourself time for this. Baked apples will keep in the refrigerator for a few days, wrapped in plastic, if you don't have time to follow through with the entire recipe at once.

        2 medium, tart apples, left whole, unpeeled
        2 cakes (½ pound; 225 gm) tofu
      ¼ cup (60 ml) plain low-fat yogurt
   1 to 2 tablespoons (15–30 ml) mild honey, maple syrup, or
          sorghum syrup
   1 to 2 tablespoons (15–30 ml) lemon juice, to taste
      ½ teaspoon (2.5 ml) ground cinnamon
¼ to ½ teaspoon (1.25–2.5 ml) freshly grated nutmeg, to taste
        1 tablespoon (15 ml) sesame tahini
        1 teaspoon (5 ml) vanilla
        2 teaspoons (10 ml) whole-wheat pastry flour

Preheat the oven to 350 degrees (180°C). Butter a small baking dish, 1-quart (1 L) casserole, or 4 pudding dishes; set aside.

Place the whole unpeeled apples in another baking dish and bake for 30 to 45 minutes, until thoroughly soft. Remove from the oven, and when cool enough to handle, core.

Place the apples in a blender along with the remaining ingredients. Blend until very smooth. Pour the mixture into the buttered baking dish. Bake at 350 degrees for 30 to 40 minutes, until firm and just beginning to brown. Cool and refrigerate. Spread on toast or serve warm, as a dessert.

This will keep, covered in the refrigerator, for up to 2 weeks.

♥ ROASTED SOYBEANS
1 CUP (250 ML)
PREPARATION TIME: 2 hours after soaking

Make these on a Sunday and have them on hand for salads, sandwiches (crack them in a blender and sprinkle them on—they're a good substitute for bacon) and snacks throughout the week. They are very crunchy and nutty.

1 cup (250 ml) dried soybeans, washed and picked over
3 cups (700 ml) water
Salt to taste

Soak the soybeans in the water overnight or for several hours. Place in a large saucepan with the water (at least twice their volume, as they swell up dramatically) and bring to a boil. Cover, reduce heat, and simmer 1 hour.

Drain the beans.

Preheat the oven to 325 degrees (165°C).

Spread the beans on a cookie sheet or in a baking pan and salt them, if you wish. Place in the preheated oven and bake for about 1 to 1½ hours, turning every 15 minutes and checking carefully when the soybeans begin to smell toasty; they will sometimes smell done before they are crunchy all the way through, but be careful not to remove them from the oven prematurely. To test for doneness, remove one from the pan, let cool, and bite through to see. If it isn't crunchy, leave the beans in about 10 to 15 minutes longer. (Be careful at this stage, though, because the roasted soybeans will burn quickly once they are done.) Remove from the oven when they are ready and allow to cool in the pan. Store in a covered jar; they will keep for months if well sealed.

SOUPS

Tamari-Bouillon Broth
Instant Tamari-Bouillon Broth
Buckwheat Noodle Soup with Green Beans
Simple Garlic Soup Provençal
Potato Leek Soup
Cheddar Cheese Soup with Vegetables
Hot and Sour Soup
Simple Miso Soup
Miso Soup with Buckwheat Noodles
Pureed Zucchini Soup
Hot or Iced Tomato Soup
Mushroom and Barley Soup
Elegant Pressure-Cooked White Bean Soup
Creamy Celery and Garlic Soup
Celery Tomato Soup with Rice
Cream of Spinach and Kasha Soup
Pureed Curry of Cauliflower Soup
Cauliflower Cheese Soup
Cream of Spinach and Potato Soup
Rosemary's Chilled Lettuce and Potato Soup
Thick Split Pea and Rice Soup
Lentil and Tomato Soup with Pasta
Very Quick Cream of Pea Soup
Chilled Buttermilk Soup
Gazpacho
Chilled Melon Soup
Peach Soup

When a soup involves standing for hours over a stock pot skimming off fat, it can be an exhausting undertaking. But a soup with a vegetable base is another story altogether. The stock I use for the soups in this section is a convenience one, Tamari-Bouillon Broth (page 62). The base of this broth is unadulterated vegetable bouillon cubes, which are now readily available in whole-foods stores and which add a lot of flavor to a soup. Of course, it's always best to make your own stock, but if you're using this book you may not have the time.

With bread and a salad, a soup makes a satisfying and easy supper. If you want a filling soup, choose a recipe like the hearty, slightly picante Lentil and Tomato Soup with Pasta (page 84) or the savory Thick Split Pea and Rice Soup on page 83. These have complementary protein in the correct proportions built right in. The Elegant Pressure-Cooked White Bean Soup on page 74, the rich Cheddar Cheese Soup with Vegetables on page 66, and all the "cream" soups like those on pages 78–80 are also quite substantial. What makes the latter "cream soups" isn't cream at all but pureed potatoes, so you needn't worry about the fat. Yet these are as rich, velvety, and sensuous as any bisque.

Lighter soups—for example, the Buckwheat Noodle Soup with Green Beans on page 63, Simple Miso Soup (page 68), and Miso Soup with Buckwheat Noodles (page 70) are often enough for me. They are comforting and fancy in their own right, and are an interesting way to start off a larger meal. They make a perfect lunch, as well.

As you cook your way through this chapter, you'll experience the flavors of China, Italy, Japan, France, Spain, and other countries. And you'll find that you can create these flavors right in your own home. The best soups I've ever had have always been homemade. At home you have time for careful tasting and adjusting of seasonings; there is always time to add final touches. You are in control, and as you stir and taste your soup you will learn to perfect it.

TAMARI-BOUILLON BROTH
6 CUPS (1.5 L)

This soup base recipe takes only minutes to prepare and tastes quite acceptable. I often make it simultaneously with my soup, just by using water, the bouillon cubes, garlic, and soy sauce where a recipe calls for water or stock, as in the Instant Tamari-Bouillon Broth that follows. Make sure you buy unadulterated vegetable bouillon cubes from whole foods stores. If they're not available, use plain water when recipes call for this broth.

> 6 cups (1.5 L) water
> 3 vegetable bouillon cubes
> 1 to 2 cloves garlic, minced or put through a press
> ¼ cup (60 ml) tamari

Combine all the ingredients in a stock pot. Bring to a boil, then reduce the heat and simmer gently until the bouillon cubes dissolve. Make sure the bouillon is dissolved.

INSTANT TAMARI-BOUILLON BROTH

Omit the garlic. Combine the water, bouillon and tamari as you make the soup you are using it for.

BUCKWHEAT NOODLE SOUP WITH GREEN BEANS
SERVES 6 TO 8
PREPARATION TIME: 10 minutes
UNSUPERVISED COOKING: 15 minutes

Although there is pasta in this soup, it's a light one. I love the contrast of textures—the soft noodles against the crisp green beans, which should remain bright green.

> 6 cups (1.5 L) Tamari-Bouillon Broth (page 62)
> ½ to 1 teaspoon (2.5–5 ml) freshly grated ginger
> ½ pound (225 gm) green beans, ends snapped off and washed, sliced if desired
> ½ pound (225 gm) buckwheat noodles
> Additional tamari to taste
> Freshly ground pepper

Bring the broth to a simmer in a stock pot or Dutch oven. Add the ginger and green beans and cook 5 minutes. Add the noodles and cook another 5 to 7 minutes. Add more tamari if you wish, some freshly ground pepper to taste, and serve.

MENU SUGGESTIONS
Main dishes: Puffed Omelet with choice of filling (page 183); Southern Spoonbread (page 189); Tofu Cutlets (page 131)
Salads: Leftover Beans Salad (page 294); Oriental Salad (page 297); Cottage Cheese and Tomato Salad with Miso Dressing (page 296)
Desserts: Gingered Fruit (page 312); Prune Soufflé (page 307), unless you are serving a main dish with eggs; Pineapple with Mint

SIMPLE GARLIC SOUP PROVENÇAL
SERVES 4
PREPARATION TIME: 5 minutes at most
COOKING TIME: 10 minutes

When I have a cold or the flu there is one consolation—garlic soup. Garlic is a natural antiseptic, antibiotic, and purgative. For centuries it has been used as a cure for colds, stomach ailments, and high blood pressure. It is a true restorative.

But you don't have to be sick to enjoy this easy soup. It certainly doesn't taste like medicine, and it doesn't give you garlic breath. The version below is the simplest I've seen.

This light soup would go well with any of the main dishes or salads.

      6 cups (1.5 L) water
   1½ teaspoons (7 ml) salt
8 to 10 large cloves garlic, minced or put through a press
      1 teaspoon (5 ml) dried sage
      1 small bay leaf
      1 teaspoon (5 ml) dried thyme
      2 eggs
         Freshly ground pepper to taste
      4 slices bread, toasted or sautéed in butter or olive oil

Bring the water to a boil in a medium saucepan and add the salt, garlic, and herbs. Simmer 10 minutes.

Beat the eggs in a large bowl. Stirring all the while with a whisk or wooden spoon, strain the broth into the bowl. Adjust the seasoning and serve at once, garnishing each serving with a crouton.

MENU SUGGESTIONS
Main dishes: Avocado Tacos (page 263); Fettuccine with Pesto (page 215); Risi e Bisi (page 108)
Salads: Tossed Green Salad (page 280); Tomato and Mozzarella

Salad (page 282); Tabouli with Pressure-Cooked Garbanzos (page 286)

Desserts: Noodle Kugel (page 318); Tofu Noodle Kugel (page 319); Rice or Leftover Grains Pudding (page 321)

POTATO LEEK SOUP
SERVES 6

PREPARATION TIME: 10 to 15 minutes
SUPERVISED COOKING: 5 minutes
UNSUPERVISED COOKING: 30 minutes
ADDITIONAL WORK: 2 to 5 minutes

This soup is a classic. It's easy, filling, and satisfying; warming and delicious any time of year. It keeps several days in the refrigerator I once lived on a big pot of it for a week in southern France; the landlady had left us with a huge basket of potatoes, and there was only one thing to do with them.

2 tablespoons (30 ml) butter or safflower oil
3 cups (700 ml) sliced leeks, white part only
2 tablespoons (30 ml) whole-wheat pastry flour or un-bleached white
2 quarts (2 L) Tamari-Bouillon Broth (page 62) or 3 or 4 vegetable bouillon cubes dissolved in hot water
2 pounds (1 kg) potatoes, unpeeled, diced
Salt and freshly ground pepper to taste
3 to 4 tablespoons (45–60 ml) dry vermouth or sherry, or more to taste
FOR GARNISH: 2 to 3 tablespoons (30–45 ml) minced fresh parsley

Heat the butter in a heavy-bottomed soup pot or saucepan and add the leeks. Stir and cover the pan. Cook slowly over medium-low heat for 5 minutes, until the leeks are tender and fragrant but not browned. Stir in the flour and cook, stirring, 2 to 3 minutes, until just beginning to brown. Beat in 2 cups (475 ml) of the hot broth and stir to blend thoroughly. Add the remaining broth and the potatoes and bring to a simmer. Add some salt, cover, and simmer 25 to 30 minutes, until the potatoes are tender and the broth aromatic.

Add the vermouth or sherry and salt and pepper to taste. With the back of a spoon mash some of the potatoes against the side of the pot, until the soup has the desired thickness. Serve garnished with minced parsley.

Note: If you want to increase the protein of this soup for a substantial meal, dissolve 1 tablespoon (15 ml) miso in ¼ cup (60 ml) of the broth and add it to the soup along with 1 cup (250 ml) slivered tofu just before serving. Reduce salt.

MENU SUGGESTIONS

Main dishes: Simple Cheese, Bread, and Mushroom Casserole (page 186); Southern Spoonbread (page 189); Broccoli or Cauliflower "Gratin" (page 143)

Salads: Tossed Green Salad (page 280); Simple Purple Cabbage and Carrot Salad with Fresh Herbs (page 298); Cucumber Yogurt Salad (page 282)

Desserts: Prune Soufflé (page 307); Strawberries or Raspberries with Red Wine (page 315)

CHEDDAR CHEESE SOUP WITH VEGETABLES
SERVES 6

PREPARATION TIME: 20 to 25 minutes
SUPERVISED COOKING: 5 to 10 minutes
UNSUPERVISED COOKING: 20 minutes

This velvety, savory soup was inspired by my friend Tani. She had me over for dinner one night and had a luscious cheese soup with sliced mushrooms in it. I liked the contrast of textures and have tried to duplicate it here.

1 tablespoon (15 ml) plus 2 teaspoons (10 ml) safflower oil
1 onion, chopped
2 medium potatoes, peeled and diced (2 cups; 475 ml)
4 cups (1 L) water
2 vegetable bouillon cubes
¼ pound (100 gm) mushrooms, sliced (2 cups; 475 ml)
1 carrot, sliced or julienned
1 clove garlic, minced or put through a press
4 to 6 tablespoons (60–90 ml) dry white wine
½ teaspoon (2.5 ml) dried thyme
Salt and freshly ground pepper to taste
2 cups (475 ml) milk
2 cups (475 ml) grated sharp Cheddar cheese
½ cup (120 ml) freshly grated Parmesan cheese
½ teaspoon (2.5 ml) crushed dried rosemary

Heat the 2 teaspoons (10 ml) oil in a heavy-bottomed soup pot or Dutch oven and sauté the onion until tender. Add the potatoes, water, and bouillon cubes. Bring to a simmer, then cover and simmer 20 minutes. Puree in batches in a blender or food processor.

Rinse out the pot and heat the 1 tablespoon (15 ml) safflower oil, the mushrooms, carrot, and garlic and sauté for about 3 minutes. Add 4 tablespoons of the wine and the thyme and continue to cook for a few minutes until the vegetables are tender and aromatic. Season with salt and freshly ground pepper and stir in the pureed potato broth. Stir in the milk and the cheeses, the rosemary, and 2 tablespoons additional wine, if desired, and heat through until the cheese is thoroughly melted. Serve immediately.

MENU SUGGESTIONS

With a green or spinach salad and bread, this soup is a filling meal. Choose a fruity dessert.

♥ HOT AND SOUR SOUP
SERVES 6
VEGETABLE PREPARATION TIME: 15 minutes
COOKING TIME: 15 minutes

This soup is a favorite of mine, and one of the easiest and best I know of. It's light and warms you with its slightly piquant, vinegary broth. Even without the traditional pork (or chicken blood, which is often an ingredient in traditional recipes) it's a true Hot and Sour Soup.

6 dried Chinese mushrooms (about 1 ounce; 25 gm)
8 cups (2 L) water
4 vegetable bouillon cubes
6 green onions, sliced, white part and green part separated
2 cakes (½ pound; 225 gm) tofu, slivered
2 tablespoons (30 ml) dry sherry or Chinese rice wine
¼ cup (60 ml) cider vinegar or Chinese rice wine vinegar, or more to taste
2 tablespoons (30 ml) tamari, or more to taste
2 tablespoons (30 ml) cornstarch or arrowroot
¼ cup (60 ml) cold water
2 eggs, beaten
¼ cup (60 ml) carrot, cut in 2-inch matchsticks
¼ cup (60 ml) bok choy or celery cut in 2-inch matchsticks
¼ to ½ teaspoon (1.25–2.5 ml) freshly ground black pepper

Before you begin cutting the vegetables, place the mushrooms in a small bowl. Bring 2 cups (475 ml) of the water to a boil and pour over

67

the mushrooms. Cover and let stand 15 minutes. Meanwhile, prepare the other vegetables.

Place the remaining 6 cups water and the bouillon cubes in a large saucepan. Drain the mushrooms in a strainer over a bowl and add their liquid to the soup pot. Bring to a simmer. Cut the mushrooms in slivers and add them to the stock, along with the white part of the green onions. Simmer 5 minutes and add the tofu. Simmer 5 more minutes and stir in the sherry, vinegar, and tamari. Dissolve the cornstarch or arrowroot in the ¼ cup (60 ml) cold water. Stir into the soup and bring to a gentle boil, stirring.

Drizzle the beaten eggs into the boiling soup, stirring with a fork or chopstick so that the egg forms shreds. When the soup becomes clear and slightly thickened, remove from the heat. Stir in the pepper (be generous—this is the "hot" part of the soup) and adjust vinegar and tamari.

Distribute the carrots, bok choy or celery, and the green onion tops among the bowls and ladle in the soup. Serve at once, passing additional pepper and vinegar so people can adjust hot and sour to taste.

MENU SUGGESTIONS

Main dishes: Fried Rice and Soy Grits with Vegetables (page 114); Chinese-Style Tofu and Vegetables with Grains (page 138); Southern Spoonbread (page 189)

Salads: Hot and Sour Buckwheat Noodle Salad (page 300), Tossed Green Salad, (page 280)

Desserts: Gingered Fruit (page 312); Oranges with Mint; Rice or Leftover Grains Pudding (page 321)

♥ Omit tamari and eggs.

SIMPLE MISO SOUP

SERVES 4 TO 6

PREPARATION TIME: 10 minutes
SUPERVISED COOKING: 10 minutes

Miso soup is a staple in most Japanese homes, where it is eaten for breakfast. It's high in protein, is very light, and for me it seems to have restorative properties.

The traditional stock for miso soup is called *dashi,* and is made with kombu—giant kelp seaweed—and bonito flakes. Since this is a vegetarian book, I have omitted the bonito flakes and use only kombu for

68

the stock. This seaweed has a very strong flavor, and it's important not to let it boil or its flavor will overpower the soup.

6 cups (1.5 L) cold water
1½ ounces (scant 40 gm) kombu (kelp; available in natural foods stores and Oriental markets)
½ teaspoon (2.5 ml) grated or minced fresh ginger (optional)
1 tablespoon (15 ml) dry sherry (optional)
3 to 4 tablespoons (45–60 ml) miso, to taste
¾ cup (180 ml) sliced fresh mushrooms
1 cake (¼ pound; 100 g) tofu, diced
½ teaspoon (2.5 ml) sesame oil (optional)
¼ cup (60 ml) chopped chives or ½ bunch watercress

Place the kombu and water in a soup pot or Dutch oven. Heat slowly, so that the water takes at least 10 minutes to come to the boiling point, but *do not* allow the water to boil. Meanwhile, prepare the vegetables and tofu.

Test the kombu to see if it is tender by piercing the fleshiest part with your thumbnail. If it is tough, continue to heat for a few minutes longer, being careful not to boil. When the kombu is soft, remove from the pot. Add the ginger and sherry, if desired.

Bring stock to a simmer. Place the miso in a bowl and whisk in ¼ cup (60 ml) of the stock. Add the miso liquid to the stock and keep at a bare simmer. (Boiling will destroy the bacillae in the miso and change the flavor.) Add the mushrooms and tofu and heat through, about 3 minutes. Add the optional sesame oil. Distribute the chives among serving bowls, ladle in the soup, and serve.

MENU SUGGESTIONS

Main dishes: Chinese-Style Tofu and Vegetables with Grains(page 138); Sweet and Sour Cabbage (page 141); Chinese-Style Snow Peas and Water Chestnuts (page 140); Fried Rice and Soy Grits with Vegetables (page 114)

Salads: Oriental Salad (page 297); Hot and Sour Buckwheat Noodle Salad (page 300); Hot and Sour Bean Sprout Salad (page 298); Tossed Green Salad (page 280)

Desserts: Prune Soufflé (page 307); Bread Pudding (page 320); Apples with Lime Juice (page 312)

MISO SOUP WITH BUCKWHEAT NOODLES
SERVES 4 TO 6
PREPARATION TIME: 10 minutes
SUPERVISED COOKING: 20 minutes

This is just like the preceding Simple Miso Soup, with the addition of nutty buckwheat noodles (soba), which make a heartier dish. It's as easy as the simpler version and takes only 10 minutes longer to cook.

Ingredients for Simple Miso Soup (page 68)
6 ounces (175 gm) buckwheat noodles (soba)

Follow the directions for Simple Miso Soup. After you add the miso to the soup, add the buckwheat noodles. Simmer without boiling; the noodles will take about 10 minutes to cook. Once they are soft, add the tofu and mushrooms and proceed as directed.

MENU SUGGESTIONS
With a salad, this soup is hearty enough to make a meal, though it would also go well with the suggestions for Simple Miso Soup, with the exception of the Hot and Sour Buckwheat Noodle Salad (page 300). Any dessert would be fine, with the exception of those based on noodles or grains.

♥ PUREED ZUCCHINI SOUP
SERVES 4 TO 6
PREPARATION TIME: 10 to 15 minutes
SUPERVISED COOKING: 15 minutes in all
UNSUPERVISED COOKING: 10 minutes

This soup is actually a coarse puree. The first time I had it, my friend Tani used the back of her spoon to mash the zucchini against the side of her cooking pot. It's a little faster if you pulse it in a blender or food processor. This is a light soup, but the milk gives it ample protein.

    1 tablespoon (15 ml) safflower oil or butter, more as needed
    2 pounds (1 kg) zucchini
    1 onion, minced
1 to 2 cloves garlic, to taste, minced or put through a press
    4 cups (950 ml) water
    2 vegetable bouillon cubes

2 cups (475 ml) milk

2 tablespoons (30 ml) mixed chopped fresh herbs (such as parsley, basil, dill, thyme) or 2 teaspoons (10 ml) dried basil

Scrub, then dice all but one half a zucchini. Slice the remaining zucchini half thin and set aside for garnish.

Heat the oil in a soup pot or Dutch oven and sauté the onion and garlic until the onion is beginning to be tender. Add the diced zucchini and sauté for about 5 minutes, stirring. Add the water and bouillon cubes and bring to a simmer. Cover and simmer for 10 minutes.

Remove from the heat and coarsely puree the vegetables and stock by pulsing in a blender or food processor, working in batches. Return to the pot and stir in the milk. Add salt and freshly ground pepper to taste, and the herbs. Heat through without boiling.

Steam or sauté the sliced zucchini until crisp-tender. Ladle the soup into bowls and float slices of cooked zucchini in each.

This soup is also good chilled.

MENU SUGGESTIONS

Main dishes: Pipérade (page 184), Braised Stuffed Artichokes in Wine (page 116), Curried Cauliflower Puree (page 153)

Salads: Tossed Green Salad (page 280); Tabouli (page 286); Leftover Grains Salad (page 293); Tomato Salad (page 284)

Desserts: Strawberries or Raspberries with Red Wine (page 315); Banana Yogurt Freeze (page 315).

♥ Omit bouillon cubes and salt. Use nonfat milk.

♥ HOT OR ICED TOMATO SOUP
serves 6

Preparation time: 10 minutes
Supervised cooking: 5 minutes
Unsupervised cooking: 15 minutes
Chilling time: 2 hours

This garlicky tomato soup warms and comforts when served hot, in cold weather, and is refreshing chilled, in the summer. It's very simple and light.

1 to 2   tablespoons (15–30 ml) olive oil, safflower oil, or butter
    3   tablespoons (45 ml) dry white wine
    4   cloves garlic, minced or put through a press
    2   tablespoons (30 ml) paprika
    5   cups (1.2 L) pureed ripe tomatoes, fresh (about 3 pounds; 1.4 kg) or canned Italian, strained
    3   cups (700 ml) water
    1   vegetable bouillon cube
    3   tablespoons (45 ml) tomato paste
      Pinch of cayenne
      Salt and freshly ground pepper to taste
1 to 3   teaspoons (5–15 ml) lemon juice, to taste
2 to 3   tablespoons (30–45 ml) chopped fresh herbs (such as basil, parsley, marjoram, thyme, dill)
For Garnish: Yogurt, alfalfa sprouts or lentil sprouts, and additional herbs

Heat 1 tablespoon (15 ml) oil in a heavy-bottomed soup pot or Dutch oven and add the garlic and white wine. Cook for 2 minutes. Add the paprika and more oil, if necessary, and sauté another minute. Stir in the tomatoes, water, bouillon, and the tomato paste. Bring to a simmer and simmer 10 to 15 minutes. Remove from the heat and add a small pinch of cayenne, lemon juice to taste, and salt and pepper. If serving hot, stir in the herbs and serve. If serving chilled, cool and chill in the refrigerator overnight or in the freezer for one hour. Just before serving, stir in the herbs and adjust the seasoning. Spoon into bowls and top each serving with a dollop of yogurt, a handful of sprouts, and more herbs.

With a salad and whole-grain bread, and some cheese or pâté for additional protein, this makes a nice light summer meal, Or try the following:

Main dishes: Kasha with Mushrooms, Water Chestnuts, and Celery (page 128); Cabbage Leaves Stuffed with Kasha (page 130); Barley Mushroom Pilaff (page 127); Southern Spoonbread (page 189); Simple Cheese, Bread, and Mushroom Casserole (page 186)

Salads: Hot and Sour Buckwheat Noodle Salad (page 300); Leftover Grains Salad (page 293); Leftover Beans Salad (page 294); Tossed Green Salad (page 280)

Desserts: Pineapple with Mint; Cantaloupe with Apricot Puree and Almonds (page 313); Noodle Kugel (page 318).

♥ Omit salt. Use 1 tablespoon safflower oil.

♥ MUSHROOM AND BARLEY SOUP
SERVES 6

PREPARATION TIME: 15 minutes
SUPERVISED COOKING: 10 minutes
UNSUPERVISED COOKING: 40 minutes

Barley and mushrooms were made for each other. This thick, savory, hearty soup is a perfect dish for a cold winter night. The soy flakes complete the protein.

```
2 to 3   teaspoons (10–15 ml) safflower oil or butter
     1   medium onion, chopped
     3   cups (700 ml) sliced fresh mushrooms (½ pound; 225 gm)
1 to 2   cloves garlic, to taste, minced or put through a press
     3   tablespoons (45 ml) dry white wine
    ½    teaspoon (2.5 ml) dried thyme
   1½    cups (350 ml) barley, washed
    ½    cup (120 ml) soy flakes
     8   cups (1.9 L) Tamari-Bouillon Broth (page 62)
         Salt and freshly ground pepper to taste
     2   tablespoons (30 ml) chopped fresh dill or 1 tablespoon (15
         ml) dried
1 to 2   tablespoons (15–30 ml) dry sherry
```

Heat the safflower oil or butter in a soup pot or Dutch oven and sauté the onion just until it's beginning to get translucent. Add the mushrooms and garlic and sauté, stirring, for 2 minutes. Add the wine and the thyme, and sauté for another 3 minutes. Add the barley and sauté stirring, for another 3 minutes. Add the soy flakes and the broth, bring to a boil, then reduce the heat and simmer for 40 minutes. Season to taste with salt and freshly ground pepper; stir in the dill and sherry and serve.

MENU SUGGESTIONS
Served with a green salad and whole-grain bread, this soup makes a meal. Serve a fruity dessert.

♥ Use water instead of Tamari-Bouillon Broth. Omit salt. With the dill, add 1 teaspoon (5 ml) thyme, ½ to 1 teaspoon (2.5–5 ml) sage. Simmer a few additional minutes before you serve.

ELEGANT PRESSURE-COOKED WHITE BEAN SOUP
SERVES 6
PREPARATION TIME: 10 minutes
SUPERVISED COOKING: 10 minutes in all
UNSUPERVISED COOKING: 45 minutes

I once served this soup twice in one week, and both times the response from my guests was, "This is a very special soup." It is definitely suitable for company, as well as for a simple family meal. The herb butter is what really makes the difference.

FOR THE SOUP:
2 cups (475 ml) dried white beans, washed and picked over
1 onion, chopped
4 cloves garlic, minced or put through a press
8 cups (1.9 L) water
3 vegetable bouillon cubes
1 large bay leaf
2 sprigs fresh parsley
   Salt and freshly ground pepper to taste
   Milk (optional)
FOR GARNISH: 1½ cups (350 ml) croutons

FOR THE LEMON-HERB BUTTER:
4 tablespoons (60 ml) butter, softened
1 medium clove garlic, minced fine or put through a press
2 tablespoons (30 ml) finely chopped fresh parsley
   Juice of 1 large lemon

74

Place all the ingredients for the soup *except* the salt, pepper, milk, and croutons in a pressure cooker and bring to a boil. Cover, bring to 15 pounds (7 kg) pressure, and cook over a medium flame for 45 minutes. Meanwhile, mix together the butter, garlic, parsley, and lemon juice, and set aside.

Remove the pressure cooker from the heat and run under cold water for several minutes. Remove the gauge and, when all the steam has escaped, carefully remove the lid.

If you don't have a pressure cooker, soak the beans overnight or for several hours. Or soak them by combining with the water and bringing to a boil. Boil 2 minutes, cover lightly, remove from heat, and let sit 2 hours. Now combine everything in a saucepan or Dutch oven and bring it to a boil. Cover, reduce heat, and cook for 1-½ to 2 hours, until tender.

Discard the bay leaf and parsley. Puree the soup in a blender in batches, and return to the pressure cooker. Add salt and freshly ground pepper to taste. Heat through, add the lemon-herb butter, and stir to melt. If desired, thin the soup out with milk. Serve garnished with toasted croutons.

MENU SUGGESTIONS

Serve this soup with a big green salad or a grain salad such as Tabouli (page 286; omit the garbanzos) or Leftover Grains Salad (page 293), which would complement the protein in the beans. Whole-grain bread is also a suitable complement.

Desserts: Strawberries in Red Wine and Preserves Syrup (page 310); Pineapple Banana Mint Sherbet (page 316); Strawberry Freeze (page 317)

♥ CREAMY CELERY AND GARLIC SOUP
SERVES 6 TO 8

PREPARATION TIME: 15 minutes
SUPERVISED COOKING: 10 minutes in all
UNSUPERVISED COOKING: 30 minutes

Every time I need one stick of celery for a dish, I'm left with the rest of the bunch, and rather than let it go limp in my refrigerator, I've taken to making soups with it. I made this beguilingly simple one on a day when I had a sore throat and knew I needed lots of garlic but also had a nice firm bunch of celery to use up. A cream of celery soup would be wonderful for dinner, I thought, but I didn't want to use milk in it. So along with the celery and garlic I cooked a potato which made the soup blend to a rich, tantalizing puree. With a salad and bread it made a marvelous dinner, two nights in a row.

> 1 tablespoon butter or safflower oil
> 1 bunch green onions (both white and green parts), chopped, or 1 small onion, chopped
> 1 head garlic, cloves separated and peeled
> 1 bunch (give or take a stalk or two) celery, sliced, leaves removed
> 1 large potato, peeled and diced
> 7 cups (1.7 L) water
> 3 vegetable bouillon cubes
> 2 sprigs fresh parsley
> Salt and freshly ground pepper to taste
> ½ cup (120 ml) freshly grated Parmesan cheese (optional)

Heat the butter in a large soup pot or Dutch oven and sauté the onion until tender, 2 to 3 minutes. Add the garlic and celery and sauté for another 2 minutes. Add the potato, water, vegetable bouillon cubes, and parsley and bring to a simmer. Cover and simmer 30 minutes. Remove the parsley and discard. Remove from the heat, add salt to taste and puree in a blender, in batches, or put through a food mill. Return to the pot and heat through. Add pepper to taste and the optional Parmesan; adjust the salt.

MENU SUGGESTIONS

Main dishes: Tofu Cutlets (page 131); Chilled Tofu with Dipping Sauces (page 132); Omelet of your choice (pages 176–184)

Salads: Curried Carrot Salad (page 284); Leftover Grains Salad (page 293); Tossed Green Salad (page 280); Tomato Salad (page 284)

Desserts: Prune Soufflé (page 307); Figs Poached in Madeira (page 311); Bread Pudding (page 320)

♥ Omit bouillon, salt, and Parmesan. Season with lemon juice (up to 2 tablespoons), thyme, and sage or basil (about 1 teaspoon; 5 ml), which you should add after pureeing the soup and before heating through; use lots of pepper. This is a marginal soup for heart patients because celery is very high in sodium.

CELERY TOMATO SOUP WITH RICE
SERVES 4

PREPARATION TIME: 15 minutes
SUPERVISED COOKING: 10 minutes
UNSUPERVISED COOKING: 30 minutes

Another good way to use celery. Celery and tomatoes contain so much sodium that they seem to season this simple soup as it cooks, and I find no need for additional salt.

    1 tablespoon (15 ml) butter or safflower oil
    1 onion, minced
    1 large clove garlic, minced or put through a press
    2 cups (475 ml) sliced celery (about ½ bunch)
    ½ cup (120 ml) sliced mushrooms (optional)
    2 tablespoons (30 ml) dry white wine
    ¼ teaspoon (1.25 ml) dried thyme
    ¼ cup (60 ml) raw brown rice
    1 cup (250 ml) peeled and diced tomato
    4 cups (250 ml) water
    2 vegetable bouillon cubes
      Freshly ground pepper
    ¼ cup (60 ml) freshly grated Parmesan or other cheese, such as Monterey Jack, Cheddar, or Gruyère

Heat the butter in a heavy-bottomed soup pot or Dutch oven and sauté the onion and garlic for 2 minutes. Add the celery and optional mushrooms and sauté another 5 minutes. Add the wine, thyme, and brown rice and sauté another 3 minutes. Add the tomatoes, water, and bouillon cubes and bring to a boil. Cover, reduce the heat, and simmer 30 minutes. Add freshly ground pepper and stir in the cheese. Stir until melted and mixed through the soup, then serve.

MENU SUGGESTIONS
Main dishes: Southern Spoonbread or Simple Cheese, Bread, and Mushroom Casserole (page 189 or 186) Tofu Cutlets (page 131) Pasta with Tofu Cream Sauce (page 209)

Salads: Tossed Green Salad (page 280); Watercress, Mushroom, and Tofu Salad (page 292); Leftover Beans Salad (page 294)
Desserts: Puffed Amaretto Omelet (page 306); Banana Yogurt Freeze (page 315); Apples with Lime Juice (page 312)

CREAM OF SPINACH AND KASHA SOUP
SERVES 6 TO 8

PREPARATION TIME: 15 minutes
SUPERVISED COOKING: 5 minutes
UNSUPERVISED COOKING: 20 to 25 minutes
ADDITIONAL WORK: 5 to 10 minutes

This rich, nutty-flavored soup will be a pleasant surprise. It's very thick, because the grains are pureed (though you must be careful not to puree them for too long or the soup will be gummy), and no butter or oil is used. You can thin it out to your own taste. Use the leftovers as a topping for baked potatoes or vegetables.

 ¾ cup (180 ml) buckwheat groats, washed
 1 egg, beaten
 1 onion, chopped
 6 cups (1.5 L) water
 3 vegetable bouillon cubes
 ½ pound (225 gm) spinach, washed and trimmed
 ¼ teaspoon (1.25 ml) freshly grated nutmeg (more to taste)
 ¼ teaspoon (1.25 ml) ground ginger
 ¼ teaspoon (1.25 ml) ground coriander
   Salt and freshly ground pepper to taste
 2 cups (475 ml) milk or buttermilk (buttermilk will give the soup a tarter flavor)
FOR GARNISH: Sunflower seeds or almond slivers and chopped fresh parsley

Mix together the buckwheat groats and the beaten egg until all the grains are coated. Heat a heavy-bottomed soup pot or Dutch oven over medium heat and add the groats. Cook, stirring all the while, until the egg is absorbed by the groats and the grains begin to smell toasty. Add the onion and water and bring to a boil. Add the bouillon cubes, then reduce the heat, cover, and simmer 20 minutes, or until the buckwheat groats are tender. Add the spinach to the soup, along with the nutmeg, ginger, and coriander, and simmer 5 minutes longer.

Puree the soup in a blender or a food processor, in batches, until only partially pureed. (Remember: don't puree too long or the soup will be gummy, owing to the starch in the kasha.) Return to the soup pot and stir in the milk or buttermilk. Add salt and freshly ground pepper to taste; heat through, stirring, and serve, garnished with sunflower seeds or slivered almonds and chopped parsley.

MENU SUGGESTIONS

This is a filling soup and can serve as a meal, with a salad, such as Leeks Vinaigrette (page 289), Warm or Chilled Cauliflower or Broccoli Vinaigrette (page 290), Jícama and Orange Salad (page 295), or Tossed Green Salad (page 280). Serve a light, fruity dessert, such as the fruit ices on pages 315–318.

♥ PUREED CURRY OF CAULIFLOWER SOUP
SERVES 6 TO 8

PREPARATION TIME: 15 minutes
SUPERVISED COOKING: 10 minutes in all
UNSUPERVISED COOKING: 20 minutes

This wonderful soup is especially nice garnished with chutney. If you don't like curry, however, you can use the same method and make Cauliflower Cheese Soup (see below). Just omit the curry and melt Cheddar cheese into the soup when you heat it through. The cheese version is seasoned with dry mustard and thyme or dill.

1 tablespoon (15 ml) butter or safflower oil
1 medium onion, chopped
1 large clove garlic, minced or put through a press
1 tablespoon (15 ml) curry powder
1 medium carrot, sliced
2 cups (475 ml) potato, peeled and diced
6 cups (1.2 L) cauliflower florets (1 large head cauliflower)
4 cups (950 ml) Tamari-Bouillon Broth (page 62)
2 cups (475 ml) buttermilk
  Salt and freshly ground pepper to taste
FOR GARNISH: Chutney and steamed cauliflower

Heat the butter in a large, heavy-bottomed soup pot or Dutch oven and sauté the onion and garlic, with the curry powder, until the onion is tender. Add the carrot, potato, 4 cups of the cauliflower, and the broth and bring to a simmer. Cover and simmer 20 minutes. Remove from the heat and puree coarsely in a blender or food processor, in batches, or put through a food mill. Return to the pot and add the buttermilk. Heat through and add salt and pepper to taste.

Slice the remaining 2 cups of cauliflower, steam briefly, and serve the soup garnished with the cauliflower and a small dollop of chutney.

MENU SUGGESTIONS

Main dishes: Picante Garbanzos (page 105); Tomatoes Stuffed with Rice and Lentils (page 113)

Salads: Tossed Green Salad (page 280); Curried Carrot Salad (page 284); Oriental Salad (page 297)

Desserts: Gingered Fruit (page 312); Baked Grapefruit with Tequila or Sherry (page 313); Apricot Soufflé (page 308)

♥ Use water instead of stock; substitute yogurt for buttermilk; omit salt.

CAULIFLOWER CHEESE SOUP

Follow the above recipe, omitting the curry powder and the chutney garnish. When you add the buttermilk, also add 1 cup (250 ml) grated Cheddar cheese (or more to taste), ½ to 1 teaspoon dry mustard (2.5–5 ml) (or to taste), and 1 teaspoon (5 ml) dried thyme or dillseed. Heat through until the cheese is melted and serve, garnished with the steamed cauliflower.

CREAM OF SPINACH AND POTATO SOUP
SERVES 6

PREPARATION TIME: 20 minutes
SUPERVISED COOKING: 10 minutes in all
UNSUPERVISED COOKING: 20 minutes

Another easy, delicious, soothing soup. This is good chilled as well as hot.

   1 tablespoon (15 ml) butter or safflower oil
   1 onion, diced
1 to 2 large cloves garlic, minced or put through a press
   2 cups (475 ml) potatoes, peeled and diced
   4 cups (950 ml) Tamari-Bouillon Broth (page 62)
   1 pound (450 gm) spinach, washed and trimmed
   1 cup (250 ml) milk
   1 cup (250 ml) plain low-fat yogurt
1 to 2 tablespoons (15–30 ml) dry white wine

1 tablespoon (15 ml) lemon juice
Salt and freshly ground pepper to taste
Freshly grated nutmeg to taste
½ cup (120 ml) freshly grated Parmesan cheese
For Garnish: Alfalfa sprouts, chopped fresh herbs (such as parsley, dill, marjoram, basil) croutons, sunflower seeds, and/or yogurt

Heat the butter in a heavy-bottomed soup pot or Dutch oven and sauté the onion, one clove of the garlic, and the potatoes until the onion is tender. Add the broth and bring to a boil. Reduce the heat, cover, and simmer 15 minutes, or until the potato is tender. Add the spinach, stir, and cook, uncovered, 5 minutes. Remove from the heat and puree the liquid and vegetables in a blender, in batches. Return to the pot and whisk in the milk, yogurt, white wine, lemon juice, and salt and pepper to taste. Return to the heat. Add the second clove of garlic, if desired, a little nutmeg, and the Parmesan. Heat through slowly and serve, or cool and chill. Serve topped with the garnishes of your choice.

MENU SUGGESTIONS

Main dishes: Egg and Poblano Tacos (page 267); Southern Spoonbread (page 189); Pipérade (page 184), Pasta with Uncooked Tomatoes and Cheese (page 207)
Salads: Coleslaw (page 295); Leftover Beans Salad (page 294); Jícama and Orange Salad with Avocados (page 295)
Desserts: Puffed Grand Marnier Omelet (page 307); Oranges with Mint; Orange Ice (page 318)

ROSEMARY'S CHILLED LETTUCE AND POTATO SOUP
SERVES 6
PREPARATION TIME: 10 to 15 minutes
SUPERVISED COOKING: 10 minutes in all
UNSUPERVISED COOKING: 25 minutes in all

I'm not sure this is actually Rosemary's soup, but every time I eat it I think of my friend Rosemary, who spent a week with us in the south of France, because hers was the first lettuce soup I'd ever had.

We had spent the afternoon picnicking at a house secluded in the mountains of Provence. There were about ten of us, and it was a long, lazy afternoon with much wine. I had left in the middle of the festivities to drive to Marseille to pick up a friend who was flying in from London for a romantic weekend, and the rest of the crew was to make dinner.

When I got back to La Sara, our own big stucco house, dinner preparations were indeed under way. Apparently everybody had just gotten home from the picnic, and I was impressed to see how the group had rallied after the inebriated afternoon. Rosemary had said she was going to make a lettuce soup, and she had pulled it off. There hadn't been enough time to chill it properly, but it was marvelous as it was, served from a great big blue-and-white bowl, not quite hot and not quite cold. How could anything made with cooked lettuce be so rich and exciting?

I finally got around to making my own version a few days after a catering job, when I had two large heads of leaf lettuce that I was determined to use one way or another. The soup I made was thick and hot, just right on a cold winter night. Had it been spring or summer I would have chilled it and garnished it with fresh herbs for a splendid, refreshing potage.

This is a good way to use up lettuce when your garden is producing abundantly.

           1 tablespoon (15 ml) butter or safflower oil
           1 onion, chopped
    3 to 4 cloves garlic, to taste, minced or put through a press
           2 cups (475 ml) peeled, diced potatoes
           5 cups (1.2 L) Tamari-Bouillon Broth (page 62)
           6 cups (1.5 L) lettuce, any variety, shredded
        1½ cups (350 ml) plain low-fat yogurt
           Salt and freshly ground pepper to taste
FOR GARNISH: Croutons, chopped fresh herbs (such as parsley, dill, marjoram, basil), alfalfa sprouts, sunflower seeds, yogurt and /or Parmesan cheese

Heat the butter in a heavy-bottomed soup pot or Dutch oven and sauté the onion and 2 cloves of the garlic until the onion is tender. Add the potatoes and broth and bring to a simmer. Cover and cook 15 minutes, or until the potato is tender. Add the lettuce and the remaining 1 or 2 cloves garlic; stir and cover. Cook 10 minutes longer and remove from the heat. Puree the vegetables and liquid in a blender, in batches, or put through a food mill, and return to the pot. Stir in the yogurt. Add salt and freshly ground pepper to taste and heat through, but do not boil. Or cool and chill several hours. Serve topped with the garnishes of your choice.

MENU SUGGESTIONS
Main dishes: Any of the pasta dishes would be appropriate; also, Spicy

Eggplant Miso Sauté with Bulgur (page 122); Pipérade (page 184) Braised Stuffed Artichokes in Wine (with or without stuffing, page 116); Green Beans à la Provençal (page 147)

Salads: Leftover Beans Salad (page 294); Tabouli with Pressure-Cooked Garbanzos (page 286); Tomato Salad (page 284); Curried Carrot Salad (page 284)

Desserts: Figs Poached in Madeira (page 311); Strawberries in Champagne (page 311); Peaches with Marsala (page 314)

♥ THICK SPLIT PEA AND RICE SOUP
SERVES 6

PREPARATION TIME: 5 to 10 minutes
SUPERVISED COOKING: 5 minutes
UNSUPERVISED COOKING: 1 hour

With a nice green salad, this hearty, thick soup is definitely a meal in itself. The rice and split peas complement each other for complete protein. You can make it as garlicky as you want, and for a variation season it with curry. Those who miss the usual pork flavor in pea soup may be compensated by the unique, chewy texture of the brown rice.

```
      1 tablespoon (15 ml) safflower or peanut oil
      1 onion, chopped
      1 medium carrot, sliced
 2 to 4 cloves garlic, to taste, minced or put through a press
 1 to 3 teaspoons (5–15 ml) curry powder, to taste (optional)
      2 cups (475 ml) split peas, washed and picked over
      1 cup (250 ml) brown rice, washed
      8 cups (1.9 L) water
      1 bay leaf
        Salt and freshly ground pepper to taste
```

Heat the oil in a large, heavy-bottomed soup pot or Dutch oven and sauté the onion, carrot, half the amount of garlic you wish, and optional curry powder to taste until the onion is tender. Add the split peas, rice, water, and bay leaf and bring to a boil. Reduce the heat, cover, and simmer 1 hour, or until the peas are tender. Add the remaining garlic halfway through the cooking. Check from time to time and add more water if the soup becomes too thick. Add salt and freshly ground pepper to taste and serve.

MENU SUGGESTIONS
Serve with a big salad: Tossed Green Salad (page 280); Tomato Salad

(page 284), or Lettuce Salad with Oranges (page 281) would all be good. Serve fresh fruit for dessert; pineapple would be very refreshing.

♥ Omit salt; use 2 teaspoons (10 ml) safflower oil.

♥ LENTIL AND TOMATO SOUP WITH PASTA
SERVES 6 TO 8

PREPARATION TIME: 10 to 15 minutes
SUPERVISED COOKING: 10 minutes in all
UNSUPERVISED COOKING: 1 hour

This soup is another meal in itself. It's like an easy version of *pasta e fagiole,* and has a robust, slightly picante flavor. The pasta and lentils are complementary. This will keep well for a few days.

  1 tablespoon (15 ml) safflower oil
  1 onion, chopped
3 to 4 cloves garlic, to taste, minced or put through a press
  2 cups (475 ml) lentils (¾ pound; 350 gm), washed and picked over
  7 cups (1.7 L) water
  1 pound (450 gm) tomatoes, peeled, seeded, and chopped
  1 bay leaf
  1 dried hot red pepper
  1 teaspoon (5 ml) dried oregano
  1 tablespoon (15 ml) fresh basil or 1 teaspoon (5 ml) dried
    Salt and freshly ground pepper to taste
  4 ounces (100 gm) whole-wheat noodles, any shape (broken if long)
FOR GARNISH: ¼ cup (60 ml) chopped fresh parsley, ½ cup (120 ml) freshly grated Parmesan cheese

Heat the oil in a heavy-bottomed soup pot or Dutch oven and sauté the onion and half the amount of garlic you wish until the onion is tender. Add the lentils, water, tomatoes, and bay leaf and bring to a boil. Add the red pepper, then lower the heat, cover, and simmer 30 minutes. Remove the red pepper and add the remaining garlic; cover and simmer another 30 minutes, or until the lentils are tender and the broth aromatic. Add the oregano, basil, and salt and pepper to taste. About 10 minutes before you wish to serve, add the noodles and cook until tender. Sprinkle on the parsley and serve, garnishing each serving with Parmesan.

See the suggestions for Thick Split Pea and Rice Soup (page 83). This hearty soup only needs a salad to make a filling, balanced meal.

♥ Use 2 teaspoons (10 ml) safflower oil; omit salt and Parmesan.

♥ VERY QUICK CREAM OF PEA SOUP
SERVES 4

PREPARATION TIME: 5 minutes
COOKING TIME: 15 minutes

This soup tends to be sweet, with all the peas. You could use the same recipe substituting other frozen vegetables such as carrots or spinach.

    1 cup (250 ml) peeled, diced potato
    2 cups (250 ml) water
    2 packages (10 ounces each) frozen peas
2½ cups (600 ml) milk
    ½ cup (120 ml) dry white wine
    1 teaspoon (5 ml) marjoram
      Salt and freshly ground pepper to taste
FOR GARNISH: Plain yogurt, chopped fresh herbs and sprouts

Place the potato and water in a soup pot or Dutch oven and bring to a simmer. Simmer 10 minutes and add the peas. Simmer another 5 minutes, or until the peas are tender. Remove from the heat and puree the vegetables and liquid in a blender along with the milk, in batches, if necessary. Return to the pot, add the wine and marjoram, and heat through. Add salt and pepper to taste and serve garnished with yogurt, mint or other fresh herbs, and sprouts.

MENU SUGGESTIONS
Main dishes: Simple Cheese, Bread, and Mushroom Casserole (page 186); Spinach and Rice Gratin (page 197); Cauliflower Baked with Tomatoes, Cheese, and Sesame (page 194)
Salads: Warm or Chilled Cauliflower or Broccoli Salad (page 290); Fattoush (page 285); Tomato and Mozzarella Salad (page 282)
Desserts: Rice or Leftover Grains Pudding (page 321); Pineapple with Mint

♥ Use skim milk. Omit salt.
  Use unsalted frozen vegetables.

♥ CHILLED BUTTERMILK SOUP
SERVES 4 TO 6
PREPARATION TIME: 20 to 30 minutes in all
COOKING TIME: 15 minutes

This is cooling and delicious. Use the leftovers as a salad dressing.

2 medium potatoes, unpeeled, finely diced
2 cups (475 ml) water
  Salt
4 green onions, coarsely chopped, white and green parts separated
1 cucumber, peeled and diced
2 large ripe tomatoes, diced
4 cups (950 ml) buttermilk
3 large cloves garlic
  Juice of 1 to 2 lemons, to taste
2 tablespoons (30 ml) chopped fresh dill
1 tablespoon (15 ml) dillseeds
  Freshly ground pepper
FOR GARNISH: Alfalfa or mung sprouts, croutons, and/or sunflower seeds

Place the water and potatoes in a saucepan and simmer 15 minutes, adding the white part of the green onions toward the end to poach for a minute or two. Meanwhile prepare the cucumber and tomatoes and place in a bowl or tureen with the green part of the onions.

Remove half the onions and potatoes with a slotted spoon and add to the bowl of prepared vegetables. Puree the remaining potatoes and onions in their liquid, in a blender, along with the 2 cups of buttermilk, the garlic, and lemon juice until smooth. Pour into the bowl of vegetables and stir in the remaining 2 cups buttermilk, the dill, and dillseeds. Add freshly ground pepper, and either chill and serve or serve at once, garnished with sprouts, croutons, or sunflower seeds, or a combination of them.

MENU SUGGESTIONS
Main dishes: Braised Stuffed Artichokes in Wine (page 116); Kasha with Mushrooms, Water Chestnuts, and Celery (page 128); Cabbage Leaves Stuffed with Kasha, with Creamy Tofu Sauce (page 130)
Salads: Hot and Sour Bean Sprout Salad (page 298); Tossed Green Salad (page 280); Tabouli with Pressure-Cooked Garbanzos (page 286)
Desserts: Orange Ice (page 318); Sliced Melon; Peaches with Marsala (page 314).
  ♥ Substitute yogurt for buttermilk. Omit salt.

♥ GAZPACHO
SERVES 6 TO 8

PREPARATION TIME: 15 to 20 minutes
CHILLING TIME: ½ hour in the freezer, or several hours in the refrigerator, unless all the ingredients are cold

There are many ways to make a gazpacho, the refreshing chilled vegetable soup that originated in Spain. Mine is a blender soup, which I then garnish with minced vegetables, tofu, and sunflower seeds to achieve a variety of textures. In the spring and summer I almost always keep a batch in the refrigerator for immediate meals. It's like drinking a salad.

FOR THE SOUP:

    4 ripe tomatoes, quartered
    2 cloves garlic
    1 small onion, peeled, poached 1 minute in boiling water, drained and quartered
    ¾ medium cucumber, peeled and coarsely chopped (use the rest for garnish)
    ¾ large carrot, coarsely chopped (use the rest for garnish)
    ¾ large green pepper, seeded and quartered (use the rest for garnish)
    2 sprigs fresh parsley
    ¼ cup (60 ml) fresh basil or 2 tablespoons (30 ml) dried
¼ to ½ cup (60–120 ml) lemon juice, to taste
    2 tablespoons (30 ml) wine vinegar
  2 to 4 tablespoons (30–60 ml) olive oil, to taste
    3 cups (700 ml) cold V-8 juice
    Salt and freshly ground pepper to taste
    ⅛ teaspoon (scant 1 ml) cayenne (optional), 1 small jalapeño, seeded (optional) or 1 banana pepper, seeded (optional)

FOR GARNISH:

    1 cup (250 ml) cubed tofu
    ¼ cup (60 ml) minced cucumber
    ¼ cup (60 ml) minced green pepper
    2 large ripe tomatoes, chopped
    3 medium mushrooms, wiped clean and sliced
    ½ cup (120 ml) alfalfa, mung or lentil sprouts
  2 to 3 green onions, white part and green, chopped
    ¼ cup (60 ml) sunflower seeds
    ½ cup (120 ml) plain low-fat yogurt

Place all the vegetables and herbs in one bowl and the lemon juice, vinegar and olive oil in another. Using the V-8 juice and the lemon juice mixture to liquify, puree the vegetables in batches in a blender until smooth. Pour each batch into a bowl or plastic container. When all the vegetables have been pureed, stir the batches together and add salt and freshly ground pepper to taste. Cover and chill, either for a short time in the freezer or for a longer time in the refrigerator.

For the garnish, mix together the tofu, cucumber, green pepper and tomato. Have the mushrooms, sprouts, green onions, sunflower seeds, and yogurt in separate bowls. Place a spoonful of the vegetable-tofu mixture in each serving bowl and spoon in the soup. Lay a few mushroom slices on top Add a dollop of yogurt, a handful of sprouts and a sprinkling of sunflower seeds, and serve, passing the green onions in a bowl.

Note: If you don't have time to chill the soup, you can add an ice cube to each serving.

MENU SUGGESTIONS
Main dishes: Asparagus Timbale (page 193); Corn Pudding (page 196); Potatoes Gruyère (page 198); Potato and Refried Bean Tacos (page 264); Whole-Grain Pasta with Butter and Herbs (page 254)
Salads: Leftover Grains Salad (page 293); Leftover Beans Salad (page 294); Cold Pasta Salad (page 302)
Desserts: Strawberries or Raspberries with Red Wine (page 315); Strawberry Sherbet (page 317); Pineapple Banana Mint Sherbet (page 316)

♥ Omit the olive oil and the salt.

♥ CHILLED MELON SOUP
SERVES 6 TO 8
PREPARATION TIME: 15 minutes
CHILLING TIME: If ingredients are cold, the soup should be cold enough to serve at once. Otherwise, chill 30 minutes in the freezer.

This refreshing, light, and beautiful soup makes a felicitous opening course for a dinner party. My guests were ecstatic the first time I made it. I followed it with Mexican food and the combination was perfect. This soup could also work as a dessert.

   4 cups (950 ml) finely chopped ripe cantaloupe (1 cantaloupe)
   4 cups (950 ml) finely chopped ripe honeydew (1 small honeydew)

  1 cup (250 ml) fresh orange juice, strained
⅓ cup (80 ml) fresh lime juice
  1 cup (250 ml) chilled champagne
FOR GARNISH: ½ cup (120 ml) heavy cream, whipped; ½ cup (120 ml) sliced strawberries, peppermint leaves

Have the fruit chilled, if possible. Reserve and chill ½ cup (120 ml) each chopped cantaloupe and honeydew. Puree the remaining melon, in batches, in a blender with the orange juice and lime juice. Stir in the chopped melon. Serve immediately, or chill 30 minutes in the freezer or several hours in the refrigerator. It's best to serve this soon, because the orange juice takes on too acidic a taste if it stands very long. Just before serving, stir in the champagne.

  Serve in chilled bowls, garnished with whipped cream, strawberries, and mint.

MENU SUGGESTIONS

This makes a nice light first course and goes especially well with Mexican foods, though it wouldn't really clash with many things that followed. Avoid, of course, melon desserts.

Main dishes: Pasta with Uncooked Tomatoes and Cheese (page 207); Baked Macaroni and Cheese (page 211); Avocado Tacos (page 263); Green Tomato, Corn, and Tofu Tacos (page 270)

Salads: Jícama and Orange Salad with Avocados (page 295); Hot and Sour Buckwheat Noodle Salad (page 300); Guacamole (page 283); Tabouli with Pressure-Cooked Garbanzos (page 286)

Desserts: Rice or Leftover Grains Pudding (page 321); Bread Pudding (page 320); Banana Yogurt Freeze (page 315)

  ♥ Omit whipped cream.

♥ PEACH SOUP
SERVES 6

PREPARATION TIME: 15 minutes
CHILLING TIME: Can be served immediately if all the ingredients are cold, or chill 30 minutes in the freezer.

This is so good you'll want to eat the leftovers for breakfast, or even for dessert.

    3 pounds (1.4 kg) ripe peaches, peeled (see note below)
    ¼ cup (60 ml) mild honey
    3 tablespoons (45 ml) fresh lemon or lime juice, or more to taste
    5 cups (1.2 L) buttermilk
    1 cup (250 ml) fresh orange juice
    3 tablespoons (45 ml) peach brandy or Marsala
    ½ teaspoon (2.5 ml) ground cinnamon
    ½ teaspoon (2.5 ml) freshly grated nutmeg
    ¼ teaspoon (1.25 ml) ground ginger
    ½ teaspoon (2.5 ml) ground cardamom
    ½ teaspoon (2.5 ml) vanilla
    FOR GARNISH: ½ cup (120 ml) slivered almonds

Set aside 6 of the peaches. Remove the pits from the remaining fruit and puree in a blender or food processor, or put through a food mill, along with the honey and lemon or lime juice. Place the puree in a large bowl and stir in the buttermilk, orange juice, brandy or Marsala, spices, and vanilla. Slice the reserved peaches and add to the soup. Serve immediately or cover and chill 30 minutes in the freezer. Serve each bowl garnished with slivered almonds.

Note: Peel peaches like tomatoes, by submerging in boiling water for ten seconds, then running under cold water. Skins should come off easily.

MENU SUGGESTIONS
Because of the buttermilk, Peach Soup is higher in protein than other fruit soups, and would make a good beginning to a salad-oriented summer meal, or even a good dessert.

Main dishes: Mushroom Tacos (page 269); Chinese-Style Snow Peas and Water Chestnuts (serve with Couscous) (page 140)
Salads: Oriental Salad (page 297); Leftover Grains Salad (page 293); Warm Potato Salad with Caraway (page 291)
Desserts: Puffed Amaretto Omelet (page 306); Bread Pudding (page 320); Rice or Leftover Grains Pudding (page 321)

   ♥ Omit almonds; reduce honey to 2 tablespoons (30 ml), or less.

GRAINS, LEGUMES, TOFU, AND VEGETABLES

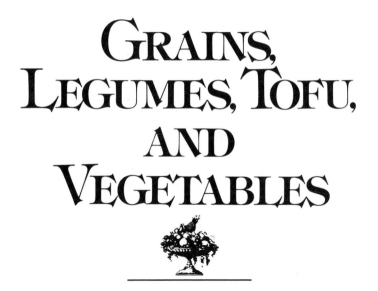

*Auxiliary recipe

91

FAST VEGETARIAN FEASTS

BARLEY MUSHROOM PILAFF

KASHA WITH MUSHROOMS, WATER CHESTNUTS, AND CELERY

CABBAGE LEAVES STUFFED WITH KASHA, WITH CREAMY TOFU SAUCE*

TOFU CUTLETS

CHILLED TOFU WITH DIPPING SAUCES (3 SAUCES)

MISO TOPPINGS FOR TOFU AND GRAINS (5 TOPPINGS)

TOFU VEGETABLE CURRY

CHINESE-STYLE VEGETABLES WITH COUSCOUS

CHINESE-STYLE TOFU AND VEGETABLES WITH GRAINS

CHINESE-STYLE SNOW PEAS AND WATER CHESTNUTS

SWEET AND SOUR CABBAGE

CELERY POTATO "GRATIN"

BROCCOLI OR CAULIFLOWER "GRATIN"

CHINESE CABBAGE WITH SESAME AND GINGER

SZECHUAN-STYLE SWEET AND SOUR CHINESE CABBAGE

GREEN BEANS AMANDINE

GREEN BEANS À LA PROVENÇAL

STEAMED, PRESSURE-COOKED, OR BAKED BEETS, AND BEET GREENS

BRUSSELS SPROUTS WITH LEMON-MUSTARD BUTTER

CARROTS COOKED IN VODKA

CARROTS WITH DILL

THIN-SLICED CAULIFLOWER WITH SESAME SEEDS AND GINGER

CAULIFLOWER COOKED IN RED WINE

CURRIED CAULIFLOWER PUREE

BAKED CELERY POTATO PUREE

DELICATE CORN FRITTERS, OR "CORN OYSTERS"

COOKED CURRIED CUCUMBERS

EGGPLANT, POTATOES, AND MUSHROOMS BRAISED IN WHITE WINE

MUSHROOMS WITH WHITE WINE AND HERBS

OKRA AND TOMATOES

MINTED FRESH PEAS WITH LETTUCE

PEPPERS, TOMATOES, AND HERBS

POTATOES WITH WHITE WINE AND HERBS

POTATOES SIMMERED WITH SAGE, TOMATOES, AND PEAS

BAKED POTATOES

PRESSURE-COOKED POTATOES

SOUFFLÉED RUTABAGA PUREE

PATTYPAN SQUASH STUFFED WITH SAVORY ALMOND FILLING

*Auxiliary recipe

Grains, Legumes, Tofu, and Vegetables

Zucchini with Rosemary or Other Herbs
Simple Picante Zucchini
Baked Yams or Sweet Potatoes with Lime
Baked Sweet Potato and Rum Casserole
Broiled Tomatoes
Florentine Tomatoes
Turnips with Apples and Port
Turnips with Lemon and Honey

The dishes in this chapter are those which, to me, comprise the *stuff* of vegetarian cuisine. Grains, legumes, tofu, and vegetables are the basis for my own diet, and in fact are the foods that feed most of the world. It's through learning how to work with them that you will reap the most important benefits of vegetarian cuisine. If you choose the bulk of your meals from these recipes, your diet will be naturally low-fat, economical, sustaining, and delicious.

Grains are a very important staple for people on a restricted diet. They are low in sodium and fat and high in protein and nutrients, especially when eaten in combination with beans. Contrary to popular belief, grains are *not* fattening. They're high in carbohydrates, but the kind of complex, nutrient-filled carbohydrates that burn readily. It's the fats and sugars that stay with you and add pounds. I've watched people, including myself, lose a few pounds a week eating as great a quantity of grains as they desired at three meals a day. They ate no dairy products or oils, and because of the absence of fats it was easy to lose weight.

Grains have lent themselves to use by almost all of the world's cuisines, and classic dishes based on them have been prepared in the same way for centuries. I have borrowed dishes like Spanish rice and Italian risotti and have adapted them to brown rice; the results are outstanding, and very easy; much easier, in fact, than their Italian counterparts. My risotti are savory and complex with herbs, wine, and Parmesan. You can even use the leftovers—if there are any—as stuffings for eggplant or tomatoes, adding yet another dimension to this dish.

Brown rice, however, is not the only grain. You can make fabulous pilaffs with barley and mushrooms (page 127), or nutty kashas full of crunchy water chestnuts and celery (page 128). Millet, bulgur, and couscous will provide tasty, nutritious beds for a variety of vegetable dishes whose flavors will evoke fantasies or memories of countries all around the globe—hot Oriental dishes like Spicy Eggplant Miso

93

Sauté with Bulgur (page 122), pungent vegetable and tofu curries, picante squash dishes, and heady Provençal combinations.

To assure that the protein is complete with these main-course dishes, grains will usually be accompanied by legumes, often in the form of soy flakes (as in Brown Rice "Risotto" with Soy Flakes, page 107, or Easy Hiziki and Squash Dinner with Soba and Soy, page 101) or soy grits (as in Fried Rice and Soy Grits with Vegetables, page 114). Rice and lentils go together in some of the recipes, and tofu often comes up in sautéed vegetable dishes like the curries and Chinese-style vegetables. Tofu, of course, is nutritionally complete in itself, which makes recipes like Tofu Cutlets (page 131) and Chilled Tofu with Dipping Sauces (page 132) particularly handy (not to mention delectable). If the dishes do not have complete proteins, I will recommend that they be accompanied by a complementary food.

This section will provide you with a lot of new ideas for tofu. You may have been working with it for a long time, but find that you're still mainly sautéing it with vegetables. The versatile Tofu Cream Sauce, which is the basis for the vegetable gratins on pages 142 and 143, will be quite a revelation; and the dipping sauces (pages 132–133) and miso spreads (pages 134–135) will be a welcome departure from the familiar soy sauce.

The first half of this chapter consists of recipes that can serve as main-dish meals because they are based on or served with grains, legumes, or tofu. The remaining recipes are vegetable-oriented dishes, everything from Baked Potatoes (page 164) to exotic Chinese Cabbage with Sesame and Ginger (page 144). You'll find recipes for many vegetables you may have been reluctant to buy in the past—things like rutabaga and turnips. A number of recipes utilize squash, broccoli, and cauliflower, foods we tend to buy over and over again and fall into ruts with. I could fill a book with potato dishes but have restricted myself here to five.

Although these vegetable recipes all make delicious side dishes, they can also be the basis for a simple light supper. When fresh vegetables are in season, I'm often satisfied with a plateful of steamed asparagus, corn on the cob, and fresh tomatoes and, for protein, rice with soyflakes, chilled tofu, or an omelet. Sometimes, though, I just want vegetables. A salad and a baked potato topped with yogurt is one of my favorite meals. As with all of the recipes in this book, the vegetable-based dishes could also serve as accompaniments to meat.

There is as much variety among the simpler vegetable dishes as there is among the more substantial main-dish ones. You'll find down-home dishes like Okra and Tomatoes (page 159), savory combinations like Eggplant, Potatoes, and Mushrooms Braised in White Wine (page 157) or Potatoes Simmered with Sage, Tomatoes, and Peas (page 162), sweet creations like Turnips with Apples and Port (page 172), and spicy Szechuan-Style Sweet and Sour Chinese Cabbage (page 145). And remember that all of these vegetables are marvelous by themselves, simply steamed or sautéed in a little oil.

This chapter will be especially helpful for those of you who want to reduce your salt, cholesterol, and fat consumption. As you will see by the number of heart symbols (♥) by the recipes, almost every one can be altered. Exceptions are some of the dishes that depend on miso, which is very salty, or on a large amount of butter. Unfortunately, Tofu Cream Sauce just doesn't taste good without miso, so if you are on a no-sodium diet, you should avoid it.

It has become increasingly important to me to develop dishes that contain not only no meat, but also very little, if any, dairy products or eggs, because these recipes are so low in fats (a proven dietary contributor to heart disease). In the seventy-odd recipes that follow, each designed to serve 4 to 6 people, I count only about fifteen eggs, and two of those are optional.

Many of the recipes that follow are ones that will intimidate newcomers to this cuisine—where all those ingredients you've never used will come up. When you see bulgur or couscous or miso called for in a recipe you might be tempted to turn to the Pasta or Cheese and Eggs chapters. But don't; it's only through working with these foods that you will learn how good they can be, or find out which ones you do like and which you don't. I know how personal eating habits are; it's difficult to adjust to a new diet, to foods that are unrecognizable. I think bulgur and garbanzos are gorgeous, but I've had people walk right by my beautifully composed taboulis, refusing to touch the salads because they looked so unfamiliar to them. You have to open yourself up to these foods in the same way you have to open yourself up to new cultures and foods when you travel. It will be a gastronomic adventure, full of delicious discovery. Remember that unfamiliar tastes are not necessarily *bad* ones. Our palates, like our minds, can continue to grow throughout our lives—and aren't we lucky they do, because there will never be a shortage of new combinations of flavors and textures or techniques for preparing food.

GENERAL COOKING DIRECTIONS FOR GRAINS

Different grains require different cooking times: brown rice, barley, and millet take about 40 to 45 minutes; buckwheat groats take about 30 minutes; and whole wheat, rye, and triticale take about 50 minutes. The fastest grains, and so the most convenient, are bulgur and couscous, which have actually been precooked and dehydrated. "Cooking" them is just a matter of rehydrating.

Though most grains do take a long time to cook, I still consider them a convenience food, because their cooking needs no supervision. Because grains keep well in the refrigerator for at least three days, you can also always cook twice the quantity you need. You'll then have them already on hand for the many "auxiliary" recipes in this book that call for cooked grains.

It's easy to start a pot of rice and tend to other things, either preparing other dishes or simply relaxing and visiting with your family or friends. A timer will tell you when the grains are done. And you don't have to eat the cooked cereals right away; their quality won't suffer if they stand.

A portion of dry grains usually expands 2½ times when cooked. So allowing for ½ cup (120 ml) per person per serving, 1 cup (250 ml) raw grains will feed 4 to 6 people.

SIMPLE COOKED GRAINS

BROWN RICE, BARLEY
Use 1 part grains to 2 parts water or stock; add ¼ teaspoon (1.25 ml) salt per cup (250 ml) of grains (omit salt on low-sodium diet). Combine the grains and water or stock in a saucepan and bring to a rolling boil. Add salt, cover and reduce heat. Simmer until most of the liquid is absorbed, about 35 minutes. Remove the lid and cook, uncovered, for 5 to 10 minutes longer to separate the grains. **Soy grits**, which cook in the same way, can be cooked along with grains.

MILLET
Use 1 part millet to 2½ parts water or stock. For a nutty flavor and fluffier grain, begin by heating 1 to 2 teaspoons (5–10 ml) safflower oil in your saucepan. Sauté the millet until it begins to smell toasty and the grains are coated with oil, about 3 to 5 minutes. Add the water or stock and bring to a boil. Add salt (¼ teaspoon per 1 cup

96

of millet), then cover and reduce the heat. Simmer 35 minutes and remove the lid. Continue to simmer until the liquid is absorbed, about 10 minutes longer.

BUCKWHEAT GROATS (KASHA)

Use 1 part groats to 2 parts water or stock. Beat 1 egg in a bowl and mix in the buckwheat groats until they are coated. Heat a dry skillet and sauté the groats with the egg until the egg is absorbed and the grains begin to smell toasty. Meanwhile, bring the water or stock to a simmer. When the grains are thoroughly dry, pour in the simmering liquid. If you wish, add a little chopped onion and celery and $\frac{1}{4}$ to $\frac{1}{2}$ teaspoon (1.25–1.5 ml) salt. Bring to a boil, then reduce the heat, cover, and cook 30 minutes. Remove the lid and continue cooking until all the liquid is absorbed about 5 to 10 minutes.

WHEAT BERRIES, WHOLE RYE, WHOLE TRITICALE

Use 1 part grains to 3 parts water. Combine the grains and water and bring to a boil. For each cup (250 ml) of grains, add $\frac{1}{4}$ teaspoon (1.25 ml) salt, then cover and reduce the heat. Simmer for 50 minutes. Remove from the heat and pour off any excess liquid.

BULGUR

Use 1 part bulgur to 2 parts water, with $\frac{1}{4}$ teaspoon (1.25 ml) salt for each cup of grains. Combine the bulgur and salt in a bowl. Bring the water to a boil and pour over the bulgur. Let stand until most of the water is absorbed and the bulgur is soft and fluffy, about 20 to 30 minutes. Pour off excess water. *Note:* Bulgur can also be soaked for a longer time in cold water or in a dressing, as it is in tabouli. If you have the time for this procedure, the grains will absorb all the wonderful flavors of the dressing.

COUSCOUS

Use 1 part couscous to 2 parts lukewarm, salted water ($\frac{1}{4}$ teaspoon per 1 cup of couscous). Pour the water over the couscous and let stand for 10 minutes. Fluff with a fork.

♥ PRESSURE-COOKED BEANS
SERVES 6

PREPARATION TIME: 5 minutes

SUPERVISED COOKING: 5 minutes

UNSUPERVISED COOKING: 60 minutes (30 minutes if beans have been soaked)

The pressure cooker is a godsend for most varieties of beans. However, never try to cook soybeans, soy flakes or grits, split peas or lentils in one, or they'll clog the device and cause an explosion.

        1 tablespoon (15 ml) safflower oil
        1 onion, chopped
 4 to 6 cloves garlic, to taste, minced or put through a press
        2 cups beans (475 ml), such as black, kidney, pinto, white, or lima, washed and picked over
        1 jalapeño pepper, cut in half, seeds removed (optional)
        1 green pepper, chopped (optional), more if desired
 2 to 3 tablespoons (30–45 ml) chopped fresh cilantro (optional)
        1 teaspoon (5 ml) dried herbs (optional)
        1 bay leaf
        6 cups (1.5 L) water
          Salt to taste
          Fresh herbs (optional)

Heat the safflower oil in the pressure cooker and sauté the onion and 2 cloves of the garlic until the onion is tender. Add the beans, optional peppers and herbs, remaining garlic (to taste), bay leaf, and the water and bring to a boil. Cover and bring to 15 pounds (7 kg) pressure. Turn heat to medium and cook 60 minutes.

Remove from the heat and run under cold water for several minutes. Remove the gauge, and when all the steam has been released, carefully remove the lid.

Add salt to taste, fresh herbs and, if you like, additional chopped green pepper. Heat through and serve with cornbread, grains or a grain salad, tortillas or bread and a salad.

MENU SUGGESTIONS
Salads: Tossed Green Salad (page 280); Lettuce Salad with Oranges (page 281); Jícama and Orange Salad with Avocados (page 295)

Dessert suggestions: Orange Ice (page 318); Oranges with Mint; fresh fruit

♥ Reduce oil to 2 teaspoons (10 ml); omit salt.

♥ SLOW-COOKED BEANS, WITH OR WITHOUT A SLOW COOKER

This has become my favorite method for cooking beans. If I begin them at night I wake up in the morning starving, because the entire house smells so wonderful. If I put them in in the morning, when I come home the house smells as if I'd been busy in the kitchen all day. I don't have a slow cooker, but use my oven. This method is actually the same as that used by the Indians all over Mesoamerica, although they leave their beans on top of the heat source and cook them all day. When you cook beans slowly the broth becomes very thick and rich and the legumes more tender. If you've had trouble digesting beans in the past, try this recipe, because the cellulose becomes very soft.

1 part beans, washed and picked over
4 parts water
1 large onion, chopped, for every 2 cups (475 ml) beans
4 cloves garlic, at least, for every 2 cups (475 ml) beans (to taste)
  Optional: herbs such as cilantro and parsley, 1 green pepper, chopped, or 1 jalapeño pepper, cut in half and seeded

Put all the ingredients into a large ovenproof pot or Dutch oven, or into a slow cooker, and cover. If not using a slow cooker, set your pot in a 200- to 220-degree (95°–105°C) oven (this is the low setting on mine), close the oven door, and leave all day or night. It takes about 6 to 8 hours for a thick, soupy broth to develop. Salt the beans after they are cooked, and correct the seasoning.

Note: If you're going to be away from the house for more than 6 hours, increase the water by 1 to 2 cups (250–475 ml).

♥ Omit salt.

99

♥ PRESSURE-COOKED BLACK BEANS AND TRITICALE (or Other Beans and Grains)

SERVES 4

SUPERVISED COOKING: 5 minutes
UNSUPERVISED COOKING: 60 minutes

I especially like triticale cooked with beans, partly because it won't become mushy like brown rice and other faster-cooking grains. Wheat berries or whole rye would also be suitable for preparation in this manner. Whatever grain you use, the dish is hearty, filling, and high in protein. (The beans, of course, can also be slow cooked, and the grains stirred in.) The beans and grains are a natural complement and with a big salad and a vegetable make an easy, plain meal. And they make a perfect filling for green peppers (see page 103). Make twice what you need and the next night use them for stuffing.

    1   tablespoon (15 ml) safflower oil
    ½   onion, chopped
    4   cloves garlic, minced or put through a press
    1   cup (250 ml) black beans (or pintos, kidneys, or red beans), washed and picked over
    1   cup (250 ml) whole triticale (or wheat berries or whole rye)
    7   cups (1.7 L) water
        Salt to taste

Heat the oil in a pressure cooker and add the onion and half the garlic. Sauté until the onion is tender, then add the beans, triticale, remaining garlic, and the water. Bring to a boil, cover, and bring to 15 pounds (7 kg) pressure. Turn heat to medium and cook 60 minutes. Remove from the heat and run under cold water for several minutes. Remove the gauge, and when all the steam has escaped, remove the lid. Add salt to taste, adjust the garlic, and heat through.
    This freezes well and will last several days in the refrigerator.

MENU SUGGESTIONS

Salads: Tossed Green Salad (page 280)
Desserts: Orange Ice (page 318); Strawberry Sherbet (page 317); Oranges with Mint

    ♥ Reduce oil to 2 teaspoons (10 ml); omit salt.

♥ EASY HIZIKI AND SQUASH DINNER WITH SOBA AND SOY

SERVES 4 TO 6

PREPARATION TIME: 15 minutes

SUPERVISED COOKING: 20 to 25 minutes

UNSUPERVISED COOKING: 30 minutes (for the soy flakes; can be done while you prepare and cook the vegetables)

I can still remember making this dish for the first time, about a year ago. I love the texture of the soy flakes against the noodles and squash. The buckwheat noodles and soy flakes together make complete protein. The hiziki, tamari, and ginger give the dish an Oriental character.

$\frac{1}{4}$ cup (60 ml) hiziki seaweed

3 cups (700 ml) water

$1\frac{1}{2}$ cups (350 ml) soy flakes

2 tablespoons (30 ml) safflower oil

1 onion, sliced

2 large cloves garlic, minced or put through a press

2 teaspoons (10 ml) minced or grated fresh ginger

2 tablespoons (30 ml) sesame seeds

4 cups (950 ml) diced (small) butternut squash (1 large)

Tamari to taste

8 ounces (225 gm) buckwheat noodles

1 teaspoon salt

Up to 1 tablespoon (15 ml) sesame oil (optional)

Place the hiziki in a bowl and add water to cover. Bring the 3 cups (700 ml) water to a boil in a 2-quart (2 L) saucepan and add the soy flakes. Cover and simmer 30 minutes, while you prepare and cook the vegetables and start a large pot of water heating for the noodles. Drain the soy flakes and retain the liquid.

The hiziki will be soft in 5 or 10 minutes—the amount of time it will take you to prepare the vegetables. Drain (retain the water) and squeeze out the remaining water from the hiziki.

Heat 1 tablespoon safflower oil in a wok or large heavy-bottomed skillet and sauté the onion, garlic, and ginger until the onion begins to turn translucent. Add the sesame seeds, hiziki, and squash, and $\frac{1}{4}$ cup (60 ml) liquid, either from the hiziki or from the soy flakes, or water. Cook, stirring, for 10 to 20 minutes, until the squash is tender. Stir in the soy flakes and add tamari to taste. Cover and keep the heat low, stirring occasionally, while you cook the buckwheat noodles.

Bring the pot of water to a rolling boil and add salt and remaining tablespoon (15 ml) safflower oil. Add the noodles, stir, and cook 4 to 5 minutes, until al dente. Lift out of the boiling water with a slotted spoon or a wire-mesh deep-fry skimmer and place in a warm casserole or bowl. Sprinkle with a little tamari and optional sesame oil, toss, and spoon on the hiziki and squash mixture. Serve at once.

MENU SUGGESTIONS

Any green vegetable, simply steamed

Salads: Tossed Green Salad (page 280); Jícama and Orange Salad with Avocados (page 295)

Desserts: Pears Poached in Wine (page 309); Apples with Lime Juice (page 312); Pineapple with Mint

♥ Use 1 tablespoon (15 ml) oil and water as necessary for vegetables; omit tamari and optional sesame oil.

♥ GREEN PEPPERS STUFFED WITH BEANS AND GRAINS*
SERVES 4

PREPARATION TIME: 15 minutes
UNSUPERVISED COOKING TIME: 30 to 40 minutes

This is a perfect idea for using up leftover beans and grains. Unlike many versions of this recipe, where you fuss around skinning or batter-frying the peppers, mine calls for them to be just slightly baked, with the filling bubbling on the inside and cheese or tofu sauce melted on top. That way the peppers retain a fresh taste and crunchy texture, and are a nice contrast to the filling. Some people prefer their peppers baked longer, so that they're soft. I leave it to your own taste.

3 cups (700 ml) Pressure-Cooked Black Beans and Triticale (page 100), or any cooked beans with grains
4 large sweet green peppers or 8 small ones
2 tablespoons (30 ml) chopped fresh cilantro (optional)
4 ounces (100 gm) Monterey Jack cheese, grated, or 4 ounces (100 gm) tofu, blended with 1 tablespoon (15 ml) tamari, 2 tablespoons (30 ml) water, and 1 teaspoon (5 ml) sesame tahini until smooth

Preheat the oven to 350 degrees (180° C). Oil a deep baking dish.
Pour off the liquid from the beans and retain.
Remove the tops from the green peppers by cutting straight across the tops just below the point they begin to curve in. Carefully remove the seeds and membranes with your fingers and discard. Chop the tops, minus the stems, into small dice and stir into the cooked beans and grains. Add the optional cilantro and stir well.
Fill the peppers with as much of the beans and grains as they will hold. Moisten each portion of filling with about 2 tablespoons (30 ml) of the liquid from the beans and grains. Top with the grated cheese or the blended tofu sauce.
Place the peppers in the oiled baking dish and cover. Bake 20 to 40 minutes, depending on how soft you wish them. Serve hot.

MENU SUGGESTIONS
Serve accompanied by a green or spinach salad, sliced tomatoes and if you wish, another simply steamed vegetable. For dessert serve something fruity, such as pineapple with mint, Pineapple Banana Mint Sherbet (page 316), or Strawberries or Raspberries with Red Wine (page 315).

♥ Use tofu and omit tamari.

*Auxiliary recipe: requires leftover beans and grains.

♥ BLACK-EYED PEAS
SERVES 6

PREPARATION TIME: 5 to 10 minutes
SUPERVISED COOKING: 5 minutes
UNSUPERVISED COOKING: 45 to 60 minutes, or 25 minutes in a pressure cooker

It's a custom in the South to eat black-eyed peas on New Year's Day for good luck. Were it not for this ritual I might never have known the pleasures of this down-home legume, which has become one of my favorites, right up there with black beans. I'm sure that good fortune must accompany them.

Black-eyed peas produce a broth that has a distinct, savory character all its own, one I get cravings for; it's soupy and satisfying. These beans are softer than most legumes, require no soaking (though you can cut the cooking time if you do soak them), and take only 45 minutes to cook. If you soak them and cook them in a pressure cooker, they take only 10 minutes.

I can't imagine eating this legume without cornbread, and another nice way to serve them is with fresh spinach added to the broth just before serving. That adds to their down-home character.

1 tablespoon (15 ml) safflower oil
1 onion, chopped
2 cloves garlic, or more to taste, minced or put through a press
2 cups (475 ml) dried black-eyed peas, washed and picked over
8 cups (2 L) water
1 teaspoon (5 ml) tamari or 1 vegetable bouillon cube (optional)
1 bay leaf
1 teaspoon salt, or to taste
  Freshly ground pepper to taste
2 cups raw fresh spinach, trimmed and washed (optional)

Heat the oil in a Dutch oven, soup pot, or flameproof bean pot and gently sauté the onion and garlic until the onion is tender. Add the peas and water and bring to a boil. Add the bay leaf and optional tamari, cover, reduce heat and simmer 45 minutes, or until the beans are tender and the broth aromatic. Add salt and freshly ground pepper to taste. Just before serving, add the spinach, if desired.

Note: This recipe can also be made with a pressure cooker. Cook 10 minutes if the beans have been soaked, 25 if not.

MENU SUGGESTIONS

Cornbread is a must, and will complete the protein. Otherwise, complete with the addition of a grain or wholegrain bread or a dairy product. Remember that these can occur in a salad or dessert. Other good country-style side dishes like Okra and Tomatoes (page 159), Coleslaw (page 295); Corn on the Cob, and Cucumbers Vinaigrette (pg 283) would be suitable.

Desserts: Peach Banana Freeze (page 316); Peaches with Marsala (page 314); fresh watermelon or other fruit.

♥ Omit salt and tamari or bouillon; add more garlic and some chopped fresh tomatoes.

♥ PICANTE GARBANZOS
SERVES 6

PREPARATION TIME: 5 to 10 minutes
SUPERVISED COOKING: 5 minutes
UNSUPERVISED COOKING: 50 to 60 minutes, with a pressure cooker

I'd never had spicy garbanzos before I tried these, and they are delightful. I have cooked them in both a pressure cooker and in a slow oven, and I prefer the latter because it leaves the beans with a better texture. You can just put everything in the oven before you go to work, turn it on low, and when you come home, dinner will be ready. The dish is hearty and will warm you all over.

1 tablespoon (15 ml) olive oil
2 onions, chopped
3 cloves garlic, minced or put through a press
2 cups (475 ml) dried garbanzos, washed and picked over
1 teaspoon (5 ml) dried thyme
2 quarts (2 L) water
1 pound (450 gm) tomatoes, canned or fresh, peeled and coarsely chopped
1 dried red chili, seeds removed
Salt and lots of freshly ground pepper (up to ½ teaspoon; 2.5 ml)

SLOW-COOKER METHOD

Place all the ingredients except the salt and pepper in the cooker and turn to a high setting to bring to a boil. Turn to low, and leave to cook about 8 hours or longer. Season with salt and freshly ground pepper.

PRESSURE-COOKER METHOD

Heat the oil in the cooker and sauté the onion and garlic for about 5 minutes. Add the remaining ingredients except the salt and pepper. Bring to a boil, cover, and bring to 15 pounds (7 kg) pressure. Cook over medium heat for 50 minutes. Remove from the heat and run under cold water for several minutes. Remove the gauge, and when all the steam has escaped, carefully remove the lid. Return to the stove to heat through, and season to taste with salt and freshly ground pepper.

MENU SUGGESTIONS

Serve with grains, whole-grain bread, or cornbread and a salad and /or steamed vegetable. If you serve with a grain or dairy products, you will obtain complete protein. This could come in the form of dessert, such as Rice or Leftover Grains Pudding (page 321) or either of the Noodle Kugels on pages 318–319. Or it could be a salad such as the Cold Pasta Salad (page 302) or Leftover Grains Salad (page 293). Other nice salads with this are Middle Eastern Beet Salad (page 288) and Curried Carrot Salad (page 284).

♥ Substitute 2 teaspoons (10 ml) safflower oil for the olive oil; omit salt.

♥ BROWN RICE "RISOTTO" WITH SOY FLAKES

SERVES 6

PREPARATION TIME: 15 minutes
SUPERVISED COOKING: 5 to 10 minutes
UNSUPERVISED COOKING: 45 minutes

Preparing a classic risotto, made with Arborio rice, is a tedious process, because to make it correctly you must be on your feet, constantly stirring the rice and adding broth. I tried to make such a risotto using brown rice, but no matter how long I stirred and how much broth I added, the rice never seemed to get cooked. So I decided to make it like a pilaff, adding all the stock after the rice had absorbed the wine. Inauthentic as it may be, it is as delicious as any risotto I ever ate in Italy.

The combination of rice and soy makes this a high-protein dish.

        6 dried Chinese mushrooms
 4 to 5 cups (950 ml–1.2 L) Tamari-Bouillon Broth, to which
      ½ teaspoon (2.5 ml) Marmite, Savorex, or Vegex has been
        added
        1 tablespoon (15 ml) butter, with additional butter (or saf-
        flower oil, if you prefer) as needed
      ¼ cup (60 ml) minced onion
        1 clove garlic, minced or put through a press
   1½ cups (350 ml) brown rice, washed
      ¾ cup (180 ml) soy flakes
        1 cup (250 ml) dry white wine
1 to 1½ cups (250–350 ml) broccoli florets, sliced zucchini, or
        chopped asparagus (optional)
      ½ teaspoon (2.5 ml) dried herbs (such as thyme, oregano,
        basil, rosemary) or 1 to 2 teaspoons (5–10 ml) chopped
        fresh herbs
        2 tablespoons (30 ml) chopped fresh parsley
 3 to 4 tablespoons (45–60 ml) freshly grated Parmesan cheese,
        plus more as desired
        Salt and freshly ground pepper to taste
        1 egg, beaten with ¼ cup (60 ml) hot broth (optional)

Soak the mushrooms in hot water to cover for 15 to 30 minutes, until tender. Meanwhile, prepare the vegetables and herbs, grate cheese, or wash lettuce for a salad. Squeeze the liquid from the mushrooms and strain it and the soaking liquid into the broth. Rinse the mushrooms thoroughly and sliver.

Bring the broth to a simmer in a saucepan.

Heat the butter and oil in a large, heavy-bottomed Dutch oven and sauté the onion and garlic until the onion is translucent. Add the rice and soy flakes and sauté, stirring, for 2 to 3 minutes, until the rice is completely coated with oil (add more butter or oil if necessary).

Add the white wine and cook over moderate heat, stirring, until the wine has almost been absorbed. Pour in 4 cups (950 ml) of the simmering stock and add the slivered mushrooms. Bring to a boil, then reduce the heat, cover, and simmer 30 minutes. Add the broccoli, additional stock (if the rice seems dry), and herbs. Cover and cook another 5 to 10 minutes, to desired doneness. Stir in the parsley, Parmesan, salt, and freshly ground pepper to taste. Stir in the optional egg beaten with broth and serve. Pass additional Parmesan.

MENU SUGGESTIONS

Soups: Simple Garlic Soup Provençal (page 64); Simple Miso Soup (page 68)

Salads: Tossed Green Salad (page 280); Tomato and Mozzarella Salad (page 282)

Desserts: Prune Soufflé (page 307); Pears Poached in Red Wine (page 309)

♥ Omit Parmesan, salt, and butter (use oil instead); use plain water for broth and omit Marmite; increase amount of herbs.

♥ RISI E BISI

SERVES 4

PREPARATION TIME: 15 minutes (25 if you're shelling the peas)
SUPERVISED COOKING: 5 to 10 minutes
UNSUPERVISED COOKING: 45 minutes

I use brown rice for this as I do in my "risotto," again relieving me of the task of standing over the pot and stirring. In all the recipes that I have seen for this classic Venetian dish, the peas are cooked as long as the rice, so that they end up with the dull green color and mushy texture of canned peas. In my version I add the peas just before the end of the cooking time. They remain a beautiful green and retain a nice firm texture, colorful against the rice.

This particular combination is soupier than a risotto and thicker than a soup. I always eat it with a spoon, so that none of the luscious broth gets away.

- 3 cups (700 ml) Tamari-Bouillon Broth, (to which an additional ½ teaspoon [2.5 ml] Marmite, Savorex, or Vegex has been added), more if needed
- 1 tablespoon (15 ml) butter
- 1 teaspoon (5 ml) olive oil
- 1 small onion, chopped
- 1 to 2 cloves garlic, minced or put through a press
- 1 cup (250 ml) brown rice
- ½ cup (120 ml) dry white wine
- 2 pounds (1 kg) unshelled fresh peas or 1 package (10 ounces; 275 gm) frozen, preferably thawed
- ½ teaspoon (2.5 gm) dried herbs (such as thyme, oregano, marjoram, rosemary)
- ½ cup (120 ml) freshly grated Parmesan cheese, more as desired
- Salt and freshly ground pepper to taste
- 3 tablespoons (45 ml) chopped fresh parsley

Bring the broth to a simmer in a saucepan.

Heat the butter and olive oil in a large, heavy-bottomed Dutch oven and sauté the onion and garlic until the onion is translucent. Add the rice and sauté, stirring, for an additional 2 to 3 minutes, until the rice is completely coated with butter and oil.

Add the white wine and cook over moderate heat, stirring, until the wine has almost been absorbed. Pour in the simmering broth and bring to a boil. Cover, reduce the heat, and simmer for 35 minutes. Add the peas and the herbs and cook another 10 minutes for fresh peas, 5 minutes for the frozen (10 minutes if they are not yet thawed). Add more stock if the rice seems dry. Stir in the Parmesan and lots of freshly ground pepper. Add salt to taste and add the parsley. Serve at once in warm soup bowls, passing more Parmesan if desired.

Note: The peas and rice are complementary in this dish, and the protein is high.

MENU SUGGESTIONS
See suggestions for Brown Rice "Risotto" with Soy Flakes (page 107). Tomato side dishes, such as Broiled Tomatoes (page 170) or

Florentine Tomatoes (page 171); Tomato Salad (page 284) would also be nice.

♥ Omit butter; substitute safflower oil for the olive oil; omit Parmesan and salt; increase amount of dried herbs; use water instead of stock, and omit Marmite.

♥ EGGPLANT STUFFED WITH RICE AND SOY "RISOTTO" OR RISI E BISI*

SERVES 4

PREPARATION TIME: 15 minutes
SUPERVISED COOKING: 10 minutes
UNSUPERVISED COOKING: 45 minutes

2 small eggplants
2 tablespoons (30 ml) olive oil
¼ cup (60 ml) water
1 to 1½ cups (250–350 ml) Brown Rice "Risotto" with Soy Flakes or Risi e Bisi
Salt and freshly ground pepper
FOR GARNISH: Fresh parsley and lemon wedges

Slice each eggplant in half lengthwise. Cut two deep lengthwise slits into the flesh on the flat side of each half, cutting down to the skin but not through it. Preheat the oven to 400 degrees (200°C) and oil a baking dish into which all the eggplant can fit.

Heat the olive oil in a large, heavy-bottomed skillet and sauté the eggplant halves, flat side down, for 5 minutes. Pour in the water and continue to cook for 5 minutes, or until the water has evaporated. Remove from the heat and allow the eggplants to cool until you can handle them.

Spread each slit apart, cutting out a little flesh if it won't give, and fill each with about 2 tablespoons (30 ml) of the "risotto" or Risi e Bisi (or more). The filling can flow out of the slits, and you can top the eggplant with what remains. Place the eggplant halves in the prepared baking dish rounded side down. Cover well and bake 45 minutes, or until the eggplants are tender.

Serve on a platter, garnished with parsley and lemon wedges.

*Auxiliary recipe: requires leftover Brown Rice "Risotto" with Soy Flakes (page 107) or Risi e Bisi (page 108)

MENU SUGGESTIONS

Soups: See suggestions for Brown Rice "Risotto" with Soy Flakes (page 107) or Risi e Bisi (page 108).

Vegetable side dishes: Brussels Sprouts with Lemon-Mustard Butter (page 149); simple steamed vegetables

Salads: Fattoush (page 285); Tossed Green Salad (page 280); Tomato Salad (page 284)

Desserts: Banana Yogurt Freeze (page 315); Puffed Dessert Omelet (page 306)

♥ Substitute 1 tablespoon (15 ml) safflower oil for the olive oil and use a nonstick skillet; omit salt.

♥ RED WINE "RISOTTO" WITH CAULIFLOWER
SERVES 4 TO 6

PREPARATION TIME: 10 minutes
SUPERVISED COOKING: 5 minutes
UNSUPERVISED COOKING: 40 to 50 minutes

I came across a recipe for a traditional risotto cooked in a combination of red wine and stock in a book of Venetian recipes and couldn't resist adapting it to brown rice. Cauliflower is the perfect vegetable to incorporate into this dish, because it too absorbs the winey color. The splendid flavors of this dish are subtly suggested by the deep purple color.

  2 cups (475 ml) red wine
  2 cups (475 ml) Tamari-Bouillon Broth
  1 tablespoon (15 ml) butter or safflower oil
  ¼ cup (60 ml) minced onion
1 to 2 cloves garlic, to taste, minced or put through a press
  1½ cups (350 ml) brown rice
  ½ cup (120 ml) soy grits
  2 cups (475 ml) cauliflower florets
  1 cup (250 ml) freshly grated Parmesan cheese
    Freshly ground pepper to taste

Bring the red wine and the broth to a simmer together in a saucepan.
  Heat the butter in a large, heavy-bottomed saucepan and sauté the onion and garlic until the onion is tender. Add the rice and soy grits and cook, stirring, for 2 to 3 minutes, until the grains are coated.
  Slowly add the simmering wine and broth, stirring, and bring to a

boil. Cover, then reduce the heat and simmer 30 minutes. (At this point the rice and soy grits should be cooked al dente, still a bit crunchy but able to be bitten through.) Add the cauliflower, stir once, cover, and cook an additional 5 to 10 minutes. Stir in half the Parmesan and lots of freshly ground pepper. If the mixture is too soupy for you (it should be somewhat more liquid than plain cooked grains or a pilaff), cook, uncovered, a little while longer. Otherwise, remove from heat and serve hot, passing the rest of the Parmesan in a bowl.

MENU SUGGESTIONS
See menu suggestions for Brown Rice "Risotto" with Soy Flakes (page 107) and Risi e Bisi (page 108). Any green vegetable would also make a nice side dish, as well as making your plate more colorful.

♥ Use 2 teaspoons (10 ml) safflower oil; omit Parmesan; use water instead of broth.

♥ BROWN RICE AND LENTILS
SERVES 4 TO 6
PREPARATION TIME: 10 minutes
UNSUPERVISED COOKING: 40 minutes

I have a close friend who went off into the wilderness a few years ago with fifty pounds of brown rice, fifty pounds of lentils, a gallon of tamari, and a few pounds of garlic and onions. He lived for six months on this food and never tired of it. He cooked the rice and lentils together and sprouted the rest of the lentils for salads.

I'm not sure I could go six months on this diet without tiring of it, but I certainly would feel great; I do love rice and lentils enough to eat them often. They constitute a basic protein combination; they can be prepared in the same pot, because they take about the same amount of time to cook; and they taste wonderful together. They are good alone, plain or seasoned, as a stuffing for other vegetables (for example, green peppers, winter or summer squash, or see the recipe for Tomatoes Stuffed with Rice and Lentils, page 113), or as the basis for a marinated salad.

```
      1  onion, chopped
 2 to 4  cloves garlic, to taste, minced
      1  cup (250 ml) brown rice, washed
      1  cup (250 ml) dried lentils, washed and picked over
```

1 bay leaf
4 cups (950 ml) water
   Salt to taste
   Tamari to taste

Place all the ingredients but the tamari in a 2-quart (2 L) saucepan and bring to a boil. Reduce the heat, cover, and cook 40 minutes. Uncover and cook another 15 minutes, or until the liquid has evaporated. Season with tamari.

MENU SUGGESTIONS

Vegetable side dishes: Any vegetables, simply steamed; Turnips with Lemon and Honey (page 173); Thin-Sliced Cauliflower with Sesame Seeds and Ginger (page 151); Broiled Tomatoes (page 170)

Salads: Tossed Green Salad (page 280); Curried Carrot Salad (page 284); Tomato Salad (page 284); Jícama and Orange Salad with Avocados (page 295); Oriental Salad (page 297)

Desserts: Apples with Lime Juice (page 312); Gingered Fruit (page 312)

♥ Omit salt and tamari.

♥ TOMATOES STUFFED WITH RICE AND LENTILS*
SERVES 4 TO 6
PREPARATION TIME: 15 minutes
UNSUPERVISED COOKING: 20 to 30 minutes

6 large, firm tomatoes
3 cups (700 ml) cooked Brown Rice and Lentils
¼ cup (60 ml) chopped fresh parsley
¼ to ½ cup (60–120 ml) freshly grated Parmesan cheese, to taste

Preheat the oven to 350 degrees (180°C). Oil a 1½- or 2-quart (1.5–2 L) baking dish.

Cut the tops off the tomatoes by slicing horizontally about ¼ inch (0.7 cm) down from the top. Squeeze or scoop out the seeds and discard, and carefully cut out the inside flesh using a small sharp knife. The remaining shell should be about ½ inch thick. Dice the removed flesh and mix with the rice and lentils. Mix in the parsley.

Fill the tomatoes as full as possible (they should each be able to

*Auxiliary recipe: requires leftover Brown Rice and Lentils (page 112)

hold about ½ cup). Top with the grated Parmesan and bake in the preheated oven 20 to 30 minutes. Serve hot.

Note: Any other grain dish, such as Risi e Bisi or Brown Rice "Risotto" with Soy Flakes, may be substituted for the Rice and Lentils.

MENU SUGGESTIONS
Any green vegetable, simply steamed, with or without sauce
Salads: Tossed Green Salad (page 280); Curried Carrot Salad (page 284); Lettuce Salad with Oranges (page 281)
Dessert of your choice

♥ Omit Parmesan.

♥ FRIED RICE AND SOY GRITS WITH VEGETABLES*
SERVES 4
PREPARATION TIME: 10 to 15 minutes
SUPERVISED COOKING: 10 minutes

This is another of my standbys. It's a reliable dish for family and guests, and a satisfying dinner that takes only minutes and provides complete protein.

Of course, any vegetable you have on hand can be used in this recipe, and even just one or two different kinds of vegetables make as delicious a dish as a variety of them would.

> 2 tablespoons (30 ml) safflower oil
> 1 onion, sliced
> 1 clove garlic, minced
> ¼ teaspoon (1.25 ml) ground ginger
> 1 carrot, sliced on the diagonal
> ¼ cup (60 ml) raw peanuts or sunflower seeds (optional)
> 1 stalk celery, trimmed and sliced ¼ inch thick on the diagonal
> 2 tablespoons (30 ml) sesame seeds
> 1 zucchini, sliced ¼ inch thick on the diagonal, or 1 cup (250 ml) broccoli florets
> 3 cups (700 ml) cooked Brown Rice and Soy Grits (page 96)
> 1 to 2 tablespoons (15–30 ml) tamari
> 2 eggs, beaten

*Auxiliary recipe: requires leftover Brown Rice and Soy Grits (page 96)

Heat 1 tablespoon (15 ml) of the oil in a wok or large, heavy-bot-tomed skillet. Add the onion, garlic, and ginger and sauté, stirring, just until the onion begins to turn translucent. Add the carrot and optional peanuts or sunflower seeds and sauté 1 minute, then add the celery and sesame seeds. Stir-fry 1 to 2 minutes, then add the zucchini or broccoli. Stir-fry 2 to 3 minutes, until the vegetables become bright green.

Add the other tablespoon (15 ml) of oil and the rice and soy grits. Cook, stirring, over medium-high heat for 2 minutes. Add the tamari and the eggs. Cook, stirring, until the eggs are cooked through, about 2 minutes, and serve.

MENU SUGGESTIONS

Soups: Hot and Sour Soup (page 67); Simple Miso Soup (page 68); Curried Cauliflower Soup (page 79), Simple Garlic Soup Provençal (page 64)

Salads: Curried Carrot Salad (page 284); Tossed Green Salad (page 280); Cucumber Yogurt Salad (page 282); Hot and Sour Bean Sprout Salad (page 298)

Desserts: Gingered Fruit (page 312); Apples with Lime Juice (page 312); Pineapple Banana Mint Sherbet (page 316)

♥ Use only 1 tablespoon (15 ml) safflower oil in all and a nonstick skillet; omit tamari and eggs; add 3 tablespoons (45 ml) chopped cilantro just before removing from the heat.

♥ BRAISED STUFFED ARTICHOKES IN WINE
SERVES 6

PREPARATION TIME: 15 minutes
UNSUPERVISED COOKING: 45 minutes
ADDITIONAL WORK: 5 minutes

I spent a recent summer in Provence, where I cooked to my heart's content. It seemed that every time I went to one of the many wonderful local markets I came home with artichokes. Sometimes they were large, round, and meaty; at other times, smaller and less bulbous, but always a beautiful mixture of shades of green and purple, and always a treat.

I kept cooking them the same way, and we never tired of them. I braised them in wine, with lemon and garlic and herbs, then thickened the poaching broth with arrowroot and used it as a sauce. I had poached artichokes in wine before, but it was only that summer that it occurred to me to use the heady poaching liquid as a sauce—economical, unfattening, and wonderful to eat.

When I got home I began making meals out of poached artichokes. This recipe involves stuffing them with a simple mixture of brown rice and soy flakes, then dressing them up with the sauce, which makes the humble grains quite elegant.

You can either cut the cooked artichokes in half and lay them flat to stuff them, or serve them whole, filling the entire cavity with the rice and soy flakes. It depends on the size of your meal.

    1 cup (250 ml) brown rice
    ⅔ cup (160 ml) soy flakes
    3 cups (700 ml) water
3 to 6 artichokes, depending on whether you are serving them whole or halved
    2 cups (475 ml) dry white wine
    1 vegetable bouillon cube
    2 tablespoons (30 ml) olive oil
    8 large cloves garlic, each cut in thirds
    ½ small or medium onion, sliced
    1 carrot, sliced
      Juice of ½ lemon, plus more to taste

    1 bay leaf
    2 sprigs fresh parsley
    ½ teaspoon (2.5 ml) crushed coriander seeds
       Salt and freshly ground pepper to taste
    ½ teaspoon (2.5 ml) mild honey (optional)
       Additional lemon juice, to taste
    2 teaspoons (10 ml) arrowroot or cornstarch, or 2 egg yolks

Bring the rice and soy flakes to a boil in 2½ cups (600 ml) of the water. Cover, reduce heat, and simmer for 40 minutes and remove from the heat. Meanwhile, prepare the artichokes.

With a sharp knife, cut the stem and top quarter off each artichoke. Use scissors to remove the top, thorny parts of the outer leaves.

Combine the remaining ½ cup water and all the rest of the ingredients except the honey and arrowroot or egg yolks in a large, heavy-bottomed saucepan (or divide the mixture between two pans, if the artichokes won't all fit in one). Stand the artichokes in the pan upside down, cover, and bring to a simmer. Poach for 45 minutes to an hour, until a leaf will pull away easily and the stems, when tested with a fork, are tender. Remove from the pan and place on a platter. When cool enough to handle, carefully separate the inner leaves, pull out the small, thorny purple ones and scoop out the chokes. Or cut in half lengthwise and scoop out the chokes.

Fill the cavities of the artichokes with the cooked rice and soy flakes. Fill spaces between the leaves as well.

Strain the poaching liquid into a small saucepan. Add salt and freshly ground pepper to taste and, if the liquid seems bitter, add the honey. Add more lemon juice to taste.

If you are using arrowroot or cornstarch to thicken: Shortly before you wish to serve, bring the poaching liquid to a simmer, dissolve the arrowroot or cornstarch in a little water, and carefully stir into the poaching liquid. Stir until it thickens slightly and pour over the artichokes. Serve at once.

If you are using egg yolks: Beat the yolks in a small bowl. Bring the poaching liquid to a simmer and stir a little into the egg yolks, mixing well. Turn the heat under the poaching liquid very low, so that it will not boil and curdle the eggs. Slowly stir the egg yolk mixture into the liquid and cook, stirring with a wooden spoon, until the sauce coats the spoon. Pour over the artichokes and serve.

MENU SUGGESTIONS

Soups: Rosemary's Chilled Lettuce and Potato Soup (page 81); Hot or Iced Tomato Soup (page 72); Chilled Buttermilk Soup (page 86)

Vegetables: Bulgur and Purple Cabbage with Apples and Onions (page 124); simple steamed vegetables

Salads: Warm Potato Salad with Caraway (page 291); Warm or Chilled Cauliflower or Broccoli Salad (page 290); Tomato Salad (page 284)

Desserts: Strawberry Sherbet (page 317); Cantaloupe with Apricot Puree and Almonds (page 313); Pineapple Banana Mint Sherbet (page 316)

♥ Use either arrowroot or cornstarch to thicken sauce, not the egg yolks. Omit olive oil, bouillon cube, and salt.

♥ CURRIED RICE WITH LENTILS
SERVES 6
PREPARATION TIME: 20 minutes
UNSUPERVISED COOKING: 40 minutes

This has always been one of my standbys. It's good by itself, topped with yogurt and chutney or raisins, and it makes a fine stuffing for acorn squash. If you double the quantities below, you'll have more than enough for an evening's meal and stuffing for acorn squash the following night.

1 to 2   tablespoons (15–30 ml) safflower oil
  ½   onion, chopped
  3   cloves garlic, minced or put through a press
  ¼   teaspoon (1.25 ml) ground ginger
  ½   teaspoon (2.5 ml) turmeric
2 to 3   teaspoons (10–15 ml) curry powder, to taste
  1   cup (250 ml) brown rice, washed
  ¾   cup (180 ml) dried lentils, washed and picked over
  4   cups (950 ml) water
  2   vegetable bouillon cubes

Salt to taste
½ cup (120 ml) raisins or currants
¼ cup (60 ml) sunflower seeds
1 large, tart apple, or 2 medium, diced
FOR GARNISH: 1 cup (250 ml) plain low-fat yogurt and ¼ cup (60 ml) raisins or chutney

Heat 1 tablespoon oil in a heavy-bottomed soup pot, 2-quart (2 L) saucepan, or Dutch oven and sauté the onion with 1 clove of the garlic until it begins to turn translucent. Add the ginger, turmeric, and curry powder and sauté for a few minutes longer. Add more oil, if necessary, and the rice, and sauté for 2 minutes. Add the lentils, water, bouillon cubes, remaining garlic, raisins, and sunflower seeds and bring to a boil. Cover, reduce the heat, and simmer for 25 minutes. Add the apples and simmer, covered, for another 10 to 15 minutes, or until the water is absorbed. Serve topped with yogurt and the additional raisins or other garnishes.

MENU SUGGESTIONS

This recipe is good accompanied by a green salad or Curried Carrot Salad (page 284) and a steamed vegetable like broccoli, cauliflower, zucchini, or spinach. It would also go well with Turnips with Lemon and Honey (page 173), Thin-Sliced Cauliflower with Sesame Seeds and Ginger (page 151).

Desserts: Baked Grapefruit with Tequila or Sherry (page 313); Gingered Fruit (page 312); Fruit and Cheese Platter (page 322)

♥ Omit bouillon cubes and salt. Reduce raisins to ¼ cup (60 ml) and sunflower seeds to 2 tablespoons (30 ml).

♥ ACORN SQUASH STUFFED WITH CURRIED RICE*
SERVES 4 TO 6

PREPARATION TIME: 5 minutes
UNSUPERVISED COOKING: 45 minutes

3 large acorn squash, cut in half, seeds and membranes removed
2 tablespoons (30 ml) butter
3 cups (700 ml) Curried Rice with Lentils
1 apple, cored and sliced
1 cup (250 ml) plain low-fat yogurt
FOR GARNISH: ¼ cup (60 ml) raisins, currants, or chutney

Preheat the oven to 375 degrees (190° C) and oil a 2- or 3-quart (2–3 L) baking dish.

Rub the cut surface of the squash with the butter. Fill with the Curried Rice with Lentils, until the mixture flows over the sides of the cavities. Cover the remaining exposed edges of the squash with the apple slices.

Place the squash in the baking dish, flat side up, and fill the dish with ½ inch (1.5 cm) of water. Cover the dish and bake for 45 minutes, until the squash is tender and succulent. Serve topped with yogurt and raisins, currants, or chutney.

MENU SUGGESTIONS
Serve with a large green salad and an optional steamed green vegetable. Gingered Fruit (page 312) makes a nice dessert.

♥ Substitute 1 tablespoon (15 ml) safflower margarine for the butter.

*Auxiliary recipe: requires Curried Rice with Lentils (page 118)

♥ ZUCCHINI STUFFED WITH GRAINS*

SERVES 6

PREPARATION TIME: 25 to 30 minutes
UNSUPERVISED COOKING: 30 minutes

I can think of no better way to serve the huge squashes that gardens produce in the summer than stuffing them with the pleasing, nutty combination below. With the tamari and ginger in the sauce, the dish has a somewhat oriental flavor.

2 to 3 pounds (1–1.4 kg) zucchini or summer squash, cut in half lengthwise
1 to 2 tablespoons (15–30 ml) safflower oil, as needed
1 medium onion, chopped
1 clove garlic, minced or put through a press
2 carrots, sliced diagonally or in matchsticks
⅓ cup (80 ml) raw peanuts
1 stalk celery, trimmed and sliced diagonally
3 cups (700 ml) cooked bulgur, millet, or couscous
1 cup (250 ml) fresh peas, steamed until bright green and tender, or 1 cup (250 ml) frozen peas, thawed
Salt and freshly ground pepper to taste
1 tablespoon (15 ml) tamari

FOR THE SAUCE:
¼ cup (60 ml) tamari
½ cup (120 ml) sesame tahini
1 teaspoon (5 ml) grated or minced fresh ginger
2 teaspoons (10 ml) dry sherry
Hot water as desired

Preheat the oven to 325 degrees (165°C). Oil a baking dish large enough to hold the squash.

Steam the squash for 5 minutes (10 minutes if very large). Scoop out the seeds and stringy part of the pulp.

Heat 1 tablespoon (15 ml) of the oil and sauté the onion and garlic until the onion is tender. Add the carrots, peanuts, and celery and sauté for 5 minutes. Add a little more oil and stir in the cooked grains, peas, and salt and pepper to taste. Add tamari and toss a few minutes. Remove from the heat.

*Auxiliary recipe: requires cooked bulgur or millet

Stuff the squash with the grain and vegetable mixture and place in an oiled baking dish. Bake for 30 minutes.

Meanwhile, prepare the sauce by mixing the tamari, tahini, ginger, and sherry. Thin with hot water to desired consistency.

Remove the baked stuffed squash from the oven, pour on the sauce and serve.

MENU SUGGESTIONS

Soups: Chilled Buttermilk Soup (page 86); Rosemary's Chilled Lettuce and Potato Soup (page 80)

Salads: Tossed Green Salad (page 280); Oriental Salad (page 297); Hot and Sour Bean Sprout Salad (page 298)

Desserts: Peaches with Amaretto (page 314); Puffed Amaretto or Grand Marnier Omelet (pages 306–307); Sliced Melon

♥ Use 2 teaspoons (10 ml) safflower oil. Omit tamari and sauce.

♥ SPICY EGGPLANT MISO SAUTÉ WITH BULGUR
SERVES 4

PREPARATION TIME: 15 minutes
SUPERVISED COOKING: 15 minutes

The combination of the tofu, eggplant, and miso in this dish makes it seem almost meaty. The high-protein miso gives it a special savory flavor, and the red pepper and ginger give it flair and a Szechuan quality. If you don't like your food picante, simply leave out the red pepper. I like this recipe best with bulgur, but it would be equally good with rice, millet, or other grains.

1½ cups (350 ml) bulgur
3 cups (700 ml) boiling water
¼ cup (60 ml) miso
3 tablespoons (45 ml) water
1 tablespoon (15 ml) mild honey
2 teaspoons (10 ml) sesame oil
2 tablespoons (30 ml) safflower oil
1 medium eggplant (about 1½ pounds; 700 gm), peeled and diced small
1 clove garlic, minced or put through a press
1 teaspoon (5 ml) minced or grated fresh ginger
¼ to ½ pound (100–225 gm) pressed tofu, to taste, diced (see Tofu Cutlets, page 131 for directions)

1 bunch green onions, sliced, both green and white parts
¼ to ½ teaspoon (1.25–2.5 ml) hot red pepper flakes, or 1 small
dried red pepper, seeds removed, crumbled

Place the bulgur in a heatproof serving dish and pour on the boiling water. Let stand while you prepare the rest of the ingredients.

In a small bowl, mix together the miso, water, honey, and sesame oil. Set aside.

Heat the oil in a wok or a large, heavy-bottomed skillet and sauté the eggplant for 5 minutes, stirring. Add the garlic and ginger and sauté for 2 minutes. Add the tofu and sauté for 5 minutes. Add the miso mixture and stir-fry for 3 to 4 minutes. Add the green onions and pepper flakes and cook, stirring, until the onions are tender.

Pour off any water that hasn't been absorbed by the bulgur. Fluff with a fork and top with the eggplant mixture. Serve at once.

MENU SUGGESTIONS

Soups: Hot and Sour Soup (page 67), Simple Garlic Soup Provençal (page 64),
Salads: Tossed Green Salad (page 280); Oriental Salad (page 297); Watercress, Mushroom, and Tofu Salad (page 292)
Desserts: Bread Pudding (page 320); Apricot Soufflé (page 308); Puffed Amaretto Omelet (page 306)

♥ BULGUR AND PURPLE CABBAGE WITH APPLES AND ONIONS

SERVES 4

PREPARATION TIME: 15 minutes
SUPERVISED COOKING: 15 minutes

I love this combination. The apples and the spices go beautifully with cabbage. This dish is traditionally cooked longer than indicated here, but I like the apples to remain crisp.

        1 cup (250 ml) bulgur
    1½ cups (350 ml) boiling water
        1 tablespoon (15 ml) safflower oil
        2 onions, sliced
        3 large, tart apples, cored and sliced
        4 cups (950 ml) purple cabbage (1 pound; 450 gm), shredded
        3 tablespoons (45 ml) apple cider vinegar or red wine vinegar
      ¼ cup (60 ml) raisins
      ½ teaspoon (2.5 ml) ground cloves
      ½ teaspoon (2.5 ml) ground allspice
        1 teaspoon (5 ml) ground cinnamon
      ¾ cup (180 ml) beer or apple juice
        2 tablespoons (30 ml) mild honey
        1 cup (250 ml) plain low-fat yogurt

Place the bulgur in a heatproof serving dish and pour on the boiling water. Let stand while you prepare the vegetables and apples.

Heat the oil in a wok or a heavy-bottomed skillet and add the onions. Sauté over medium heat until they begin to brown. Add the apples and sauté for about 2 minutes, then add the cabbage, vinegar, raisins, spices, beer, and honey. Stir together and cook over medium-low heat for 5 to 10 minutes, or longer, to taste.

Transfer the bulgur to a warm serving dish, spoon on the cabbage mixture, and top with yogurt. Serve immediately.

MENU SUGGESTIONS:

Soups: Elegant Pressure-Cooked White Bean Soup (page 74); Simple Miso Soup (page 68)
Side dishes: Artichokes Braised in Wine (omit the stuffing) (page 116); a simple steamed vegetable
Salads: Tossed Green Salad (page 280); Leftover Beans Salad (page 294); Watercress, Mushroom, and Tofu Salad (page 292)

Desserts: Tofu Noodle Kugel (page 319); Puffed Grand Marnier Omelet (page 307)

♥ Reduce raisins to 2 tablespoons (30 ml) and honey to 1 tablespoon (15 ml).

PURPLE CABBAGE, TOFU, ONIONS, AND WINTER SQUASH WITH MISO
SERVES 4

PREPARATION TIME: 15 minutes
SUPERVISED COOKING: 20 to 25 minutes

There is something unusually satisfying about the taste of browned onions with purple cabbage. The tofu, miso, and grains give the dish ample protein. The colors of the yellow-orange squash against the purple cabbage are nice, and the dish is pungent with fresh ginger.

    2 tablespoons (30 ml) miso
    ¼ cup (60 ml) water
    2 teaspoons grated or minced fresh ginger or ½ teaspoon (2.5 ml) dried
    1 teaspoon (10 ml) sesame oil
    2 tablespoons (30 ml) safflower oil
    2 onions, sliced
    2 cakes (½ pound (225 gm)) tofu, pressed, if desired (see Tofu Cutlets, page 131, for directions), and diced
    1 tablespoon (15 ml) sesame seeds
    2 cups (475 ml) finely diced, peeled butternut squash
    4 cups (950 ml) purple cabbage, shredded (1 pound; 450 gm)
2 to 3 cups (475–700 ml) hot, cooked grains (such as millet, couscous, or brown rice cooked with soy grits or plain)

Mix together the miso, water, 1 teaspoon (5 ml) of the fresh ginger (or ¼ teaspoon dried) and the sesame oil in a small bowl and set aside.

Heat a wok or heavy-bottomed skillet and add 1 tablespoon (15 ml) of the safflower oil. Add the onions and sauté over a medium flame until they begin to brown. Add the remaining teaspoon (5 ml) of fresh ginger (or ¼ teaspoon dried) and the tofu and sauté for 3 minutes. Add the sesame seeds, butternut squash, and remaining safflower oil and stir-fry, adding a little water from time to time if the squash begins to stick, for about 10 minutes, or until the squash is tender. Add the cabbage and more water if necessary and cook, stirring, for 2 to 3 minutes.

Stir the miso mixture and mix into the vegetables. Cook several minutes, stirring, and serve over the grains of your choice.

MENU SUGGESTIONS

Salads: Lettuce Salad with Oranges (page 281); Oriental Salad (page 297); Hot and Sour Bean Sprout Salad (page 298)

Desserts: Apples with Lime Juice (page 312); Baked Grapefruit with Tequila or Sherry (page 313)

♥ UPAMA (Curried Cream of Wheat with Vegetables)
SERVES 4 TO 6

PREPARATION TIME: 15 minutes

SUPERVISED COOKING TIME: 15 minutes

Upama (pronounced UP-ma) is a curried cream of wheat, almost an Indian version of polenta. Because cream of wheat cooks so quickly, this is a fast meal. You can use either the regular packaged cereal, Cream of Wheat, or a product now widely available in natural foods stores called Bear Mush. This is a darker, whole-wheat version, and I think it's tastier. The finished product should be stiff, like polenta. It's good topped with yogurt. If you want to complement the protein further, cook the tofu along with the vegetables.

1 to 2 tablespoons (15–30 ml) safflower oil or butter, as needed
1 medium onion, peeled and sliced
1 tablespoon (15 ml) curry powder
½ teaspoon (2.5 ml) ground ginger
1 tablespoon (15 ml) mustard seeds
2 cakes (½ pound) tofu, diced (optional)
2 cups (475 ml) broccoli or cauliflower florets
3 tablespoons (45 ml) slivered almonds or cashews, or a mixture
3 tablespoons (45 ml) raisins
5 cups (1.2 L) water
2 cups of Cream of Wheat
½ teaspoon (2.5 ml) salt
2 tablespoons (30 ml) chopped fresh cilantro
1 cup (250 ml) plain low-fat yogurt

Heat the oil in a Dutch oven or wok and add the onion, curry powder, ginger, mustard seeds, and optional tofu. Sauté until the onion is tender and the seeds begin to pop. Add the broccoli, nuts, and raisins, adding more oil if necessary, and sauté for 3 to 5 minutes, stirring. Pour in the water and bring to a boil. Add the salt. Stir in

126

the Cream of Wheat *very* slowly, pouring in a slow, steady stream and stirring continually. When the mixture is smooth and thick, remove from the heat, top with the yogurt, and serve.

MENU SUGGESTIONS

Soups: Pureed Curry of Cauliflower Soup (page 79); Peach Soup (page 90)

Side dishes: Cooked Curried Cucumbers (page 156); Picante Garbanzos (page 105)

Salads: Curried Carrot Salad (page 284); Tossed Green Salad (page 280); Cucumber Yogurt Salad (page 282)

Desserts: Fresh fruit; Pineapple Banana Mint Sherbet (page 316); Orange Ice (page 318)

♥ Omit salt.

♥ BARLEY MUSHROOM PILAFF
SERVES 6

PREPARATION TIME: 15 to 20 minutes
SUPERVISED COOKING: 10 minutes
UNSUPERVISED COOKING: 30 minutes

Here's another recipe using that inspired combination, barley and mushrooms. The addition of the flaked soybeans makes the protein complete, and it produces a filling main dish.

Use any leftovers as a stuffing for zucchini, cabbage, or eggplant.

```
        1  quart (1 L) Tamari-Bouillon Broth (page 62), plus more as
           needed
 1 to 2  tablespoons (15–30 ml) safflower oil or butter, as needed
        2  onions, sliced thin
        2  large cloves garlic, minced or put through a press
        1  pound (450 gm) fresh mushrooms, sliced thin
        1  sweet green pepper, seeded and membranes removed,
           sliced
        2  tablespoons (30 ml) dry white wine
      ½  teaspoon (2.5 ml) thyme
        2  cups (475 ml) barley, washed
      ½  cup (120 ml) soy flakes
           Salt and freshly ground pepper to taste
        2  tablespoons (30 ml) chopped fresh dill or 1 tablespoon (15
           ml) dried dillweed
```

Preheat the oven to 350 degrees (180°C).

In a large saucepan, slowly bring the broth to a boil.

Heat a large, lidded flameproof casserole or Dutch oven and add 1 tablespoon of the oil. Sauté the onions and 1 clove of the garlic until the onion begins to turn translucent. Add the remaining garlic, the mushrooms, and green pepper and sauté for 2 minutes, adding more oil, if necessary. Add the white wine and thyme and sauté for 3 minutes. Stir in the barley and soy flakes and sauté for 3 minutes. Stir in the boiling broth, salt and pepper to taste and the dill. Bring to a boil, cover, and place in the oven.

Bake 30 to 40 minutes, until the barley is tender, checking from time to time to make sure the liquid does not evaporate. If it does, simply add about ½ cup (120 ml) more broth or water at a time, until the barley is tender.

MENU SUGGESTIONS

Side dishes: Simply steamed green vegetable; Turnips with Lemon and Honey (page 173); Thin-Sliced Cauliflower with Sesame Seeds and Ginger (page 151)

Salads: Tossed Green Salad (page 280); Cucumber Yogurt Salad (page 282)

Desserts: Pears Poached in Red Wine (page 309); Prune Soufflé (page 307)

♥ Substitute water for the broth and omit salt. Increase the garlic to 4 cloves and add 1 teaspoon (5 ml) or more of savory dried herbs, such as thyme, rosemary, sage, or oregano.

♥ KASHA WITH MUSHROOMS, WATER CHESTNUTS, AND CELERY
SERVES 6

VEGETABLE PREPARATION TIME: 10 to 15 minutes
SUPERVISED COOKING: 10 to 15 minutes
UNSUPERVISED COOKING: 20 minutes

I love buckwheat groats, and kasha is one of the few dishes my father would eat when I first became a vegetarian, years ago—his Russian mother cooked kasha all the time, so it was familiar. (Now, of course, he eats many of the dishes I cook.) Kasha reheats very well in the oven, so cook twice as much as you need. You can use any leftovers for the auxiliary recipe that follows, Cabbage Leaves Stuffed with Kasha.

1½ cups (350 ml) buckwheat groats, washed
1 egg, beaten
3 cups (700 ml) boiling water
1 tablespoon (15 ml) safflower oil
1 small onion, chopped
1 clove garlic, minced or put through a press
1 cake (¼ pound; 100 gm) tofu, diced (optional; will complement the protein)
1 tablespoon (15 ml) tamari (if using tofu)
6 mushrooms, sliced
1 tablespoon (15 ml) dry sherry
2 stalks celery, sliced
½ small can water chestnuts, drained
Salt and freshly ground pepper to taste

Mix the buckwheat groats with the egg and stir together to coat well. Heat a heavy, dry skillet and add the groats. Stir over medium heat until all the egg is absorbed and the groats are beginning to toast. Add the boiling water. When the mixture comes to a boil, reduce the heat, cover, and simmer 20 minutes, or until the liquid is absorbed. Meanwhile, prepare the vegetables.

When the kasha is cooked, heat the oil in a large, heavy-bottomed skillet and sauté the onion with the garlic until the onion is just beginning to get tender. Add the optional tofu and tamari, and sauté 3 minutes. Add the mushrooms and sauté, stirring, for a minute, then add the sherry and sauté 3 minutes. Add the celery and water chestnuts and sauté 2 minutes. Stir in the kasha, and cook another 2 or 3 minutes. Season to taste with salt and freshly ground pepper. Serve hot.

MENU SUGGESTIONS

Any green vegetable, simply steamed
Soups: Hot or Iced Tomato Soup (page 72); Pureed Zucchini Soup (page 70); Simple Miso Soup (page 68)
Main dishes: Tofu Cutlets, (page 131), if you don't use tofu in the kasha
Salads: Tossed Green Salad (page 280); Leftover Beans Salad (page 294); Cucumber Yogurt Salad (page 282)
Desserts: Figs Poached in Madeira (page 311); Banana Yogurt Freeze (page 315); Fruit and Cheese Platter (page 322)

♥ Omit egg; sauté dry kasha in a dry skillet until it begins to smell toasty. Omit tamari and salt.

CABBAGE LEAVES STUFFED WITH KASHA, WITH CREAMY TOFU SAUCE*

SERVES 4

PREPARATION TIME: 20 to 30 minutes
UNSUPERVISED COOKING TIME: 20 minutes

Just in case you're considering freezing this, don't. The cabbage leaves become like cardboard.

FOR THE CABBAGE LEAVES:
 2 cups (475 ml) Kasha with Mushrooms, Water Chestnuts, and Celery from the preceding recipe
12 large green cabbage leaves

FOR THE TOFU SAUCE (makes 1½ cups; 350 ml):
 2 cakes (½ pound; 225 gm) tofu
 1 tablespoon (15 ml) miso
 1 tablespoon (15 ml) sesame tahini
 ½ cup (120 ml) plain low-fat yogurt
 1 tablespoon (15 ml) lemon juice
 Pinch of freshly grated nutmeg

Preheat the oven to 350 degrees (180°C). Oil a 2-quart (2 L) baking dish. Steam the cabbage leaves for about 3 minutes, in a large covered saucepan or wok, until tender and pliable. Rinse under cold water and drain on paper towels.

In a blender or food processor, blend together the ingredients for the tofu sauce until smooth.

Place 2 heaping tablespoons (30 ml) Kasha mixture in the middle of each cabbage leaf. Spread a teaspoon (5 ml) of sauce over the kasha. Fold in the sides of the leaf and roll up, starting at the stem end. Place seam side down in the baking dish.

Pour ½ cup (120 ml) water in the dish and cover with foil or a lid. Bake for 20 minutes. Top with the remaining sauce and serve.

MENU SUGGESTIONS

Soups: Hot or Iced Tomato Soup (page 72); Pureed Zucchini Soup (page 70)

Salads: Tossed Green Salad (page 280), Coleslaw (page 295, to use up the remaining cabbage); Tomato Salad (page 284)

Any green vegetable, simply steamed

Desserts: See suggestions for previous recipe.

*Auxiliary recipe: requires leftover Kasha with Mushrooms, Water Chestnuts, and Celery (page 128)

TOFU CUTLETS
SERVES 4

PREPARATION TIME: 10 minutes
UNSUPERVISED MARINATING AND PRESSING: 1 hour, in all
SUPERVISED COOKING: 10 minutes

When pressed and sautéed or broiled, tofu takes on a texture that somewhat resembles that of chicken breasts—I think it even tastes a bit like chicken. This dish can be prepared far ahead of time: you can always marinate the pressed tofu longer than specified and even keep pressed tofu in the marinade for several days in the refrigerator. You can also make a delicious sandwich with tofu cutlets. Serve them on a bun or whole-wheat bread with tomatoes, sprouts, and mustard or ketchup or barbecue sauce.

    4 cakes (1 pound; 450 gm) tofu
    ¼ cup (60 ml) water
    ½ cup (120 ml) tamari
    1 tablespoon (15 ml) mild honey
    1 teaspoon (15 ml) grated or finely minced fresh ginger
1 to 2 cloves garlic, minced or put through a press
    2 tablespoons (30 ml) sesame tahini
    1 tablespoon (15 ml) safflower oil (more as needed)

To press the tofu: Wrap the tofu in a dish towel, in a single layer. Place on a baking sheet, and set another baking sheet or a cutting board on top. Place a saucepan full of water or an equivalant weight (at least 2 pounds; 1 kg) on the top sheet or cutting board and leave for 30 minutes or longer. Pressed tofu is now ready to marinate or cook, or can be kept in water in the refrigerator.

To prepare the cutlets: In a bowl, mix together the water, tamari, honey, ginger, garlic, and tahini. With a skewer, poke 6 to 8 holes in each square of pressed tofu. Marinate the tofu in the mixture for at least 30 minutes. (If you don't have time to marinate the tofu, you can simply cook it and use the marinade as a sauce.)

To broil: Preheat the broiler. Place the tofu on a baking sheet brushed with oil and broil for 5 minutes on each side. Serve immediately.

To sauté: Heat a large, heavy-bottomed skillet. Add the oil, and sauté the tofu for 5 minutes on each side. Serve immediately.

MENU SUGGESTIONS

A vegetable side dish such as Florentine Tomatoes (page 171), Green Beans Amandine (page 146), or Green Beans à la Provençal (page 147) would be welcome here. You can serve either a substantial salad like Leftover Beans Salad (page 294) or Hot and Sour Buckwheat Noodle Salad (page 300) or a lighter one like Warm or Chilled Cauliflower or Broccoli Salad (page 290), Tossed Green Salad (page 280), or Middle Eastern Beet Salad (page 288). Either Peach Banana Freeze (page 316) or Strawberries in Red Wine and Preserves Syrup (page 310) would make a fitting dessert.

CHILLED TOFU WITH DIPPING SAUCES
SERVES 4

PREPARATION TIME: 5 to 15 minutes, depending on the number of dipping sauces you make

My closest friends know that I like tofu plain. At first they thought this somewhat extreme, until I introduced them to it with these dipping sauces. That's the way it's often served as a starter in Japanese restaurants. The tofu will be a delicate sponge for the ginger sauces, especially if it is very fresh.

    4 cakes (1 pound; 450 gm) tofu, each cut into ½-inch (1.5 cm) strips
    Any or all of the sauces which follow.

Keep the tofu chilled in individual bowls of ice-cold water. Place dipping sauces in small bowls at each place. Serve.

SIMPLE DIPPING SAUCE FOR TOFU AND VEGETABLES
1 CUP (250 ML)

    ½ cup (120 ml) vegetable stock or water
    ¼ cup (60 ml) tamari
3 to 4 tablespoons (45–60 ml) *sake* or dry sherry
    1 tablespoon (20 ml) grated fresh ginger

Combine the stock, tamari, and *sake* or sherry in a small saucepan. Heat just to the boiling point and add the ginger. Remove from the heat and allow to cool.

TERIYAKI SAUCE
¾ CUP (180 ML)

¼ cup (60 ml) tamari
¼ cup (60 ml) *sake* or dry sherry
2 tablespoons (30 ml) mild honey
1 tablespoon (15 ml) freshly grated ginger or 1½ teaspoons (7 ml) ground ginger
2 cloves garlic, minced or put through a press
1 tablespoon (15 ml) sesame oil
¼ teaspoon (1.25 ml) dry mustard

Combine all the ingredients in a small bowl.

TAHINI-TAMARI SAUCE
¾ TO 1 CUP (180–250 ML)

One of my favorite meals is a slice of tofu spread with this scrumptious sauce and served with sprouts on a piece of whole-grain bread. This sauce also goes very nicely with simply steamed or raw vegetables, and is a good topping for Fried Rice and Soy Grits with Vegetables (page 114), Chinese-Style Tofu and Vegetables with Grains (page 138), and Zucchini Stuffed with Grains. Keep it on hand in the refrigerator.

¼ cup (60 ml) tamari
½ cup (120 ml) sesame tahini
1 teaspoon (5 ml) freshly grated ginger
2 teaspoons (10 ml) dry sherry
Hot water

Combine the tamari, tahini, ginger, and sherry. Thin out to the desired consistency with hot water.

MENU SUGGESTIONS
Soups: Buckwheat Noodle Soup with Green Beans (page 63); Potato Leek Soup (page 65)
Vegetable and Grain dishes: Chinese-Style Vegetables with Couscous (page 137); Bulgur and Purple Cabbage with Apples and Onions (page 124)
Salads: Oriental Salad (page 297); Hot and Sour Bean Sprout Salad (page 298); Hot and Sour Buckwheat Noodle Salad (page 300); Jícama and Orange Salad (page 295)
Desserts: Strawberry Freeze (page 317); Cantaloupe with Apricot Puree and Almonds (page 313); Rice or Leftover Grains Pudding (page 321)

MISO TOPPINGS FOR TOFU AND GRAINS

These miso-based toppings are adapted from recipes in *The Book of Miso* by William Shurtleff and Akiko Aoyagi (Brookline, Mass.: The Autumn Press, Inc., 1976). They are very thick, like pastes, and extremely salty: a little goes a long way. If you have high blood pressure, or are prone to it, they are not for you.

Spread any of these out thinly on tofu or top grains with about ¼ to ½ teaspoon (1.25–2.5 ml) per serving (or more, to taste). These will keep for a long time in the refrigerator, covered.

SIMPLE SIMMERED RED MISO
⅓ CUP (80 ML)

¼ cup (60 ml) red or barley miso
4 teaspoons (20 ml) mild honey
1 tablespoon (15 ml) water
1 tablespoon (15 ml) white wine or *sake*

Combine all the ingredients and place in a small, heavy-bottomed skillet or saucepan. Bring to a simmer, stirring, and cook 2 to 3 minutes, stirring constantly. Remove from the heat and allow to cool.

SIMMERED RED MISO WITH GINGER
⅓ CUP (80 ML)

¼ cup (60 ml) red, barley or hacho miso
2 tablespoons (30 ml) mild honey
2 tablespoons (30 ml) *sake*
1 tablespoon (15 ml) water
2 teaspoons (10 ml) freshly grated or minced ginger

Mix together all the ingredients and proceed as in Simple Simmered Red Miso above.

PEANUT MISO
½ CUP (120 ML)

This is one of my favorites. I especially like it spread on jícama.

¼ cup (60 ml) salt-free crunchy peanut butter
2 tablespoons (30 ml) red, barley, or hacho miso
2 tablespoons (30 ml) mild honey
2 tablespoons (30 ml) water
1 teaspoon (5 ml) freshly grated ginger (optional)

Mix together all the ingredients and proceed as in Simple Simmered Red Miso above.

SESAME MISO
½ cup (120 ml)

Substitute sesame tahini or ground roasted sesame seeds for the peanut butter and proceed as in Peanut Miso (above).

MISO "SOUBISE"
2 cups (475 ml)

Preparation time: 5 to 10 minutes
Supervised cooking: 15 minutes

This recipe could be considered an Oriental version of a *soubise,* the French onion sauce. The onions cook down gently and combine nicely with the miso, whose flavor is not as intense as in the simmered miso recipes. Mix this sauce into cooked grains or use it as a topping for tofu or steamed vegetables.

1 to 2 tablespoons (15–30 ml) sesame oil
4 medium onions, thinly sliced
2 tablespoons (30 ml) barley, red or hacho miso
¼ cup (60 ml) water
2 tablespoons (30 ml) *sake,* dry sherry, or dry white wine

Heat the oil in a heavy-bottomed skillet and sauté the onions over medium heat for 5 minutes, or until completely soft. Dissolve the miso in the water and stir into the onions. Cover and simmer for 10 minutes, stirring occasionally. Add the sake, and continue cooking, uncovered, for 3 to 5 minutes longer. Serve over grains, tofu, or vegetables.

MENU SUGGESTIIONS

Vegetable side dishes: Turnips with Lemon and Honey (page 173); Carrots Cooked in Vodka (page 150)

Salads: Tossed Green Salad (page 280); Watercress, Mushroom, and Tofu Salad (page 292); Curried Carrot Salad (page 284); Leftover Beans Salad (page 294)

Desserts: Strawberry Freeze (page 317); Prune Soufflé (page 307); Puffed Grand Marnier Omelet (page 307)

♥ TOFU VEGETABLE CURRY (Slower-Cooking Vegetables)
SERVES 4 TO 6
PREPARATION TIME: 15 minutes
SUPERVISED COOKING: 15 minutes
UNSUPERVISED COOKING: 15 minutes

> 2 potatoes, diced
> 2 cups (475 ml) diced, peeled eggplant
> 2 tablespoons (30 ml) butter, safflower oil, or peanut oil
> 1 onion, sliced
> 1 clove garlic, minced or put through a press
> 1 teaspoon (5 ml) minced fresh ginger or ¼ teaspoon (1.25 ml) ground
> 2 cakes (½ pound; 225 gm) tofu, pressed and diced (see page 131 for instructions on pressing)
> 1 tablespoon (15 ml) curry powder
> ¼ cup (60 ml) peanuts, almonds, or sunflower seeds
> ½ cup (120 ml) raisins
> 1 cup (250 ml) buttermilk or plain low-fat yogurt
> Salt to taste
> 2 tablespoons (30 ml) chopped fresh cilantro (optional)
> 2 to 3 cups (475–700 ml) hot cooked grains, such as millet, couscous, or brown rice

Steam the potatoes and peeled eggplant for 15 minutes.

Meanwhile, heat the butter in a heavy-bottomed skillet, Dutch oven, or wok and add the onion, garlic, and ginger. Sauté over medium-low heat for a minute or two, then add the tofu and the curry powder. Sauté gently for about 10 minutes, stirring.

Add the steamed potato and eggplant, peanuts, and raisins and sauté another 5 minutes. Season to taste with salt, then remove from the heat. Cool a moment, then stir in the buttermilk or yogurt and the optional cilantro.

Serve over the hot cooked grains, with chutney on the side.

VARIATION (Faster-Cooking Vegetables)
Substitute ¾ pound zucchini and ¾ pound cauliflower for the potatoes and eggplant. Omit the steaming, and sauté them for 3 to 5 minutes after you have sautéed the onion, garlic, spices, and tofu. Then add the raisins, etc., and proceed with the recipe.

MENU SUGGESTIONS
Soups: Chilled Buttermilk Soup (page 86); Peach Soup (page 90); Chilled Melon Soup (page 88)

Salads: Cucumber Yogurt Salad (page 282); Coleslaw (page 295); Curried Carrot Salad (page 284)

Desserts: Banana Yogurt Freeze (page 315); Gingered Fruit (page 312)

♥ Use 1 tablespoon (15 ml) safflower oil and cook in a nonstick skillet; reduce peanuts to 2 tablespoons (30 ml) and raisins to 3 tablespoons (45 ml); omit salt; use the yogurt.

♥ CHINESE-STYLE VEGETABLES WITH COUSCOUS
SERVES 6

PREPARATION TIME: 15 minutes
SUPERVISED COOKING: 10 to 15 minutes

This dish once marked the beginning of a romance. The romance didn't last too long, but I'm still enticing people with Chinese-Style Vegetables with Couscous. To balance the protein I make it with either tofu or cooked soy flakes, which I prefer. It's a very light dish, but throughly satisfying.

FOR THE SAUCE:

¼ cup (60 ml) tamari

2 tablespoons (30 ml) water

1 tablespoon (15 ml) dry sherry

1 teaspoon (5 ml) mild honey

½ teaspoon (2.5 ml) freshly grated ginger or ¼ teaspoon (1.25 ml) ground

1 tablespoon (15 ml) sesame oil

1 tablespoon (15 ml) Pernod or ½ teaspoon (2.5 ml) crushed anise seeds

FOR THE VEGETABLES:

1½ cups (350 ml) warm water or soy flakes cooking liquid, or a combination

1 cup (250 ml) couscous

1 tablespoon (15 ml) plus 1 teaspoon (5 ml) safflower oil

1 clove garlic, minced or put through a press

1 teaspoon (5 ml) grated or minced ginger

1 small onion, sliced

2 cakes (½ pound) tofu, diced, or 1 cup cooked soy flakes

1 pound (450 gm) zucchini, sliced ¼ inch (0.7 cm) thick

½ pound (225 gm) asparagus, trimmed and cut in 1- or 2-inch (2.5–5 cm) pieces

1 tablespoon (15 ml) chopped cilantro (optional)

Mix together the ingredients for the sauce and set aside.

Place the couscous in a bowl and pour on 1½ cups (350 ml) warm water or cooking liquid from the soyflakes, or a combination of the two.

Heat the 1 tablespoon oil over medium heat in a wok or heavy-bottomed skillet and add the garlic and ginger. Sauté a few seconds, being careful not to burn, and add the onion. Stir-fry until the onion begins to soften. Add the tofu, if using, and a tablespoon (15 ml) of the sauce. Stir-fry for 2 minutes and add the zucchini. Add a couple tablespoons (30 ml) of water if the food is beginning to stick. Stir-fry the zucchini for 2 to 3 minutes, or until it begins to turn translucent, and add the asparagus and a little more water. Stir, cover, and cook for 2 to 3 minutes. Add the 1 teaspoon (5 ml) oil to the pan and stir in the soyflakes, if using, and the couscous. Stir together and add 3 to 4 tablespoons (45–60 ml) of the sauce, to taste, and the optional cilantro. Toss together and serve, passing the remaining sauce.

MENU SUGGESTIONS
Soups: Hot and Sour Soup (page 67); Simple Miso Soup (page 68)
Salads: Tossed Green Salad (page 280); Curried Carrot Salad (page 284); Hot and Sour Bean Sprout Salad (page 298)
Desserts: Prune Soufflé (page 307); Apricot Soufflé (page 308); Orange Ice (page 318)

♥ Omit tamari; reduce sesame oil to 1 teaspoon (5 ml).

♥ CHINESE-STYLE TOFU AND VEGETABLES WITH GRAINS
SERVES 6
PREPARATION TIME: 15 minutes
COOKING TIME FOR VEGETABLES: 10 to 15 minutes

This stir-fry is the first "vegetarian" dish I learned. It differs from the previous dish in that it contains tomatoes, which give the dish a hint of sweetness, as well as carrots, celery, and crunchy peanuts. I like it with any grain.

1 tablespoon (15 ml) safflower oil, plus more as necessary
1 teaspoon (5 ml) freshly grated ginger, or ¼ teaspoon (1.25 ml) ground
1 clove garlic, minced
1 small onion, sliced

2 cakes (½ pound; 225 gm) tofu, pressed if time allows (see instructions, Tofu Cutlets, page 131) and diced
2 tablespoons (30 ml) tamari
1 large or two small carrots, sliced on the diagonal
1 stalk celery, sliced on the diagonal
¼ cup (60 ml) raw peanuts
1 pound (450 gm) sliced summer squash or broccoli florets
2 tomatoes, sliced
¼ teaspoon (1.25 ml) dried basil
1 tablespoon (15 ml) arrowroot or 2 teaspoons (10 ml) cornstarch dissolved in a small amount of water
2 tablespoons (30 ml) dry sherry (optional)
2 cups hot, cooked grains, such as brown rice, bulgur, millet, couscous, or wheat berries

Heat the tablespoon of safflower oil over medium heat in a wok or large, heavy-bottomed skillet and add the ginger and garlic. Sauté for a few seconds, being careful not to burn, and add the onion. Stir-fry until the onion begins to look translucent, then add the tofu and 1 tablespoon (15 ml) tamari. Stir-fry for 2 to 3 minutes and add the carrots and a tablespoon (15 ml) or two (30 ml) of water if the pan is dry. Cook, stirring, for a few minutes, until the centers of the carrots begin to look yellow, then add the celery and peanuts. Stir-fry for a minute or two, until the celery begins to turn a brighter green, and add the squash or broccoli. Add a little more water if the pan is dry and stir-fry for 3 to 5 minutes, until the vegetables are just beginning to turn bright green. Add the tomatoes and basil, cover and cook for 5 to 10 minutes over low heat.

Meanwhile, stir a tablespoon of tamari and the sherry into the dissolved arrowroot or cornstarch. Uncover the vegetables, add the arrowroot mixture, and stir until the vegetables are glazed.

Remove from the heat and serve over hot cooked grains.

MENU SUGGESTIONS

Soups: Simple Miso Soup (page 68); Hot and Sour Soup (page 67)
Salads: Hot and Sour Bean Sprout Salad (page 298); Curried Carrot Salad (page 284); Tossed Green Salad (page 280)
Desserts: Prune or Apricot Soufflé (pages 307 and 308); Noodle Kugel (page 318) or Tofu Noodle Kugel (page 319); any fruit dessert

♥ Omit tamari.

♥ CHINESE-STYLE SNOW PEAS AND WATER CHESTNUTS
SERVES 6

PREPARATION TIME: 10 minutes
SUPERVISED COOKING: 10 minutes at most

FOR THE SAUCE:
- ¼ cup (60 ml) tamari
- 2 tablespoons (30 ml) water
- 1 tablespoon (15 ml) dry sherry
- 1 teaspoon (5 ml) mild flavored honey
- ½ teaspoon (2.5 ml) grated fresh ginger, or ¼ teaspoon (1.25 ml) dried
- 1 tablespoon (15 ml) sesame oil
- 1 tablespoon (15 ml) Pernod, or ½ teaspoon (2.5 ml) crushed anise seeds
- 1 tablespoon (15 ml) cornstarch or arrowroot

FOR THE VEGETABLES:
- 1 pound (450 gm) snow peas, strings removed
- 4 green onions, both white part and green, chopped
- 1 4-oz. (100 gm) can water chestnuts, drained and sliced
- 2 teaspoons (10 ml) safflower or peanut oil

First mix together the ingredients for the sauce.

Steam the snow peas, green onions, and water chestnuts together for 5 to 10 minutes, to taste. Heat the oil in a large, heavy-bottomed skillet or wok and transfer the vegetables to it. Toss a few seconds to coat with oil, and add the sauce. Cook, stirring, over medium-high heat just until the sauce thickens and glazes the vegetables. This should take less than a minute.

MENU SUGGESTIONS

Soups: Buckwheat Noodle Soup with Green Beans (page 63); Potato Leek Soup (page 65); Hot and Sour Soup (page 67)

Main dishes: Chilled Tofu with Dipping Sauces (page 132); Tofu Cutlets (page 131); Grains with Miso Toppings (page 134); Simple Soba with Sesame Oil (page 214)

Salads: Hot and Sour Bean Sprout Salad (page 298); Hot and Sour Buckwheat Noodle Salad (page 300); Curried Carrot Salad (page 284); Simple Cabbage and Carrot Salad with Herbs (page 298)

Desserts: Fruit ices would be especially good, but anything would be suitable.

♥ Omit tamari. Reduce sesame oil to 1 teaspoon.

♥ SWEET AND SOUR CABBAGE
SERVES 6
PREPARATION TIME: 10 to 15 minutes
SUPERVISED COOKING TIME: 15 to 20 minutes

Few dishes are simpler and cheaper than this one.

> 1 tablespoon (15 ml) safflower or peanut oil, more as needed
> 1 onion, sliced
> 2 carrots, sliced on the diagonal
> ¼ cup (60 ml) raw peanuts
> 1½ to 2 pounds (700 gm–1 kg)(about ½ head), green cabbage, shredded or chopped
> ½ cup (120 ml) mung bean sprouts
> 2 tomatoes, sliced
> ¼ cup (60 ml) mild honey
> ¼ cup (60 ml) wine vinegar or cider vinegar
> 1 tablespoon (15 ml) arrowroot or 2 teaspoons (10 ml) cornstarch
> tamari to taste
> 2 cakes tofu, pressed if desired (see page 131), diced (optional)
> 1 tablespoon (15 ml) tamari (optional)

Heat the 1 tablespoon oil in a wok or a large skillet over medium-high heat. Add the onion and stir-fry until it begins to soften. Add the carrots and peanuts and continue to stir-fry for 2 to 3 minutes. Add the cabbage and bean sprouts and stir-fry for 2 to 3 minutes, then add the tomatoes and toss together. Add a couple tablespoons (30 ml) water, cover and cook over medium-low heat for 10 minutes.

Meanwhile, combine the honey and vinegar and stir well. Stir in the arrowroot or cornstarch to dissolve. Uncover the vegetables, stir in the sauce and cook, stirring, until the sauce thickens and glazes the vegetables. Add tamari to taste.

Serve at once over hot, cooked grains.

Note: For additional protein add the tofu along with the onions. Sauté, adding the tamari, and proceed with the recipe.

MENU SUGGESTIONS
Soups: Buckwheat Noodle Soup with Green Beans (page 63); either of the Miso soups (pages 68 and 70)
Salads: Jícama and Orange Salad with Avocados (page 295); Leftover

Beans Salad (page 294); Watercress, Mushroom, and Tofu Salad (page 292); Cottage Cheese and Tomato with Miso Dressing (page 296)

Desserts: Prune or Apricot Soufflé (pages 307 and 308); Pears Poached in Red Wine (page 309); fresh fruit; Puffed Grand Marnier Omelet (page 307)

♥ Omit tamari.

CELERY POTATO "GRATIN"
SERVES 4 TO 6
PREPARATION TIME: 10 to 15 minutes
UNSUPERVISED COOKING: 35 minutes in all

Because it's made with a creamy tofu sauce instead of the traditional high-fat white sauce with cheese, this recipe isn't really a gratin. But I like it better than the traditional version, and the simple tofu sauce just can't be beat. This sauce does bake differently from a white sauce, for it firms up rather than melting; But it still retains its creamy quality, and the casserole comes out bubbling and mouth-watering. You can have the sauce on hand in the refrigerator—it will stay good for at least a week, if you can resist eating it all before that—or you can prepare it in minutes while the vegetables are steaming.

This particular recipe is a good way to use up celery when it begins to become limp, though cauliflower, broccoli, or squash can be substituted (see the following recipe).

2 medium potatoes, peeled and sliced about ¼ inch (0.7 cm) thick (2 cups; 475 ml)
2 cups (475 ml) sliced celery (½ to 1 inch; 1.5–2.5 cm)
2 cakes (½ pound; 225 gm) tofu
1 tablespoon (15 ml) miso
1 tablespoon (15 ml) sesame tahini
1 tablespoon (15 ml) lemon juice
½ cup (120 ml) plain low-fat yogurt or water
1 teaspoon (5 ml) unbleached flour
Freshly ground black pepper

Preheat the oven to 400 degrees (200°C). Butter a 2-quart (2 L) casserole or gratin dish.

Put the sliced potatoes in a steamer. Bring the water to a boil, and after the potatoes have been steaming for 5 minutes, add the celery. Steam the vegetables for 10 minutes longer.

Meanwhile, blend together the remaining ingredients except for the pepper until completely smooth, using a blender or food processor.

Drain the steamed vegetables and refresh under cold water. Toss with black pepper to taste. Place in the baking dish and cover with the tofu sauce. Gently move the vegetables around so that the sauce can coat them all.

Bake for 20 minutes. (The top will brown and firm up a little.) Serve bubbling hot.

MENU SUGGESTIONS

Soups: Simple Garlic Soup Provençale (page 64); Hot or Iced Tomato Soup (page 72); Gazpacho (page 87)

Salads: Tossed Green Salad (page 280); Leftover Beans or Grains Salad (pages 293 and 294)

Side dishes: Southern Spoonbread (page 189)

Desserts: Peaches with Amaretto (page 314); Apples with Lime Juice (page 312); Strawberries or Raspberries with Red Wine (page 315)

BROCCOLI OR CAULIFLOWER "GRATIN"
SERVES 4 TO 6

Follow the recipe for Celery Potato "Gratin" (above), but substitute 4 cups (950 ml) briefly steamed broccoli or cauliflower florets, or a combination, for the celery and potatoes. Menu suggestions are the same.

♥ CHINESE CABBAGE WITH SESAME AND GINGER
PREPARATION TIME: 10 minutes
SUPERVISED COOKING: 5 minutes

Chinese cabbage, or celery cabbage, is too often overlooked in the supermarket. It has a subtle cabbage flavor all its own, and a marvelous crisp texture.

Most stir-fry recipes are cooked over higher heat than I use, because they utilize more oil. After burning garlic and ginger time after time, I realized that I should not try to follow the Chinese technique for stir-frying, but should use moderate heat. So let my burned garlic and ginger be an example, and don't make the same mistake.

1 tablespoon (15 ml) mild honey
2 tablespoons (30 ml) tamari
1 tablespoon (15 ml) vinegar
Juice of ½ lemon
1 tablespoon (15 ml) cornstarch
1 teaspoon (5 ml) sesame oil
1 tablespoon (15 ml) safflower or peanut oil
1 clove garlic, minced or put through a press
1 teaspoon (5 ml) grated or minced fresh ginger
2 pounds (1 kg) Chinese cabbage, cut crosswise in 2-inch slices
2 tablespoons (30 ml) sesame seeds

Mix together the honey, tamari, vinegar, lemon juice, and cornstarch in a small bowl. Stir to dissolve the cornstarch and stir in the sesame oil. Set aside.

Heat the 1 tablespoon oil in a wok or large heavy-bottomed skillet over moderate heat and add the garlic and ginger. Sauté for a couple of seconds and add the cabbage and sesame seeds. Stir-fry for 2 to 3 minutes, until the cabbage begins to wilt, then stir in the honey-tamari mixture. Cook until the cabbage is glazed and serve at once, with grains or a grain and soy combination.

MENU SUGGESTIONS
Soups: Simple Miso Soup (page 68); Miso Soup with Buckwheat Noodles (page 70); Hot and Sour Soup (page 67); Pureed Curry of Cauliflower Soup (page 79)
Main dishes: Tofu Cutlets (page 131) or Chilled Tofu with Dipping Sauces (page 132)

Salads: Tossed Green Salad (page 280); Cottage Cheese and Tomato Salad with Miso Dressing (page 296); Curried Carrot Salad (page 284)

Desserts: Tofu Noodle Kugel (page 319); Noodle Kugel (page 318); Strawberry Sherbet (page 317)

♥ Use 2 teaspoons (10 ml) safflower oil; omit tamari and sesame oil.

♥ SZECHUAN-STYLE SWEET AND SOUR CHINESE CABBAGE
SERVES 4

PREPARATION TIME: 10 minutes
SUPERVISED COOKING: 5 minutes

This is a provocative dish for those who like spicy food. The miso gives it a satisfying, gutsy flavor.

      2 tablespoons (30 ml) tamari
      2 tablespoons (30 ml) vinegar
  1½ tablespoons (23 ml) mild honey
      1 tablespoon (15 ml) cornstarch
      1 tablespoon (15 ml) sesame oil
      1 tablespoon (15 ml) safflower oil
  ½ to 1 teaspoon (2.5–5.0 ml) hot red pepper flakes, minced dried hot red pepper (seeds removed), or minced fresh hot red pepper (seeds removed)
      1 tablespoon (15 ml) miso (optional)
      2 pounds (1 kg) Chinese cabbage, sliced crosswise into 2-inch (5 cm) pieces
  2 to 3 cups (475–700 ml) hot, cooked grains, such as millet, couscous, or brown rice

Mix together the tamari, vinegar, and honey. Stir in the cornstarch. When it is dissolved, stir in the sesame oil. Set aside.

Heat the safflower oil in a wok or large, heavy-bottomed skillet over moderate heat and add the red pepper and optional miso. Stir-fry for a few seconds and add the cabbage. Stir-fry for 2 to 3 minutes, until the cabbage begins to wilt, then add the tamari mixture. Cook for 1 minute, or until the cabbage is glazed. Serve immediately, with the hot, cooked grains.

Menu suggestions

Soups: Hot and Sour Soup (page 67); Potato Leek Soup (page 65)

Main dishes: Tofu Cutlets (page 131) or Chilled Tofu with Dipping Sauces (page 132)

Salads: Hot and Sour Buckwheat Noodle Salad (page 300); Oriental Salad (page 297)

Desserts: Any of the sherbets or frozen fruit ices on pages 315–318.

♥ Omit miso; reduce safflower oil to 2 teaspoons (10 ml) and use a nonstick skillet; reduce tamari to 1 teaspoon (5 ml) and omit sesame oil.

GREEN BEANS AMANDINE
SERVES 4

Preparation time: 10 minutes
Supervised cooking: 10 minutes

This dish is one of the earliest memories I have of green beans. However, back then it was easier to find young, tender beans. Today's tough, gnarled variety are hardly worth the trouble, but in the spring and summer, when locally grown produce abounds, you can cook green bean dishes often and make up for lost time.

```
        1  pound (450 gm) tender string beans
        2  tablespoons (30 ml) butter or safflower oil
       ½  cup (120 ml) slivered almonds
1 to 2  cloves garlic, minced or put through a press
        1  teaspoon (5 ml) lemon juice
        1  teaspoon (5 ml) dried marjoram
           Salt and freshly ground pepper to taste
```

Trim the beans and, if you wish, cut diagonally into julienne strips. Steam until crisp-tender, about 5 minutes, and set aside.

Heat the butter in a heavy-bottomed skillet and add the almonds. Brown a minute or two over medium heat and stir in the beans and garlic. Cook, tossing, for about 3 minutes. Add the lemon juice, marjoram, and salt and pepper to taste, and serve as a side dish.

♥ GREEN BEANS À LA PROVENÇALE
SERVES 6

PREPARATION TIME: 20 minutes
SUPERVISED COOKING: 10 minutes
UNSUPERVISED COOKING: 25 minutes

A heady mixture of garlic, onion, tomatoes, and green beans, this always transports me to the southern part of France.

    3 pounds (1.4 kg) tender green beans, trimmed
    1 tablespoon (15 ml) olive oil
    1 onion, thinly sliced
    3 cloves garlic, minced or put through a press
1½ pounds (725 gm) firm, ripe tomatoes, peeled, seeded, and chopped
    1 bay leaf
    2 sprigs fresh thyme or ½ teaspoon (2.5 ml) dried
    4 sprigs fresh parsley
    ¼ cup (60 ml) vegetable bouillon (made from vegetable bouillon cube and water)
    1 tablespoon (15 ml) chopped fresh basil or oregano or 1 teaspoon (5 ml) dried
    2 tablespoons (30 ml) dry white wine
      Salt and freshly ground pepper to taste

Steam the beans for 5 minutes and refresh under cold water.

Heat the olive oil in a heavy-bottomed lidded skillet or Dutch oven and add the onion and garlic. Sauté until the onion is tender, then add the tomatoes, bay leaf, thyme, parsley, and bouillon. Cover and simmer 15 minutes. Remove the bay leaf and parsley sprigs, and thyme if you've used them.

Add the green beans to the tomato mixture, cover, and simmer 5 minutes. Uncover and add the basil and wine, then raise the heat and cook over high heat, stirring, until the mixture thickens. Season with salt and pepper.

MENU SUGGESTIONS

Main dishes: Whole grains of your choice or a grain and any soy combination; Simple Cheese, Bread, and Mushroom Casserole (page 186); any of the Omelets on pages 176–183

Salads: Tossed Green Salad (page 280); Warm or Chilled Cauliflower Vinaigrette (page 290); Warm Potato Salad with Caraway (page 291)

Desserts: Sliced Melon; Strawberries in Champagne (page 311); Peaches with Amaretto (page 314)

♥ Substitute safflower oil for the olive oil and water for the bouillon; omit salt.

♥ STEAMED, PRESSURE-COOKED, OR BAKED BEETS AND BEET GREENS
SERVES 4
PREPARATION TIME: 5 minutes
UNSUPERVISED STEAMING: 20 minutes, or 12 to 18 minutes in a pressure cooker
UNSUPERVISED BAKING: 30 to 60 minutes, depending on size

People can be quite emphatic in their antipathy for beets. I didn't much care for them as a child, probably because I only knew canned beets, but somewhere along the line I got over my dislike, and as an adult I've always liked them. I like their sweet, earthy taste and crunchy texture, and always feel as if I'm eating one of the healthiest vegetables around. I eat them simply steamed, with their greens. They are one of the longer-cooking vegetables, and I suggest that, unless you use a pressure cooker, you quarter them. Scrub the skins and remove them only after the beets are cooked. For pressure cooking, beets should be left whole.

Beets can also be baked. It takes some time, but this is unsupervised. The flavor of baked beets is even more intense.

I prefer beet greens to other greens, like mustard and collards, which are quite tough and metallic tasting. Beet greens are fairly mild, and similar in taste to spinach, though a bit more metallic. They are quite high in iron and vitamins, and should not be overlooked.

TO STEAM BEETS
Cut the tops off 1 pound (450 gm) beets, leaving about ¼ inch (0.7 cm) of stem attached, and scrub the skins. Cut large beets in quarters and place on the steamer rack. Steam for 15 minutes. Meanwhile, trim the greens, discarding the tough stems. Add to the beets and cook for another 5 to 10 minutes, until the beets are tender. Remove from the heat, peel the beets (holding on to them with a towel), and serve with the greens, as a side dish.

TO PRESSURE-COOK BEETS
Leave the beets whole and scrub the skins. Cut off the tops, leaving

about ¼ inch (0.7 cm) of stem attached. Place the beets on a rack in the pressure cooker and add 1 cup (250 ml) water. Cover and bring to 15 pounds (7 kg) pressure. Cook small beets for 12 minutes, over medium heat, larger beets for 15 to 18 minutes. Meanwhile, steam the trimmed greens separately for 5 minutes.

Remove the pressure cooker from the heat, run under cold water until all the steam escapes, and remove the lid. Peel the beets and serve with the greens, as a side dish.

TO BAKE BEETS

BAKING TIME: 30 minutes to 1 hour, depending on the size of the beets

Baking brings out the maximum flavor of beets, just as it does for sweet potatoes.

Preheat oven to 325 degrees (160°C).

Scrub the beets and trim the tops, leaving 1 inch of stem. Wrap them in aluminum foil and bake for 30 to 60 minutes, depending on the size, until they can be easily pierced with a fork. Remove the skins and eat.

BRUSSELS SPROUTS WITH LEMON-MUSTARD BUTTER
SERVES 4

PREPARATION TIME: 5 minutes
UNSUPERVISED COOKING: 10 to 15 minutes

The lemon-mustard butter in this is delicious with any number of vegetables, so don't restrict yourself to Brussels sprouts.

    1 pound (450 gm) Brussels sprouts
    4 tablespoons (60 gm) butter
       Juice of ½ lemon
    1½ teaspoons (7 ml) prepared Dijon-style mustard

Trim the ends of the Brussels sprouts, and with a sharp knife cut an X into each stem end. Place in a steamer and steam 10 to 15 minutes, until tender. Meanwhile, warm a serving dish.

Melt the butter in a small heavy-bottomed saucepan. Stir in the lemon juice and mustard and mix well.

Transfer the cooked Brussels sprouts to the warm serving dish, pour on the butter, and toss. Serve as a side dish.

♥ CARROTS COOKED IN VODKA
SERVES 4

PREPARATION TIME: 5 minutes
UNSUPERVISED COOKING: 10 minutes

This may seem strange at first glance, but carrots, like people, get a nice lift from vodka. Try it.

- ½ pound (225 gm) carrots, sliced thinly on the diagonal (2 cups; 475 ml)
- ¼ cup (60 ml) vodka
- 1 tablespoon (15 ml) minced or grated orange zest
- ½ teaspoon (2.5 ml) mild honey
- 1 teaspoon (5 ml) butter or safflower margarine

Place all the ingredients except the butter in a medium saucepan. Cover and simmer over medium-low heat for 10 minutes. Toss with the butter or margarine and serve as a side dish.

♥ Omit butter or margarine.

♥ CARROTS WITH DILL
SERVES 4

PREPARATION TIME: 5 minutes
UNSUPERVISED COOKING: 10 minutes

- ½ pound (225 gm) carrots, sliced thinly on the diagonal (2 cups; 475 ml)
- 1 teaspoon (5 ml) butter or safflower margarine
- 1 tablespoon (15 ml) chopped fresh dill
  Freshly ground pepper to taste

Steam the carrots for 10 minutes. Toss with the butter, dill. and pepper in a warm serving dish and serve as a side dish.

♥ Omit butter or margarine.

♥ THIN-SLICED CAULIFLOWER WITH SESAME SEEDS AND GINGER

SERVES 4

PREPARATION TIME: 10 minutes
SUPERVISED COOKING: 10 minutes

The sweet and sour flavor of this cauliflower dish is delightful.

1 large head cauliflower (1½ to 2 pounds; 700 gm–1 kg)
1 tablespoon (15 ml) mild honey
2 tablespoons (30 ml) tamari
1 tablespoon (15 ml) vinegar
Juice of ½ lemon
1 tablespoon (15 ml) cornstarch
1 teaspoon (5 ml) sesame oil or sesame tahini
1 tablespoon (15 ml) sesame, safflower, or peanut oil
1 teaspoon (5 ml) grated or minced fresh ginger
2 cloves garlic, minced or put through a press
2 tablespoons (30 ml) sesame seeds
FOR GARNISH: 1 tablespoon chopped fresh cilantro (optional)

Trim the cauliflower and cut the entire head into thin slices; then cut the florets from the stalk and discard the stalk. Steam 5 minutes, refresh with cold water, and set aside.

In a small bowl mix together the honey, tamari, vinegar, lemon juice, cornstarch, and sesame oil. Set aside.

Heat the tablespoon (15 ml) of oil in a heavy-bottomed skillet or wok and add the ginger, garlic, and sesame seeds. Sauté just until the ginger and garlic begin to turn golden, then stir in the cauliflower. Toss the cauliflower to heat through, stir in the honey-tamari mixture and serve, garnished, if you like, with chopped cilantro. Serve as a side dish; for menu suggestions see Curried Cauliflower Puree (page 153).

♥ Omit tamari; omit sesame oil or tahini; reduce sautéing oil to 2 teaspoons (10 ml) and use safflower oil; use nonstick skillet.

♥ CAULIFLOWER COOKED IN RED WINE
SERVES 4

PREPARATION TIME: 5 minutes
SUPERVISED COOKING: 10 to 15 minutes

My guests—and I—can never believe how good this dish is. Briefly steamed cauliflower is finished with wine and garlic over high heat, and then tossed with Parmesan. It's tantalizing and has a beautiful red color.

1 medium head cauliflower (1 to 1½ pounds; 450–700 gm), cut into florets
1 tablespoon (15 ml) safflower oil
1 large clove garlic, minced or put through a press
¼ teaspoon (1.25 ml) dried thyme
  Freshly ground pepper to taste
½ cup (120 ml) dry red wine
¼ cup (60 ml) freshly grated Parmesan cheese

Steam the cauliflower for 5 to 10 minutes, to taste. Refresh under cold running water.

Heat the oil in a heavy-bottomed skillet and sauté the garlic and cauliflower for 1 minute. Add the thyme, pepper, and wine and turn up the heat. Cook, tossing over high heat, until the wine has evaporated. Transfer to a warm serving dish, sprinkle on the Parmesan, and serve with grains or as a side dish.

MENU SUGGESTIONS
Main Dishes: Corn Pudding (page 196); Pasta with Uncooked Tomatoes and Cheese (page 207)
Salads: Tossed Green Salad (page 280); Leftover Beans Salad (page 294)
Desserts: Strawberry Sherbet (page 317); Bread Pudding (page 320); melon

♥ Omit Parmesan.

♥ CURRIED CAULIFLOWER PUREE
SERVES 4

PREPARATION TIME: 10 minutes
UNSUPERVISED COOKING: 15 minutes
SUPERVISED COOKING: 5 minutes
ADDITIONAL WORK: 5 minutes

The idea of sprinkling anise and currants over cauliflower was inspired by a sultana-anise paste I enjoyed on tandoori breads at my favorite Indian restaurant, Khan's, in London. I thought the anise and currants would make a nice accompaniment to curries, and they do.

     1 large head cauliflower (2 pounds; 1 kg), broken into florets
1½ cups (350 ml) plain low-fat yogurt
     1 tablespoon (15 ml) curry powder
     1 teaspoon (5 ml) ground cumin
     ½ teaspoon (2.5 ml) ground cardamom
     ½ teaspoon (2.5 ml) ground coriander
     Salt and freshly ground pepper to taste
1 to 2 teaspoons (5–10 ml) anise seeds
     3 tablespoons (45 ml) currants
     2 tablespoons (30 ml) sunflower seeds or pine nuts, toasted
FOR GARNISH: Fresh cilantro or parsley sprigs

Preheat the oven to 300 degrees (150°C).

Select 8 small, pretty florets from the cauliflower and steam 5 minutes. Refresh under cold water and set aside.

Steam the remaining cauliflower until very tender, about 15 minutes. Puree in a food processor or put through a food mill. Combine the yogurt and spices, except for the anise seeds, and stir into the puree. Season to taste with salt and pepper. Place in a serving dish and sprinkle the top with the anise seeds, pine nuts, and currants. Place the cauliflower florets you had set aside around the sides of the dish. Heat through in the oven for 10 minutes. Garnish with cilantro and serve.

MENU SUGGESTIONS

Main dishes: Brown Rice and Lentils (page 112); Barley Mushroom Pilaff (page 127); Tofu Cutlets (page 131)
Vegetables: Any green vegetable, simply steamed
Salads: Any grain or bean salad; Tossed Green Salad (page 280); Curried Carrot Salad (page 284)

Desserts: Tofu Noodle Kugel (page 319); Noodle Kugel (page 318); Orange Ice (page 318); Oranges with Mint

♥ Omit salt.

♥ BAKED CELERY POTATO PUREE
SERVES 4

PREPARATION TIME: 10 minutes
UNSUPERVISED COOKING: 50 minutes in all

The first time I had this dish was in one of the best restaurants in which I've ever eaten, Le Petit Montmorency, in Paris. Daniel Bouché, the gifted chef, is very creative with vegetables and cooks after my own heart, using very little flour and butter. This tasted like a high class, low-calorie version of mashed potatoes, and I couldn't wait to get home and figure out the recipe.

      1 bunch celery, leaves removed, stalks trimmed and cut in 1-inch (2.5 cm) pieces
      1 pound (450 gm) baking potatoes, peeled and cut in chunks
    ¼ cup (60 ml) chopped onion
      Salt and freshly ground pepper to taste
¼ to ½ cup (60–120 ml) buttermilk, as needed
    ¼ cup (60 ml) freshly grated Parmesan cheese (optional)
      1 tablespoon (15 ml) butter

Preheat the oven to 400 degrees (200° C). Oil a 1½- or 2-quart (1.5–2 L) gratin or baking dish.

Steam the potatoes, celery, and onion together for about 20 minutes, or until the potatoes are tender. Remove from the heat and puree or put through a food mill.

Add salt and pepper to taste, and moisten with buttermilk. It should have the consistency of smooth, well-buttered mashed potatoes. Stir in the optional Parmesan.

Spoon the puree into the prepared baking dish and dot the top with the butter. Bake for 30 minutes, or until the top begins to brown. Serve as a side dish.

♥ Omit salt, Parmesan, and butter. Substitute plain low-fat yogurt for buttermilk. This is a marginal dish for heart patients, because celery is very high in sodium.

DELICATE CORN FRITTERS, OR "CORN OYSTERS"

SERVES 6

PREPARATION TIME: 20 minutes

SUPERVISED COOKING: 10 minutes

I'm not sure why the traditional name for these delicate, luscious fritters is "corn oysters." It is certainly not due to their texture, which is feather-light but not slippery. It may be because they are the size of a silver dollar, which reminds one of little round oysters. They are as much a treat as oysters—and nobody ever died of a bad corn oyster.

I like mine plain, but you could serve them with a little maple syrup.

- 2½ cups (600 ml) fresh or frozen corn kernels (4 medium ears), either grated off the ear or cut off and coarsely pureed in a food processor
- 2 teaspoons (10 ml) whole-wheat flour, or unbleached white
  Salt and freshly ground pepper to taste
- 1 egg, separated, plus 1 egg white
- 1 tablespoon (15 ml) butter or safflower oil

Toss the corn with the flour, salt, and pepper. Beat in the egg yolk. Beat the 2 egg whites until stiff but not dry and fold into the corn mixture.

Heat a heavy-bottomed skillet (Silverstone works beautifully for these) and melt 1 tablespoon of the butter. Drop the corn mixture into the pan by heaping teaspoonfuls (5 ml), so that the fritters are about the size of a silver dollar. (You can make them larger if you wish.) Cook on both sides until golden brown, and serve immediately. Or transfer to a serving dish and hold in a warm oven for up to 30 minutes.

MENU SUGGESTIONS

Soups: Elegant Pressure-Cooked White Bean Soup (page 74)

Main dishes: Slow-Cooked Beans (page 99) or Pressure-Cooked Beans (page 98)

Salads: Tossed Green Salad (page 280); Simple Cabbage and Carrot Salad with Fresh Herbs (page 298)

Desserts: Pears Poached in Red Wine (page 309); Strawberry Sherbet (page 317)

♥ COOKED CURRIED CUCUMBERS
SERVES 4 TO 6

PREPARATION TIME: 15 minutes
SUPERVISED COOKING: 5 minutes
UNSUPERVISED COOKING: 20 minutes

The idea of cooked cucumbers came as a surprise to me. I first had them this way in ratatouille, and was amazed by the fact that they retained their texture, becoming succulent yet remaining crunchy. Cooked cucumbers are perfect in a curry, because they taste so cool against the spicy flavors. I like this dish both hot and cold, and it will hold a day or so in the refrigerator.

    4 cucumbers
    1 tablespoon (15 ml) butter or safflower oil
    1 small onion, sliced
    1 teaspoon (5 ml) curry powder, or more to taste
    1 cup (250 ml) dry white wine
      Salt to taste
    1 tablespoon (15 ml) chopped fresh parsley or cilantro

Peel the cucumbers, then cut in half lengthwise and scoop out the seeds. Slice ¼ to ½ inch (0.7–1.5 cm) thick.

Heat the butter or safflower oil in a heavy-bottomed, lidded skillet or saucepan and sauté the onion and curry powder until the onion is tender. Add the cucumber and sauté for 3 minutes, then add the wine. Bring to a simmer, then cover and cook over medium-low heat for 20 minutes. Raise the heat and boil off the wine, uncovered. Season to taste with salt, garnish with chopped parsley, and serve, or chill and serve cold. This makes a nice side dish for the Tofu Vegetable Curry on page 136.

♥ Omit salt.

♥ EGGPLANT, POTATOES, AND MUSHROOMS BRAISED IN WHITE WINE

SERVES 6

PREPARATION TIME: 20 minutes
SUPERVISED COOKING: 15 minutes
UNSUPERVISED COOKING: 30 to 40 minutes

This heady, aromatic dish will make your kitchen smell very inviting, and while it simmers in the oven, you'll have time to make a salad and dessert, and to cook some grains.

2 pounds (1 kg) eggplant, cut in half lengthwise and scored
3 tablespoons (45 ml) olive oil
1 medium onion, sliced thin
4 cloves garlic, minced or put through a press
1 pound (450 gm) mushrooms, stemmed and cut in half
1 cup (250 ml) coarsely chopped ripe tomatoes
½ teaspoon (2.5 ml) dried thyme
1 cup (250 ml) dry white wine
1 cup (250 ml) vegetable bouillon (made with vegetable bouillon cube and water)
1 pound (450 gm) boiling potatoes, unpeeled and diced
Salt and freshly ground pepper to taste
¼ cup (60 ml) fresh chopped parsley
½ cup (120 ml) freshly grated Parmesan cheese

Preheat the oven to 500 degrees (260°C). Brush a baking sheet with olive oil and place the scored eggplant on it, flat side down. Bake for 10 to 15 minutes, then remove from the oven and turn the heat to 350° (180°C).

Heat 1 tablespoon (15 ml) of the oil in a flameproof casserole or Dutch oven and sauté the onion and half the garlic, gently, until the onion is tender. Add the mushrooms and sauté for 3 minutes. Stir in another tablespoon (15 ml) of olive oil, the remaining garlic, the tomatoes, thyme, wine, broth, and potatoes. Add a little salt and bring to a simmer. Simmer for 5 minutes while you dice the eggplant, which should by now be cool enough to handle. You can leave the peel on or scoop out the pulp and dice it.

Add the remaining tablespoon of olive oil, the eggplant, and half the parsley and cook, stirring, for about 10 minutes. Cover and place in the oven. Bake 30 to 40 minutes, until tender and aromatic. Adjust the salt and add freshly ground pepper to taste. Garnish with the remaining parsley and serve. Pass the Parmesan in a bowl for people to spoon on if they wish.

MENU SUGGESTIONS
Serve as a main dish with a brown rice/soy grits mixture, or as a side dish with an egg and cheese dish such as an omelet (pages 176–183) or Southern Spoonbread (page 189)

Salads: Tossed Green Salad (page 280); Tomato Salad (page 284)

Desserts: Orange Ice (page 318); Prune Soufflé (page 307), unless serving with an eggy main dish; Puffed Grand Marnier Omelet (page 307), unless serving with an eggy main dish

♥ Omit olive oil; use 1 tablespoon (15 ml) safflower oil in all, and cook the vegetables in the safflower oil and wine as needed; omit salt and Parmesan.

♥ MUSHROOMS WITH WHITE WINE AND HERBS
SERVES 4 TO 6
PREPARATION TIME: 10 to 15 minutes
SUPERVISED COOKING: 15 minutes

Mushrooms were made to be cooked in white wine with garlic and herbs. Their own flavor is subtle, and they're porous, so they absorb all the savory flavors they're cooked with and become quite aromatic. The kitchen smells marvelous as they cook, and you've hardly done a bit of work.

1 tablespoon (15 ml) butter or olive oil
1½ pounds (700 gm) mushrooms, stems trimmed, and left whole or thickly sliced
1 teaspoon (5 ml) dried herbs (thyme, rosemary, basil, parsley, or marjoram, in any combination) or 1 tablespoon (15 ml) fresh chopped herbs
2 cloves garlic, minced or put through a press
¼ cup (60 ml) dry white wine
Salt and freshly ground pepper to taste
2 tablespoons (30 ml) chopped green onion tops or chives

Heat the butter in a heavy-bottomed skillet or wok and add the mushrooms and herbs. Sauté for 10 minutes over medium heat, stirring, and add the garlic and white wine. Cook, stirring, for about 4 minutes, turning the heat high toward the end of the cooking time and cooking, stirring, until the liquid evaporates. Add salt and pepper to taste and the green onion tops. Cook another minute and serve, as a side dish.

♥ Substitute 2 teaspoons (10 ml) safflower oil for the butter or olive oil; omit salt.

♥ OKRA AND TOMATOES
SERVES 4 TO 6

PREPARATION TIME: 10 to 15 minutes
COOKING TIME: 20 to 25 minutes

I didn't discover how much I loved okra until fairly recently, when I cooked a lot of it on a month-long study involving heart patients, and several people had requested it. I found that one of the marvelous things about this vegetable is that, no matter how long you cook it, it never seems to lose its texture. I like to cook most green vegetables only until the heat brings out their maximum bright-green color; if they become drab, I feel that I've cooked them too long. But because okra is often tough, it must be cooked into the olive-green stage. However, it seems that it achieves its maximum flavor there, and still remains crunchy.

I have been given lots of advice on how to avoid the "slime" okra produces, but as is true of the advice I've received on avoiding tears while peeling onions, none of these methods has proven entirely successful. It does help, I think, if, when you slice the okra at the stem end you slice just below the stem, before the seeds begin. And adding vinegar to an okra mixture while it's cooking may minimize the slime. I especially love okra in the following recipe, combined with tomatoes, onions, and garlic.

     1 tablespoon (15 ml) safflower oil
     1 large onion, chopped
     2 cloves garlic, minced or put through a press
     1 pound (450 gm) okra, trimmed and sliced ¼ to ½ inch (0.7–1.5 cm) thick
1 to 2 tablespoons (15–30 ml) wine vinegar
2 to 3 tablespoons (30–45 ml) white wine
     1 pound (450 gm) ripe tomatoes, sliced (canned may be substituted)
     1 teaspoon (5 ml) dried basil, oregano, or marjoram
       Salt and freshly ground pepper to taste

Heat the safflower oil in a heavy-bottomed skillet and sauté the onion and 1 clove of the garlic until the onion is tender. Add the okra and 1 tablespoon vinegar and sauté until the okra becomes bright green, about 5 minutes. Add 2 tablespoons wine, tomatoes, remaining garlic, and the basil and cook, stirring from time to time, for 10 to 15 minutes, until the okra is tender and the mixture aromatic. Season to taste with salt, freshly ground pepper, and, if you like, a little more vinegar and/or wine.

MENU SUGGESTIONS

For a nice country-style meal serve this with corn on the cob or Rice and Soy Grits or Flakes (page 107), Black-Eyed Peas (page 104) and Rich Jalapeño Cornbread (page 53), Coleslaw (page 295) or Potato Salad (page 291).

♥ Reduce oil to 2 teaspoons (10 ml); omit salt. Use only *unsalted* canned tomatoes.

♥ MINTED FRESH PEAS WITH LETTUCE
SERVES 6
PREPARATION TIME: 10 minutes
UNSUPERVISED COOKING: 10 to 15 minutes

A refreshing minty, healthy dish for spring.

3 pounds (1.4 kg) unshelled, tender, fresh green peas (shelled, 3 cups; 700 ml)
5 leaves Boston lettuce, cut crosswise into 1-inch pieces
1 to 2 tablespoons (15–30 ml) butter (optional)
1 to 2 tablespoons (15–30 ml) chopped fresh mint
Salt and freshly ground pepper to taste

Shell the peas and steam them until bright green and tender, about 10 to 15 minutes. Melt the butter in a heavy-bottomed skillet and add the lettuce. When it wilts (in about a minute), add the peas and mint and toss to coat with the butter. Add salt and freshly ground pepper and serve at once, as a side dish.

♥ Omit butter and salt.

♥ PEPPERS, TOMATOES, AND HERBS
SERVES 4

PREPARATION TIME: 15 minutes
SUPERVISED COOKING: 10 minutes
UNSUPERVISED COOKING: 20 minutes

I have a clear memory of this dish cooking in a big frying pan in the kitchen of the house I grew up in. It was one of my stepmother's specialties. She liked to use marjoram and different kinds of peppers —long, mild yellow-green Italian peppers and sweet green peppers, and sometimes beautiful sweet red ones. It's a lovely dish, and is good cold as well as hot.

1 to 2 tablespoons (15–30 ml) olive oil
1 small onion, minced
1 clove garlic, minced or put through a press
4 large sweet green peppers, sliced, or a mixture of peppers (about 1 pound; 450 gm), such as Italian peppers, sweet red, and sweet green
3 large tomatoes (1 pound; 450 gm), sliced, or 1 pound (450 gm) canned, sliced
2 teaspoons (10 ml) minced fresh basil or 1 teaspoon (5 ml) dried
1 teaspoon (5 ml) minced fresh marjoram or ½ teaspoon (2.5 ml) dried
Salt and freshly ground pepper to taste

Heat 1 tablespoon of the oil in a heavy-bottomed skillet and sauté the onion and garlic until the onion is tender, about 3 to 5 minutes. Add the peppers, adding more oil if you need it, and sauté for 5 minutes. Add the tomatoes and herbs and stir together, then cover and cook over medium-low heat for 20 minutes. Season to taste with salt and freshly ground pepper. Serve as a side dish.

♥ Substitute 2 teaspoons (10 ml) safflower oil for the olive oil; omit salt. Make sure canned tomatoes are unsalted.

♥ POTATOES WITH WHITE WINE AND HERBS
SERVES 4 TO 6

PREPARATION TIME: 15 minutes
SUPERVISED COOKING TIME: 10 minutes
UNSUPERVISED COOKING: 20 to 30 minutes

Potatoes are an ideal convenience food—they can be stored for a long time and used in dozens of ways. This is one of the most mouthwatering potato dishes I've ever eaten. The potatoes brown slightly as they cook, while absorbing the flavors of the wine and herbs. Your kitchen will smell very inviting.

1 to 2 tablespoons (15–30 ml) butter, olive oil, or safflower oil
1 teaspoon (5 ml) unbleached flour
4 medium boiling potatoes, peeled and sliced very thin (about 4 cups)
1 medium onion, sliced thin
1 clove garlic, minced or put through a press
Salt and freshly ground pepper to taste
¾ cup (180 ml) dry white wine
¾ cup (180 ml) Tamari-Bouillon Broth (page 62)
1 teaspoon (5 ml) chopped fresh rosemary or ½ teaspoon (2.5 ml) crushed dried
2 teaspoons (10 ml) minced fresh thyme or marjoram or 1 teaspoon dried (5 ml)
2 teaspoons (10 ml) minced fresh parsley

Heat the butter in a large, heavy-bottomed skillet (a nonstick variety, such as Silverstone, is best for this). Add the flour and the sliced potatoes, the onion, garlic, and salt and pepper. Sauté, stirring, over medium-high heat until the onion and potatoes begin to brown, about 10 minutes. Add the remaining ingredients except the parsley; stir, then reduce the heat, cover, and simmer for 20 minutes, or until the liquid is absorbed and the potatoes tender. Add the parsley and serve, as a side dish.

♥ Use 1 tablespoon (15 ml) safflower oil instead of butter or olive oil; omit flour and salt; use water instead of broth.

♥ POTATOES SIMMERED WITH SAGE, TOMATOES, AND PEAS
SERVES 6
PREPARATION TIME: 20 to 25 minutes
SUPERVISED COOKING: 10 minutes
UNSUPERVISED COOKING: 1 hour

Sage is an herb whose magic I discovered a few summers ago in a marvelous Florentine restaurant, where I was served spinach *gnocchi* that had been finished in butter with sage. They were amazing to me, and the sage flavor was quite distinguishable. I began trying the herb with several different varieties of vegetables, and think it goes especially well with potatoes. This stew needs very little attention as it simmers; a stir every now and again will suffice.

Fresh sage is really preferable in this recipe, but if you must use dried, don't use rubbed sage, but the whole dried leaves.

1 to 2 tablespoons butter, safflower oil, or olive oil
   1 medium onion, sliced
   1 tablespoon (15 ml) fresh sage leaves, torn into pieces, or 1 teaspoon dried (5 ml)
   2 pounds (1 kg) potatoes, unpeeled, sliced
   1 pound (450 gm) tomatoes, fresh or canned (with liquid), peeled, seeded, and sliced
   ⅔ cup (160 ml) dry white wine
   ½ cup (120 ml) vegetable bouillon made with vegetable bouillon cube and water (omit if using liquid from canned tomatoes)
   2 cups (475 ml) fresh peas (unshelled, 2 pounds; 1 kg), or 1 package (10 ounces; 275 gm) frozen
      Salt and freshly ground pepper to taste
   ½ cup (120 ml) freshly grated Parmesan cheese

Heat 1 tablespoon (15 ml) of the butter in a heavy-bottomed saucepan or Dutch oven and sauté the onion with the sage until the onion is tender. Add the potatoes and toss with the onions for 1 minute, then add the tomatoes, wine, and broth or liquid from the canned tomatoes and bring to a simmer. Cover and cook slowly over a low flame for 1 hour, or until the potatoes are tender, stirring occasionally. Stir in the peas and continue to simmer until the peas are tender and bright green, 5 to 10 minutes. Add salt and freshly ground pepper to taste and stir in the Parmesan. Remove from the heat and serve.

This makes a sublime side dish with any of the egg and cheese dishes in the following chapter. It can also serve as a substantial main dish. For dessert, serve a puffed omelet or soufflé and you'll get enough protein. Tossed Green Salad (page 280) is my favorite with this.

♥ Use 1 tablespoon (15 ml) safflower oil; omit salt and Parmesan; increase amount of sage, if you wish. Use liquid from canned tomatoes only if no salt has been added; otherwise, use water.

♥ BAKED POTATOES
SERVES 4

PREPARATION TIME: 5 minutes
UNSUPERVISED COOKING: 40 to 60 minutes, depending on the size

I've often insisted that I could be happy dining at a steakhouse as long as it served baked potatoes. Along with a salad they are a favorite light supper. Now that I understand that potatoes aren't "fattening," I eat them whenever I please. Of course, I don't slather them with butter; yogurt or Tofu Cream Sauce (page 130) moistens and seasons potatoes just as well, if not better. A generous amount of freshly ground pepper is essential, and fresh herbs are always welcome.

As far as vegetables go, potatoes are relatively high in protein—one 4-ounce (100 gm) potato has about 2.1 grams of protein—as well as in vitamins and minerals. In fact, my nutrition teacher once told me that if a person were stranded on a desert island and could choose only one food, potatoes should be the one, because they have some quantity of almost every nutrient. They also have the advantage of keeping well.

If you don't have time to bake your potatoes, a pressure cooker gives quite good results. Leave them whole and steam them in the cooker and they will become as flaky as baked potatoes in only 15 minutes.

    4 medium or large Idaho or Maine baking potatoes
    1 teaspoon (5 ml) butter
    ½ cup (120 ml) plain low-fat yogurt or Tofu Cream Sauce (page 57), or additional butter (or safflower oil) to taste
      Freshly ground pepper
    2 tablespoons chopped fresh herbs

Preheat the oven to 425 degrees (220°C).

Scrub the potatoes and rub with the butter. Puncture the skins once with a fork.

Bake for 40 minutes to an hour, until tender all the way through when pierced. Remove from the oven, slit down the middle, and top with yogurt, Tofu Cream Sauce, and butter, (or safflower oil). Grind on pepper and top with herbs. The potatoes can also be scooped out, mashed with the above ingredients, and spooned back in their skins.

♥ PRESSURE-COOKED POTATOES

Scrub the potatoes and pierce once with a fork. Place on a rack in a pressure-cooker and pour in 1½ cups (350 ml) water. Cover and bring to 15 pounds (7 kg) pressure. Reduce the heat to medium and cook for 15 minutes. Remove from the heat and run the pressure cooker under cold water until all the steam escapes.

Serve with the toppings for baked potatoes, above.

♥ Brush with safflower oil instead of butter; top with yogurt.

♥ SOUFFLÉED RUTABAGA PUREE
SERVES 4 TO 6

PREPARATION TIME: 10 to 15 minutes
UNSUPERVISED COOKING: 30 to 35 minutes in all

Rutabagas never interested me until I discovered how wonderful turnips, which are closely related, could be. When I did begin to work with the clumsy-looking waxed bulbs, I was pleased with the results. They taste very much like turnips, though stronger, and their apricot color wins my heart every time. Don't skimp on the black pepper in this dish—rutabagas need it.

    2 pounds (1 kg) rutabagas, peeled and diced small
    1 cup (250 ml) peeled, diced potato
    3 tablespoons (45 ml) chopped onion
    2 eggs, separated, at room temperature
    ½ cup (120 ml) skim milk or plain low-fat yogurt
       Salt and freshly ground pepper to taste
       Juice of 2 oranges

Preheat the oven to 375 degrees (190°C) and butter a 2-quart (2 L) soufflé or baking dish.

Steam the rutabaga with the potato and onion until it is tender, about 15 to 20 minutes. Meanwhile, beat the egg whites until stiff peaks form. Set aside.

When the rutabaga is tender, puree it with the potato and onion in a food processor or put through a food mill. Beat in the milk, orange juice, salt and lots of freshly ground pepper, and the egg yolks. Fold in the egg whites and carefully spoon the mixture into the prepared baking dish.

Bake for 15 to 20 minutes, until beginning to brown.

Soups: Hot or Iced Tomato Soup (page 72); Pureed Zucchini Soup (page 70)

Side dishes: Tomatoes Stuffed with Rice and Lentils (page 113); Cooked Curried Cucumbers (page 156); Beets and Beet Greens (page 148)

Salads: Tossed Green Salad (page 280); Leftover Beans Salad (page 294)

Desserts: Pears Poached in Red Wine (page 309); Figs Poached in Madeira (page 311)

♥ Omit eggs and salt. Puree ingredients and heat through at 325 degrees (165°C).

PATTYPAN SQUASH STUFFED WITH SAVORY ALMOND FILLING
SERVES 6 TO 8

PREPARATION TIME: 10 minutes
SUPERVISED COOKING: 8 to 10 minutes
UNSUPERVISED COOKING: 30 minutes

With the light green of the squash against the orange of the grated carrots and golden brown of the almonds, this dish is as beautiful as it is delicious. If you can get small new squash from local gardens they make an appealing hors d'oeuvre.

1½ pounds (700 gm) pattypan squash, preferably young and small
2 tablespoons (30 ml) butter
½ small onion, minced
1 large clove garlic, minced or put through a press
½ cup (120 ml) unblanched almonds, finely chopped (you can do this quickly in a blender)
1 medium carrot, finely grated
2 tablespoons (30 ml) chopped fresh parsley
1 teaspoon (5 ml) chopped fresh thyme or rosemary or ½ teaspoon (2.5 ml) dried
Heaping ¼ cup (60 ml) freshly grated Parmesan Cheese
Salt and freshly ground pepper to taste

Preheat the oven to 325 degrees (165°C) and oil a 2- or 3-quart (2 or 3 L) baking dish.

Cut each squash in half horizontally across the scalloped "edge" and steam 5 minutes. Refresh under cold water and scoop out the seeds and pulp from the centers, being careful not to cut through the outer surface. Place the squash on a baking sheet, cut side down, while you prepare the filling.

Heat 1 tablespoon (15 ml) of the butter in a large, heavy-bottomed skillet and sauté the onion and garlic until the onion is tender. Add the almonds and a little more butter, if necessary, and cook for a minute or two, then add the carrot and cook for a few minutes longer, until the carrot begins to turn golden. Add the parsley and other herbs, remove from the heat, add salt and pepper to taste, and stir in the Parmesan.

Melt the remaining butter in a small saucepan and use it to brush the cut surfaces of the squash. Fill the cavities with the almond mixture, then place the squash in the buttered casserole, filled side up. Cover with foil and bake for 30 minutes, or until the squash is tender.

MENU SUGGESTIONS
Soups: Gazpacho (page 87); Elegant Pressure-Cooked White Bean Soup (page 74)

Any grain would be suitable or serve another steamed vegetable, or a baked potato or sweet potato (see page 169).

Salads: Fattoush (page 285); Guacamole (page 283); Leeks Vinaigrette (page 289); Tossed Green Salad (page 280)

Desserts: Leftover Grains Pudding (page 321); Puffed Amaretto Omelet (page 306); melon; Apples with Lime Juice (page 312)

♥ ZUCCHINI WITH ROSEMARY OR OTHER HERBS
SERVES 4 TO 6
PREPARATION TIME: 5 to 10 minutes
SUPERVISED COOKING: 10 to 15 minutes
UNSUPERVISED COOKING: 10 minutes

1 tablespoon (15 ml) butter, olive oil, or safflower oil
1 small or medium onion, sliced thin
1 medium clove garlic, minced or put through a press
4 medium zucchini, washed and sliced about ¼ inch (0.7 cm) thick
½ teaspoon (2.5 ml) crushed dried rosemary or 1 teaspoon (5 ml) dried basil or marjoram (double quantities if using fresh herbs)
1 tomato, peeled and chopped
⅓ cup (80 ml) vegetable bouillon (made from a vegetable bouillon cube and water)
Salt and freshly ground pepper to taste
2 to 3 tablespoons (30–45 ml) freshly grated Parmesan cheese (optional)

Heat the butter in a heavy-bottomed skillet or wok and sauté the onion and garlic gently for 5 minutes. Add the zucchini and rosemary and sauté, stirring, for 3 to 5 minutes. Add the tomato and broth, then cover, reduce the heat, and cook for 10 minutes. Add salt and freshly ground pepper to taste and serve, sprinkling each serving with Parmesan, as a side dish.

♥ Use 2 teaspoons (10 ml) safflower oil and cook in a nonstick skillet; substitute water for the broth; omit salt and Parmesan.

♥ SIMPLE PICANTE ZUCCHINI
SERVES 4 TO 6

PREPARATION TIME: 15 minutes
SUPERVISED COOKING: 5 minutes
UNSUPERVISED COOKING: 10 to 15 minutes (with occasional stirring)

A special way to prepare zucchini, this goes well with Mexican food, especially tacos.

    1 tablespoon (15 ml) safflower oil
    1 small onion, chopped
    1 clove garlic, minced or put through a press
 1½ pounds (700 gm) zucchini, washed and sliced ¼ to ½ inch (0.7–1.5 cm) thick
 1½ pounds (700 gm) tomatoes, chopped
    1 serrano chili, minced
      Salt and freshly ground pepper to taste
    1 tablespoon (15 ml) chopped cilantro

Heat the oil in a wok or a large, heavy-bottomed skillet and sauté the onion until tender. Add the garlic, zucchini, tomatoes, chili, and salt. Cook, stirring, for 1 minute, then cover and cook over medium-low heat for 10 to 15 minutes, until tender. Add freshly ground pepper to taste and the cilantro, and serve.

MENU SUGGESTIONS
This makes a nice accompaniment to the taco dishes on pages 261–270, and to any of the egg and cheese dishes on pages 176–199. It can also be served simply, with grains or a grain-soy combination, or with a tofu dish. Accompany it with Lettuce Salad with Oranges (page 281) and a fruit ice or sherbet (pages 315–318).

♥ Use 2 teaspoons (10 ml) safflower oil; omit salt.

♥ BAKED YAMS OR SWEET POTATOES WITH LIME
SERVES 4

PREPARATION TIME: 5 minutes
UNSUPERVISED COOKING: 40 minutes to an hour, depending on the size

The best way to cook sweet potatoes or yams is to bake them in their skins. This allows all the sweetness to emerge, and the resulting product, simple as it is, is irresistible. It was a surprise to me to find how much their flavor is enhanced with lime juice, traditional in Latin America.

Prepare and bake the yams or sweet potatoes as in Baked Potatoes (page 164). When they are done, slit open and mash in for each potato the juice of ¼ to ½ lime, along with a small pat of butter, if you wish.

Sweet potatoes can also be steamed in a pressure cooker. Follow the directions for Pressure-Cooked Potatoes (page 165).

♥ Same as for Baked Potatoes.

♥ BAKED SWEET POTATO AND RUM CASSEROLE
SERVES 6

PREPARATION TIME: 20 minutes
UNSUPERVISED COOKING: 45 to 60 minutes

This heady casserole will make you very hungry as it bakes, for it smells as if you have several apple pies in the oven. It's a perfect dish for Thanksgiving, as well as for any other festive occasion.

2 tart apples, cored and diced
Juice of ½ lime
2 pounds (1 kg) sweet potatoes, peeled and diced
⅓ cup (80 ml) raisins
¼ cup (60 ml) sunflower seeds or sliced almonds
2 tablespoons (30 ml) butter
1½ cups (350 ml) apple cider
¼ to ⅓ cup (60–80 ml) rum, to taste
2 tablespoons (30 ml) mild honey

Salt to taste
½ teaspoon (2.5 ml) ground allspice
½ teaspoon (2.5 ml) ground cinnamon
¼ teaspoon (1.25 ml) ground mace
1 teaspoon (5 ml) ground ginger

169

Preheat the oven to 400 degrees (200°C) and butter a 2-quart (2 L) casserole.

Toss the diced apples with the lime juice in a bowl, then add the sweet potatoes, raisins, and sunflower seeds.

Combine the butter, cider, rum, honey, salt, and spices in a saucepan. Heat over low heat until the butter is melted. Pour over the sweet potato mixture and toss.

Turn into the buttered casserole, cover, and bake for 45 minutes to 1 hour, until the sweet potatoes are thoroughly cooked and glazed. Serve hot.

MENU SUGGESTIONS

Serve this with Southern Spoonbread (page 189) or another cheese and egg dish (pages 176–199), or with a light soup, such as Simple Miso Soup (page 68) or Pureed Zucchini Soup (page 70).

Salads: Tossed Green Salad (page 280); Watercress, Mushroom, and Tofu Salad (page 292)

Desserts: Gingered Fruit (page 312); Baked Grapefruit with Tequila or Sherry (page 313); Oranges with Mint

♥ Omit butter and salt; reduce raisins to 3 tablespoons (45 ml); omit sunflower seeds or almonds; use 3 tablespoons (45 ml) rum.

♥ BROILED TOMATOES
SERVES 4 TO 6
PREPARATION TIME: 10 to 15 minutes
UNSUPERVISED COOKING: 5 to 7 minutes

The pungent flavors of the garlic and herbs make these sliced tomatoes an especially versatile side dish.

3 medium tomatoes (1 pound; 450 gm), sliced horizontally
3 tablespoons (45 ml) olive oil
1 large clove garlic, minced or put through a press
¼ teaspoon (1.25 ml) dried tarragon
1 teaspoon (5 ml) chopped fresh basil or ½ teaspoon (2.5 ml) dried
1 teaspoon (5 ml) chopped fresh parsley
Salt and freshly ground pepper to taste
2 tablespoons (30 ml) freshly grated Parmesan cheese
¼ cup (60 ml) whole-wheat bread crumbs

Heat the broiler and place the sliced tomatoes on an oiled baking sheet or in a gratin dish.

Mix together the olive oil, garlic, tarragon, basil, and parsley and drizzle over the tomatoes. Sprinkle with salt and freshly ground pepper to taste. Mix together the Parmesan and bread crumbs and sprinkle over the tops.

Place under the broiler and broil for 5 to 7 minutes, until the bread crumbs brown and the cheese melts. Serve as a side dish.

♥ Omit olive oil, Parmesan, and salt.

FLORENTINE TOMATOES
SERVES 4 TO 6
PREPARATION TIME: 15 to 20 minutes
SUPERVISED COOKING: 15 minutes
UNSUPERVISED COOKING: 20 to 30 minutes

The walnuts in this recipe add a crunchy variation to the texture of the spinach. I love the color contrast of the dark green against the tomatoes, and the simple combination of these vegetables is always very pleasing.

    1½ pounds (700 gm) fresh spinach, stemmed and washed thoroughly, or 2 packages (10 ounces or 275 gm each) frozen, chopped, thawed
    1 tablespoon (15 ml) butter
    ¼ cup (60 ml) finely minced onion
    ¼ cup (60 ml) finely chopped walnuts
      Freshly grated nutmeg to taste
      Salt and freshly ground pepper to taste
    2 eggs, separated
    2 tablespoons (30 ml) cream or milk
    ¼ cup (60 ml) freshly grated Parmesan cheese
    3 to 4 tomatoes, cut in half horizontally, seeded, pulp removed (reserve pulp for filling, if desired)

Preheat the oven to 350° (180°C) and oil a 2-quart (2 L) baking dish or gratin dish.

If you are using fresh spinach, blanch, squeeze dry, and chop fine. If you are using thawed frozen spinach, squeeze dry and chop even finer.

Heat the butter in a heavy-bottomed, nonaluminum skillet (spinach reacts with aluminum and develops a metallic taste) and sauté the onion until tender. Add the spinach and walnuts and cook for 2 minutes, tossing. Remove from the heat and season to taste with nutmeg, salt, and freshly ground pepper.

Stir the egg yolks, cream, Parmesan, and optional pulp from the tomatoes into the spinach mixture. Beat the egg whites until they form stiff peaks and fold in.

Fill the tomatoes with the mixture and place in the oiled baking dish. Bake for 30 minutes until the top begins to brown. Serve as a side dish.

♥ TURNIPS WITH APPLES AND PORT
SERVES 4 TO 6
PREPARATION TIME: 10 TO 15 MINUTES
COOKING TIME: 8 MINUTES

Someone once asked me to name some vegetables I thought were unfairly maligned or too often ignored. Without hesitation I answered, "Turnips." I quickly added that I didn't think the tough, overgrown ones you find throughout the year in most produce sections were worth much. But in the spring you can find small, young, tender turnips, which are sweet, crisp, and delicious. They readily combine with other flavors, and have a special affinity for port. This recipe may convince even the most closed-minded turnip haters.

    1½ pounds (700 gm) young, tender turnips, peeled and diced
     1 tablespoon (15 ml) butter
     2 tart apples, peeled, cored, sliced thin, and tossed in lemon
        juice
        Freshly ground pepper
    ¼ cup (60 ml) port

Steam the turnips until crisp-tender, about 5 minutes. Set aside.

Heat the butter in a skillet and add the apples and turnips. Sauté for 3 to 5 minutes, grind in plenty of pepper and add the port. Turn up the heat and cook, stirring, until the port reduces and glazes the apples and turnips, which should only take a few minutes. Serve at once, with plain cooked grains and soygrits or flakes, or as a side dish with any of the grain dishes in this section, or a cheese and egg dish from the next chapter, and a big green salad. Another vegetable, simply steamed, would also be welcome. A soufflé or puffed omelet for dessert, if you are serving this with a grain-oriented dish, would add substantial protein to the meal.

♥ Substitute 2 teaspoons (10 ml) safflower oil for the butter.

♥ TURNIPS WITH LEMON AND HONEY
SERVES 4 TO 6

PREPARATION TIME: 10 minutes
COOKING TIME: 10 minutes

Here again, if you can find tender turnips, is an exceptional combination of flavors. I was first introduced to this dish at a Vietnamese restaurant in Paris called Tanh Dinh.

1½ pounds (700 gm) young, tender turnips, peeled and sliced thin
1 tablespoon (15 ml) mild honey
Juice of 1 large lemon (¼ cup; 60 ml)
2 teaspoons (10 ml) cornstarch or arrowroot
1 tablespoon (15 ml) safflower oil
½ to 1 teaspoon (2.5–5 ml) minced or grated fresh ginger, to taste
Freshly ground pepper to taste

Steam the turnips for 5 minutes, until crisp-tender. Remove from the heat and retain the cooking liquid.

In a small bowl, mix together the honey, lemon juice, cornstarch, and 3 to 4 tablespoons (45–60 ml) of liquid from the turnips.

Heat the oil in a skillet and sauté the ginger for 1 minute. Add the turnips and sauté, stirring, for a few minutes, until tender. Stir in the lemon-honey mixture and add pepper to taste, then heat through and serve.

MENU SUGGESTIONS

Serve with a grain and soy grits or soy flakes combination, or a grain dish like Kasha with Mushrooms, Water Chestnuts, and Celery (page 128), Barley Mushroom Pilaff (page 127), or Tabouli with Pressure-Cooked Garbanzos (page 286). A steamed green vegetable would also be nice.

Salads: Oriental Salad (page 297); Tossed Green Salad (page 280); Simple Cabbage and Carrot Salad with Fresh Herbs (page 298)
Desserts: Prune or Apricot Soufflé (pages 307 and 308); Apples with Lime Juice (page 312)

CHEESE AND EGGS

OMELETS
SIMPLE FLAT OMELETS
TORTILLAS ESPAÑOLAS
PUFFED ASPARAGUS OMELET
PIPÉRADE
MIGAS
SIMPLE CHEESE, BREAD, AND MUSHROOM CASSEROLE
GRUYÈRE PUFFS
SOUTHERN SPOONBREAD
DEEP-FRIED SPOONBREAD SQUARES*
ASPARAGI ALLA PARMIGIANA
ASPARAGI ALLA PARMIGIANA WITH POACHED EGGS
BROCCOLI TIMBALE
ASPARAGUS TIMBALE
CHEESE, STRING BEAN, AND SESAME CASSEROLE
CAULIFLOWER BAKED WITH TOMATOES, CHEESE, AND SESAME
CORN PUDDING
SPINACH AND RICE GRATIN*
POTATOES GRUYÈRE
TURNIPS GRUYÈRE

Although I feel that many meatless cookbooks rely too heavily on
eggs and dairy products, which are so high in fats, and that too many
vegetarian entrées in restaurants consist of heavy-handed vegetable

*Auxiliary recipe

174

dishes predictably slathered with cheese, these products certainly have their place at a table that is cutting down on meat. In this book they are indeed welcome, for few foods cook more quickly than eggs. And because their protein makeup is of such high quality, eggs seem to have a completeness about them. I eat egg dishes about once a week, and whether I'm having a plain boiled egg, an omelet, or a luscious timbale, I always feel that I've eaten just enough.

Cheese and egg dishes can be plain or fancy. While Pipérade (page 184), Migas (page 185) and Spinach and Rice Gratin (page 197) make an ideal easy Sunday night dinner, an Asparagus or Broccoli Timbale (pages 192 and 193) is a suitable dish for a more formal dinner. Gruyère Puffs (page 188) can turn a soup-oriented dinner into a party, and after you've experienced a Puffed Asparagus Omelet (page 183) you'll never get into an omelet rut again.

One of my favorite recipes in this chapter is Southern Spoonbread (page 189). I discovered it a few years ago when I was writing an article for *Texas Monthly* on Texas breads. When I made it I realized that spoonbread was really a pudding, and almost as impressive as a soufflé. I've always liked cornmeal, and this is a marvelous way to use it.

One of the greatest virtues of these dishes is that their flavors are subtle and won't clash with accompanying foods. They make perfect accompaniments to light soups like Buckwheat Noodle Soup with Green Beans (page 63) and the miso soups (pages 68 and 70). But even if a soup contains grains, pasta, or potatoes, a cheese or egg dish would not be too much to follow it with. You could also accompany many of these recipes with a small side serving of pasta, like Whole-Grain Pasta with Butter and Herbs (page 214) or Simple Soba with Sesame Oil (page 214). And any of the vegetable dishes from the previous chapter would be welcome. Cheese and eggs have complete protein, which is why they're such good components in vegetable-oriented dishes. Of course, I don't think Asparagi alla Parmigiana (page 190), with its small amount of Parmesan, would constitute a main dish, but it certainly would if you added poached eggs to it (Asparagi alla Parmigiana with Poached Eggs, page 191). If you wish a simple, light meal, most of these dishes can even stand alone, with a salad.

As delicious and easy as all these dishes are, I would caution you against *focusing* your diet on them. One of the main reasons many people are cutting down on meat is to reduce the fat content in their diets. Eggs and dairy products are high in saturated fats, and you won't be doing yourself a great favor if you replace the meat on your plate with an omelet every night. A few times a week is fine. On remaining nights, choose from the filling, mouthwatering dishes in the other chapters in this book.

If you do eat these products sparingly, then most of you won't have to worry when you indulge. I for one can never resist Brie or Buchéron (a rich French goat cheese), but since I don't eat these goodies every day, I never decline them when they're offered. The fact that my diet is usually a low-fat one doesn't mean I don't enjoy or appreciate butter, cream, and cheese.

OMELETS

PREPARATION TIME: Including fillings, no more than 10 minutes

One of the most obvious fast vegetarian feasts is, of course, the omelet. A friend tells me that she and her husband eat omelets the way others eat hamburgers. They're certainly as easy to make, and infinitely more delicate.

You can fill an omelet with practically anything—vegetables, fruits, cheese, herbs, and even chutneys. I often surprise people with my fruit fillings, combinations like strawberries and Brie, or spiced apples and Cheddar or nuts. Avocados are a sensuous filling, and sprouts and herbs produce an omelet bursting with life. The suggestions here should just get you started. Remember, too, that these creations are a good way to use up leftovers. One of the best omelets I've ever had was concocted ten years ago on a hot morning in South Texas. We'd had a rich eggplant Parmesan the night before, and used up the remains the following morning as the filling in a terrific omelet. I used to have a "Breakfast in Bed Catering Service" in Austin, and my clients were particularly fond of a ratatouille omelet.

A richer, actually heavenly, version of this dish is the puffed omelet. This is made by separating the eggs, beating the egg whites stiff and folding in the beaten yolks along with the filling. It's cooked briefly on one side and folded as it is turned out of the pan. What you get is a dish that resembles a soufflé—and you've prepared it on the top of the stove in one minute! I, who don't often eat eggs, could hardly stop myself from devouring these while I was testing recipes. They are truly special, and make fabulous dessert omelets as well as main dishes.

For a 2-egg omelet (1 serving):

2 teaspoons (10 ml) butter
2 eggs

Salt and freshly ground pepper to taste

1 teaspoon (5 ml) milk or cream (optional)

¼ cup (60 ml) of the filling of your choice (see below)

Have everything you need ready, including the serving plate. The folded omelet is prepared very quickly.

Heat an 8-inch (20 cm) well-seasoned or nonstick omelet pan (see equipment section, page 23) slowly, over a medium-low flame for 1 minute, to melt the butter in the pan. Meanwhile, break the eggs into a bowl, add a little salt and pepper and the optional milk or cream, and beat 30 times with a fork or whisk.

Add the butter; it will sizzle. Tip the pan from side to side to coat the bottom evenly, then turn up the heat to medium. As soon as the sizzling stops, and not a moment later, pour in the egg mixture. Tilt the pan with a rotating wrist motion so that the bottom is evenly coated with egg. As soon as you see that a thin layer of egg at the bottom is cooked (which is almost immediately) shake the pan vigorously by pushing it away from you and then jerking it toward you. It is the motion of the pan that assures a fluffy omelet and prevents it from browning. If the jerking motion is not moving the egg mixture enough for the uncooked egg at the top to flow beneath the cooked layer, lift the edge of the cooked layer with a spatula to allow the uncooked egg to flow onto the hot surface of the pan.

After a few shakes of the pan, place your filling in the center of the omelet, making a line of filling across its diameter. Jerk the pan so the omelet folds over on itself. (If you are afraid of spilling the eggs out over the side of the pan, fold the omelet over with a spatula.) Tilt the pan and roll the omelet out onto the serving plate, helping it along if necessary with the spatula. This entire operation should take about 1 minute.

Keep in mind that the center of the omelet should be undercooked, since it continues to cook by its own heat for a minute or so after the omelet has been removed from the pan. Also, be prepared for a few failures at first. I went through 3 dozen eggs during the 2 days I gave myself to master the omelet.

For further filling suggestions, see *The Vegetarian Feast* (Harper & Row, 1979), page 171.

MENU SUGGESTIONS

Soups: Hot or Iced Tomato Soup (page 72); Very Quick Cream of Pea Soup (page 85); Gazpacho (page 87); Potato Leek Soup (page 65)

Side dishes: Baked Potato (page 164); Baked Yams or Sweet Potatoes with Lime (page 169); Steamed, Pressure-Cooked, or Baked Beets and Beet Greens (page 148); any simply steamed vegetable
Salads: Tossed Green Salad (page 280); Oriental Salad (page 297); Tomato Salad (page 284); Cold Pasta Salad (page 302)
Desserts: Strawberries in Champagne (page 311); Baked Grapefruit with Tequila or Sherry (page 313); Apples with Lime Juice (page 312)

FILLINGS

CHEESE FILLING

This is a standard. I like Swiss Gruyère or Jarlsberg best, with a little Parmesan to give it even more character. Other good cheeses are undyed Cheddar, Emmenthaler, or Monterey Jack. Brie makes a sinfully rich, marvelous filling to be enjoyed occasionally. Use 2 to 4 tablespoons (30–60 ml) cheese per omelet.

STEAMED VEGETABLE FILLING

Diced or sliced zucchini, chopped asparagus, chopped broccoli florets or cauliflower, steamed until tender, are all wonderful. Combine with a tablespoon or two of Parmesan or other cheese, and perhaps one or two tablespoons of fresh herbs, such as parsley, basil, dill, or fennel, for an even more interesting omelet.

HERB FILLING

I mix the fresh herbs right into the eggs here and proceed as if I were making a plain omelet. Use 1 tablespoon (15 ml) of your choice of the following for each omelet: fresh chopped parsley, fresh chopped basil, or fresh chopped dill. Or 1 to 2 teaspoons (5–10 ml) of the following: fresh rosemary, fresh thyme, or fresh marjoram. You can also enhance the filling with fresh garlic (1 small clove) and/or a tablespoon (15 ml) of Parmesan.

LEFTOVER SPAGHETTI SAUCE FILLING

Use any of the tomato sauces on pages 203–206. Spoon ¼ cup (60 ml) of heated sauce into each omelet. Sprinkle on 1 teaspoon (5 ml) grated Parmesan cheese and, if you wish, a teaspoon (5 ml) of sunflower seeds before folding the omelet. Top with grated Parmesan and chopped fresh parsley.

MUSHROOM FILLING
FOR 4 TWO-EGG OMELETS

1 tablespoon butter or safflower oil
2 cups sliced fresh mushrooms
1 clove garlic, minced or put through a press
3 green onions, white part and green, chopped
Large pinch of dried thyme
Salt and freshly ground pepper to taste

Heat the butter or oil in a heavy-bottomed skillet and add the mushrooms, garlic, and green onions. Sauté five minutes and add a large pinch of thyme and the salt and freshly ground pepper to taste. Sauté another 3 to 5 minutes, until the mushrooms are tender. Remove from the heat.

STRAWBERRY AND BRIE FILLING
ENOUGH FOR 4 TWO-EGG OMELETS

This makes a heavenly breakfast in bed, as my friend Elizabeth found out on her thirtieth birthday.

1 to 1½ cups (250–350 ml) sliced fresh strawberries
2 ounces (50 gm) Brie cheese, sliced

Fill each omelet with ¼ cup (60 ml) strawberries and a couple of slices of Brie.

Note: 1 tart apple, cored and sliced, may be substituted for the strawberries.

APPLE AND CHEESE FILLING
ENOUGH FOR 4 TWO-EGG OMELETS

1 tart apple, cored and sliced thin
Juice of ½ lemon or lime
2 ounces (50 gm) Gruyère or Cheddar cheese, sliced thin or grated

Toss the apple with the lemon or lime juice. Divide equally with the cheese among the omelets.

BEAN SPROUT AND HERB FILLING
ENOUGH FOR 4 TWO-EGG OMELETS

1 cup (250 ml) sprouts (alfalfa, mung, lentil, sunflower, or a combination)
3 tablespoons (45 ml) chopped fresh herbs (try cilantro for a zesty twist)

Divide equally among the omelets.

CURRIED ORANGE FILLING
ENOUGH FOR 4 TO 6 TWO-EGG OMELETS

1 tablespoon (15 ml) butter
1½ teaspoons (7 ml) curry powder
2 oranges, peeled and sectioned
½ cup (120 ml) plain yogurt (optional)
¼ cup (60 ml) chutney

Heat the butter in a skillet and sauté the curry powder for 1 minute. Add the orange sections and sauté, stirring, for 3 minutes. Remove from the heat, place in a bowl, and stir in the optional yogurt. Divide among the omelets and serve with chutney.

SIMPLE FLAT OMELETS

Flat omelets, called *frittate* in Italy and *tortillas* in Spain, are very popular in these two countries, as well as in southern France. They aren't as quick to prepare as the folded omelet, but their advantage is that they are good served hot, at room temperature, or even chilled. Cut into squares or wedges, they make a marvelous picnic food or hors d'oeuvre. In Spain they are standard *tapa* fare in bars, *tapas* being hors d'oeuvres that are served along with drinks in the evening, before dinner. *Tapas* come in such a variety, and I was so curious about everything when I was in Spain, that I was never hungry by the time dinnertime, late in that country, rolled around.

For a simple flat omelet for 1:

1 tablespoon (15 ml) butter
1 teaspoon (5 ml) safflower oil
2 eggs
    Salt and freshly ground pepper to taste
1 teaspoon (5 ml) milk or cream
    Any of the fillings listed for the folded omelets on pages 178–180, in the amounts suggested for each

Heat the butter and oil in an 8-inch (20 cm) omelet pan or frying pan over a medium flame. Mix together the eggs, salt, pepper, and milk in a bowl. Beat about 30 times. Stir in the filling of your choice.
    Heat the broiler.
    Let the butter foam, and when the foam subsides pour the egg mixture into the pan and lower the heat to medium low. When a thin

layer of egg at the bottom has set, begin to shake the pan gently and continue cooking for about 5 minutes, until the omelet has set on the bottom and is almost set on the top. Place the pan under the broiler for about 2 minutes to finish it off. It should puff up. (Don't let it brown or it will be tough.) Remove from the heat and serve, cut in wedges, or remove from the pan with a spatula, cool, and chill.

Note: Sometimes flat omelets stick to the bottom of the pan. They will come loose if you slowly and patiently work a spatula beneath them. The reason I use the broiler to finish this sort of omelet instead of the traditional method of sliding it onto a plate and flipping it back into the pan is that I would panic whenever mine stuck and I couldn't get it out of the pan—it just wouldn't slide— and I'd often break the omelet in my determination. If it is stuck after being broiled, you can work it out of the pan gently with a spatula without breaking it.

TORTILLAS ESPAÑOLAS (Spanish Omelets)
SERVES 4
PREPARATION TIME: 10 to 15 minutes
SUPERVISED COOKING: 35 minutes

These are a little more complicated than the folded, Simple Flat or Puffed omelets. They are full of textures and colors, and when sliced they look like pretty mosaics. I have seen gorgeous stacks of them, of all different varieties, in bars in Spain. They looked like tortilla layer cakes. You begin these by sautéing onions and potatoes in olive oil until the potatoes are tender. Then you may add other ingredients, such as peppers, mushrooms, carrots or peas, and the eggs. The mixture cooks slowly, covered, for about 15 minutes, and is finished underneath the broiler.

The simplest version of this dish is given first, with variations following. Like the Simple Flat Omelet, a tortilla makes a wonderful cold hors d'oeuvre, lunch, or picnic.

2 tablespoons (30 ml) olive oil
1 large russet potato (about ½ pound; 225 ml), scrubbed and diced fine
½ medium onion, chopped
Salt and freshly ground pepper to taste
5 eggs

Heat 1 tablespoon (15 ml) of the olive oil in a 10- or 12-inch (25–30 cm) skillet or well-seasoned omelet pan and sauté the onion and potato over a medium flame until the potato is crisp-tender, about 15 to 20 minutes. Add the remaining tablespoon (15 ml) of oil as necessary. Add any of the ingredients below and sauté the mixture for another 5 minutes. Stir frequently so the vegetables don't stick.

Heat the broiler.

Put the eggs in a bowl and beat with a fork or whisk 30 times. Add salt and freshly ground pepper to taste. Pour into the skillet and tilt the pan to spread evenly over the surface: The eggs should just cover the vegetables. Turn the heat low, cover, and cook for 10 to 15 minutes, until the eggs are just about set.

Uncover and finish for 2 to 3 minutes under the broiler. Remove from the heat and serve, cut in wedges, or remove from the pan with a spatula and cool on a plate. Serve hot, warm, at room temperature, or chilled.

Note: If you don't want to use all the olive oil that the recipe calls for, reduce it to 1 tablespoon (15 ml). Steam the potatoes for 10 minutes, until crisp-tender, and add to the onions when the onions are tender.

VARIATIONS

Any or all of these additions will enhance your tortilla.

1 small green pepper or pimiento, or 1 of each, seeded and diced: Add to the onion and potato when the onion is tender.

1 medium zucchini or summer squash, diced: Add to the onion and potato after they have been sautéed for about 10 minutes. Continue to sauté until the potatoes are soft.

1 medium carrot, diced: Steam the carrot for 5 minutes. Add to the onion and potato when the potato is just about tender.

½ cup (120 ml) fresh peas or chopped fresh asparagus: Steam the vegetables until crisp-tender, about 5 minutes for asparagus, 5 to 10 minutes for peas. Add to the pan a minute or two before you add the eggs.

1 clove garlic, minced or put through a press: Add when the onion is tender.

1 cup (250 ml) sliced mushrooms plus 1 clove minced garlic: Add to the onion and potato mixture when the onion is tender. Sauté until the potato is tender.

½ cup (120 ml) sliced black olives: Add shortly before you add the eggs.

MENU SUGGESTIONS

Like the other omelets, Tortillas Españolas will go with any of the soups, salads, and desserts that don't call for eggs. Gazpacho (page 87) would make a nice authentic soup for a Spanish meal, and I would choose a fruity dessert.

PUFFED ASPARAGUS OMELET

PREPARATION TIME: 5 minutes

COOKING TIME: 1 MINUTE

The puffed omelet is an amazing phenomenon. I learned the technique for dessert omelets (see page 266) from my friend Ann Clark, who has spent six years in France and teaches regional French cooking. Her dishes are simple and authentic.

This resembles a soufflé made in a pan. Yet, unlike a soufflé, it takes only 5 minutes to prepare. It's made like a regular omelet, except you separate the eggs and beat the whites, then fold in the whites. What you end up with is something elusive and light that will melt in your mouth.

The asparagus is particularly pleasing to me, but you can, instead, use any of the suggested omelet fillings on pages 178–180.

For each omelet:

¼ cup (60 ml) chopped tender asparagus
2 eggs, separated
    Salt and freshly ground pepper to taste
    Pinch or two of freshly grated nutmeg
2 teaspoons (10 ml) butter

Steam the asparagus 5 minutes, until crisp tender.

Beat the egg whites in a bowl until they form stiff peaks. Beat the egg yolks in another bowl and add salt, freshly ground pepper, and nutmeg.

Gently fold the yolks into the whites, along with the asparagus.

Heat an 8-inch well-seasoned or nonstick omelet pan over medium heat and add the butter. When the foam subsides and the butter just begins to color, gently pour in the omelet mixture. Do not stir. Cook for exactly 1 minute. The bottom should now be brown; the top will be very soft. Turn onto a plate, folding in half as you turn it out. Serve at once.

Note: When you first make this, you might worry that it will taste like raw eggs, because the whites seem almost uncooked. It doesn't. There is enough heat to set the whites and make them so light that they melt in your mouth, and the yolks, which settle a bit, contribute to the delicious browned surface.

MENU SUGGESTIONS

The same as those for regular omelets and Tortillas Españolas, pages 176 and 181.

PIPÉRADE
SERVES 4 TO 6

PREPARATION TIME: 15 TO 20 minutes
SUPERVISED COOKING: 20 minutes

I was often inspired to make this dish the summer I lived in France, where you can find beautiful peppers—green, red, and yellow. (The two times I was in Italy I wished for a kitchen, because the peppers there often approach the size of small pumpkins! This multidimensional version of scrambled eggs comes from the Basque region of Spain and southern France, and usually contains ham. But with all those peppers to give the dish body, the ham is hardly necessary.

  2 tablespoons (30 ml) olive oil or butter
  1 onion, sliced
  2 cloves garlic, minced or put through a press
  3 sweet green peppers, seeded and sliced in thin strips
  2 sweet red peppers, seeded and sliced in thin strips (if unavailable, use additional green peppers)
  2 medium ripe tomatoes, peeled, seeded, and chopped
    Salt and freshly ground pepper to taste
  ½ teaspoon (2.5 ml) dried oregano
  ½ teaspoon (2.5 ml) dried marjoram
  6 eggs

Heat the oil in a large, heavy-bottomed frying pan, and sauté the onions and garlic until tender. Add the green and red peppers and cook a few more minutes, until they begin to soften, then add the tomatoes, salt, pepper, oregano, and marjoram. Stir to mix and cook, covered, over low heat for about 15 minutes, until the mixture is saucelike and fragrant.

Beat the eggs in a bowl with a fork or whisk and pour into the vegetable mixture. Stir constantly, as for scrambled eggs, over low heat. When the eggs have set, remove from the heat and serve.

This dish would go well with any of the light soups, such as Simple Miso Soup (page 68). Serve with a Tossed Green Salad, (page 280) or Watercress, Mushroom, and Tofu Salad (page 292), and, if you wish, a simple steamed vegetable.

Desserts: Pears or Peaches poached in Red Wine (pages 309–310); Figs Poached in Madeira (page 311) or Peaches with Marsala (page 314)

MIGAS
SERVES 4

PREPARATION TIME: 15 minutes
SUPERVISED COOKING: 15 minutes

I get regular cravings for *migas,* which are usually eaten for breakfast. At least once a month I find myself at one of Austin's most popular Tex-Mex restaurants, standing in line with all the other Austinites who have awakened with *migas* cravings, waiting for a table. It's always worth the wait.

Migas are scrambled eggs with fried corn tortillas, onions, tomatoes, and chilis. They are really a version of *chilaquiles,* and are one of my favorite Mexican dishes. They make a satisfying dinner as well as a breakfast, and are a great way to use up stale tortillas. If your tortillas are fresh, simply cut them into 6 or 8 wedges and dry them out in a 250-degree oven for 20 to 30 minutes.

½ pound (225 gm) tomatoes
8 eggs
Salt and freshly ground pepper to taste
1 to 2 tablespoons (15–30 ml) safflower oil
6 to 8 stale corn tortillas, cut into wedges in sixths or eighths
½ small onion, minced
2 serrano chilis, seeded and minced
1 teaspoon (5 ml) butter
1 tablespoon (15 ml) chopped fresh cilantro (optional)
½ cup (120 ml) grated Cheddar cheese (optional)

Place the tomatoes under the broiler and cook until they blister, turning to blister on all sides. Remove from the heat and chop. (This step may be omitted if you are short on time.)

Beat the eggs in a bowl with a fork or whisk and add the salt and freshly ground pepper.

Heat one tablespoon of the oil and sauté the dried tortillas until they are just beginning to stiffen, about 3 to 5 minutes. Add the onion and continue to sauté until tender, adding more oil if necessary. Add the tomatoes and chilis and sauté for another 5 minutes.

Turn the heat to low and add the butter. When it has melted stir in the beaten eggs and mix slowly, as you would scrambled eggs. When the eggs are set, add the optional cilantro and cheese. Serve at once, with hot sauce on the side, and fresh tortillas.

MENU SUGGESTIONS

Gazpacho (page 87) or any of the light soups, such as Simple Miso Soup (page 68). Serve a Tossed Green Salad (page 280), or Jícama and Orange Salad with Avocados, (page 295) and a cooling dessert such as one of the sherbets or frozen fruit ices on pages 315–318.

SIMPLE CHEESE, BREAD, AND MUSHROOM CASSEROLE
SERVES 6 TO 8
PREPARATION TIME: 15 minutes
UNSUPERVISED COOKING: 35 to 45 minutes

A friend and I were once invited to cook on a forty-foot sailboat off the coast of Honduras for a crew of six men. My friend Barbara had been on one of these chartered boats, and was worried about how I'd do in the galley. "You'll never be able to pull it off," she whispered anxiously to me. "They stock those boats with nothing but canned foods. You won't have any spices, not even any garlic!"

I told her not to worry, I liked such challenges. She was right about the canned food, but the boat was also generously supplied with eggs, cheese, and milk. With those resources I came up with a number of dishes—potato soups, and sauces and custards—to gussy up the canned fare. This Simple Cheese and Bread Casserole (at the time it lacked mushrooms) was the biggest hit. After dinner that night, the men extended our three-day invitation to a week.

    1 tablespoon (15 ml) butter
    1 cup (250 ml) mushrooms, sliced
    4 green onions, both green part and white, chopped
    2 tablespoons (30 ml) dry white wine
    8 ounces (225 gm) Cheddar cheese, grated

4 to 6 slices whole-wheat bread
    4 eggs
    2 cups (475 ml) milk, whole or skim, or 1½ cups (350 ml) milk and ½ cup (120 ml) dry white wine
    ½ teaspoon (2.5 ml) dried thyme
    ½ teaspoon (2.5 ml) dry mustard
      Salt and freshly ground pepper to taste

Preheat the oven to 350 degrees (180°C) and oil a 2-quart (2 L) casserole or soufflé dish.

Heat the butter in a heavy-bottomed skillet and sauté the mushrooms and green onions until the mushrooms begin to get tender. Add the 2 tablespoons (30 ml) wine and continue to sauté until the wine evaporates, about 3 to 5 minutes. Set aside.

Toss the cooked mushrooms with the cheese and layer this mixture with the bread in the prepared casserole. Beat together the eggs, milk, optional wine, thyme, and mustard. Add a little salt and freshly ground pepper and pour over the cheese and bread.

Bake for 35 to 45 minutes, until puffed and browned.

MENU SUGGESTIONS
Serve with a simple steamed vegetable, or a green vegetable dish such as Green Beans Amandine (page 146), Green Beans à la Provençal (page 147), or Brussels Sprouts with Lemon-Mustard Butter (page 149). For salad serve either Tossed Green Salad (page 280), Tomato Salad (page 284) or Oriental Salad (page 297).
Desserts: Pineapple with Mint; Strawberries in Red Wine and Preserves Syrup (page 310); Oranges with Mint

GRUYÈRE PUFFS
SERVES 6 TO 8

SUPERVISED COOKING: 10 minutes
UNSUPERVISED COOKING: 40 to 45 minutes

These buttery, rich delights are certainly not something I'd eat every day, but they are so special that I can't resist them from time to time. They are a marvelous accompaniment to soups.

    1 cup (250 ml) water
    6 tablespoons (90 ml) unsalted butter
    ½ teaspoon (2.5 ml) salt
    ⅛ teaspoon (.625 ml) freshly ground pepper
    1 cup (250 ml) sifted whole-wheat pastry flour
    4 eggs, at room temperature
    1 cup grated Gruyère cheese

Preheat the oven to 425 degrees (220°C) and lightly oil or butter a baking sheet.

Place the water, butter, salt, and pepper in a 1- or 2-quart (1 or 2 L) saucepan and heat until the butter is melted and the mixture is boiling rapidly.

Add the flour to the water all at once and continue to cook, stirring, until the mixture forms a ball and leaves the sides of the pan clean. Remove from the heat and cool slightly.

Beat in the eggs, one at a time, incorporating each thoroughly before adding the next. Stir in all but 2 tablespoons (30 ml) of the cheese.

Place rounded tablespoons (15 ml) of the dough on the prepared baking sheet. You can make a ring, leaving about 2 inches (5 cm) in the center, or place them in rows, like cookies. Sprinkle the remaining cheese over the dough and bake 40 to 45 minutes, until puffed and golden.

SOUTHERN SPOONBREAD
SERVES 6 TO 8

PREPARATION TIME: 5 to 10 minutes
SUPERVISED COOKING: 15–25 minutes
UNSUPERVISED COOKING: 30 minutes

Spoonbread, a traditional dish in the South, deserves more attention in the rest of the country. It is really like a pudding or a soufflé, and is as elegant as it is basic. It apparently originated when a cook put too much water into a cornbread batter, and the baked bread had to be spooned out of the pan. I also like spoonbread cold, and cut it into squares for hors d'oeuvres. Or you can deep-fry the leftovers for a slightly different hors d'oeuvre or side dish (see page 190).

        1 cup (250 ml) water
    ½ teaspoon (2.5 ml) salt
        1 cup (250 ml) cornmeal
    1½ cups (350 ml) milk
    ½ teaspoon (2.5 ml) honey
        2 tablespoons (30 ml) butter
        3 eggs, separated
          Kernels from 1 ear of corn (optional)
        1 jalapeño pepper, minced, or a small sweet green pepper, minced

Preheat the oven to 350 degrees (180°C). Oil or butter a 2-quart (2 L) soufflé dish, 9- or 10-inch (23 or 25 cm) cast-iron skillet, or a 2-quart (2 L) baking dish.

Bring the water to a boil in a 1-quart (1 L) heavy-bottomed saucepan or the top of a double boiler. Add the salt and very slowly pour in the cornmeal, stirring continually with a wooden spoon. Stir in the milk and cook over a low flame or over boiling water, stirring continually, for 10 to 15 minutes, until you have a thick, smooth mixture. Remove from the heat and stir in the honey and butter. Stir in the egg yolks, one at a time.

Beat the egg whites until they form stiff peaks. Stir one fourth of the whites into the cornmeal mixture until just mixed. Gently fold in the rest, along with the optional corn kernels and minced pepper.

Spoon the mixture into the prepared baking dish and bake for 30 minutes, until puffed and beginning to brown. Serve at once. Chill leftovers.

MENU SUGGESTIONS
Serve with a light soup, any of the vegetable side dishes, and the salad of your choice.

DEEP-FRIED SPOONBREAD SQUARES*

PREPARATION TIME: 5 minutes
SUPERVISED COOKING: 15 minutes

The contrast of crisp outside and creamy inside here is heavenly.

> Leftover Southern Spoonbread
> 2 oz. (50 gm) mozzarella cheese, sliced thin (optional)
> 2 to 4 cups (.5 L to 1 L) safflower oil, for deep frying

Cut the spoonbread into ½-inch (1.5 cm) slices. If using mozzarella, make little sandwiches by layering a slice of cheese between two squares of the spoonbread.

Heat the oil over a medium flame until it reaches 370 degrees (190° C) on a fat thermometer. Maintain an even flame so that the oil retains its temperature. Deep-fry the spoonbread squares until they turn golden brown and float to the surface. Drain on paper towels and serve.

ASPARAGI ALLA PARMIGIANA (Asparagus with Parmesan)
SERVES 4

PREPARATION TIME: 10 minutes in all
UNSUPERVISED COOKING: 15 minutes

I once went to one of the fanciest restaurants in Florence twice in one day just to eat this dish. I was alone and felt less strange about eating so little when I noticed the man at the next table. He ate first a bowl full of peas, with little specks of ham, then a large plate of cherries. Like me, he knew what he wanted.

> 2 pounds (1 kg) asparagus, trimmed
> Salt and freshly ground pepper to taste
> ⅔ cup (160 ml) freshly grated Parmesan cheese
> 1 to 2 tablespoons (15–30 ml) butter

Steam the asparagus just until bright green, about 3 minutes. Refresh under cold water.

Preheat the oven to 450 degrees (235°C).

Butter a 2-quart (2 L) baking dish. Layer the asparagus side by side, overlapping in rows with the tops covering the ends so that the tips

*Auxiliary recipe: requires leftover Southern Spoonbread (page 189)

are all exposed. Sprinkle each row with Parmesan and dot with butter.

Bake on the upper rack of the oven until a light crust begins to form and the mixture is bubbling. Remove from the oven, allow to stand a moment, then serve, as a side dish.

ASPARAGI ALLA PARMIGIANA WITH POACHED EGGS
SERVES 4

PREPARATION TIME: 10 minutes
SUPERVISED COOKING: 5 minutes
UNSUPERVISED COOKING: 15 minutes

This simple meal makes a very nice brunch or luncheon, as well as a satisfying supper. The yolks of the poached eggs run into the tips of the asparagus, which are coated with melted Parmesan. Result: delicious!

> 1 tablespoon (15 ml) vinegar
> 2 pounds (1 kg) asparagus, trimmed
> Salt and freshly ground pepper to taste
> ⅔ cup (160 ml) freshly grated Parmesan cheese
> 1 to 2 tablespoons (15–30 ml) butter
> 4 slices toasted whole-wheat bread or English muffins (optional)
> 8 eggs

Preheat the oven to 450 degrees (235°C). Butter a large saucepan, fill with water, and add the vinegar.

Steam the asparagus just until bright green and crisp-tender, about 3 minutes. Refresh under cold water.

Butter a 2-quart (2 L) baking dish and layer the asparagus side by side, overlapping rows as in Asparagi alla Parmigiana (page 190). Sprinkle each row with Parmesan and dot with butter. Bake 15 minutes in the preheated oven. Meanwhile, toast the optional bread and bring the buttered pot of water to a simmer.

When the asparagus is ready, remove from the oven and begin to poach the eggs. Swirl the water as you add the eggs, and poach for 4 minutes. Remove the eggs from the water with a slotted spoon, dip briefly into a bowl of cool water to stop the cooking and rinse off the vinegar, and drain on a dish towel.

For each serving, place a piece of optional toast on a warm plate, and top with a few pieces of asparagus. Place 2 poached eggs on top of the asparagus, pour over any juices that remain in the baking pan, grind on pepper, and serve.

A big green salad goes nicely with this. Also Broiled Tomatoes (page 170). Serve a springtime dessert, like Strawberries in Champagne (page 311) or Peaches with Amaretto (page 314).

BROCCOLI TIMBALE
SERVES 6
PREPARATION TIME: 20 minutes
UNSUPERVISED COOKING: 50 to 60 minutes

A timbale is a molded custard baked in a *bain marie* (a baking dish partially filled with water) and unmolded for serving. It is as elegant as a soufflé but not nearly as temperamental: it can stand for a while before serving and can even be reheated or served cold. You can use any steamed green vegetable in a timbale, but I especially like broccoli and asparagus.

> 2 cups (475 ml) broccoli florets (about 1 pound broccoli; 450 gm)
> 4 eggs
> 1½ cups (350 ml) milk (whole or skim)
> ¼ to ½ teaspoon (1.25–2.5 ml) salt
> ½ teaspoon (2.5 ml) paprika
> Freshly ground pepper to taste
> ½ cup (120 ml) freshly grated Parmesan cheese
> 2 tablespoons (30 ml) chopped fresh parsley
> Sliced tomatoes and parsley for garnish

Preheat the oven to 325 degrees (165°C) and butter a 2-quart (2 L) soufflé dish, mold, or Bundt pan generously.

Steam the broccoli for 5 minutes and refresh under cold water. Chop fine (this can be done in a food processor) and set aside.

Beat the eggs in a bowl. Heat the milk in a saucepan until the surface just begins to tremble; remove from the heat, cool a moment, and slowly whisk into the eggs. Stir in the broccoli, salt, paprika, pepper, Parmesan, and parsley. Pour into the prepared soufflé dish.

Place the dish in a pan of hot water and place in the oven. Bake for 50 minutes, or until set (a knife should come out clean) and just beginning to brown. Remove from the oven, cool for 10 minutes, and carefully unmold onto a serving platter. Surround with sliced tomatoes and parsley and serve.

This is also good with a light tomato sauce (page 204), and menu suggestions for Asparagus Timbale (page 193). You could also serve a baked potato or a baked sweet potato (see pages 164 and 169). Any dessert without eggs would be appropriate.

ASPARAGUS TIMBALE
SERVES 4 TO 6
PREPARATION TIME: 20 minutes
UNSUPERVISED COOKING: 45 minutes

This light custard with asparagus is similar to the Broccoli Timbale (page 192), but the addition of Gruyère cheese gives it a nuttier flavor.

    2 teaspoons (10 ml) safflower oil
    ¼ cup (60 ml) finely chopped onion
    2 pounds (1 kg) fresh asparagus, trimmed
    4 eggs
    1 cup (250 ml) milk
      Salt and freshly ground pepper to taste
      Pinch of freshly grated nutmeg
    ⅔ cup (160 ml) grated Gruyère cheese
    ¼ cup (60 ml) freshly grated Parmesan cheese

Preheat the oven to 325 degrees (165°C) and butter a 2-quart (2 L) soufflé dish, mold, or Bundt pan generously.

Heat the oil in a small pan and sauté the chopped onion until tender. Remove from the heat. Steam the asparagus for 5 minutes and refresh under cold water. Cut into ½-inch (1.5 cm) pieces.

Beat the eggs in a bowl. Heat the milk in a saucepan until the surface begins to tremble; remove from the heat, cool a moment, and beat slowly into the eggs. Stir in the salt, pepper, nutmeg, cheeses, onion, and chopped asparagus. Pour into the prepared soufflé dish.

Place the dish in a pan of hot water and pour in the egg mixture. Bake for 45 minutes, or until a knife inserted in the center comes out clean. Let the timbale stand at room temperature for 10 minutes, then run a knife around the edge. Carefully reverse onto a warm serving dish and serve, or chill and serve.

This is good with the Simple Tomato Sauce on page 204 or plain, with a Tossed Green Salad (page 280) or Tomato Salad (page 284).

CHEESE, STRING BEAN, AND SESAME CASSEROLE
SERVES 4 TO 6
PREPARATION TIME: 25 minutes
UNSUPERVISED COOKING: 30 to 40 minutes

I love the thick crust of sesame that forms on the top of this dish as it bakes. The cheese and wine combine here to produce a marvelous, heady aroma and taste. If you use a Swiss cheese in this recipe, such as Gruyère, the casserole will be similar to the traditional dish "Swiss string beans."

    1 cup (250 ml) sesame seeds
    1 pound (450 gm) tender string beans, trimmed and cut in half
    ½ cup (120 ml) minced onion
    2 tablespoons (30 ml) whole-wheat flour
      Salt to taste
    ½ cup (120 ml) plain low-fat yogurt
    ½ cup (120 ml) dry white wine
    1 cup (250 ml) grated Gruyère, Swiss, or mozzarella cheese
    1 tablespoon (15 ml) butter or safflower margarine

Preheat the oven to 350 degrees (180°C) and oil or butter a 2-quart (2 L) baking dish or soufflé dish.

Heat a dry skillet over moderate heat and add the sesame seeds. Cook, stirring or shaking the pan, until the seeds begin to smell toasty, about 5 minutes. (They will begin to pop at this point.) Remove from the heat and transfer to a food processor, blender, or mortar. Grind to a coarse meal.

Steam the beans for 3 to 5 minutes, until crisp-tender. Refresh under cold water. Toss with the minced onion, flour, salt, yogurt, and wine. Turn into the prepared baking dish and top with the cheese. Spread the ground sesame seeds over the top and dot with the butter.

Bake for 30 minutes, or until the top browns.

MENU SUGGESTIONS
Hot or Iced Tomato Soup (page 72); Potato Leek Soup (page 65); Gazpacho (page 87)
Salad of your choice
Dessert of your choice

CAULIFLOWER BAKED WITH TOMATOES, CHEESE, AND SESAME

SERVES 4 TO 6

PREPARATION TIME: 15 minutes
SUPERVISED COOKING: 20 minutes, in all
UNSUPERVISED COOKING: 30 minutes

Ground toasted sesame seeds are fast becoming a favorite topping of mine for baked dishes. They go especially well with cheese, as their nutty flavors combine so nicely.

1 cauliflower, broken into florets
1 tablespoon (15 ml) safflower oil
1 medium onion, sliced or chopped
1 pound (450 gm) ripe tomatoes, peeled, seeded, and sliced, or use canned
½ cup (120 ml) grated Gruyère or mozzarella cheese
¼ cup (60 ml) freshly grated Parmesan cheese
¼ cup (60 ml) ground toasted sesame seeds (see preparation in Cheese, String Bean, and Sesame Casserole page 194)

Steam the cauliflower for 5 to 10 minutes, to taste, and refresh under cold water.

Preheat the oven to 375 degrees (190°C) and oil a 2-quart baking dish or soufflé dish.

Heat the safflower oil in a heavy-bottomed skillet and sauté the onion until tender. Add the tomatoes and cook, uncovered, stirring occasionally, for 10 to 15 minutes. Add the cauliflower and toss together.

Fill the prepared baking dish with the cauliflower mixture. Toss together the cheeses and sesame seeds and spread over the top.

Bake for 30 minutes, or until the top begins to brown.

MENU SUGGESTIONS

Soups: Creamy Celery and Garlic Soup (page 76); Celery Tomato Soup with Rice (page 77); Miso Soup with Buckwheat Noodles (page 70)
Salad and dessert of your choice
You could also serve this with another vegetable dish.

CORN PUDDING
SERVES 4 TO 6

PREPARATION TIME: 15 minutes
SUPERVISED COOKING: 8 minutes
UNSUPERVISED COOKING: 30 minutes

Corn pudding is a very comforting dish, and as special as a soufflé, if not quite as dramatic.

    1 tablespoon (15 ml) butter or safflower oil
    ¼ cup (60 ml) finely minced onion
    1 small sweet green pepper, seeded and minced
    2 cups (475 ml) fresh corn, either grated or cut from the cob, coarsely pureed in a food processor
    4 eggs, two of them separated
    ¼ cup (60 ml) milk
    Salt and freshly ground pepper to taste
    ¼ teaspoon (1.25 ml) paprika

Preheat the oven to 375 degrees (190°C) and butter a 2-quart (2 L) soufflé dish.

Heat the butter in a heavy-bottomed skillet and sauté the onion and green pepper until the onion is tender, about 3 minutes. Add the corn and sauté, stirring, for another 3 minutes. Cool a few minutes.

Beat the whole eggs and the two egg yolks together with the milk. Add the corn mixture and salt and freshly ground pepper to taste. Stir in the paprika.

Beat the egg whites until they form stiff peaks, and fold into the corn mixture. Carefully turn into the buttered soufflé dish and bake for 30 minutes, or until the top is browned and the mixture set.

MENU SUGGESTIONS
This dish would go well with a tomato-based soup such as Hot or Iced Tomato Soup (page 72) or Gazpacho (page 87), a green vegetable, and any salad. Okra and Tomatoes (page 159) or Black-Eyed Peas (page 104) would make a nice down-home meal with it, along with Coleslaw (page 295).

SPINACH AND RICE GRATIN*
serves 4 to 6

Preparation time: 20 minutes using frozen spinach, 30 using fresh
Unsupervised cooking: 30 minutes

- 2 pounds (1 kg) raw spinach, washed and stemmed, or 2 packages (10 ounces or 275 gm each), frozen, thawed
- 1 tablespoon (15 ml) butter or safflower oil
- ½ medium onion, minced
- ½ teaspoon (2.5 ml) dried thyme or rosemary, or a combination
  Pinch of freshly grated nutmeg
- 1½ cups (350 ml) cooked brown rice (½ cup [120 ml] raw)
- 1 cup (250 ml) grated Swiss or mozzarella cheese
- ¼ cup (60 ml) freshly grated Parmesan cheese
  Salt and freshly ground pepper to taste
- 2 tablespoons (30 ml) whole-wheat bread crumbs

Preheat the oven to 350 degrees (180°C) and butter a 2-quart (2 L) casserole.

If using fresh spinach, blanch, squeeze dry, and chop fine. If using thawed frozen, squeeze dry and chop.

Heat the butter in a heavy-bottomed skillet and sauté the onion until tender. Add the spinach and toss a minute or two. Add the thyme and/or rosemary and nutmeg and remove from the heat. Toss with the rice and cheeses and add salt and freshly ground pepper to taste.

Turn the mixture into the prepared casserole and sprinkle the bread crumbs over the top. Bake for 30 minutes.

See menu suggestions for Corn Pudding (page 196).

*Auxiliary recipe: requires cooked brown rice

POTATOES GRUYÈRE
SERVES 6

PREPARATION TIME: 20 minutes
UNSUPERVISED COOKING: 1½ hours

Although this has to bake for a long time, the actual preparation is so easy that it belongs in this collection. This dish is protein-rich and filling, but not nearly as laden with fat as a traditional potato gratin. It goes well with a light soup, and I always like to see tomatoes served on the side.

> 1 small onion, chopped (½ cup; 120 ml)
> 2 tablespoons (30 ml) butter or safflower margarine
> 1½ cups (360 ml) plain, low-fat yogurt
> 8 ounces (225 gm) Gruyère or other Swiss cheese, grated
> ¼ cup (60 ml) freshly grated Parmesan cheese
> 2 tablespoons (30 ml) chopped fresh chives or green onion tops
> 5 large Russet potatoes, unpeeled and sliced thin
> Salt and freshly ground pepper to taste
> ½ cup (120 ml) whole-wheat bread crumbs

Preheat the oven to 350 degrees (180°C) and butter a 2-quart (2 L) baking dish or casserole.

Sauté the onion in 2 teaspoons (10 ml) of the butter until tender. Remove from the heat.

Combine the yogurt, cheeses, onion, and chives or green onion tops.

Place half the potatoes in a layer on the bottom of the prepared baking dish. Salt and pepper them and cover with half the yogurt mixture.

Repeat with another potato layer and the remaining yogurt mixture. Top with the bread crumbs, dot with the butter, and cover. Bake for 1½ hours.

MENU SUGGESTIONS

Soups: Hot or Iced Tomato Soup (page 72); Gazpacho (page 87); Simple Garlic Soup Provençal (page 64)

Vegetable Side Dishes: Simple steamed vegetables; Brussels Sprouts with Lemon-Mustard Butter (page 149); Florentine Tomatoes (page 171)

Salads: Tossed Green Salad (page 280); Watercress and Mushroom Salad (omit tofu) (page 292); Tomato Salad (page 284)

Desserts: Strawberry Sherbet (page 317); Orange Ice (page 318); Figs Poached in Madeira (page 311)

TURNIPS GRUYÈRE
SERVES 4 TO 6

PREPARATION TIME: 20 minutes
UNSUPERVISED COOKING: 30 to 45 minutes

This recipe is much like Potatoes Gruyère (page 198), but lighter. You must use young, tender turnips; if your turnips are mealy or dry, they'll become rubbery as they cook.

2 pounds (1 kg) young, tender turnips, peeled and sliced thin
1½ cups (350 ml) milk
2 large cloves garlic, minced or put through a press
¾ cup (180 ml) chopped green onion
   Salt and freshly ground pepper to taste
1 cup (250 ml) plain low-fat yogurt
¼ cup (60 ml) freshly grated Parmesan cheese
½ cup (120 ml) grated Gruyère cheese
   Fresh parsley for garnish

Preheat the oven to 400 degrees (200°C) and butter a 1½-quart (1.5 L) baking dish or gratin dish.

Combine the turnips, milk, garlic, green onions, and salt and pepper in a saucepan. Bring to a simmer, stirring, and remove from the heat. Let cool a few minutes, then stir in the yogurt and Parmesan. Turn into the prepared baking dish and top with the grated Gruyère. Bake for 30 to 45 minutes, until the top begins to brown. Garnish with parsley and serve.

See menu suggestions for Potatoes Gruyère (page 198).

PASTA

PASTA WITH TOMATO SAUCE
SIMPLE TOMATO SAUCE
TOMATO SAUCE WITH SOY GRITS*
TOFU TOMATO SAUCE
PASTA WITH UNCOOKED TOMATOES AND CHEESE
PASTA WITH COTTAGE CHEESE OR RICOTTA AND TOMATO SAUCE
PASTA WITH TOFU CREAM SAUCE
SPINACH AND WHOLE-WHEAT FETTUCCINE WITH WILD MUSHROOMS
AND CHEESE
BAKED MACARONI AND CHEESE
BAKED MACARONI WITH TOFU CREAM SAUCE
FETTUCCINE WITH OIL, GARLIC, AND ZUCCHINI
PASTA WITH BROCCOLI, CALABRIAN STYLE
SIMPLE SOBA WITH SESAME OIL
WHOLE-GRAIN PASTA WITH BUTTER AND HERBS
FETTUCCINE WITH PESTO
PESTO WITH MISO
PASTA WITH PICANTE TOMATO SAUCE

I get cravings for pasta the way others get cravings for ice cream. The recipes in this chapter were, in fact, the seeds of this book. Shortly after *The Vegetarian Feast* came out, my friend Marina wrote me a letter requesting some fast, filling one-dish meals, and mentioned some

*Auxiliary recipe

pasta creations she and her husband Reid had made. That inspired me to explore the possibilities. Later, when friends began to complain that vegetarian cooking was time consuming, I countered with some of the quick dishes in the following pages. I remember ecstatically writing a column right after developing Pasta with Cottage Cheese or Ricotta and Tomato Sauce (page 208)—I had just prepared a hot meal from scratch in seven minutes.

Now, of course, I could fill an entire book with quick, easy pasta dishes. It was a revelation to me when I began to see how adaptable pasta was, how well it went with foods other than the usual tomato. I was delighted with heady combinations like pasta with Broccoli, Calabrian style (see the one on page 213, which has raisins and nuts in it). When I cooked for heart patients for a month, a favorite dish was pasta tossed with simply steamed vegetables—like squash, carrots, and broccoli—and sprinkled with cracked roasted soybeans, which gave it a bacon flavor. In an Italian restaurant in London, one of my favorite dishes had hot red peppers in it—a picante pasta! It, too, opened new doors.

If you don't eat dairy products, try the Pasta with Tofu Cream Sauce (page 209) or the Baked Macaroni with Tofu Cream Sauce (page 211). These are rich and heavenly, as creamy as a cheese dish with a fraction of the fat.

When I cooked for a group of people who had never eaten whole-grain foods, I thought I'd start with something they'd recognize, like spaghetti. I made a vegetarian tomato sauce and tossed it with the pasta, and to my dismay they hardly touched it—because the noodles were brown! Since they're heavier than enriched pasta, whole-wheat noodles may not appeal to everyone, but I love their nutty flavor. Lots of shapes are available; some seem to be more successful than others. I have never liked whole-wheat elbow macaroni because the noodles are too hard and pasty; spirals, however, always turn out just right—perfectly al dente, and the sauces ooze seductively around the coils. I also prefer fettuccine noodles to spaghetti. There are now a number of different pasta varieties available, including those made with sesame and soy, whole wheat and soy, spinach, and artichoke. For marvelous, nutty Oriental dishes, try buckwheat noodles (soba).

No matter what shape noodle or what sauce you offer them, most people, old and young, enjoy pasta. An Italian friend once remarked that the one thing all the tourists in Italy have in common is that they like the food.

A NOTE ON MENUS

These recipes won't all come accompanied with menu suggestions. As a rule, other dishes should be light. If you do serve a soup, avoid those that contain cheese or potatoes, unless the pasta dish you've prepared doesn't use much cheese. I like to accompany pasta dishes with either a big crisp green salad, Lettuce Salad with Oranges (page 281) if the dish has an abundance of tomatoes, or Tomato and Mozzarella Salad (page 282). If the pasta dish is low in dairy products, a soufflé or puffed omelet, either as a main dish or dessert, would be appropriate. Whole grain pasta has the same amino acid pattern as whole grains, so beans, eggs, and dairy products would all be complementary. The menu sections in the front and back of the book will give you more ideas.

GENERAL DIRECTIONS FOR COOKING PASTA

Warm a serving dish or plates. To cook 8 ounces to 1 pound of pasta, bring a large pot of water, at least 7 quarts (about 7 L), to a rolling boil. Add 2 to 3 teaspoons (10–15 ml) salt, which will make the water bubble furiously, and a tablespoon (15 ml) or two (30 ml) of safflower oil, to prevent the pasta from sticking together. Drop in the pasta and give it a stir. A pegged pasta fork is good for this, but any spoon will do. Cook until the pasta is firm but not starchy—al dente—testing the noodles by biting one after they have cooked for a few minutes. When they are done, pour in some cold water and turn off the heat to stop the cooking, and immediately lift the pasta out of the water with a slotted spoon or a wide-mesh deep-fry skimmer. Place on the serving dish and top with sauce. Serve at once.

The most important things to remember in these instructions are not to overcook the noodles and to keep them hot after they're done. Avoid overcooking them by testing soon enough in the cooking process. If you can bite all the way through a noodle, it's done. Keep the pasta hot by quickly lifting it from the pot into a warm serving dish with the slotted spoon or skimmer. Some of the boiling water will be transferred with the noodles, keeping them hot and preventing them from sticking together.

One pound (450 gm) of pasta will feed 4 to 6 people. Use a pound (450 gm) for four big eaters, or for six with moderate appetites.

♥ PASTA WITH TOMATO SAUCE
SERVES 4 TO 6

PREPARATION TIME: see sauces; 10 minutes in all for pasta

¾ to 1 pound (350 gm) pasta of your choice, preferably whole-wheat pasta

1 recipe Simple Tomato Sauce, Tofu Tomato Sauce, or Tomato Sauce with Soy Grits (recipes follow)

1 to 2 tablespoons (15–30 ml) safflower oil

2 or more teaspoons (10 ml) salt

½ to 1 cup (120–250 ml) freshly grated Parmesan cheese, to taste

2 tablespoons (30 ml) fresh chopped parsley for garnish

Make the tomato sauce of your choice. While it is simmering bring a large pot of water to a boil. When the sauce is ready, add a tablespoon or two (15 ml–30 ml) of oil to the water, and at least 2 teaspoons (10 ml) salt. Add the pasta and cook al dente, so that it is still firm to the bite (time will vary according to the type of pasta; keep testing it. It shouldn't take more than 5 minutes in most cases).

Have a large serving bowl, platter, or individual bowls warmed and ready. Remove the pasta from the cooking water with a large slotted spoon or a wire deep-fry skimmer and place in the serving dish, platter, or individual bowls. Pour on the sauce, sprinkle on the Parmesan and serve.

♥ Omit Parmesan. See individual sauce recipes for substitutions.

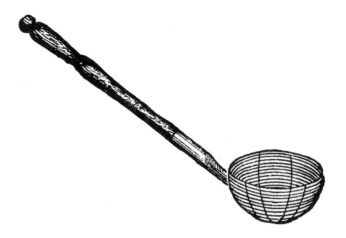

♥ SIMPLE TOMATO SAUCE
3 CUPS (700 ML)

PREPARATION TIME: 15 minutes
SUPERVISED COOKING: 5 minutes
UNSUPERVISED COOKING: 20 minutes

It's amazing how good a very simple tomato sauce like this is. Until I began working with this, I always used to cook my tomato sauces for hours. The longer-cooking ones are darker and richer, but this has all the freshness and lightness of ripe tomatoes. Unfortunately, it's difficult to find good red, ripe tomatoes these days. But, unlikely as it may seem, canned tomatoes work very well here, especially ones imported from the San Marzano region in Italy.

     1 tablespoon (15 ml) olive oil or butter
     1 small onion, chopped
     2 cloves garlic, minced or put through a press
     3 pounds (1.4 kg) ripe tomatoes, seeded and pureed, or 3 pounds (1.4 kg) canned tomatoes, seeded and pureed
       Salt and freshly ground pepper to taste
       Pinch of ground cinnamon
1 to 2 teaspoons (5–10 ml) chopped fresh basil or ½ teaspoon (2.5 ml) dried (optional)
  ½ to 1 teaspoon (2.5–5 ml) dried oregano (optional)

Heat the oil in a 4- or 5-quart heavy-bottomed saucepan and saute the onion and garlic until the onion is translucent. Add the tomatoes, then stir and simmer gently, uncovered, for 20 minutes. Add salt, freshly ground pepper, cinnamon, and the optional herbs and simmer a little longer if you wish. Remove from the heat and serve.

♥ Use 2 teaspoons (10 ml) safflower oil instead of olive oil or butter; omit salt. Only use fresh tomatoes, as canned are full of salt, or find an unsalted brand.

♥ TOMATO SAUCE WITH SOY GRITS*
MAKES 1 QUART

PREPARATION TIME: 15 minutes
SUPERVISED COOKING: 5 minutes
UNSUPERVISED COOKING: 40 minutes

The soy grits here add complete protein to this sauce, and give it a somewhat meaty consistency. It's very hearty, and because of the longer cooking time and the addition of tomato paste, it's darker and richer than the Simple Tomato Sauce (above).

1 tablespoon (15 ml) olive oil or butter
1 small onion, chopped
2 cloves garlic, or more to taste, minced or put through a press
3 pounds (1.4 kg) ripe tomatoes, seeded and pureed, or 3 pounds (1.4 kg) canned tomatoes, seeded and pureed
1 cup (250 ml) cooked soy grits (½ cup raw) (see page 96)
1 6-oz. can tomato paste
1 to 2 teaspoons (5–10 ml) fresh basil or ½ to 1 teaspoon (2.5–5 ml) dried
1 to 2 teaspoons (5–10 ml) dried oregano
Salt and freshly ground pepper to taste
Pinch of ground cinnamon

Heat the oil or butter in a large, heavy-bottomed saucepan and sauté the onion and the garlic until the onion is translucent. Add the tomatoes, soy grits, and tomato paste and bring to a simmer. Cover and simmer gently for 30 minutes. Add the herbs, salt and pepper to taste, and cinnamon. Simmer another 10 minutes. Remove from the heat and serve.

♥ Use 2 teaspoons (10 ml) safflower oil in place of the olive oil or butter. Omit salt. Do not use canned tomatoes, or find an unsalted brand.

*Auxiliary recipe: requires cooked soy grits

♥ TOFU TOMATO SAUCE

1½ quarts (about 1.5 L)

Preparation time: 15 minutes
Supervised cooking: 20 minutes
Unsupervised cooking: 40 minutes

The tofu here adds a substantial amount of protein to the sauce, and gives it nice body. As always, the tofu absorbs all the savory flavors of the tomatoes and garlic.

    2 tablespoons (30 ml) olive oil or safflower oil
    1 small onion, minced
    3 cloves garlic, minced or put through a press
    2 cakes (½ pound; 225 gm) tofu
    1 tablespoon (15 ml) tamari
    3 pounds (1.4 kg) fresh tomatoes, seeded and pureed, or 3 pounds
       (1.4 kg) canned, seeded and pureed
    1 small 6 ounce can tomato paste
    2 teaspoons (10 ml) chopped fresh basil, or 1 teaspoon (5 ml)
       dried
    1 teaspoon (5 ml) dried oregano
       Salt and freshly ground pepper to taste
       Pinch of ground cinnamon

Heat 1 tablespoon (15 ml) of the oil in a large, heavy-bottomed saucepan and sauté the onion with 1 clove of the garlic until the onion is tender. Add the remaining oil, the tofu, and tamari and cook, mashing the tofu with the back of your spoon, until the tofu begins to stick to the pan, about 5 to 10 minutes. Add the tomatoes, tomato paste, and remaining garlic and bring to a simmer; cook, covered, for 30 minutes. Add the herbs, salt and pepper to taste, and cinnamon and cook, uncovered, for another 10 minutes. Remove from the heat and serve.

   ♥ Use 2 teaspoons (10 ml) safflower oil; omit tamari and salt.

♥ PASTA WITH UNCOOKED TOMATOES AND CHEESE
SERVES 4 TO 6
PREPARATION TIME: 20 to 25 minutes, in all

This is one of the easiest pasta dishes I can think of. All the ingredients taste so fresh, and the diced mozzarella melts and stretches with every bite of the hot pasta. All the contrasts here, the tart capers, crunchy nuts, succulent tomatoes, and soft, mellow noodles make this a special favorite with guests. It makes a dinner party quite simple, as all the ingredients can be prepared in advance, needing only to be tossed with the pasta in a large bowl or casserole at serving time.

$3/4$ pound (350 gm) fettuccine, preferably whole-wheat
8 ripe tomatoes, seeded and diced
$1/2$ cup (120 ml) coarsely chopped walnuts or pecans
$1/4$ cup (60 ml) chopped fresh basil
3 tablespoons (45 ml) chopped fresh parsley
$1/4$ cup (60 ml) capers, rinsed
$1/2$ pound (225 gm) mozzarella cheese, diced
Freshly ground pepper to taste
3 to 4 tablespoons (45–60 ml) olive oil
$1 1/2$ cups (350 ml) freshly grated Parmesan cheese (6 ounces)

Bring a large pot of water to a boil. Meanwhile toss together the tomatoes, nuts, herbs, capers, and mozzarella in a bowl. Season with pepper.

Have a large (4- to 6-quart; 4–6 liter) casserole warmed and ready. Cook the pasta al dente and spoon into the casserole. Toss with the olive oil, then with the tomatoes mixture and 1 cup (250 ml) of the Parmesan. Serve at once on warm plates, and pass the additional $1/2$ cup (120 ml) Parmesan in a bowl.

♥ Omit capers, mozzarella, Parmesan, and olive oil. This is still a very nice dish with only the uncooked tomatoes and herbs.

♥ PASTA WITH COTTAGE CHEESE OR RICOTTA AND TOMATO SAUCE
Serves 4 to 6
Preparation time: 10 minutes

Here is another easy sauce. As a base, you can use leftover tomato sauce from another meal, a decent brand of bottled tomato sauce, or fresh tomatoes. Blended with cottage cheese or ricotta and Parmesan, it makes a creamy mixture, with the added lift of cayenne.

You can use any kind of pasta for this dish. I like green fettuccine, partly because it looks so pretty against the light orange sauce.

¾ pound (350 gm) pasta
2 cups (475 ml) cottage cheese or ricotta
2 cups (475 ml) either homemade tomato sauce (such as Simple Tomato Sauce, page 204) an unadulterated brand of prepared tomato sauce, or chopped ripe tomatoes
1 clove garlic, pureed or put through a press (only if using chopped ripe tomatoes)
Pinch of ground cinnamon
Pinch of freshly grated nutmeg
Freshly ground pepper to taste
Pinch or two of cayenne pepper
½ cup (120 ml) freshly grated Parmesan cheese

Begin heating the water for your pasta.

Meanwhile, blend together the cottage cheese or ricotta with the tomatoes and garlic until smooth in a blender or food processor. Transfer to a saucepan and heat through while you cook the pasta. Be careful not to boil the sauce or the cheese will curdle. Add the cinnamon, nutmeg, pepper, and cayenne.

Have warmed bowls or a warmed serving dish ready. When the pasta is cooked al dente, spoon into the bowls or serving dish, top with the sauce and Parmesan, toss, and serve at once.

♥ Use low-fat cottage cheese and omit Parmesan and salt. Use unsalted tomato sauce.

PASTA WITH TOFU CREAM SAUCE
SERVES 4 TO 6

PREPARATION TIME: 10 minutes, in all

This is like a slimming version of Fettuccine Alfredo, with all the creaminess and none of the fat. I think it's an exciting discovery.

¾ pound (350 gm) whole-wheat pasta, any shape
2 cakes (½ pound; 225 gm) tofu
½ cup (120 ml) plain low-fat yogurt
1 tablespoon (15 ml) sesame tahini
1 heaping tablespoon (15 ml) miso
1 tablespoon (15 ml) fresh lemon juice
  Pinch of freshly grated nutmeg
1 cup (120 ml) freshly grated Parmesan cheese
  Freshly ground pepper to taste

Begin heating water to cook the pasta. Meanwhile, blend together the tofu, yogurt, tahini, miso, lemon juice, and nutmeg in a food processor or blender until completely smooth.

Cook the pasta al dente and spoon into a warm serving dish. Toss with the tofu cream sauce and the Parmesan, and grind in plenty of pepper. Serve at once.

♥ SPINACH AND WHOLE-WHEAT FETTUCCINE WITH WILD MUSHROOMS AND CHEESE

SERVES 4

PREPARATION TIME: 45 minutes, including the unsupervised soaking of the mushrooms
UNSUPERVISED SOAKING: 45 minutes
COOKING TIME: 5 minutes

I brought some dried *cèpes* and *girolles* back from France once and waited for the right opportunity to use them, knowing that it would be with pasta for some special occasion. I served this dish for a friend's birthday dinner, and everybody was intrigued by the sort of "meaty things" in the pasta, which also contained diced mozzarella, Parmesan, and lots of parsley and freshly ground pepper.

½ cup (120 ml) dried mushrooms, such as cèpes, morels, shiitake, or a combination
¾ cup (180 ml) white wine
1 tablespoon (15 ml) butter
1 cup (250 ml) sliced fresh mushrooms (3 to 4 ounces; 75–100 gm)
1 clove garlic, minced or put through a press
¼ teaspoon (1.25 ml) dried thyme
½ pound (225 gm) mozzarella cheese, diced
1 cup (250 ml) chopped fresh Italian parsley
1 cup (250 ml) freshly grated Parmesan cheese
¾ to 1 pound (350–450 gm) fettuccine, preferably a combination of spinach and whole-wheat
¼ cup (60 ml) olive oil, plus oil for the pot
Freshly ground pepper

Soak the dried mushrooms in hot water to cover for 15 to 30 minutes, until soft. Drain and rinse thoroughly, to remove all the grit, which will be plentiful. Place in a bowl and pour in ½ cup (120 ml) of the white wine. Soak while you prepare the remaining ingredients, or for about 15 minutes.

Heat the butter in a heavy-bottomed skillet and sauté the fresh mushrooms until they begin to get tender. Add the garlic, remaining ¼ cup (60 ml) wine, and the thyme and continue to cook until the wine has evaporated. Remove from the heat and place the cooked mushrooms in a large bowl. Drain the dried mushrooms, slice, and add to the cooked mushrooms. Mix in the mozzarella, parsley, and ¾ cup (180 ml) of the Parmesan.

Bring a large pot of water to a boil. Have a warmed serving dish ready. Add salt and a little oil to the water and cook the pasta al dente. Spoon into the serving dish, toss with the olive oil, and add the mushroom mixture. Toss, adding freshly ground black pepper to taste, and serve at once. Pass the remaining Parmesan in a bowl.

♥ Omit cheese. Substitute 2 teaspoons safflower oil for the butter.

BAKED MACARONI AND CHEESE

PREPARATION TIME: 30 minutes
UNSUPERVISED BAKING: 30 minutes

If you have been curious enough to turn to this page, what with all the packaged versions of this dish that the name brings to mind, you'll be pleasantly surprised.

There are several versions of Baked Macaroni and Cheese. Most use a béchamel sauce in addition to the cheese. This is too rich for my tastes. This simpler version is not only much faster to put together, it doesn't weigh on your stomach and stay with you the way richer recipes do. And it's still creamy and delicious, as the cheese melts all around the pasta.

You can use flat noodles or elbow macaroni for this. I like to use a combination of spinach and whole-wheat noodles. With the tomatoes and the cheese, the resulting dish looks like the Italian flag.

½ pound (225 gm) sharp Cheddar cheese, grated
¼ pound (100 gm) Parmesan cheese, grated
2 to 3 pinches freshly grated nutmeg
     Freshly ground pepper
¾ pound (350 gm) flat noodles or elbow macaroni
2 tablespoons (30 ml) olive oil
2 pounds (1 kg) ripe tomatoes, seeded and sliced thin, or 2 cans (1 pound each or 450 gm) tomatoes, drained and sliced thin
2 tablespoons (30 ml) dry white wine
1 cup (250 ml) whole-wheat bread crumbs
1 tablespoon (15 ml) butter

Preheat oven to 375 degrees (190° C) and butter a 3– to 4–quart (3–4 L) casserole. Start the water heating for the pasta.

Grate the cheeses and mix them together. Toss with the nutmeg and the pepper.

Cook the pasta to slightly firmer than al dente. Drain and toss with the 2 tablespoons (30 ml) olive oil.

Layer one third of the tomatoes over the bottom of the casserole. Top with one third of the pasta. Top the pasta with one third of the cheese. Repeat the layers twice, ending with the cheese. Sprinkle on the white wine, spread the bread crumbs over the top, and dot with butter.

Bake, uncovered, for 20 to 30 minutes, until the top browns and the casserole is bubbling. Serve very hot, with a big tossed green salad.

Note: The sauce in Pasta with Tofu Cream Sauce (page 209) can be substituted for the Cheddar cheese, with very nice results.

FETTUCCINE WITH OIL, GARLIC, AND ZUCCHINI
SERVES 4 TO 6
PREPARATION TIME: 25 to 30 minutes, in all

This is based on the Italian Pasta Aglio e Olio, pasta with oil and garlic, with the added feature of zucchini that has been cut in matchsticks and briefly steamed, then tossed with the pasta and the oil, garlic, and Parmesan. It is a garlic lover's dream dish, and one that I can never resist.

    1 pound (450 gm) zucchini, cut in 2 inch julienne strips
    ⅓ cup (80 ml) olive oil
 2 to 3 teaspoons (10–15 ml) finely minced garlic
    ¾ pound (350 gm) fettuccine, preferably whole-wheat
 ½ to 1 cup (120–250 ml) freshly grated Parmesan cheese, to taste, plus additional for the table
    3 tablespoons (45 ml) chopped fresh parsley
      Other chopped fresh herbs to taste (optional), such as basil, sage, thyme, marjoram
      Salt and freshly ground pepper to taste

Steam the zucchini 5 minutes and remove from the heat. Begin bringing water to a boil in a large pot for the pasta.

Meanwhile, heat the olive oil with the garlic in a small pan over very low heat. The garlic should simmer very gently, never turning brown, but just golden. (If it cooks too quickly it will burn.) It should simmer for about ten minutes. When it is golden and the oil aromatic, remove from the heat.

Have a warmed serving dish ready. Cook the pasta al dente, and when it is done, spoon into the serving dish and toss with the oil and garlic, and the remaining ingredients. Serve at once, passing additional Parmesan.

♥ PASTA WITH BROCCOLI, CALABRIAN STYLE
SERVES 4 TO 6

PREPARATION TIME: 15 minutes
SUPERVISED COOKING (JUST OCCASIONAL STIRRING): 20 minutes

When I first came across this style of serving pasta it seemed very strange to me. I couldn't imagine the combination of tomatoes, broccoli, and raisins in a pasta dish, and put off making it until a friend in New York served it to me, and it was wonderful. The raisins are quite a tasty component; when I cooked for a number of heart patients who couldn't have any salt or dairy products, the dish was a big hit, because the raisins provided the zip that might have otherwise been missing.

  1 large bunch broccoli (2 pounds; 1 kg), broken into florets
  2 teaspoons (10 ml) safflower oil
  2 large cloves garlic, minced or put through a press
  2 pounds (1 kg) ripe tomatoes, cut into strips
¼ cup (60 ml) raisins
  2 tablespoons (30 ml) pine nuts or sunflower seeds
     Salt and freshly ground pepper to taste
¾ pound (350 gm) pasta, preferably whole-wheat
  2 tablespoons (30 ml) minced fresh parsley

Steam the broccoli until tender but still bright green, about 10 minutes. Refresh under cold water and set aside.

Begin heating water for the pasta.

Heat the oil in a heavy-bottomed skillet or saucepan and sauté the garlic until golden. Add the tomatoes and simmer for 15 minutes, uncovered, stirring occasionally. Add the raisins and pine nuts and simmer for another 5 minutes. Season to taste with salt and freshly ground pepper.

Have a large serving dish warmed and ready. Cook the pasta al dente and spoon into the serving dish. Spoon on the tomato mixture and the broccoli and toss. Sprinkle with the parsley and serve.

♥ Omit salt. Use 3 tablespoons raisins.

♥ SIMPLE SOBA WITH SESAME OIL
SERVES 4 TO 6
PREPARATION TIME: 5 minutes

Soba, or buckwheat noodles, have a rich, nutty flavor, which is enhanced by the sesame oil. This is an excellent accompaniment to most vegetable dishes.

    1 tablespoon (15 ml) safflower oil
    2 teaspoons (10 ml) salt
    ¾ pound (350 gm) buckwheat noodles (soba)
    3 tablespoons (45 ml) sesame oil
    1 tablespoon (15 ml) tamari (optional)

Bring a large pot of water to a boil and add the safflower oil and salt. Add the buckwheat noodles and cook al dente, about 5 minutes. Remove from the cooking water with a slotted spoon or wire deep-fry skimmer and toss with the sesame oil and optional tamari. Serve as a side dish.

♥ Use 1 tablespoon (15 ml) sesame oil. Omit salt and oil in cooking water and omit the tamari.

♥ WHOLE-GRAIN PASTA WITH BUTTER AND HERBS
SERVES 4 TO 6
PREPARATION TIME: 10 minutes
UNSUPERVISED COOKING: 4 minutes

This simple pasta dish is bursting with all the fresh, herby flavors of spring.

    1 tablespoon (15 ml) safflower oil
    2 teaspoons (10 ml) salt
    1 pound (450 gm) whole-grain pasta
    1 tablespoon (15 ml) olive oil
    3 tablespoons (45 ml) unsalted butter
    ¼ cup (60 ml) chopped fresh parsley
    ¼ cup (60 ml) chopped fresh basil
    ¼ cup (60 ml) mixed chopped fresh herbs (such as sage, thyme, marjoram, rosemary, oregano); optional
    ½ cup (120 ml) freshly grated Parmesan cheese

Bring a large pot of water to a boil and add the safflower oil and salt. Have ready a warmed serving dish. Cook the pasta al dente and transfer to the serving dish with a slotted spoon or wire deep-fry skimmer. Toss at once with the olive oil, butter, herbs, and Parmesan. Serve hot, or chill and serve as a salad.

Soups: Cheddar Cheese Soup with Vegetables (page 66); Hot or Iced Tomato Soup (page 72); Pureed Zucchini Soup (page 70)
Salads: Tossed Green Salad (page 280); Tomato Salad (page 284); Tomato and Mozzarella Salad (page 282)
Desserts: Any in this collection

♥ Omit butter and Parmesan; use safflower oil instead of olive oil; omit salt in cooking water.

FETTUCCINE WITH PESTO
SERVES 4, GENEROUSLY
PREPARATION TIME: 20 minutes

A pesto is a marvelous fast feast, especially if you make it in a food processor or blender. The traditional *pesto genovese* is a heady paste consisting of basil, garlic, olive oil, pine nuts or walnuts, Parmesan and Romano. There is nothing like it. My friends Gay and Dan grow nothing but basil in their not-too-small garden, and eat pesto all through the summer. I like to join them often in this ritual.

Because the quantities of fresh basil that *pesto genovese* requires aren't always available, I decided to experiment with parsley and spinach, and found that the resulting pestos were perfectly respectable, delicious, in fact. They don't have that deep unmistakable flavor of basil, but they do have a fresh, herbal essence, and with the garlic and cheeses and olive oil, they are just as gutsy and aromatic. They also have a better color: the basil pesto tends to be a drab green color, whereas the parsley version, and to a lesser degree the spinach, remain bright green.

While I was developing pestos it occurred to me that it would be possible to make a dairyless version, one lower in fat, by substituting miso for the cheeses. Miso has qualities in common with Parmesan and Romano: it is quite salty and is produced by fermentation. And it has the complexity of cheese. Indeed, my notion worked. My pesto made with miso had the same kind of complete taste and finish as the original, and all the flavors of the ingredients come through. Texture is one of the most important elements of a pesto, and none of that has been lost. This new pesto will be a boon to those who don't eat (or want to cut down on) dairy products.

2 cups (475 ml) tightly packed fresh basil
2 tablespoons (30 ml) broken pine nuts or shelled walnuts
2 large cloves garlic, peeled
Salt
½ cup (120 ml) olive oil
½ cup (120 ml) freshly grated Parmesan cheese
2 tablespoons (30 ml) freshly grated Romano cheese
2 tablespoons (30 ml) safflower or vegetable oil
¾ to 1 pound (350–450 gm) fettucine; whole-grain, spinach, or semolina
2 tablespoons (30 ml) unsalted butter
2 tablespoons (30 ml) hot water from the pasta

Start the water heating for the pasta.

Place the basil, pine nuts, garlic, and ¼ to ½ teaspoon salt, if desired, in a food processor fitted with the steel blade or a blender jar. Pulse several times to begin chopping and blending the ingredients. Then turn on machine at high speed and pour in the olive oil in a steady stream. Blend until the mixture is a smooth paste. If you are using a blender you'll have to stop and start the machine occasionally to give the ingredients a stir. When the ingredients are pureed, transfer to a bowl and stir in the cheeses. Blend thoroughly.

When the water comes to a boil, add a generous amount of salt and the safflower oil. Have ready a warmed serving dish. Cook the pasta al dente and transfer to the serving dish with a slotted spoon or wire deep-fry skimmer. Toss with the butter. Add the 2 tablespoons (30 ml) of water from the pasta to the basil mixture and toss with the pasta. Or you can transfer the fettuccine to individual serving dishes and place a little butter and a generous amount of pesto on each serving.

FOR PARSLEY PESTO
Substitute 2 cups (475 ml) tightly packed parsley for the basil, or use part parsley, part basil, in any proportion.

FOR SPINACH PESTO
Substitute 2 cups (475 ml) tightly packed, washed, and stemmed spinach for the basil, or use part spinach, part basil, in any proportion.

Use 2 additional tablespoons (30 ml) walnuts or pine nuts.

Add 10 minutes to the preparation time, to account for washing the spinach.

TO STORE PESTO IN THE REFRIGERATOR

Prepare the herb or vegetable paste, but do not mix in the cheese. Top the paste with a thin film of olive oil and cover tightly. It will keep this way for weeks, even months. Stir in the cheese when you are serving the pesto. Pesto can also be frozen: omit the cheeses, top with olive oil and cover tightly. Thaw and stir in cheeses before serving.

MENU SUGGESTIONS

Soups: Hot or Iced Tomato Soup (page 72); Simple Garlic Soup Provençal (page 64)

Salads: Tomato and Mozzarella Salad (page 282); Tossed Green Salad (page 280); Tomato Salad (page 284)

Desserts: Preferably a fruit dessert, or a fruit ice (see pages 315–318)

PESTO WITH MISO
1 CUP (250 ML)

This version of pesto works especially well with spinach.

- 2 cups (475 ml) firmly packed spinach, basil, or parsley, or a combination
- 2 to 4 tablespoons (30–60 ml) broken pine nuts or walnuts, to taste
- 2 large cloves garlic, peeled
- ¼ cup (60 ml) olive oil
- ¼ cup (60 ml) water, or an additional ¼ cup (60 ml) olive oil
- 2 tablespoons (30 ml) hacho or red miso
- 2 tablespoons (30 ml) water from the pasta

Place the herbs or spinach, the pine nuts, and the garlic in a blender or food processor. Pulse several times to begin chopping and blending the ingredients. Then turn on the machine and pour in the olive oil in a steady stream and water. Blend until the mixture is a smooth paste. Add the miso and continue blending until it is thoroughly incorporated.

Cook your pasta and proceed as in Fettuccine with Pesto (see preceding recipe).

♥ PASTA WITH PICANTE TOMATO SAUCE
SERVES 4 TO 6

PREPARATION TIME: 15 minutes

SUPERVISED COOKING: 5 to 10 minutes

UNSUPERVISED COOKING, WITH OCCASIONAL STIRRING: 20 to 30 minutes

The first time I ever ate pasta like this was at my parents' favorite Italian restaurant in London, Sam Rufilo. This was everybody's favorite dish. I don't know why I'd never thought of adding something picante to a spaghetti sauce before.

    1 tablespoon (15 ml) olive oil
    2 large cloves garlic, minced or put through a press
    3½ pounds (1.5 kg) tomatoes, fresh or canned, seeded and coarsely pureed
    3 tablespoons (45 ml) chopped fresh basil or 1 tablespoon (15 ml) dried
    1 teaspoon (5 ml) crushed or minced dried red pepper
      Salt
    1 tablespoon (15 ml) safflower oil
    1 pound (450 gm) either small shell macaroni, tube macaroni, or other available pasta
    ½ cup (120 ml) freshly grated Parmesan cheese

Heat the olive oil in a large, heavy-bottomed saucepan or skillet and sauté the garlic gently until it begins to color, about 1 to 2 minutes. Add the tomatoes, basil, and red pepper and bring to a simmer, stirring. Cook, uncovered, over moderate heat, stirring occasionally, for 20 to 30 minutes, until the sauce thickens. Season to taste with salt.

Meanwhile, bring a large pot of water to a boil. Have ready a warmed serving dish. Add salt and a tablespoon of safflower oil and add the pasta. Cook al dente. Remove from the boiling water with a slotted spoon or deep-fry skimmer and place in a warm serving dish. Toss with half the sauce and the ½ cup Parmesan. Pour the rest of the sauce on the top of the pasta or place the remaining sauce on individual servings. Serve at once.

MENU SUGGESTIONS

Accompany this with a crisp green salad and serve a cooling sherbet or fruit ice for dessert (see pages 315–318).

♥ Use 2 teaspoons (10 ml) safflower oil instead of olive oil; omit the Parmesan (you really won't miss it with this satisfying spicy sauce) and salt. Omit safflower oil in pasta water.

FISH

3 Court Bouillons
Fish Fumet
Tuna or Swordfish à la Marseillaise
Baked Whiting with Tomato-Caper Sauce
Cod Fillets with Tomato-Mint Sauce
Steamed Whole Sea Bass or Flounder à la Chinoise
Trout en Papillote with Lemon and Dill
Fish Fillets Baked en Papillote with Garlic and Mushrooms
Snapper Fillets en Papillote with Green Salsa
Broiled Salmon Steaks
Salmon Fillets Simmered in Sake
Fillets of Sole with Cucumbers and Dill
Flounder or Sole Amandine
Broiled Fish with Coriander Sauce
Broiled or Grilled Flat Fish with Sorrel Puree
Poached Fish with Egg-Lemon Sauce
Poached Redfish with Baby Artichokes
Grilled or Broiled Mackerel or Bluefish with Cumin and
Coriander
Fish au Gros Sel
Smoked Salmon with Red Peppercorns
Spicy Shrimp Salad
Ceviche
Lulu's Escabeche aux Sardines

When I first became a vegetarian, in 1972, I stopped eating all meat, poultry, and fish. I can even remember my last bite of lobster; it tasted too rich for me at that time, and I knew that I wouldn't be eating it again for a while.

I started eating fish again about four years later, during a seventies-style, very low-budget beach vacation in southern Mexico. We slept in hammocks in a thatch lean-to owned by a woman named Marta, who did all the cooking. The meals were simple: eggs, frijoles, tortillas, and the day's Pacific catch, which Marta would fry or grill. I considered my diet; I could eat either greasy eggs every day or that beautiful fresh fish, and my choice was obvious. It's been ten years, yet I can still taste that succulent grilled mackerel. I've been eating fish ever since.

After that I usually ordered fish in restaurants, especially when I traveled. I was living in Austin, Texas, and I loved the redfish dishes that most of the Austin restaurants offered. It was there that I discovered how much I adored ceviche. I learned to make it in a class offered by a Peruvian woman at the cooking school where I was then teaching; hers was an interesting version, garnished with sweet potatoes and corn on the cob, which looked beautiful against the lettuce leaves that served as a bed for the tart, glistening morsels of fish.

But it wasn't until I moved to Paris, in 1981, that I really began to work with seafood. Maybe it was because I just didn't see it in the shops I marketed at in Austin, but I was a little nervous about fish and mystified by it. I loved to eat it, but I wasn't confident about my ability to cook it.

This lasted until I got a job as a private cook for the sculptress Niki de Saint Phalle, after I'd been in Paris about eight months. Niki had put an ad in the paper that read: "Artist living near Fontainebleau seeks assistant who can cook health food. Must drive and be free to travel." She might as well have said "Calling Martha Rose Shulman." It was a perfect job for me. I would go out to her house, about thirty miles from Paris, two or three times a week and make dishes that would last a few days, like bean pâtés and grain salads and soups; and on the days I cooked, Niki would invite people for dinner. She always wanted me to do fish for these dinners, so when I wasn't out at her house cooking I read fish cookbooks and tested recipes in order to build up a repertoire. You will find some of the dishes I cooked for her in this chapter—Trout en Papillote with Lemon and Dill (page 236). Broiled Salmon Steaks (page 239), Fillets of Sole with Cucumber and Dill (page 242), to name a few; given the fact that I had to prepare food for the rest of the week on the same day I was catering Niki's dinner party, I didn't exactly have all day to dabble in time-consuming, elaborate dishes. These meals were fast vegetarian feasts.

After I'd been in Paris a little over a year I began my Supper Club chez Martha, which consists of paying dinners for twenty-five people that I do once or twice a month in my home. I often serve fish at these dinners: Baked Whiting with Tomato-Caper Sauce (page 232), Poached Fish with Egg-Lemon Sauce (page 247) and my Ceviche (page 255) have pleased many palates; they are the kind of dishes that are perfect for entertaining, because everything up to the final cooking of the fish can be done in advance.

In fact, that's what makes fish so perfect for this book. It is such easy, satisfying fare. A plain grilled tuna, swordfish, or salmon steak, seasoned with nothing more than fresh lemon juice and accompanied with steamed fresh vegetables and a crisp tossed salad can be a perfect meal. It takes very little to dress it up a bit—soy sauce and ginger, or a scrumptious tomato-caper sauce or green salsa, as you will find in the following pages.

Then there's the nutritional value that fish delivers, at only about 125 calories per 4-ounce serving. Fish contain anywhere from 16 to 25 percent protein (one 4-ounce serving can supply half your daily protein needs), a large amount of calcium, and a relatively small amount of fat. But here the fat is "good." Curiously enough, all fish, but especially the fattier types like mackerel and salmon, contain fatty acids that cut through cholesterol buildup.

WHAT'S SO FISHY ABOUT FISH? BUYING, STORING, AND PREPARING

Buying Fish: I am impressed with the variety and availability I see in the fish markets in the United States. As the consumption of meat decreases, the demand for good-quality fish must be on the rise, and I'm glad to see all the reliable fish sellers. Success with fish begins at the market.

If a fish store smells "fishy," find another one. That's the first sign that the fish is not fresh. In Paris I can tell right away, when I walk through a market, if it's worth stopping at the fish stand. Fresh fish has a sweet, lively aroma, not a rank or fishy smell; it's not hard to tell the difference. The flesh should be moist, shiny, and translucent. If fillets and steaks appear dry or gray around the edges, they're past their prime. Whole fish should have clear, slightly bulging eyes, not cloudy, sunken ones. If you can, touch the fish to make sure that the flesh is firm and not soggy. It should spring back.

Most fish stores sell fish already filleted, especially larger fish like cod and snapper. If you want fillets but can buy the fish whole and have the fish seller scale, clean, and fillet it, all the better. The more there is for you to inspect, the better. If you are buying whole fish for a recipe, have the fish seller clean and scale it (except for Fish au Gros Sel, page 251; scales should be left on).

Buying Frozen Fish: Many fish are flash-frozen—sometimes after being cleaned and filleted—as soon as they're caught. The technology is very good, and there's no reason to turn up your nose at frozen fish if you can't get it fresh. But you must be careful when buying packaged frozen fish that the packages contain no leaks or ice crystals. If there are ice crystals, the fish has thawed somewhere along the line, then been refrozen. If you find packages like this at the supermarket you should point them out to the manager, because the fish could contain harmful bacteria. Also watch out for packages that give off a strong odor; it's a sure sign of rancidity.

Storing Fish: Store fish in the coldest part of the refrigerator, lightly covered with plastic wrap. Use within two days. If you can't use the fish within two days but don't want to waste it, wrap it in plastic or foil and freeze it. Date the packets; fish will keep in the freezer for up to two months. Some freshness and flavor will be lost, but not too much.

Choosing fish: The fish you choose depends upon your taste and the way you plan to cook it. If you don't like meaty, fishier fish, you won't want to try the darker, fatty-fleshed kinds like mackerel, salmon, bluefish, or swordfish. The light, white-fleshed varieties like sole, whiting, flounder, and cod are the ones for you. Fish like tuna, red snapper, and porgy or bream fall somewhere in the middle. Their flesh is denser than the white fish I mentioned, but their flavor is relatively mild. Use the chart on page 228 to help you choose. You will see from the chart that some kinds do not respond to certain cooking methods; the fattier and meatier fish, for example, do not steam or poach well because their flesh falls apart.

You can substitute one type for another in almost all fish recipes.

The cooking times for fish are uniform, and if a recipe calls for a mild, white-fleshed type like sole, you can substitute turbot, whiting fillets, or cod fillets. Swordfish steaks can be used instead of tuna; mackerel, a fatty fish, can be interchanged with bluefish, another fatty fish. Each fish does have a particular taste, but the way similar types of fish respond to various cooking methods is uniform. So let the freshness and availability of the day's catch be your final shopping guide.

Preparation: The first time I did a dinner party for Niki de Saint Phalle I bought ten small trout, which I planned to cook *en papillote* (see page 236 for the recipe). But I forgot to ask the fish seller to clean them. *Yuck.* I did the task, having learned to clean fish at Le Cordon Bleu in London, but I don't think I'll ever make that mistake again. Although my friend Lulu Peyraud insists that if you aren't the one to clean them you won't know if they're really fresh, I and most of my readers—especially those of you who are interested in fast feasts—would just as soon leave that task up to the fish seller. Space and time do not allow me to go into all the ins and outs of cleaning and scaling, cutting into steaks, boning and filleting, nor do the purposes of this book. But these techniques *are* important for those of you who are truly interested in pursuing fish cookery. My recommendation for a primer on these techniques is the Time-Life Good Cook series on *Fish.* Their instructions are clear and concise, with photographic illustrations.

COOKING METHODS

First, a word on timing. Generally speaking, if you measure the fish at the thickest point and allow 10 minutes per inch of thickness, you won't go wrong. I think, though, that your best timing device should be your eyes. Once the fish is opaque and begins to fall apart around the edges, it's done. This is the crucial moment, because cooking fish even a minute too long—especially delicate fillets—renders them dry. You should begin checking fillets after 5 minutes, steaks after 8 (unless they are very thin).

Poaching: Poaching means to cook in barely simmering liquid. All firm-fleshed fish, such as sea bass, sole, and cod lend themselves to this cooking method. The fattier fish do not. For large whole fish you need a poacher or roasting pan fitted with a rack and placed on top of the stove. The rack allows you to lift out the whole fish intact. Wrap smaller whole fish in cheesecloth and use the ends of the cheesecloth to lift the fish into and out of the liquid. Small fish, fillets, and steaks can be poached in a buttered deep skillet or any casserole large enough to accommodate all the pieces in one layer. A rack isn't necessary.

To bring out the best flavor, fish should be poached in a seasoned liquid, either a court bouillon, a fumet, or flavored stock. A court bouillon is made by simmering aromatic vegetables and herbs in salted water for 15 minutes, then adding wine, vinegar, or milk and continuing to simmer another 15 minutes. The liquid is then strained. If fish trimmings are added to the water, it becomes a fumet, with a stronger, fishier flavor. Given the time requirements in this book, my poaching recipes don't require the first step of making a court bouillon, even though it is quite simple and takes only a half hour. The broth in the Poached Fish with Egg-Lemon Sauce on page 247 involves a quick variation of the court bouillon, and the flavor of the dish is heightened at the end with the lemony sauce; and the Poached Redfish with Baby Artichokes (page 249) makes use of the cooking liquid from the artichokes. Nevertheless, I am including recipes for these poaching media, as they will be useful for other recipes. They can all be frozen, and require very little effort, so I suggest you make some up for the freezer on a Sunday.

Fish fillets should be pounded with the flat side of a knife and scored before poaching. This breaks down their fibers, so that they don't toughen up and curl when exposed to the heat.

The method for poaching is simple. Place the fish in the buttered cooking vessel and cover with tepid or room-temperature liquid. Bring to a simmer—*not a boil*—and cover with buttered wax paper or a lid. Simmer gently, never letting the temperature rise above 175 degrees (80° C), for 5 minutes per ½ inch of flesh, or until the fish becomes opaque. Gently remove from the cooking liquid, transfer to a platter, and proceed with the recipe. If you are serving the fish cold, decrease the cooking time by a few minutes and allow to cool in the poaching liquid.

Steaming: Steaming is cooking fish above, not in, liquid. Here the liquid should be boiling rapidly to ensure fast, even cooking, and as in poaching, a fish will benefit from an aromatic steaming liquid. Any fish that can be poached can be steamed, and the results will be moist and succulent. The advantage of steaming is that none of the flavor of the fish is lost in the liquid, as the fish isn't immersed.

Any lidded pot that can accommodate a fold-up steaming basket or rack will do. A Chinese steamer—either wooden or metal, or a metal steaming pot are particularly useful, as recipes often require that you place the fish first on a plate and these steamers are large enough to set a plate on. No matter what kind of steamer you use, remember to oil the rack before you place the fish on it to prevent sticking.

To achieve the most flavorful results, rub the fish with ginger or garlic, or stuff with aromatic vegetables and/or herbs to "steam in" flavor (see Steamed Whole Sea Bass or Flounder à la Chinoise, page 235). Bring about 2 inches steaming liquid (make sure that it doesn't touch the bottom of your steaming rack) to a rapid boil. Place the fish on the rack, cover tightly, and steam for 10 minutes per inch of thickness. Fish should be opaque and flake easily. Remove from the heat and proceed with the recipe.

Baking: Baking works well for any fish, especially delicate types like sole, flounder, and cod. Large whole fish are perfect candidates for baking, and can often be baked right in the sauce they will be served with. Baking, grilling, and broiling all involve the use of dry heat, and it is necessary to take care that the fish does not dry out. There are several ways to intervene. I usually bake fish in a small amount of white wine or fish fumet, to provide a little steam around the fish. You can also wrap fish in lettuce leaves to seal in juices, marinate the fish and bake in the marinade, basting often, or bake *en papillote* (see discussion of this technique below).

The oven temperature should be 425 to 450 degrees, (200 to 220° C), the baking dish lightly buttered or oiled, and the fish should be covered with lightly buttered or oiled parchment, foil, or a lid. As in other cooking methods, bake 10 minutes for each inch of thickness.

En Papillote: This is a method I am using more and more frequently. You can bake, broil, grill, or steam whole fish or fillets sealed in foil packets, which locks in moisture and aroma. The fish actually steams in its own juices, with the added flavor of the aromatics you've added to the foil packet. Place fillets or whole fish on lightly buttered or oiled double-thickness pieces of aluminum foil, about twice the size of the fish. Add salt and pepper and flavorings of your choice, such as herbs like dill or rosemary, slices of lemon, slivers of garlic, or ginger shreds. Bring the edges of the foil up over the fish, join together, and crimp tightly. Bake, broil, grill, or steam for 10 minutes per inch of thickness. I like to serve the fish right from the packets if I'm not adding a sauce; that way none of the aromatic fish juices are lost.

Broiling: The best fish for broiling are the fattier fish, like salmon, mackerel, and halibut. But meaty fish like tuna and swordfish work very well, and lean fish can also be broiled, as long as you watch the time. My favorite candidates are the meaty, steaky varieties, like salmon and tuna. There is something very satisfying about eating a nice, simply broiled fish steak. But I love the seared flavor broiling gives to any fish, and you will find a variety of recipes using this method here. To ensure that your fish stays moist, marinate for 20 minutes or longer in some kind of liquid with a little oil (see Broiled Salmon Steaks, page 239, and Broiled or Grilled Flat Fish with Sorrel Puree, page 246), and baste once halfway through the cooking. Preheat the broiler for about 15 minutes and make sure your rack is oiled, to prevent sticking. Place the fish 4 inches from the heat, and cook 10 minutes per inch of thickness, turning halfway through.

Grilling: Any fish that can be broiled can also be grilled, and again, the fatty and meaty varieties are good candidates (but light fish are just as delicious cooked this way). Strong-tasting fish like mackerel and sardines are also fabulous cooked over aromatic wood, as the smoky flavor compliments their own. I have delicious memories of eating fresh sardines grilled in the fireplace at Domaine Tempier, the winery I love so much in Bandol. This was during the wintertime, when sardines are large and fleshy, and the Peyrauds knew how to cook them just right, so that the skin was crisp and the flesh succulent, the whole fish aromatic with the vine branches over which they were cooked. A large plate full of these grilled treasures, washed down with the Domaine's cool, light, crisp Bandol Rosé wine and followed by a simple green salad and goat cheese made a perfect lunch.

Rules for grilling are similar to those for broiling. It helps to marinate fish, especially the less oily varieties, for 20 to 30 minutes beforehand. It is also useful to have a hinged grill (which should be oiled), so that you can turn the fish easily without the risk of breaking steaks or fillets. For whole fish a fish-shaped hinged grilling basket is very handy.

Electric or gas barbecue grills should be preheated for 15 minutes; charcoal and wood need 30 to 40 minutes to develop the ash that indicates correct cooking temperature (about 350 degrees or 180° C). Cook fish for about 10 minutes per inch of thickness, but watch extra carefully, as the heat can be altered by wind, humidity, and air currents.

Frying: Frying is not my favorite cooking method, as you know, since I try to be as low-fat a cook as possible. But certain small fish, like smelts and small sardines, can only be fried, as they will fall apart when cooked any other way. Frying exposes fish to very high heat, creating a protective seal that locks in flavor. For many fried-fish recipes, like the Flounder or Sole Amandine on page 243, clarified butter and oil can be kept to a minimum (you must use butter and oil in combination, or clarified butter, because unclarified butter alone will burn at the high cooking temperatures), especially if you use a nonstick skillet. Stir-fried, and of course deep-fried, fish, require much more oil. Clarified butter is butter from which the solid fat particles have been removed. These burn quickly when butter is used for frying at high heat. To make clarified butter, heat the butter to just simmering and skim off solids. Continue to skim until perfectly clear. Remove from the heat and store in the refrigerator.

Lean, firm-fleshed fish are the best candidates for frying. The oilier varieties will yield too rich results. They need to be dusted with a protective coating, like flour, bread crumbs, beaten egg white, and /or cornstarch, or, as in Sole Amandine, beaten egg, then ground almonds, before they are exposed to the heat. This prevents burning, and also keeps the fish in one piece.

Dealing with a large whole fish: The most difficult aspect of working with a large whole fish is handling it after it has been cooked, as it can easily fall apart. To transfer a large fish from cooking vessel to platter, grasp it firmly on the top and bottom with two large spatulas and lift quickly. If the fish has been grilled, open the hinged grill and turn the platter upside down over the fish. Hold the platter against the fish and turn platter side down. Gently lift the grill up from the fish, easing the fish off the grill with a spatula.

To separate the flesh from the cooked fish, first remove the skin by slitting from head to tail with a small sharp knife along the back and belly and lifting off the skin with fingers or a flat fish knife. Then make an incision down the middle of the fish through to the backbone, tilting the knife so that you can ease the flesh off from the bones in one or two long pieces. Remove the fillets from both sides of the backbone, then gently pull the tail up and forward toward the head, using a knife if necessary to ease the bottom fillets away from the bones. Discard head and bones and serve bottom fillets.

GETTING STARTED

Using the chart: The recipes that follow will be as satisfying and easy for the novice as they are for the practiced fish cook. To clarify things further, below is a table that will tell you at a glance how to match up fish with cooking method, what the different fish taste like, and what kind of nutritional value each kind has to offer.

Fish's taste is often linked to its fat content: Fattier (oilier) fish are usually stronger-tasting than their lean counterparts—so the higher the percentage of calories from fat (see details below), the more pronounced the flavor. Use this table to match up other fish factors as well—calories, nutrients, taste/texture, and cooking methods.

FISH (3½ ounces)	CALS.	% OF PROTEIN	% OF FAT	TASTE/ TEXTURE	BEST COOKING METHODS
Bluefish	107	19.2	3.3	Strong taste, soft flesh	Bake, broil, grill
Cod	74	17.4	0.5	Mild taste, firm texture	Poach, steam, bake, broil, grill
Flounder	94	16.3	3.2	Delicate taste, soft flesh	Steam, bake
Haddock	77	18.2	0.5	Delicate taste, firm texture	Poach, steam, bake, broil, grill
Halibut	119	18.7	4.3	Light taste, firm texture	Poach, steam, bake, broil, grill
Herring	122	17.7	2.8	Pronounced flavor, soft texture	Bake, broil, grill

FISH (3½ ounces)	CALS.	% OF PROTEIN	% OF FAT	TASTE/ TEXTURE	BEST COOKING METHODS
Mackerel	167	19.5	9.9	Strong taste, firm texture	Bake, broil, grill
Mullet	122	20.1	4.6	Nutty flavor, firm texture	Bake, broil, grill
Red Snapper	88	19.4	1.1	Light flavor, firm-fleshed	Poach, steam, bake, broil, grill
Salmon	163	19.9	9.3	Smooth taste, "steaky" and firm-fleshed	Poach, steam, bake, broil, grill
Shad	152	19.4	8.3	Strong taste, firm texture	Bake, broil, grill
Sole	83	17.9	1.0	Delicate taste, fine texture	Poach, steam, bake, broil
Striped Bass	92	18.2	3.1	Moderate to strong taste, firm texture	Poach, steam, bake, broil, grill
Swordfish	118	19.4	4.4	Strong taste, "steaky," firm, dense texture	Poach, steam, bake, broil, grill
Tilefish	95	19.1	2.1	Light flavor, firm texture	Poach, steam, bake, broil, grill
Trout	94	18.8	3.1	Moderately strong taste, firm-fleshed	Poach, steam, bake, broil, grill

FISH (3½ ounces)	CALS.	% OF PROTEIN	% OF FAT	TASTE/ TEXTURE	BEST COOKING METHODS
Tuna	145	24.7	5.1	Mild taste, firm-fleshed	Bake, broil, grill
Whiting	90	18.9	1.3	Mild flavor, firm texture	Poach, steam, bake, broil, grill

Sources:

Pennington, Jean A. T., Ph.D., R.D., and Church, Helen Nichols, B.S., *Food Values of Portions Commonly Used,* Harper & Row, Publishers, New York, 1980

Time-Life Books, Editors, *Fish,* Time-Life Books, Alexandria, Virginia, 1980

COURT BOUILLON

1 onion, sliced
1 carrot, sliced
1 leek, sliced
1 branch celery, sliced
1 bouquet garni made with 1 bay leaf, 1 sprig parsley, 1 sprig thyme
1 quart (1 l) water
1 teaspoon (5 ml) salt
2 cups (½ l) dry white wine
6 peppercorns

Combine the vegetables, bouquet garni, water, and salt and bring to a boil. Reduce heat and simmer, uncovered, 15 minutes. Add the wine and peppercorns, cover, and simmer another 15 minutes. Strain.

VINEGAR COURT BOUILLON

Substitute ½ cup vinegar (or more, to taste), for the wine. Simmer the mixture, uncovered, for 30 to 40 minutes. Strain.

MILK POACHING LIQUID

  1 cup (220 ml) milk
  4 cups (1 l) water
  1 teaspoon (5 ml) salt
1 to 2 lemons, skin and pith removed, sliced in rounds, seeds
    removed

Combine all the ingredients. The mixture is ready for poaching and
no previous cooking is required.

FISH FUMET

1 pound (500g) fish trimmings, such as heads and bones
1 quart (1 l) water
1 onion, peeled and quartered
2 cloves garlic, peeled
1 carrot, sliced
1 stalk celery, sliced
1 leek, white part only, cleaned and sliced
1 bouquet garni made with bay leaf, thyme, and parsley
1 teaspoon (5 ml) salt
1 cup dry white wine

Combine all the ingredients except the salt and wine and bring to a
simmer. Skim off all the foam that rises (it's bitter). When all the foam
has been skimmed off, cover and simmer 15 minutes. Add the white
wine and salt, cover, and simmer another 15 minutes. Strain at once
through a double layer of cheesecloth or a dish towel. Set aside.

TUNA OR SWORDFISH À LA MARSEILLAISE
SERVES 4 TO 6
PREPARATION TIME: 15 minutes
COOKING TIME: 40 minutes, in all

I first ate tuna steaks, grilled just right so that they were still succulent, at Domaine Tempier, the winery near Bandol where I cooked
with Lulu during the harvest. This fish dish, served with the garlicky,
pungent tomato-caper sauce, is one of my favorites. I use the sauce
with other fish too (see Baked Whiting with Tomato-Caper Sauce on
page 232), and I also use it for pasta and grains.

FOR THE SAUCE:

1 tablespoon (15 ml) olive oil
1 small or ½ medium onion, finely chopped
1 cup capers, rinsed and chopped in a food processor or mashed with a mortar and pestle
8 cloves garlic, peeled and chopped (can be chopped or mashed along with the capers)
2½ pounds (1.2 kg) tomatoes, chopped
Freshly ground pepper to taste

FOR THE FISH:

4 to 6 tuna or swordfish steaks, about 4 ounces (115 g) each
Olive or safflower oil

First make the sauce. Heat 1 tablespoon olive oil in a large, heavy-bottomed skillet and add the onion. Sauté for a few minutes and add the capers and garlic. Sauté, stirring for 5 minutes, and add the tomatoes. Cook, stirring from time to time, over medium-low heat for 20 to 30 minutes. Add freshly ground pepper. Set aside.

The fish can be either grilled or sautéed. Brush steaks with olive oil and cook over aromatic wood, or sauté in a skillet in 1 tablespoon olive oil over medium-high heat for approximately 10 minutes (according to thickness), turning halfway through the cooking. Watch closely, because tuna and swordfish will become cotton-dry if you overcook them. The steaks should remain pink in the middle.

Remove from the heat and serve immediately, topped with the tomato-caper sauce.

MENU SUGGESTIONS

See Baked Whiting with Tomato-Caper Sauce, below.

BAKED WHITING WITH TOMATO-CAPER SAUCE
SERVES 6

PREPARATION TIME: 15 minutes
COOKING TIME: 30 minutes

The sauce for this simple dish can be made several hours or even days in advance and kept in the refrigerator. It is the same sauce used in Tuna or Swordfish à la Marseillaise, page 231. It's so delicious that you'll probably find plenty of other uses for it, as I have. For example, it makes a terrific sauce for pasta, or topping for grains. It will go well with all kinds of fish.

FOR THE SAUCE:

1 tablespoon olive oil

1 small onion or ½ medium onion, finely chopped

1 cup capers, rinsed and chopped in a food processor or mashed with a mortar and pestle

8 cloves garlic, peeled and chopped (can be chopped or mashed along with the capers)

2½ pounds (1.2 kg) tomatoes, chopped

Freshly ground pepper to taste

FOR THE FISH:

Butter for the baking dish

6 small whiting, cleaned, heads removed

Salt and freshly ground pepper to taste

½ cup (120 ml) dry white wine

First make the sauce. Heat the olive oil in a large, heavy-bottomed skillet and add the onion. Sauté for a few minutes and add the capers and garlic. Sauté, stirring, for 5 minutes, and add the tomatoes. Cook over moderate heat, stirring occasionally, for 20 to 30 minutes. Season to taste with freshly ground pepper.

Meanwhile preheat the oven to 425 degrees (220° C). Butter a rectangular or oval baking dish. Wipe the fish and pat dry with a dish towel. Lay side by side, alternating head end to tail end, in the buttered baking dish. Salt and pepper lightly. Place the wine in a saucepan, bring to a simmer, and pour over the fish. Cover with buttered wax paper and bake 10 to 15 minutes in the preheated oven. Serve with some of the sauce on the top and more on the side.

MENU SUGGESTIONS

Soups or Starters: Pureed Zucchini Soup (page 70); Very Quick Cream of Pea Soup (page 85); Cold Pasta Salad (page 302)

Side Dishes: Whole Grain Pasta with Butter and Herbs (page 214); simply steamed vegetables of your choice; Baked Potatoes (page 164) or Pressure-Cooked Potatoes (page 165)

Salads: Tossed Green Salad (page 280); Lettuce Salad with Oranges (page 281)

Desserts: Strawberries in Champagne (page 311); Cantaloupe with Apricot Puree and Almonds (page 313)

♥ COD FILLETS WITH TOMATO-MINT SAUCE
SERVES 6

PREPARATION TIME: 15 minutes
COOKING TIME: 15 minutes

The sauce for this refreshing combination can be made several hours in advance, and will hold for a few days in the refrigerator. Other white fish, such as sole or whiting, would also work here.

FOR THE SAUCE:
2 pounds (1 kg) tomatoes, peeled and seeded
1 small clove garlic
3 tablespoons fresh mint
3 tablespoons (45 ml) red wine vinegar
2 tablespoons (30 ml) olive oil (optional)
  Salt and freshly ground pepper to taste

FOR THE FISH:
1½ pounds (750 g) cod fillets
  Salt and pepper to taste
½ cup (120 ml) dry white wine
  Butter for the baking dish

Preheat the oven to 425 degrees (220° C). Butter a baking dish large enough for the fillets.

Make the sauce. Blend together the tomatoes, garlic, mint, and vinegar in a blender, or mash together with a mortar and pestle until smooth. Drizzle in the oil and add salt and freshly ground pepper to taste. This can also be prepared like a salsa fresca, the ingredients finely chopped instead of blended together. The sauce can be chilled several hours, served at room temperature, or heated through over medium-low heat in a saucepan.

Lay the fillets side by side in the baking dish, and salt and pepper lightly, to taste. Add the wine and cover with buttered foil or wax paper. Bake 10 to 15 minutes. Serve, topping the fillets with the sauce.

Note: This could also be served cold.

MENU SUGGESTIONS
Soups or Starters: Pureed Zucchini Soup (page 70); Very Quick Cream of Pea Soup (page 85); Cold Pasta Salad (page 302)
Side Dishes: Zucchini with Rosemary or Other Herbs (page 167); Mushrooms with White Wine and Herbs (page 158); simply steamed vegetables

Salads: Tossed Green Salad (page 280); Jícama and Orange Salad with Avocados (page 295); Cucumber Yogurt Salad (page 282)
Desserts: Orange Ice (page 318); Strawberries in Champagne (page 311); Apples with Lime Juice (page 312)

♥ Omit olive oil and salt.

♥ STEAMED WHOLE SEA BASS OR FLOUNDER À LA CHINOISE
SERVES 4

PREPARATION TIME: 30 minutes
COOKING TIME: 15 minutes

This makes a dramatic-looking main dish for a dinner party. It's light, succulent, and redolent with ginger.

1 sea bass, flounder, or other lean, light-fleshed fish, cleaned and scaled with head and tail left on, weighing about 2 pounds (1 kg)
3 tablespoons (45 ml) shredded fresh ginger
4 tablespoons (60 ml) dry sherry
2 tablespoons (30 ml) soy sauce
1 teaspoon (2.5 ml) mild-flavored honey
2 teaspoons (10 ml) Pernod
3 large scallions, cut in ½-inch-wide shreds
3 tablespoons (45 ml) safflower oil

Fill your steamer with water to within 1 to 2 inches of the bottom of the steaming basket.

Rinse and dry the fish. Score diagonally at 1-inch (2 cm) intervals across each side. Place on a heatproof plate that will fit into your steamer.

Slice the ginger very thin, then cut in julienne-type slivers.

Mix together the sherry, soy sauce, honey, and Pernod. Brush the fish inside the slits and all over the surface with this mixture. Stuff some of the ginger into the slits and sprinkle the rest over the surface. Retain the sauce for serving with the fish.

Bring the water in your steamer to a boil. Carefully place the platter on the rack (wear mitts). Steam the fish for about 15 minutes, or until it is opaque and flakes easily with a fork or chopstick. Add more boiling water if necessary.

Remove the fish from the heat and carefully transfer to a serving platter. Pour on whatever juices have collected on the plate and sprinkle with the scallions. Heat the oil in a saucepan until very hot but not smoking, and carefully pour it over the fish. Serve at once, passing the remaining sauce.

MENU SUGGESTIONS

Soups or Starters: Hot and Sour Soup (page 67); Buckwheat Noodle Soup with Green Beans (page 63); Simple Miso Soup (page 68), Hot and Sour Buckwheat Noodle Salad (page 300)

Side dishes: Hot cooked grains or buckwheat pasta; Chinese-Style Snow Peas and Water Chestnuts (page 140); Chinese Cabbage with Sesame and Ginger (page 144)

Salads: Oriental Salad (page 297); Cold Marinated Zucchini, Oriental Style (page 301); Hot and Sour Bean Sprout Salad (page 298)

Desserts: Orange Ice (page 318); Pineapple Banana Mint Sherbet (page 316); Baked Grapefruit with Tequila or Sherry (page 313)

♥ Omit soy sauce. Omit oil.

♥ TROUT EN PAPILLOTE WITH LEMON AND DILL
SERVES 4

PREPARATION TIME: 20 minutes
COOKING TIME: 15 minutes

Cooking in an aluminum pouch—en papillote—is about the simplest and one of the most satisfying ways to prepare fish. Whether you cook the entire fish in the foil, as in this recipe, or you use fillets, the fish steams in its own liquid and no flavor or moisture are lost. The shallots and dill give this trout a fine taste.

4 small trout, each weighing about 6 ounces (170 g), cleaned and scaled
4 teaspoons (20 ml) safflower oil
8 sprigs fresh dill
4 teaspoons (20 ml) lemon juice
  Salt and freshly ground pepper to taste
2 shallots, minced
4 tablespoons (60 ml) dry white wine or vermouth
2 lemons, peeled, with white pith removed, sliced in thin rounds

Preheat the oven to 425 degrees (220° C). Rinse the trout and wipe dry.

Cut four double thicknesses of aluminum foil, each twice the size of the trout. Brush each with a teaspoon of safflower oil and lay a fish on each one.

Stuff the cavities of the fish with two sprigs dill and sprinkle with lemon juice. Season the fish with salt and freshly ground pepper to taste. Top the fish with the shallots, a few lemon slices, and white wine or vermouth.

Join the edges of the foil and pinch together, crimping the edges well so that none of the juice escapes. Place the papillotes in a baking dish and bake for 10 to 15 minutes in the preheated oven (test one after 10 minutes to see if the fish flakes easily with a fork and is opaque). Serve the fish from the pouches at once (do not open them), placing a pouch on each plate.

MENU SUGGESTIONS

Soups and Starters: Warm or Chilled Broccoli Vinaigrette (page 290); Gazpacho (page 87); Simple Garlic Soup Provençal (page 64)

Side Dishes: Tomatoes Florentine (page 171); Brussels Sprouts with Lemon-Mustard Butter (page 149); Mushrooms with White Wine and Herbs (page 158)

Salad of your choice

Desserts: Prune Soufflé (page 307); Strawberries in Red Wine (page 315); Peaches with Marsala or Amaretto (page 314)

♥ Omit salt.

♥ FISH FILLETS EN PAPILLOTE WITH GARLIC AND MUSHROOMS
SERVES 4

PREPARATION TIME: 20 minutes
COOKING TIME: 15 minutes

This simple, light preparation, fragrant with rosemary but not over-whelmed by the herb, is great for a dinner party. You can prepare the papillotes way ahead of time and put them in the oven during the first course. The fish is so light that you could serve a substantial first course like Fettucine with Pesto (page 215), and your guests won't be weighed down. These fillets should be eaten right from the packets so you don't lose any of the juice.

1 pound (500 g) fillets of sole, snapper, sea bass, or other white-
  fleshed fish
1 tablespoon (15 ml) safflower oil, or olive oil, or butter
  Salt and freshly ground pepper to taste
8 large mushrooms or 16 medium, cleaned and sliced
8 cloves garlic, cut in lengthwise slivers
2 tablespoons (30 ml) dry white wine
2 lemons, cut in thin slices
4 large sprigs fresh rosemary, or 2 teaspoons dried
  Additional lemon for garnish

Preheat the oven to 425 degrees (220° C)

Cut squares of double-thickness aluminum, each about twice the
size of the fillets. Brush with oil or butter.

Place a fillet on each square and sprinkle with salt and pepper. Top
with the mushrooms and garlic slivers. Sprinkle with white wine and
lay three or four slices of lemon over the mushrooms and garlic. Lay
the rosemary over the lemon slices or sprinkle each fillet with ½
teaspoon dried rosemary. Bring the edges of the foil together over
the fish and seal, crimping them together well so that no juice escapes.

Place the packets in a baking dish and bake in the oven for 10 to
15 minutes (check one after 10 minutes; the fish should be opaque
and should flake easily). Serve at once, placing a packet on each plate
and passing additional lemon wedges, as well as additional salt and
pepper.

MENU SUGGESTIONS

Soups or Starters: Fettucine with Pesto (page 215); Fettucine with Oil,
  Garlic, and Zucchini (page 212); Chilled Lettuce and Potato Soup
  (page 81)
Side dishes: Peppers, Tomatoes, and Herbs (page 161); Broiled
  Tomatoes (page 170); Florentine Tomatoes (page 171)
Salads: Tossed Green Salad (page 280); Tomato and Mozzarella
  Salad (page 282); Cucumbers Vinaigrette (page 283)
Desserts: Puffed Amaretto Omelet (page 306); Figs Poached in
  Madeira (page 311); Peaches Poached in Red Wine (page 309)

♥ Omit salt. Use 2 teaspoons safflower oil.

♥ SNAPPER FILLETS EN PAPILLOTE WITH GREEN SALSA
SERVES 6

PREPARATION TIME: 20 minutes
COOKING TIME: 10 to 15 minutes

Here red snapper fillets are baked in foil, then topped with the picante Green Tomato Sauce on page 262. Serve this with fresh corn tortillas and refried black beans for a fine Mexican dinner.

1 recipe Green Tomato Sauce, page 262
6 red snapper fillets, about 1½ (750 g) pounds in all
    Salt and freshly ground pepper
2 lemons, thinly sliced

Make the Green Tomato Sauce according to the instructions.
    Meanwhile, preheat the oven to 425 degrees (220° C).
    Butter 6 squares of double-thickness aluminum, each about twice the size of the fillets. Place the fillets on the squares, salt and pepper lightly and top with several slices of lemon. Bring the edges of the foil up around the fillets and seal tightly. Place on a baking sheet and bake in the preheated oven for 10 to 15 minutes.
    Remove the fish from the foil and drizzle on any liquid. Top with sauce and serve, passing extra sauce on the side.

MENU SUGGESTIONS
Soups or Starters: Chilled Melon Soup (page 88); Gazpacho (page 87); Guacamole (page 283); Jícama and Orange Salad with Avocados (page 295)
Side Dishes: Refried black beans; Simple Picante Zucchini (page 168); steamed new potatoes or cooked grains
Desserts: Peach Banana Freeze (page 316); Cantaloupe with Apricot Puree and Almonds (page 313); Strawberry Sherbet (page 317)

♥ Omit salt. Use safflower oil for the foil.

♥ BROILED SALMON STEAKS
SERVES 4

PREPARATION TIME: 5 minutes
MARINATING TIME: 20 minutes
COOKING TIME: 10 minutes

In 1984 I spent the month of August in Eugene, Oregon. It was the sunny season, the best time to be there. I was working on a book, and every day when I finished my work I'd go for a swim, then I'd often stop at the nearby fish market, where they would invariably have the best salmon I've ever tasted. I'd usually cook it just like this, and serve it with sweet corn and homegrown tomatoes, because they were at their peak too.

     Juice of 1 lime
  2 tablespoons (30 ml) soy sauce
  1 teaspoon (5 ml) mild-flavored honey (optional)
  1 tablespoon (15 ml) safflower oil
  1 tablespoon (15 ml) chopped fresh ginger
  2 cloves garlic, minced or put through a press
  4 salmon steaks, about ¾ inch (1½–2 cm) thick

Combine the lime juice, soy sauce, honey, safflower oil, ginger, and garlic. Mix together well and place in a baking dish. Lay the salmon steaks in this mixture and let marinate for 20 minutes, turning once.
     Meanwhile, preheat the broiler.
     Place the baking dish with the salmon in it 3 to 4 inches from the heat and broil the steaks 4 to 5 minutes on each side, basting once on each side. Serve at once.

MENU SUGGESTIONS

This goes beautifully with whole baked tomatoes, which you can cook in the oven while you are preheating the broiler and cooking the fish. The Broiled Tomatoes on page 170 or the Florentine Tomatoes on page 171 also work well, along with simple steamed potatoes or corn on the cob. Also see soup, salad, and dessert suggestions for Salmon Fillets Simmered in Sake, page 241. Also for dessert, any of the ices in this book.

  ♥ Omit soy sauce.

♥ SALMON FILLETS SIMMERED IN SAKE
SERVES 4 TO 6
PREPARATION TIME: 25 minutes
COOKING TIME: 15 minutes, in all

This is a dish for the ginger lover, inspired by a recipe in Bruce Cost's wonderful *Ginger East to West* (Aris Books). The salmon fillets will be succulent and heady with sake, ginger, and the fragrant mushroom soaking liquid.

1 ounce (30 g) Chinese mushrooms or dried cepes
1 cup (225 ml) boiling water
1½ pounds (750 g) salmon fillets
1 cup (225 ml) sake
4 tablespoons shredded ginger
1 teaspoon (5 ml) mild-flavored honey
2 tablespoons (30 ml) soy sauce
1 teaspoon (5 ml) sesame oil
Chopped fresh coriander for garnish (optional)

Place the mushrooms in a bowl and pour on boiling water. Let sit 20 minutes, or until softened. Strain through a fine cheesecloth and retain liquid. Rinse the mushrooms and cut in slivers.

Rinse the fish, remove small bones, and pat dry.

Combine the sake and liquid from the mushrooms in a flameproof casserole or pan wide enough to accommodate the fillets, and add the ginger in a layer. Lay the fish over the ginger and bring to a simmer. Cover and simmer 3 minutes.

Combine honey and soy sauce and sprinkle over the fish. Cook uncovered 4 more minutes, or until the fish flakes easily with a fork.

Remove the fish fillets, place on a warm platter, and reduce the sauce by half. Add the mushroom slivers to the sauce and pour over the fish. Sprinkle on the sesame oil and serve, garnishing if you wish with chopped fresh coriander.

MENU SUGGESTIONS

Soups or Starters: Buckwheat Noodle Soup with Green Beans (page 63); Cream of Spinach and Kasha Soup (page 78); Cream of Spinach and Potato Soup (page 80)

Side Dishes: Green Beans Amandine (page 146); simply steamed vegetables; Whole Grain or Buckwheat Pasta with Butter and Herbs (page 214)

Salads: Tossed Green Salad (page 280); Lettuce Salad with Oranges (page 281); Warm or Chilled Broccoli Vinaigrette (page 290)

Desserts: Baked Grapefruit with Tequila or Sherry (page 313); Pineapple Banana Mint Sherbet (page 316); Apples with Lime Juice (page 312)

♥ Omit soy sauce.

♥ FILLETS OF SOLE WITH CUCUMBERS AND DILL
SERVES 4

PREPARATION TIME: 20 to 25 minutes
COOKING TIME: 10 to 15 minutes

The cucumbers here are beautifully seasoned with dill, garlic, and shallots. They provide a moist bed and coverlet for the fillets of sole. You could assemble this dish early in the day and just pop it in the preheated oven 10 to 15 minutes before dinner.

      Butter or safflower oil for the baking dish
 1 cucumber, peeled and cut in thin rounds
 4 tablespoons chopped fresh dill
 1 pound (500 g) fillets of sole
      Salt and freshly ground pepper to taste
 2 large cloves garlic, minced
 2 shallots, minced
 1 tablespoon chopped fresh parsley (optional)
      Juice of 2 lemons
 ¼ cup (60 ml) dry white wine (more if needed)

Butter or oil an attractive baking dish, large enough to accommodate the fillets in one layer. Lay half the sliced cucumbers over the bottom. Sprinkle with a third of the dill.

Rinse the sole fillets and pat dry. Score on the diagonal a few times with a sharp knife, and lay on top of the cucumbers. Lightly salt and pepper, and sprinkle on the garlic, shallot, parsley, another third of the dill, and the lemon juice. Top with the remaining cucumbers. Cover with plastic and marinate in the refrigerator for one hour.

Preheat the oven to 425 degrees (220° C).

Sprinkle the remaining dill over the cucumbers. Pour on the white wine and make sure the entire surface of the baking dish is covered (add a little more if it isn't). Cover with buttered foil or wax paper and place in the oven. Bake for 10 to 15 minutes (10 minutes per inch of thickness of the fish), until the fish is tender and flakes easily with a fork. Remove from the oven and serve from the baking dish, scooping up cucumbers from below and above the fish.

MENU SUGGESTIONS

Soups or Starters: Pureed Curry of Cauliflower Soup (page 79); Simple Garlic Soup Provençal (page 64); Potato Leek Soup (page 65)

Side Dishes: Baked Potatoes (page 164); cooked grains of your choice;

Mushrooms with White Wine and Herbs (page 158); Broiled Tomatoes (page 170)

Salads: Tossed Green Salad (page 280); Tomato Salad (page 284); Tabouli (page 286)

Desserts: Figs Poached in Madeira (page 311); Banana Yogurt Freeze (page 315); Strawberry Freeze (page 317)

♥ Omit salt.

FLOUNDER OR SOLE AMANDINE
SERVES 4

PREPARATION TIME: 10 minutes
COOKING TIME: 6 to 8 minutes

This recipe is derived from my first kitchen flop. It was back when I was just learning to cook, and in those days the family kitchen was stocked with garlic powder and garlic salt (we threw them out a few years later). Every time I wanted to learn a new recipe my stepmother would either give me her recipe, written out neatly on an index card, or point me to the proper book. For sole amandine she told me to salt the fillets lightly with garlic salt and pepper, dip them in egg and ground almonds and fry them in clarified butter. I followed her instructions, but either I confused garlic powder for garlic salt, or I did not go lightly on the garlic salt. Whatever I did, my brothers, whom I was unfortunately responsible for feeding that night, gagged on the fish and never let me forget the incident. Perhaps I became a cook to redeem myself.

1 pound (500 g) flounder or sole fillets
¼ cup (30 g) almonds, coarsely ground
1 tablespoon chopped fresh parsley
2 egg yolks
1 tablespoon (15 ml) milk
1 clove garlic, minced or put through a press
Salt and freshly ground pepper
1 tablespoon (15 ml) safflower oil
1 tablespoon (15 ml) butter (or use 2 tablespoons clarified butter in all)

Rinse the fish fillets and pat dry. Combine the almonds and parsley on a plate. Beat together the egg yolks, milk, and garlic.

Heat together the oil and butter, or the clarified butter in a wide, heavy-bottomed skillet over medium-high heat. Lightly salt and pepper the fish and dip in the egg-yolk mixture. Dip the moistened fillets in the ground almonds and coat on both sides.

Fry the coated fillets in the hot butter and oil or clarified butter for 3 to 5 minutes on each side (depending on their thickness), until browned and cooked through. Serve at once.

MENU SUGGESTIONS
Soups or Starters: Pasta with Broccoli, Calabrian Style (page 213); Hot or Iced Tomato Soup (page 72); Gazpacho (page 87)

Side Dishes: Pasta with Butter and Herbs (page 214); simply steamed vegetables; Green Beans à la Provençale (page 147)

Salads: Tossed Green Salad (page 280); Tomato Salad (page 284); Warm or Chilled Cauliflower or Broccoli Vinaigrette (page 290)

Desserts: Fruit and Cheese Platter (page 322); Orange Ice (page 318); Peaches with Marsala or Amaretto (page 314)

♥ BROILED FISH WITH CORIANDER SAUCE
SERVES 6

PREPARATION TIME: 25 minutes
MARINATING TIME FOR FISH: 15 to 60 minutes
COOKING TIME: 10 minutes

This intriguing coriander sauce would go equally as well with vegetables or grains as it does with grilled or broiled fish. You can thin it out with more of the prune water if you wish; I like the thick version. I also use it as a dip for vegetables and as a spread.

FOR THE FISH:
6 4-ounce (115 g) halibut, cod, swordfish, or tuna steaks
2 tablespoons (30 ml) lemon juice
4 tablespoons (60 ml) safflower oil

FOR THE CORIANDER SAUCE:
6 prunes, pitted
1 cup (30 g) fresh coriander leaves, tightly packed
½ cup (15 g) chopped fresh parsley
¼ cup (60 ml) fresh lime juice
2 cloves garlic, peeled
½ teaspoon peeled fresh ginger, chopped
¼ teaspoon salt
¼ teaspoon freshly ground pepper

FISH

2 to 4 tablespoons (30 to 60 ml) olive or safflower oil, to taste
¼ cup (60 ml) sesame tahini
Cooking water from the prunes, as needed

Marinate the fish in the lemon juice and safflower oil for 15 minutes to an hour, or longer.

Place the prunes in a saucepan and cover with 1 cup (225 ml) water. Bring to a simmer and cook over low heat for 15 minutes. Drain prunes and retain the liquid. Meanwhile prepare the remaining ingredients for the sauce.

In a blender or food processor fitted with the steel blade combine the cooked prunes with all the remaining ingredients except the oil, tahini, and cooking water from the prunes. Blend or process until you have a fairly smooth paste. Add the tahini and continue to blend. Add 2 to 4 tablespoons oil, depending on how thick you want your sauce and also depending on how runny your tahini is. If you have a very oily, runny tahini, use less oil. Thin out to desired consistency (it can be anywhere from dip consistency to sauce consistency) with the cooking water from the prunes.

Preheat the broiler or prepare a grill. Cook the steaks for 8 to 10 minutes, depending on the thickness, turning halfway through the cooking. Serve at once with the sauce on the side.

MENU SUGGESTIONS

Soups or Starters: Chilled Buttermilk Soup (page 86); Cheddar Cheese Soup with Vegetables (page 66); Asparagus or Broccoli Timbale (pages 192–193)

Side Dishes: Cooked grains or whole-grain pasta; simply steamed vegetables; Delicate Corn Fritters (page 155); Broiled Tomatoes (page 170); Florentine Tomatoes (page 171)

Salads: Tossed Green Salad (page 280); Tomato Salad (page 284); Jícama and Orange Salad with Avocado (page 295)

Desserts: Orange Ice (page 318); Strawberry Freeze (page 317); Gingered Fruit (page 312)

♥ Halve the quantity of prunes, tahini, and oil throughout. Omit salt.

♥ BROILED OR GRILLED FLAT FISH WITH SORREL PURÉE

SERVES 4

PREPARATION TIME: 25 minutes
COOKING TIME: 20 to 25 minutes in all

One of my favorite fish preparations in France is simply grilled *barbue* (brill) or turbot on a bed of sorrel or with a sorrel sauce. Both the brill and turbot are flat fish, similar to sole or flounder. Any white flat fish will do for this recipe. The sharp, acidic flavor of the sorrel contrasts nicely with the mild flavor of the fish.

> 2 whole flat fish, such as brill, turbot, sole, lemon sole, or flounder, about 10 ounces (285 g) each, cleaned, skins removed
> Salt and freshly ground pepper
> ¼ cup (60 ml) freshly squeezed lemon juice
> 1 tablespoon (15 ml) safflower oil
> 2 tablespoons (30 ml) butter
> 1¼ pounds (565 g) sorrel, washed, stemmed, and coarsely chopped
> 2 tablespoons (30 ml) either crème fraîche, heavy cream, or plain low-fat yogurt (optional)
> Lemon wedges for garnish

Rinse the fish and pat dry. Season with salt and pepper. Combine the lemon juice and safflower oil, and marinate the fish in the mixture for 20 minutes, turning once, while you prepare the sorrel. Meanwhile light the broiler or prepare your grill.

Heat the butter in a large, heavy-bottomed skillet (not aluminum or cast iron, as the metals will react with the sorrel). Add the sorrel and cook gently, stirring over medium-low heat until it reduces to a purée. It will change color as soon as it begins to cook, from bright green to olive drab (though the flavor remains vibrant), and it will cook down quickly, in about 10 minutes. Mash the sorrel gently with the back of your spoon, taste and season with salt and pepper. If the flavor is too intense, thin out with crème fraîche, heavy cream, or plain low-fat yogurt. Keep warm while you cook the fish.

Grill or broil the fish for 5 minutes on each side and remove from the heat. Divide the sorrel evenly among four plates. Fillet the fish and place two fillets on top of each portion of sorrel. Serve at once, garnishing with lemon wedges.

Soups or Starters: Potato Leek Soup (page 65); Hot or Iced Tomato Soup (page 72); Pasta with Cottage Cheese or Ricotta and Tomato Sauce (page 208)

Side Dishes: Baked Potatoes (page 164); Carrots Cooked in Vodka (page 150); Broiled Tomatoes (page 170)

Salads: Tossed Green Salad (page 280); Tomato Salad (page 284); Curried Carrot Salad (page 284)

Desserts: Prune Soufflé (page 307); Pears Poached in Red Wine (page 309); Strawberries in Red Wine and Preserves Syrup (page 315)

♥ Omit salt. Substitute 2 teaspoons (10 ml) safflower oil for the butter and use a nonstick skillet to cook the sorrel. Use plain low-fat yogurt to thin out sorrel.

POACHED FISH WITH EGG-LEMON SAUCE
SERVES 4

PREPARATION TIME: 20 minutes
COOKING TIME: 40 minutes, in all

The sauce here is something like hollandaise with none of the fat. It's a beautiful dish to look at and I love the lemony taste. I have served it hot and also chilled, which is fabulous. I served it this way for one of my summer dinners in Paris, and it was a big hit. The tarragon adds a very special touch.

2 cups water (500 ml), light vegetable bouillon or fish stock
1 cup (225 ml) dry white wine
1 lemon, thinly sliced
4 black peppercorns
1 bay leaf
1 sprig parsley
1 leek, white part only, cleaned and sliced
Salt to taste
2 large flat white fish, such as sole, brill, turbot, flounder, or plaice, filleted, skins removed (you should have 1 pound (500 g) fillets in all)
4 egg yolks
Juice of 1 to 2 large lemons, to taste
2 tablespoons (30 ml) chopped fresh tarragon
Thin slices of lemon for garnish

Butter a large, flat flameproof casserole large enough to accommodate the fish fillets in one layer. Add one cup of the water or stock, the wine, the thinly sliced lemon, peppercorns, bay leaf, parsley, leek, and salt and bring to a simmer. Simmer 10 minutes while you prepare the fish.

Rinse the fish fillets and pat dry with paper towels. Using the flat side of a large knife, pound the fillets to break down the muscle fibers so that they won't curl when you poach them. Now make two or three diagonal slashes, about $\frac{1}{8}$ inch deep, across the fillets on the skin side.

Add a cup of cold water or stock to the poaching liquid to cool it down. Place the fish fillets in the stock, cover with a piece of buttered parchment, and bring to a simmer over medium heat. Reduce heat and poach the fish for 10 minutes, until fillets are opaque and flake easily. Remove the fish from the liquid with a slotted spatula and place on a serving dish. Keep warm in a very low oven. Strain the liquid into a saucepan. Turn up the heat and reduce to about 1 cup (225 ml). Remove from the heat and let cool a moment.

Beat together the egg yolks and lemon juice (use juice of one lemon at first, then add more if you want a more lemony sauce); add a ladleful or so of the hot stock to this, stir together well, and return mixture to the remaining stock. Stir over low heat until the mixture reaches a creamy consistency, being careful not to bring to a simmer or the eggs will scramble. Remove from the heat and adjust lemon juice, salt, and pepper. Pour over the fish fillets, sprinkle with tarragon and serve, garnishing with thin slices of lemon.

MENU SUGGESTIONS

Soups or Starters: Very Quick Cream of Pea Soup (page 85); Hot or Iced Tomato Soup (page 72); Tabouli with Pressure Cooked Garbanzo Beans (the garbanzos may be omitted) (page 286)

Side Dishes: Simply steamed green vegetable of your choice; Florentine Tomatoes (page 171); Broiled Tomatoes (page 170)

Desserts: Fruit and Cheese Platter (page 322); Strawberries in Red Wine and Preserves Syrup (page 310); Cantaloupe with Apricot Puree and Almonds (page 313)

♥ POACHED REDFISH WITH BABY ARTICHOKES
SERVES 4

PREPARATION TIME: 10 minutes
COOKING TIME: 40 to 45 minutes (mostly unsupervised)

This will be a fast feast only if you can find the tiny purple baby artichokes, which will cook in 30 to 35 minutes. If you can only find larger artichokes, but can also find a few more minutes, follow the recipe and cook the artichokes a little longer, until a leaf pulls away easily. This recipe will work with other types of fish, such as snapper or cod.

    1 pound (500 g) small purple baby artichokes, washed, ends
        trimmed, and cut in half lengthwise
 2½ cups (570 ml) dry white wine
 1½ cups (340 ml) water, as needed
    Juice of ½ lemon
    1 small carrot, sliced
  ½ onion, sliced
    4 large garlic cloves, sliced
    1 bay leaf
    1 sprig parsley
    6 black peppercorns
    Salt to taste
    1 pound (500 g) redfish fillets
    1 lemon, cut in wedges

Combine all the ingredients except the fish and lemon wedges in a casserole or lidded skillet wide enough to eventually accommodate the fish fillets, and bring to a simmer. Cover and cook 30 to 35 minutes over low heat or until the artichokes are tender and a leaf pulls away easily. Meanwhile rinse the fish fillets and pat dry. Remove the artichokes and place on a platter. Discard the bay leaf and parsley.

Add the fish fillets to the casserole, placing them side by side, and add a little more wine or water if fillets are not immersed in the liquid. Simmer 10 minutes, or until the fish is opaque and flakes easily with a fork.

Carefully remove the fillets with a slotted spatula and place on the platter with the artichokes. Turn up the flame and reduce the liquid by half. Adjust salt and pour over the fish and artichokes. Serve, garnishing each portion with lemon wedges.

MENU SUGGESTIONS

Soups and Starters: Potato Leek Soup (page 65); Hot or Iced Tomato Soup (page 72); Warm Potato Salad with Caraway (page 291)

Side Dishes: Baked Potatoes (page 164); Whole Wheat Pasta with Butter and Herbs (page 214); Steamed green vegetables of your choice

Salads: Tossed Green Salad (page 280); Tomato Salad (page 284)

Desserts: Strawberry Sherbet (page 317); fresh fruit

♥ Omit salt.

♥ GRILLED OR BROILED MACKEREL OR BLUEFISH WITH CUMIN AND CORIANDER
SERVES 4

PREPARATION TIME: 15 minutes
MARINATING TIME: 20 minutes
COOKING TIME: 10 to 15 minutes

Oilier, fishy fish like mackerel and bluefish are good candidates for this recipe. You could, however, use a milder fish like flounder or sea bass. The marinade is such a nice combination of flavors that you should not miss trying it, no matter what your fish preference is.

          4 medium-sized mackerel or bluefish, cleaned, heads removed
          1 teaspoon (5 ml) curry powder
          3 cloves garlic, minced or put through a press
          1 tablespoon (15 ml) ground cumin
¼ to ½ teaspoon (1.25 to 2.5 ml) salt, to taste
          ⅓ cup (90 ml) dry white wine
          ¼ cup (60 ml) safflower oil
          ¼ cup (60 ml) lemon juice
    3 to 4 tablespoons (45 to 60 ml) chopped fresh coriander, to taste
          Lemon slices or wedges for garnish

Slash the fish diagonally 2 or 3 times on each side.

Preheat the grill or broiler.

Mix together the curry powder, garlic, cumin, salt, white wine, safflower oil, and lemon juice. Place in a wide bowl and marinate the fish in the mixture for 20 minutes, turning from time to time.

Brush the fish with the marinade, working some of it into the slits, and grill or broil for five to seven minutes on each side, basting once.

Meanwhile heat the marinade to a simmer. When the fish is done, pour on the marinade, sprinkle with the coriander and serve, garnished with lemon slices or wedges.

MENU SUGGESTIONS

Soups or Starters: Curried Carrot Salad (page 284); Fattoush (page 285); Hot and Sour Bean Sprout Salad (page 298); Chilled Melon Soup (page 88)

Side Dishes: Hot cooked grains or plain cooked pasta tossed with butter; Cooked Curried Cucumbers (page 156); Broiled Tomatoes (page 170)

Desserts: Puffed Grand Marnier Omelet (page 307); Peach Banana Freeze (page 316); Orange Ice (page 318)

♥ Omit salt. Reduce oil to 1 tablespoon.

FISH AU GROS SEL
SERVES 4

PREPARATION TIME: 15 minutes
COOKING TIME: 20 minutes

When you first read this recipe you will think: "How can a cook who is concerned with low-sodium diets print a recipe like this in good conscience?" It does seem a bit contradictory, but in fact all the salt acts as a shell for the fish, which retains all of its juices and is protected from the saltiness by its skin. Fish prepared in this fashion is incredibly succulent. Remove the skin before serving and you won't get any of the coarse salt with the superb, delicate fillets. A number of varieties of fish can be prepared in this way; the round type works the best.

5 pounds (2½ kg) coarse sea salt
1 sea bass, porgy, red snapper, sea trout, or bream, weighing 2 to 2½ pounds (1 kg), cleaned, head left on, or 4 small trout (rainbow, sea, brook, salmon), cleaned, heads left on
8 sprigs parsley
   Freshly ground pepper
   Lemon wedges for garnish

Preheat the oven to 425 degrees (220° C).

Cover with a third of the coarse salt the bottom of a baking dish just large enough to accommodate the fish.

Stuff the cavity or cavities of the fish with the parsley and sprinkle the fish with freshly ground pepper.

Place the fish on the salt and bury completely with the remaining salt. Make sure none of the skin is visible.

Bake in the oven for 25 minutes. Remove from the heat. You will hear the fish sizzling. Transfer the fish from the baking dish to a platter, shaking off the loose salt. A hard shell of salt will surround the fish. Gently break it, remove the fish, and take off the skins, which will be salty. Fillet and serve at once, with lemon wedges.

MENU SUGGESTIONS

Soups or Starters: Cream of Spinach and Potato Soup (page 80); Rosemary's Chilled Lettuce and Potato Soup (page 81); Pasta with Broccoli, Calabrian Style (page 213)

Side Dishes: Baked Potatoes (page 164); Florentine Tomatoes (page 171); Simple Picante Zucchini (page 168)

Salad of your choice

Dessert of your choice

♥ SMOKED SALMON WITH RED PEPPERCORNS
SERVES 6
PREPARATION TIME: 10 to 15 minutes

One of my favorite Paris restaurants, Le Muniche, serves a dish called Salmon Cru aux Baies Roses. It is a simple, light dish consisting of very thin slices of raw salmon, marinated in lemon juice and oil and topped with preserved red peppercorns. Red peppercorns have an intriguing flavor, and I owe many thanks to Le Muniche for introducing me to them.

I often crave this dish, and it's such a simple one to duplicate at home. Since I can't always get fresh salmon, I've come up with this smoked-salmon version; it's just as light, and the red peppercorns really make it. You can find red peppercorns preserved in a vinegar-and-water solution at most specialty food shops.

> 1 pound (500 g) smoked salmon (unsalted) or very thinly sliced fillets of salmon
> Juice of 2 limes
> 3 tablespoons (45 ml) safflower or light vegetable oil
> ½ cup (15 g) red peppercorns preserved in vinegar
> 1 to 2 additional limes, thinly sliced, for garnish

Arrange the fish on a platter and top with the lime juice and the oil. Garnish with lime slices. Pour on the red peppercorns and refrigerate, covered, for one hour. Serve with black bread or pumpernickel as a light supper, as a first course, or as a light lunch.

MENU SUGGESTIONS

Main or side dishes: Tortilla Española (page 181); Broccoli or Asparagus Timbale (page 192, 193); Corn Pudding (page 196)
Salad of your choice
Dessert of your choice

SPICY SHRIMP SALAD

SERVES 4 to 6

PREPARATION TIME: 35 minutes
COOKING TIME FOR SHRIMP: up to 1 minute
CHILLING TIME: 1 hour or more, but you may serve it at once

This is an intriguing combination of flavors and textures, based on a recipe from my book *The Vegetarian Feast,* where I used tofu in a similar salad. The shrimp is fabulous, and now all of you who don't like tofu will have access to a truly special dish.

For the Dressing:

 1 large tomato, peeled
 ¼ cup (7.5 g) fresh coriander leaves
 ¼ cup (7.5 g) fresh mint leaves
1 to 2 small hot green chili peppers (to taste)
 1 garlic clove, peeled
 1 teaspoon (5 ml) freshly grated ginger root
 2 green onions, both white part and green, coarsely chopped
 ¼ cup (60 ml) lemon or lime juice
 ½ cup (120 ml) plain low-fat yogurt
 2 tablespoons (30 ml) olive oil or safflower oil
 ½ teaspoon (2.5 ml) whole coriander seed
   Salt and freshly ground pepper to taste

For the Salad:

 2 pounds (1 kg) shrimp, shelled and deveined
 1 cucumber, peeled, seeded, and diced
 2 large tomatoes, peeled and chopped
 1 small green pepper, seeded and diced
 3 green onions, both white part and green, chopped
 1 orange, peeled, white pith removed, sectioned
 1 banana, sliced and tossed with 1 tablespoon lemon juice
 ½ cup (55 g) broken walnuts or pecans, plus 2 tablespoons for garnish

For Garnish:

   Leaf lettuce
 ½ cup (15 g) alfalfa sprouts
   Fresh chopped coriander
   Lime wedges

Puree all the ingredients for the dressing in a blender or food processor fitted with the steel blade. Adjust seasonings and set aside while you prepare the remaining ingredients.

Bring a large pot of water to a boil and add the shrimp. Cook 30 seconds to a minute, until they turn pink. Drain and refresh under cold water. Toss with the remaining salad ingredients, then toss with the dressing. Cover and chill for an hour or more, or serve at once.

To serve, line a platter, bowl, or individual plates with lettuce leaves, top with the salad, and garnish with alfalfa sprouts, chopped fresh coriander, a sprinkling of chopped walnuts or pecans, and a wedge of lime.

MENU SUGGESTIONS

I would serve this as a main dish for a light lunch or supper. Start with a light soup, like Gazpacho (page 87), Hot or Iced Tomato Soup (page 72), or Peach Soup (page 90). For dessert I might serve a soufflé, like the Apricot Soufflé on page 308, a Puffed Grand Marnier Omelet (page 307), or something a little more substantial, like Rice or Leftover Grains Pudding (page 321) or Noodle Kugel (page 318).

♥ CEVICHE
SERVES 4

PREPARATION TIME: 30 minutes
UNSUPERVISED MARINATING: 8 hours

Even though this dish has to marinate for at least eight hours, I'm including it here because the actual preparation time is so short. It's really just a question of squeezing limes, dicing the fish fillets and a few vegetables, covering, and chilling. Do it in the morning and dinner is a snap.

This is one of the purest, lightest ways I can think of to serve fish. There are a number of versions of ceviche; the kinds of fish, degree of piquancy, and garnishes vary from recipe to recipe. Diana Kennedy uses oily fish like mackerel or sierra, whereas others use snapper or bay scallops or redfish. In France I usually use cod or whiting fillets. I like their nice white tender flesh and mild flavor. My ceviche is always a big hit here (I admit I am very conservative when it comes to hot peppers; the French do not have Tex-Mex palates); I often serve it as a first course at my Mexican dinners.

1 pound (500 g) fish fillets, such as cod, red snapper, whiting, redfish, mackerel or sierra

Juice of 7 large limes

1 small onion, sliced

1 small clove garlic, minced or put through a press

2 canned jalapeño or serrano peppers, seeded and chopped

2 medium tomatoes, chopped

Salt and freshly ground pepper to taste

1 large or 2 small ripe avocados, diced

¼ cup (60 ml) olive oil

4 tablespoons (60 ml) chopped fresh coriander

FOR THE PLATE:

Either 6 ounces (170 g) large spinach leaves, washed and stemmed, *or* 1 head Boston or leaf lettuce

½ avocado, sliced

2 tomatoes, sliced

2 ears corn, cooked and broken into 3-inch pieces (optional)

Additional fresh coriander

Cut the fish fillets into ½-inch cubes and place in a bowl. Pour on the lime juice and toss together well. Marinate, covered, in the refrigerator for seven hours, making sure the fish is completely submerged. Stir occasionally. The fish should be opaque.

Add the onion, garlic, jalapeño or serrano peppers, chopped tomatoes, salt and pepper, avocado, and olive oil and refrigerate another hour or more. Toss with the coriander shortly before serving, and adjust seasonings.

Line salad plates with leaves of spinach, or with lettuce leaves. Top with the ceviche. Garnish with slices of avocado and tomato, and the corn on the cob. Sprinkle with coriander and serve.

This makes a good first course for a Mexican meal, or a light lunch or supper.

MENU SUGGESTIONS

Serve any of the taco dishes on pages 259–271 as a main course, and a fruit dessert. The Jícama and Orange Salad with Avocados (page 295) would be an excellent accompaniment.

♥ Omit salt, avocados, and oil. You could add extra hot peppers for added flavor.

♥ LULU'S ESCABECHE AUX SARDINES
SERVES 6 TO 8

PREPARATION TIME: 30 minutes
COOKING TIME: 25 minutes
MARINATING TIME FOR FISH AND VEGETABLES: 2 hours to 2 days

This is another recipe I learned at Domaine Tempier, the winery in the South of France. During my stay there in 1981, this was served for lunch as a first course on the first day of the harvest; the next day I left the vineyards to work in the kitchen with Lulu Peyraud. You can prepare this up to two days ahead of the time you wish to serve it; the longer the fish marinate the more vinegary they become.

6 to 8   small fresh sardines per person (about 1½ to 2 pounds) (750 g to 1 kg)
    4   tablespoons (60 ml) olive oil
    4   tablespoons (60 ml) red wine vinegar
    3   medium-sized yellow onions, chopped
    1   medium-sized carrot, minced
    3   large cloves garlic, minced or put through a press
        Salt and freshly ground pepper to taste
    2   lemons, cut in wedges
        Fresh chopped parsley for garnish

Scale the sardines, remove heads, and clean. Rinse and pat dry with paper towels.

Heat 2 tablespoons (30 ml) of the olive oil in a large, heavy-bottomed skillet and sauté the sardines on both sides over medium heat until the flesh is white and flakes easily, about 1 to 2 minutes per side, depending on the size of the fish. Remove from the pan, drain on paper towels, and place in a casserole. Toss with 2 tablespoons (30 ml) of the vinegar and set aside.

Rinse the pan, dry and heat the remaining 2 tablespoons olive oil. Add the onions, carrot, and garlic and sauté over medium heat, stirring often, until the onions are soft and golden. Add the remaining 2 tablespoons of the vinegar and continue to cook over medium-low heat for 10 minutes. Season to taste with salt and pepper and remove from the heat.

Spread the onion mixture over the sardines, cover the casserole, and refrigerate for two hours or longer, tossing occasionally. Serve topped with chopped fresh parsley and garnished with lemon wedges.

This will keep for 2 days in the refrigerator.

Serve this as a first course. Main dishes that could follow might be any of the pasta dishes or tacos in this book, or the risottos on pages 108–112. With a tossed green salad on the side and a fruit dessert, this would make a fine dinner.

♥ Reduce oil to 2 tablespoons (30 ml). Use safflower oil. Omit salt.

TACOS

SALSA FRESCA
GREEN TOMATO SAUCE
COOKED SALSA
AVOCADO TACOS
POTATO AND REFRIED BEAN TACOS*
POTATO AND EGG TACOS
POTATO AND CHEESE TACOS
POTATO, TOFU, AND TOMATO TACOS
EGG AND POBLANO TACOS
TOFU AND POBLANO TACOS
MUSHROOM TACOS
GREEN TOMATO, CORN, AND TOFU TACOS

I ate my first taco at the age of twelve on a beach in Acapulco. It was filled with refried black beans, shredded lettuce, and crumbled white cheese. I loved it and still remember the flavors vividly.

Tacos are one of those perfect dishes, like pasta, that can make an exciting dinner with very little effort. My editor says her young daughter often makes them when it's her turn to cook at home. When I was testing taco recipes for this book I couldn't throw enough taco bashes.

The recipes that follow represent only a smattering of what you can fill a taco with. Should you have leftover vegetables from a previous meal, sauté them with a chopped serrano or jalapeño pepper, add

*Auxiliary recipe

cheese or tofu and sprouts, and make tacos. As long as you have Salsa Fresca, (page 261) which takes just a few minutes to prepare, almost anything can be transformed into a Tex-Mex, if not authentic Mexican, meal. I have some friends who love to make a big pot of beans on a Monday and eat soft tacos all through the week.

When I make crispy tacos I use less oil than most cooks to fry them. The tortillas don't burn, because I watch them carefully and cook them quickly. However, if you find that it's hard for you to get the knack of this, do use a bit more oil.

If you don't want to consume any of the fat that is involved in frying the tacos, and you want even faster meals, you can make soft tacos just by warming the tortillas through in a dry skillet or, even better, steaming them before filling. Or you can make chalupas, flat crisp tortillas with the fillings mounded on top. (To prepare the tortillas for chalupas, bake in a 250-degree (120°C) oven for 15 minutes, until crisp.) By substituting soft tacos and chalupas for fried tortillas, people on a low-fat, low-salt diet can enjoy many of the recipes in this chapter. (Remember also to omit the salt, tamari, and cheese called for in recipes, and to reduce the quantity of any oil.)

Another nice way to serve tacos—and this makes it really easy for the cook—is to let people assemble their own. If you have the prepared tortillas on one plate and the fillings and garnishes in separate bowls, you can make an attractive buffet.

Menu suggestions are similar for all the taco recipes. They go well with light soups, fairly simple vegetable side dishes, and crispy salads. Picante side dishes like Simple Picante Zucchini (page 168) would match well, as do avocado dishes. One of my favorite Mexican-food night-salads is Jícama and Orange Salad with Avocados (page 295). See the menus in the front section and Appendix for further ideas.

GENERAL DIRECTIONS FOR FRIED TACOS

First heat the tortillas in a dry skillet on both sides for a few seconds so that they will be flexible. Fill them by placing the filling down the middle of the tortillas and folding the tortillas in half over the filling. Heat 2 tablespoons (30 ml) safflower oil, or more if necessary, in a heavy-bottomed skillet and sauté the filled tacos on both sides, until just beginning to crisp; you don't want them to be as hard as chalupa crisps. Drain on paper towels, and fill with garnishes.

RECOMMENDED GARNISHES FOR TACOS AND CHALUPAS:

Salsa Fresca (page 221)
Green Tomato Sauce (page 222)
Cooked Salsa (page 222)
Alfalfa sprouts
Shredded lettuce or cabbage
Yogurt
Sliced radishes
Sliced olives
Sunflower seeds
Chopped fresh cilantro
Sauce from Pasta with Tofu Cream Sauce (page 209)
Pickled hot peppers

SALSAS

These can be made fresh each time you serve tacos, or you can make the cooked salsas ahead of time and have them on hand in the refrigerator.

♥ SALSA FRESCA
1½ CUPS
PREPARATION TIME: 5 minutes

3 medium ripe tomatoes, minced (1 pound; 450 gm)
½ small onion, minced
6 sprigs cilantro, minced
2 serrano or jalapeño peppers, minced
¼ cup (60 ml) red wine vinegar
⅓ cup (80 ml) water
Salt to taste

Mix all the ingredients; serve, or chill and serve. This is best served very fresh, but it will keep for 2 days in the refrigerator.

♥ Omit salt.

♥ GREEN TOMATO SAUCE
2 CUPS
PREPARATION TIME: 20 minutes in all

This sauce isn't made with *green* tomatoes per se, but with the Mexican variety, which have a sweet flavor all their own.

3/4 pound (350 gm) Mexican green tomatoes (tomatillos)
2 serrano peppers
1 clove garlic, peeled
1/4 medium onion
    Salt to taste
2 teaspoons (10 ml) safflower oil

Remove the papery husks from the Mexican green tomatoes and place the tomatoes in a saucepan. Cover with water and bring slowly to a boil. Boil gently for 10 minutes, or until soft.

Meanwhile, roast the peppers over a flame or in a dry skillet until they blister. When cool enough to handle, remove the stems.

When the tomatoes are soft, drain them and blend all the ingredients except the safflower oil in a blender until smooth. Heat the safflower oil in a heavy-bottomed skillet and cook the sauce for about 5 minutes over medium heat. Serve.

♥ For all, omit salt.

♥ COOKED SALSA
1 1/2 CUPS
PREPARATION TIME: 5 minutes
UNSUPERVISED COOKING: 30 minutes, in all

1 1/2 pounds (700 gm) ripe tomatoes
1/4 medium onion,
1 clove garlic
2 jalapeño or serrano peppers
1 tablespoon (15 ml) safflower oil
    Salt and freshly ground pepper to taste

Heat the broiler and broil the tomatoes until blistered, turning to broil on all sides. This should take about 10 minutes. Meanwhile, heat the peppers over a flame or in a dry skillet until they blister. Remove the stems when cool enough to handle.

Blend all the ingredients except the safflower oil together in a blender until smooth. Heat the safflower oil in a skillet or heavy-bottomed saucepan and add the puree. Cook over a medium flame for 15 to 20 minutes, or until the salsa reaches a thick consistency.

♥ For all these salsas, omit salt.

AVOCADO TACOS
12 TACOS

PREPARATION TIME: 15 minutes
SUPERVISED COOKING: 10 minutes

When I began testing taco recipes for this book I had taco dinner parties, and this dish always seemed to be the favorite. The sensuous guacamole and cheese melt together when you sauté the tacos, and it all tastes quite extravagant.

    3 medium-sized ripe avocados, preferably Haas
    1 clove garlic, minced or put through a press
    ¼ cup (60 ml) finely minced onion
    ¼ teaspoon (1.25 ml) chili powder
    ¼ teaspoon (1.25 ml) ground cumin
      Juice of ½ lemon, or more to taste
      Salt to taste
    12 corn tortillas
    6 ounces (175 gm) farmer or mozzarella cheese, diced, or 1 ½ cakes (6 ounces) tofu, crumbled
2 to 3 tablespoons (30–45 ml) safflower oil
FOR GARNISH: Salsa Fresca (page 261) or Cooked Salsa (page 262), plain yogurt, alfalfa sprouts, ¼ cup (60 ml) sliced radishes, and other garnishes as desired

Mash together the avocados, garlic, onion, chili powder, cumin, and lemon juice and season to taste with salt.

Heat the tortillas in a dry skillet for a minute, or until flexible. Spread a heaping tablespoon of guacamole down the middle of each, top with the cheese and fold over.

Heat the safflower oil and sauté the filled tortillas on both sides just until crisp. Drain on paper towels briefly and serve at once, with hot sauce, yogurt, sprouts, radishes and other garnishes of your choice.

♥ POTATO AND REFRIED BEAN TACOS*

12 tacos

Preparation time: 10 minutes
Supervised cooking: 20 to 30 minutes

If you're the sort of cook who likes the idea of making a big pot of beans on Sunday and using them through the week, this will be a great dish for you. I have always liked potato tacos, as long as I have salsa to go with them, since the tacos tend to be dry without it. The beans here are seductively spiced with cumin and chili, and the tacos are filling and high in protein.

    1 pound (450 gm) new or boiling potatoes, diced
    ¼ cup (60 ml) safflower oil
    3 cups (700 ml) cooked black beans, with their liquid
    1 teaspoon (5 ml) chili powder
    1 teaspoon (5 ml) ground cumin
    1 small onion, sliced
    12 corn tortillas
       Salsa Fresca (page 261) or Cooked Salsa (page 262)
       Garnishes of your choice, such as sprouts, cilantro, yogurt

Steam the potatoes for 5 to 10 minutes, until crisp-tender.

Meanwhile heat 1 tablespoon (15 ml) of the safflower oil in a heavy-bottomed skillet and add the black beans with about ¼ cup (60 ml) of their liquid, the chili powder, and the cumin. Cook, mashing with the back of a spoon, until they form a thick paste; do not allow them to get too dry.

Remove the beans from the heat, place in a bowl, and clean the skillet.

Heat another tablespoon of safflower oil in the skillet and add the onion. Sauté until tender, then add the potatoes. Cook, stirring, until the potatoes are just beginning to brown, about 10 minutes.

Heat the tortillas in a dry skillet for a minute, or until flexible. Spread a heaping tablespoon (15 ml) of refried beans down the middle of each and top with a heaping tablespoon (15 ml) of the potato-onion mixture. Fold the tortilla in half and press together, or roll it, like an enchilada or crepe.

Just before serving, heat the remaining oil in a skillet and sauté the filled tortillas on both sides, until just beginning to be crisp. Drain on paper towels briefly and serve at once with hot sauce and other *garnishes* of your choice.

*Auxiliary recipe: requires cooked black beans

♥ Omit safflower oil. Steam the potatoes and onions together until tender. Puree the beans in a blender or food processor with the cumin and chili. Make soft tacos or chalupas with the steamed potatoes and onions and the pureed beans, as above.

POTATO AND EGG TACOS
12 tacos

Preparation time: 15 minutes
Supervised cooking: 10 to 20 minutes

This is a taco I often order at a popular Mexican restaurant in Austin and I love to make them at home. They are easier than the Potato and Refried Bean Tacos on page 264 because you need nothing prepared in advance and they are also high in protein. These require salsa (any on pages 261–262) or they'll be rather dry.

     1 pound (450 gm) new or boiling potatoes, diced
3 to 4 tablespoons (45–60 ml) safflower oil
     1 small onion, sliced
     1 teaspoon (5 ml) butter
     3 eggs, beaten
    12 corn tortillas
       Salt and freshly ground pepper to taste
    ¼ pound (100 gm) farmer cheese or mozzarella, diced (optional)
       Salsa Fresca, Green Tomato Sauce, or Cooked Salsa (pages 261–262)

For Garnish: Alfalfa sprouts, shredded lettuce, sliced radishes, and/or sliced olives

Steam the potatoes until crisp-tender, about 10 minutes.

Heat 1 tablespoon (15 ml) of the safflower oil in a heavy-bottomed skillet and sauté the onion until tender. Add the potatoes and continue to sauté until the potatoes just begin to brown, about 10 minutes.

Add the butter, and when it has melted stir in the beaten eggs. Cook, stirring, until the eggs are set. Remove from the heat.

Heat the tortillas in a dry skillet until flexible and fill with 2 heaping tablespoons of the potato-egg mixture and the optional cheese. Heat the remaining oil in the skillet and sauté the folded, filled tortillas on both sides just until crisp. Drain on paper towels and serve immediately with salsa and garnishes of your choice.

POTATO AND CHEESE TACOS
12 TACOS
PREPARATION TIME: 15 minutes
SUPERVISED COOKING: 10 to 20 minutes

See preceding recipe for Potato and Egg Tacos. Substitute 6 ounces (175 gm) of farmer or mozzarella cheese, diced, for the eggs and butter. Sauté the onions and potatoes as directed. Remove from the heat and toss with the cheese. Fill the tortillas with 2 heaping table-spoons of the mixture and fold. Fry and serve immediately with the garnishes of your choice.

♥ POTATO, TOFU, AND TOMATO TACOS
12 TACOS
PREPARATION TIME: 15 to 20 minutes
SUPERVISED COOKING: 20 to 30 minutes

The tofu-tomato mixture in these tacos begins to smell a little like chorizo, of all things, as it cooks. The mixture has a deep, rich flavor.

     1 pound (450 gm) new or boiling potatoes, diced
     2 medium ripe tomatoes
    ¼ medium onion
     1 clove garlic
     1 serrano pepper
    ¼ cup (60 ml) safflower oil
     2 cakes (½ pound; 225 gm) tofu
     2 teaspoons (10 ml) tamari
     1 teaspoon (5 ml) ground cumin
    ½ additional onion, sliced
     2 tablespoons (30 ml) chopped fresh cilantro (optional)
    12 corn tortillas
    FOR GARNISH: Salsa Fresca (page 261) and alfalfa sprouts or shred-ded lettuce

Heat the broiler.
    Steam the potatoes 5 to 10 minutes, until crisp-tender.
    Meanwhile, broil the tomatoes 5 to 10 minutes, turning often, until they blister on all sides. Remove from the oven and puree in a blender with the ¼ onion, garlic, and serrano pepper. Set aside.
    Heat 2 teaspoons (10 ml) of the safflower oil in a skillet or heavy-bottomed saucepan and add the tomato puree. Cook 5 minutes, then add the tofu, mashing it thoroughly with the back of a spoon. Add

the tamari and cumin and continue to cook, stirring, another 5 minutes. Place the mixture in a bowl and clean the pan.

Heat another tablespoon (15 ml) of oil and sauté the sliced onion for 5 minutes, until it begins to brown. Add the potatoes and sauté for another 5 minutes. Stir in the tomato mixture and remove from the heat. Add the optional cilantro and correct seasoning.

Heat the tortillas briefly in a dry skillet until flexible. Fill tortillas with 2 heaping tablespoons of the potato mixture and fold. Heat the remaining oil in the skillet and sauté gently on both sides just until crisp. Drain on paper towels and serve immediately, garnished with salsa and sprouts.

♥ Sauté the tomato puree in 2 teaspoons (10 ml) safflower oil with the tofu but omit the tamari. Instead of sautéing the ½ sliced onion and potato until they brown, steam them together until tender. Increase the cilantro, if you like, and omit all salt. Make soft tacos or chalupas, as directed.

EGG AND POBLANO TACOS
12 TACOS

PREPARATION TIME: 20 minutes
SUPERVISED COOKING: 20 minutes

This recipe, and the dish that follows, which uses tofu instead of eggs, were inspired by the Mexican Cuisine expert Diana Kennedy.

    4 fresh poblano chilies
    ½ pound (450 gm) ripe tomatoes or 1 cup (250 ml) canned, drained
    ¼ medium onion
    1 clove garlic
      Salt to taste
    ¼ cup (60 ml) safflower oil
    3 large eggs, beaten
      Freshly ground pepper to taste
   12 corn tortillas
FOR GARNISH: 1 cup (250 ml) alfalfa sprouts or shredded lettuce and sliced black olives

Heat the broiler. Place the chilies and tomatoes on a baking sheet and broil them until they blister, about 10 minutes, turning to broil on all sides. Remove from the heat and cool a moment. Place the chilies in a plastic bag and close it tightly. Let stand for 5 minutes or so.

Place the tomatoes, onion, garlic, and salt to taste in a blender jar and puree until smooth.

Peel the chilies and remove their seeds and membranes. Cut into thin strips. If your skin is sensitive, wear rubber gloves, because the chilies can burn your skin quite severely.

Heat 1 tablespoon (15 ml) of the safflower oil in a heavy-bottomed skillet and sauté the chili strips for about 3 minutes. Add the tomato puree and cook for 5 minutes, over medium-high heat, stirring. Turn the heat down to medium and stir in the beaten eggs, cook, stirring, just until set. Add salt and freshly ground pepper to taste and remove from the heat.

Heat the tortillas briefly in a dry skillet until flexible. Fill with 2 heaping tablespoons of the egg and poblano mixture. Heat the remaining safflower oil in the skillet and fry the folded, filled tortillas on both sides just until crisp. Drain on paper towels, and serve immediately, garnished with sprouts or lettuce and olives.

♥ TOFU AND POBLANO TACOS

PREPARATION TIME: 20 minutes
SUPERVISED COOKING: 25 minutes

These are just as redolent and savory as the Egg and Poblano Tacos on page 267. The tofu absorbs all those rich flavors of the peppers, tomato, and garlic.

Follow the recipe for Egg and Poblano Tacos (see preceding recipe) up to the point when you add the eggs. Instead of the eggs, add 2 cakes (½ pound; 225 gm) tofu, 2 teaspoons (10 ml) tamari, and 1 teaspoon (5 ml) ground cumin. Mash the tofu thoroughly with the back of your spoon. Cook, stirring, for 5 minutes. Add salt and freshly ground pepper to taste and remove from the heat. Stir in 2 tablespoons (30 ml) chopped fresh cilantro, then complete the recipe.

♥ Reduce oil to 2 teaspoons (10 ml). Omit salt and tamari. Make soft tacos or chalupas and omit black olives in the garnish.

♥ MUSHROOM TACOS
12 TACOS

PREPARATION TIME: 30 minutes
SUPERVISED COOKING: 20 minutes, in all

All the heavenly mushrooms in these tacos give them an almost meaty quality. Mushrooms can often take the place of meat in a dish because of their body and texture. This filling will hold for a day or two in the refrigerator.

3 to 4 tablespoons (45–60 ml) safflower oil
1 small onion, chopped
2 cloves garlic, minced or put through a press
1 pound (450 gm) mushrooms, sliced thin
¾ pound (350 gm) ripe tomatoes, peeled and chopped, or 1 ½ cups (350 ml) canned, drained, and chopped
2 serrano or jalapeño peppers, chopped
2 tablespoons (30 ml) chopped fresh cilantro
½ teaspoon (2.5 ml) ground cumin
Salt and freshly ground pepper to taste
¼ pound (100 gm) farmer cheese, diced
12 corn tortillas

FOR GARNISH: Yogurt, Salsa Fresca, alfalfa sprouts, chopped lettuce or cabbage, and sliced black olives

Heat 1 tablespoon (15 ml) of the oil in a large, heavy-bottomed skillet and sauté the onion and garlic until the onion is tender. Add the mushrooms and sauté for 5 minutes, stirring. Add the tomatoes and peppers and sauté for another 10 to 15 minutes. Add the cilantro, cumin, and salt and pepper to taste. Remove from the heat and stir in the cheese.

Heat the tortillas in a dry skillet until flexible and fill with 2 heaping tablespoons of the mushroom mixture. Heat the remaining oil in the skillet and sauté the folded, filled tortillas on both sides just until crisp. Drain on paper towels and serve immediately with the garnishes of your choice.

♥ Reduce oil to 1 tablespoon (15 ml); omit salt and farmer cheese, and add a little white wine or beer if necessary for cooking the mushrooms. Make soft tacos or chalupas as directed.

♥ GREEN TOMATO, CORN, AND TOFU TACOS
12 TACOS
Preparation time: 15 minutes
Supervised cooking: 15 to 20 minutes

Every once in a while I come up with a recipe that excites me so much that it's all I want to cook. Here the corn and tofu, made pungent and picante with the green sauce, go together beautifully, and with the sautéed corn tortillas, alfalfa sprouts, cilantro, and farmer cheese the combination is quite complete. If you don't want to include the cheese, the tacos will be just as delicious, and the protein, with the corn and tofu, will be beautifully balanced.

      ¾ pound (350 gm) green tomatoes (tomatillos), papery husks
         removed
      2 serrano peppers
      ¼ medium onion
      1 clove garlic, peeled
 3 to 4 tablespoons (45–60 ml) safflower oil, in all
      1½ cups corn kernels (2 large ears)
      3 cakes (¾ pound; 350 gm) tofu
      2 teaspoons (10 ml) tamari
         Salt to taste
 2 to 3 tablespoons (30–45 ml) chopped fresh cilantro
      ¼ pound (100 gm) farmer cheese, diced
      12 corn tortillas
For Garnish: Alfalfa sprouts or shredded lettuce, sliced radishes, Salsa Fresca or Cooked Salsa, and the remaining Green Sauce

Place the green tomatoes in a saucepan and cover with water. Bring to a boil, then reduce the heat and simmer gently for 10 minutes, or until soft. Meanwhile place the peppers directly over a flame or on a hot skillet and cook until toasted and blistered.

Drain the green tomatoes and puree in a blender with the onion, garlic, and peppers.

Heat 1 tablespoon (15 ml) of the oil and sauté the corn for 2 to 3 minutes, until it becomes bright yellow. Add the tofu and tamari and cook, mashing the tofu with a spoon and stirring, for another 5 minutes. Add 1 cup (250 ml) of the green tomato mixture and cook for another 5 minutes, stirring. Remove from the heat, add salt to taste, and stir in the cilantro and the diced cheese.

Heat the tortillas in a dry skillet until flexible. Fill with 2 heaping tablespoons of the tofu mixture. Heat the remaining safflower oil and fry the folded, filled tortillas on both sides just until crisp. Drain briefly on paper towels and serve at once, with sprouts, radishes, salsa, and the remaining green sauce as garnishes.

♥ Use 2 teaspoons (10 ml) safflower oil; omit tamari, salt, and farmer cheese. Make soft tacos or chalupas as directed.

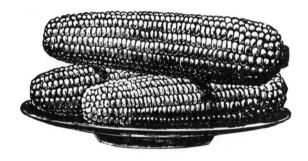

SALADS AND DRESSINGS

VINAIGRETTE
LOW-FAT VINAIGRETTE
YOGURT VINAIGRETTE
TOMATO VINAIGRETTE
AVOCADO VINAIGRETTE
TOFU MAYONNAISE
GREEN TOFU DRESSING
SESAME DRESSING
COLD SOUP DRESSING
PARSLEY SALAD DRESSING
TOSSED GREEN SALAD
LETTUCE SALAD WITH ORANGES
TOMATO AND MOZZARELLA SALAD
CUCUMBER YOGURT SALAD
CUCUMBERS VINAIGRETTE
GUACAMOLE
TOMATO SALAD
CURRIED CARROT SALAD
FATTOUSH
TABOULI WITH PRESSURE-COOKED GARBANZOS
MIDDLE EASTERN BEET SALAD
LEEKS VINAIGRETTE
WARM OR CHILLED CAULIFLOWER OR BROCCOLI VINAIGRETTE
WARM POTATO SALAD WITH CARAWAY
WATERCRESS, MUSHROOM, AND TOFU SALAD

LEFTOVER GRAINS SALAD*
LEFTOVER BEANS SALAD*
COLESLAW
JÍCAMA AND ORANGE SALAD WITH AVOCADOS
COTTAGE CHEESE AND TOMATO SALAD WITH MISO DRESSING
ORIENTAL SALAD
SIMPLE CABBAGE AND CARROT SALAD WITH FRESH HERBS
HOT AND SOUR BEAN SPROUT SALAD
HOT AND SOUR BUCKWHEAT NOODLE SALAD
COLD MARINATED ZUCCHINI, ORIENTAL STYLE
COLD PASTA SALAD

As you make your way through the recipes that follow you'll encounter a wide range of evocative flavors. There are salads from the Middle East, Mexico, India, China, and of course, beloved France.

All sorts of unexpected ingredients are welcome in salads, foods like miso, tofu, noodles, and even oranges. You may be surprised by the presence of a seasoning like cumin in Tabouli (page 246), yet how pleasing it is! Caraway in potato salad (page 291) might also seem strange, but that is equally delicious.

Not only can the salad course be a masterful creation made with fresh ingredients, but it can also be a catchall for leftovers. I often add yesterday's cooked grains to my tossed green and spinach salads, or dress leftover pasta with a vinaigrette. Add a little tofu or cheese to these and you've got a meal. Leftover cooked vegetables can also enhance this course, or can constitute a salad on their own. Cold Green Beans Amandine (page 146), for example, makes a marvelous dish when tossed with a vinaigrette.

By the same token, a leftover cold soup can serve as a terrific dressing. Gazpacho (page 87) and Chilled Buttermilk Soup (page 86) are ideal for this purpose, and are marvelous for a low-fat diet. Other delicious low-fat dressings in this chapter are Low-Fat Vinaigrette (page 275), Yogurt Vinaigrette (page 276), Tomato Vinaigrette (page 276), Tofu Mayonnaise (page 277), and Green Tofu Dressing (page 278). I'm quite enthusiastic about these. Perhaps it's because my mother didn't allow me as an overweight child to eat sweets or starches but, knowing little about the composition of foods, nonetheless drenched my salad every night with Russian Dressing made with mayonnaise and ketchup—or, in nutritional terms, fat and sugar. She

*Auxiliary recipe

273

always told me salads were "thinning," and I couldn't understand why I remained pudgy (the thick bologna and processed cheese sandwiches with mayonnaise for lunch didn't help, either). When I later learned about fats (I was thin by then), I developed a passion for creating delicious low-fat recipes, and salad dressings were an exciting challenge.

If you feel that the rest of your meal might be lacking in protein, include cheese, hard boiled eggs, roasted soybeans, or tofu in your salad, or use yogurt or tofu in your dressing. With the proper ingredients, this course could also *be* your main dish; in spring and summer a grain, pasta, or bean salad, or grains and beans combined in a salad, can be quite satisfying.

The most time-consuming, boring aspect of making a salad is washing and drying the greens. I've tested a lot of friendships by asking people to do this task for me (but only after they asked me if they could help). This is, however, the most important job; one grain of sand between the teeth will ruin this course, no matter how wonderful the ingredients are. One of my biggest fears as a professional cook is discovering the greens haven't been sufficiently washed, and I'm usually a bit tense until the salad plates are cleared. As I mention in the Useful Equipment and Related Maxims section, a salad spinner will speed up the drying process. I also recommend that you take ten minutes when you get home from the store to wash all your greens, so that you won't have to rush through this task when it comes time for dinner. Dry the leaves, keeping them whole if possible, wrap them in a towel, seal in plastic bags, and refrigerate. Then you can enjoy imaginative salads through the week with very little effort.

VINAIGRETTE
1 CUP (250 ML)
PREPARATION TIME: 5 minutes

Vinaigrette is a standard dressing that will go well with most of the salads in this chapter. Although it's always best if made shortly before you serve it, you can get away with making it in quantity or preparing one batch in advance and keeping it on hand for several days in the refrigerator.

This classic vinaigrette is a high-fat dressing, but following it are low-fat versions using yogurt, stock, blended tomatoes, or tofu in place of the oil.

Juice of ½ lemon

3 tablespoons (45 ml) wine vinegar

1 clove garlic, minced or put through a press

½ teaspoon (2.5 ml) dry mustard or 1 teaspoon Dijon mustard

¼ teaspoon (1.25 ml) dried marjoram or basil

¼ teaspoon (1.25 ml) dried tarragon

2 to 3 teaspoons (10–15 ml) chopped fresh herbs, such as basil, tarragon, marjoram, dill, or thyme, if available

Salt and freshly ground pepper to taste

½ to ¾ cup (120–180 ml) olive oil, safflower oil, or a combination, to taste

Mix together all the ingredients except the oil. Whisk in the oil and blend well. Stir well before tossing with the salad. Store in the refrigerator.

♥ LOW-FAT VINAIGRETTE
ABOUT 1 CUP (250 ML)
PREPARATION TIME: 5 minutes

When I cooked for heart patients for a month my right-hand woman Connie made this dressing and variations of it by the blenderful every morning. It's amazing how far a little oil will go. Even though Low-Fat Vinaigrette is thinner than the vinaigrettes you're used to, that little bit of oil will help it to stick to the salad. Instead of whisking the ingredients together you use a blender, which makes a fairly thick, emulsified mixture. You can vary this with any herbs or spices you wish to use.

Juice of ½ lemon

3 to 4 tablespoons (45–60 ml) wine vinegar or cider vinegar, to taste

1 clove garlic, minced or put through a press

½ teaspoon (2.5 ml) dry mustard or 1 teaspoon (5 ml) Dijon-style

¼ teaspoon (1.25 ml) dried marjoram or basil

¼ teaspoon (1.25 ml) dried tarragon

2 to 3 teaspoons (10–15 ml) chopped fresh herbs (such as basil, thyme, dill, fennel, marjoram, parsley, or chives), if available

Freshly ground pepper to taste

1 to 2 tablespoons (15–30 ml) chopped onion (optional)

2 tablespoons (30 ml) safflower oil
½ cup (120 ml) Tamari-Bouillon Broth (page 62) or water

Blend all the ingredients together in a blender for about 30 seconds. Shake before using.

♥ Use water instead of bouillon.

♥ YOGURT VINAIGRETTE
1 CUP (250 ML)
PREPARATION TIME: 5 minutes

This creamy yet low-fat dressing will add protein to your meal, and is a good idea in the summertime when you want to eat nothing but salads but have to work in protein.

Follow preceding recipe for Vinaigrette, substituting ½ to ¾ (120–180 ml) cup plain low-fat yogurt for the oil. Whisk in as you would the oil.

♥ TOMATO VINAIGRETTE
1 CUP (250 ML)
PREPARATION TIME: 5 minutes

Another low-fat, creamy dressing. It's amazing how many variations on this theme there are.

Follow recipe for Low-Fat Vinaigrette (page 275), substituting either 1 large ripe tomato or ½ cup (120 ml) tomato juice for the broth. Blend together in a blender.

AVOCADO VINAIGRETTE
1 CUP (250 ML)
PREPARATION TIME: 5 minutes

This dressing *isn't* low-fat, but it's certainly a wonderful way to use avocados.

Follow recipe for Low-Fat Vinaigrette (page 275), substituting ½ peeled ripe avocado and ¼ cup (60 ml) plain low-fat yogurt for the broth and oil. Add up to ¼ teaspoon paprika or ground cumin if you wish, or both. Blend as directed.

♥ TOFU MAYONNAISE
1 AND ⅓ CUPS (330 ML)

PREPARATION TIME: 5 minutes

This discovery has changed my life. Another one of those miraculous tofu foods, it can be put to all the uses of a mayonnaise without giving you all the fat. To use it as a dressing for salad you might want to thin it out a bit with water or yogurt. It's a very high-protein dressing, and will keep for a week in a covered container in the refrigerator.

Juice of ½ lemon (or more, to taste)
2 tablespoons (30 ml) wine vinegar or cider vinegar
1 clove garlic, minced or put through a press
1 teaspoon (5 ml) Dijon-style mustard
½ cup (120 ml) plain yogurt or buttermilk
2 cakes (½ pound; 225 gm) tofu
1 to 2 teaspoons (5–10 ml) tamari or miso, to taste
Freshly ground pepper to taste
Additional water or yogurt as desired
2 tablespoons (30 ml) olive or safflower oil (optional)

Combine all the ingredients in a blender or food processor fitted with the steel blade and blend until completely smooth. Make sure you don't leave any stray bits of tofu unblended, or the mixture will be gritty.

Refrigerate in a covered container.

Note: If you are on a low-sodium diet, this recipe and the Green Tofu Dressing that follows might not be palatable without the tamari or miso. The addition of extra vinegar might help. Try it once, and if it doesn't work, use the other low-fat vinaigrettes for your salads.

♥ Omit tamari or miso. Add more vinegar to taste. Substitute ½ teaspoon dry mustard for the Dijon-style prepared.

♥ GREEN TOFU DRESSING
1⅓ CUPS (330 ML)
PREPARATION TIME: 5 minutes

This beautiful green dressing is actually Tofu Mayonnaise but with spinach blended in. It adds a new dimension to its parent dressing. This too will keep for a week in the refrigerator.

Ingredients for Tofu Mayonnaise (page 277)
¼ to ½ cup (60–120 ml) spinach, to taste, washed and stemmed
2 tablespoons (30 ml) chopped onion (optional)

Blend all the ingredients together in a blender or food processor fitted with the steel blade until smooth. Chill in a covered container.

♥ Omit tamari or miso; add vinegar to taste.

♥ SESAME DRESSING
1 CUP (250 ML)
PREPARATION TIME: 5 minutes

The nutty taste of this dressing goes especially nicely with sprouts and spinach salads. It will keep in a covered container in the refrigerator for a week.

2 tablespoons (30 ml) vinegar (wine or cider)
Juice of ½ lemon
1 clove garlic, minced or put through a press
2 tablespoons (30 ml) sesame tahini
Salt and freshly ground pepper to taste
½ to ¾ cup (120–180 ml) plain low-fat yogurt, to taste

Mix together the vinegar, lemon juice, garlic, tahini, salt, and freshly ground pepper. Stir in the yogurt. Refrigerate in a covered container until ready to use.

♥ Omit salt.

♥ COLD SOUP DRESSING

If these seem a little too watery to you, add a tablespoon (15–30 ml) or two of olive or safflower oil and mix well.

For a salad that will serve 4 to 6 people use ¾ cup (180 ml) of any of the following soups—and note that the Buttermilk in the Chilled Buttermilk Soup will increase the protein content of your salad.

Gazpacho (page 87)
Chilled Buttermilk Soup (page 86)

Toss with the salad just before serving.

♥ Gazpacho made without the olive oil or salt, and Chilled Buttermilk Soup made with yogurt instead of buttermilk, would be appropriate.

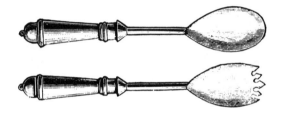

♥ PARSLEY SALAD DRESSING
1½ CUPS (350 ML)

PREPARATION TIME: 5 minutes

¼ cup (60 ml) fresh lemon juice
1 clove garlic
1 tablespoon (15 ml) chopped onion or shallot
¼ teaspoon (1.25 ml) dried tarragon
½ teaspoon (2.5 ml) dry mustard or 1 teaspoon (5 ml) Dijon-style
1 cup (250 ml) chopped fresh parsley
Salt and freshly ground pepper to taste
3 tablespoons (45 ml) water
½ cup (120 ml) olive or safflower oil

Combine all the ingredients except the oil in a blender or food processor and turn on the machine on high speed. Add the olive or safflower oil in a steady stream. Blend until smooth and adjust seasonings.

♥ Use only 2 tablespoons (30 ml) safflower oil and add ¼ cup (60 ml) water or vegetable stock. Use dry mustard.

♥ TOSSED GREEN SALAD
serves 4 to 6

Preparation time: 20 minutes (or up to 30 minutes, depending on the number of ingredients you're using)

A tossed green salad can be simple or elaborate. The more complex the rest of your meal is, the simpler your salad should be. Tender young lettuce and herbs with a nice vinaigrette (see page 274) will often suffice, while at other times a variety of vegetables, with all their textures, are welcome. A happy medium is a salad with lettuce, sliced mushrooms, chives or green onions, radishes, and herbs.

½ to ¾ pound (225–350 gm) lettuce, either Boston, red tip, leaf, romaine, or a combination

6 medium-size firm fresh mushrooms, wiped clean and sliced thin

6 radishes, sliced thin

3 to 4 green onions, both white and green parts, sliced thin

Optional:
 ½ cucumber, peeled (if waxed) and sliced thin
 1 small sweet green pepper, seeded and sliced
 2 ripe tomatoes, cut in wedges
 1 sweet red pepper, seeded and sliced
 2 to 3 tablespoons (30–45 ml) mixed fresh herbs, chopped (such as basil, marjoram, dill, thyme, fennel, rosemary)
 ½ to 1 cup (120–250 ml) sprouts (any kind)
 2 tablespoons (30 ml) sunflower seeds, roasted soybeans, walnuts, pecans, or slivered almonds
 1 to 2 cakes (¼ to ½ pound; 100–225 gm) tofu, crumbled
 2 hard-boiled eggs, sliced or diced
 ¼ cup (60 ml) grated or diced Swiss or Cheddar cheese
 ¼ cup (60 ml) freshly grated Parmesan cheese
 ¼ cup (60 ml) ripe olives, pitted
 1 avocado, sliced

Vinaigrette (page 274) or other dressing of your choice

Wash and dry the lettuce and prepare the other vegetables. Tear the lettuce in fairly large pieces and combine with the other ingredients, including any or all of the optional ones, in a large salad bowl. Toss just before serving with dressing, scattering more sprouts, herbs, and roasted soybeans or sunflower seeds over the top for garnish.

♥ Do not add nuts, cheese, eggs, or avocado; use low-fat dressings.

♥ LETTUCE SALAD WITH ORANGES
SERVES 4 TO 6
PREPARATION TIME: 20 minutes

When I plan a meal that includes lots of tomatoes, like a pasta, I love to serve this salad. It's also very good with Mexican and Indian food, because the oranges are so refreshing against the spices. I've had cooking students who were skeptical about the unusual combination of ingredients in this salad until they tasted it, and now they're making it all the time. If you can get raspberry vinegar (found in specialty food stores) for marinating the oranges before you toss the salad, you will have something very special indeed.

    1–2 tablespoons very thin slivers orange zest
       2 seedless or seeded oranges, peeled, white membranes removed, and sectioned
       1 head Boston, tender red-tipped, or romaine lettuce
1 to 2 tablespoons (15–30 ml) chopped fresh herbs, such as dill, basil, tarragon, fennel, parsley
       2 tablespoons (30 ml) chopped fresh chives or green onion tops
       3 tablespoons (45 ml) chopped pecans or walnuts
       1 recipe Vinaigrette (page 274)
         Optional: 2 tablespoons (30 ml) raspberry vinegar
                      ½ cup (120 ml) alfalfa sprouts
                3 to 4 radishes, sliced
                3 to 4 fresh mushrooms, sliced

Bring a small pot of water to a boil and blanch the orange zest slivers for ten seconds. Drain and toss with the orange sections in the raspberry vinegar, if you are using it. Marinate for up to an hour before tossing with the salad.

Wash and dry the lettuce and tear into large pieces, then toss together with the oranges, zest, herbs, chives, and pecans or walnuts. Add optional ingredients and toss with the Vinaigrette just before serving.

♥ Omit pecans or walnuts. Use low-fat vinaigrette.

♥ TOMATO AND MOZZARELLA SALAD
SERVES 4
PREPARATION TIME: 20 minutes

I have always admired this dish in Italian *trattorie;* it's colorful, simple, and delicious. The tomatoes are left intact—sliced only about three fourths of the way down—providing a colorful little "carriage" for the cheese.

- 4 small ripe tomatoes, or 2 large
- 3 ounces (75 gm) mozzarella cheese, sliced thin
  Salt and freshly ground pepper to taste
- 2 tablespoons (30 ml) wine vinegar
- 1 small clove garlic, minced or put through a press
- ¼ cup (60 ml) olive oil
- 2 teaspoons (10 ml) chopped fresh basil or other herbs (such as parsley, thyme, sage, or marjoram)
  Leaves of Boston lettuce, for serving

If using large tomatoes, cut them in half lengthwise, through the stem, and turn the halves on the cut side. Slice down to within ½ inch (1.5 cm) of the bottom, in slices about ¼ inch (0.7 cm) thick. If using whole tomatoes, turn them upside down so they rest on the stem end. Slice down to within ½ inch (1.5 cm) of the bottom.

Insert slices of mozzarella between the slices of tomato. Grind pepper over the top and sprinkle on salt. Mix together the vinegar, garlic, and olive oil. Drizzle over the tomatoes and sprinkle the fresh basil or other herbs over the top. Set a tomato on a leaf of lettuce for each serving. Serve chilled or at room temperature.

♥ Substitute tofu for the mozzarella (this is actually one of my favorite ways to eat tofu). Omit salt; substitute 2 tablespoons (30 ml) safflower oil for the olive oil.

♥ CUCUMBER YOGURT SALAD
SERVES 4 TO 6
PREPARATION TIME: 15 minutes

- 3 cucumbers, peeled (if waxed) and sliced thin
- 3 or 4 green onions, both white part and green, sliced
- 2 to 4 tablespoons (30–60 ml) chopped fresh dill
- 3 tablespoons (45 ml) vinegar
  Juice of ½ lemon

    1 clove garlic, minced or put through a press
    1 teaspoon (5 ml) Dijon-style mustard (optional)
      Salt and freshly ground pepper to taste
    2 tablespoons (30 ml) olive oil
    ¾ cup (180 ml) plain low-fat yogurt

Toss together the cucumbers, green onions, and dill.

Mix together the vinegar, lemon juice, garlic, mustard, and salt and pepper. Stir in the olive oil and the yogurt. Toss with the cucumbers and serve, or chill and serve.

♥ Omit salt and olive oil. Omit mustard or substitute ½ teaspoon dry mustard.

♥ CUCUMBERS VINAIGRETTE

Substitute 1 Bermuda onion, sliced, for the green onions. Substitute ½ cup vinegar and ¼ cup water for the yogurt. Marinate for ½ to 1 hour if possible.

GUACAMOLE
SERVES 4 TO 6
PREPARATION TIME: 10 minutes

You can prepare this salad in a food processor, but use the pulse action carefully or the mixture will become too smooth, like a dip.

This dish depends heavily on the quality of the avocados. The best ones are dark, with a pebbled skin; avoid altogether the large shiny ones from Florida, which are watery and tasteless.

    2 or 3 ripe avocados, preferably Haas
        1 large tomato, peeled and seeded
        1 clove garlic, minced or put through a press (optional)
    2 to 4 tablespoons (30–60 ml) finely minced onion, to taste
           Juice of ½ lemon or lime, or to taste
           Salt, cumin, and chili powder to taste
           Optional: 1 or 2 serrano peppers, minced (for a picante
                     guacamole)
                 1 to 2 tablespoons (15–30 ml) chopped fresh
                        cilantro

Cut the avocados in half, remove the seeds, and scoop out the flesh. Place in a bowl with the tomato and the optional garlic and mash until smooth, allowing the avocado to retain some of its texture. Stir in the onion, lemon juice, salt, cumin, chili powder, and optional serranos and cilantro.

Note: If you are not serving Guacamole right away, cover and refrigerate. The top will turn brownish, but this is just on the surface and can be scraped off.

♥ TOMATO SALAD
SERVES 4 TO 6
PREPARATION TIME: 10 minutes

        1½ pounds (700 gm) ripe tomatoes, sliced thin
          1 cup (250 ml) alfalfa sprouts
          2 tablespoons (30 ml) chopped chives
    2 to 3 tablespoons (30–45 ml) chopped fresh basil
          2 tablespoons (30 ml) chopped fresh parsley
          1 tablespoon (15 ml) other chopped fresh herbs (optional)
          1 recipe Vinaigrette (page 274)

Place the tomatoes on a platter and garnish with the sprouts. Sprinkle on the chives, basil, parsley, and other herbs and pour the dressing over all. Serve immediately, or chill and serve.

♥ Omit vinaigrette. Douse tomatoes with red wine vinegar.

♥ CURRIED CARROT SALAD
SERVES 4 TO 6
PREPARATION TIME: 20 minutes

This splendid salad is a recipe from Nina, who was my neighbor one summer in the south of France. She had a small, informal restaurant where she served some of the best food I've ever eaten. I think my favorite dish of hers was this curried shredded carrot salad. My friends and I couldn't believe how wonderful it was the first time we had it; we polished off a huge bowl of it, even though we knew it was just the first of many courses. Carrot salads before this one had always been somewhat dull—either simple vinaigrettes or sweet, with raisins. Curry adds a completely new dimension.

        2 pounds (1 kg) carrots, scrubbed and grated
    ¼ to ½ cup (60–120 ml) capers, to taste, rinsed

¼ cup (60 ml) grated onion
Juice of 1 lemon
2 to 3 teaspoons (10–15 ml) good curry powder
½ teaspoon (2.5 ml) ground cumin
¼ teaspoon (1.25 ml) ground allspice
Pinch of cayenne
Salt and freshly ground pepper to taste
¼ cup (60 ml) safflower oil

Toss the carrots with the capers and onion. Mix together the lemon juice, curry powder, cumin, allspice, cayenne, and salt and pepper. Toss with the carrots. Add the oil and toss again. Taste and correct the seasoning, adding more curry powder if you wish.

♥ Omit capers; omit salt; use only 2 tablespoons (30 ml) safflower oil.

♥ FATTOUSH
SERVES 4 TO 6
PREPARATION TIME: 15 to 20 minutes

Fattoush is a Middle Eastern salad consisting of diced cucumbers, tomatoes, and bread. It's fragrant with mint and parsley and is tossed with a yogurt vinaigrette. There are many textures and flavors at play here, which make this simple salad an exciting one.

2 cucumbers, peeled (if waxed or bitter) and chopped
2 large ripe tomatoes, chopped
4 green onions or ½ Bermuda onion, minced
½ cup (120 ml) chopped fresh parsley
¼ cup (60 ml) chopped fresh mint
½ cup (120 ml) watercress or sunflower greens
½ cup (120 ml) lemon juice
Salt and freshly ground pepper to taste
1 to 2 cloves garlic, to taste, minced or put through a press
1 cup (250 ml) plain low-fat yogurt
¼ cup (60 ml) olive oil
1 cup (250 ml) bite-sized pieces French bread or pita, lightly toasted

Toss the cucumbers, tomatoes, green onion, parsley, mint, and greens together in a glass or wooden salad bowl.
Mix together the lemon juice, salt, pepper, garlic, and yogurt.

Whisk in the olive oil. Toss with the herbs and vegetables. Just before serving, add the bread and toss again.

♥ Omit salt and olive oil.

♥ TABOULI WITH PRESSURE-COOKED GARBANZOS
SERVES 6 TO 8
PREPARATION TIME: 20 to 25 minutes
UNSUPERVISED COOKING FOR THE BEANS: 45 minutes

There are many variations of tabouli, the Middle Eastern salad made with bulgur and fresh herbs. The one below, with the garbanzos, has complete protein built right in. If you don't have time or don't have garbanzos, you could leave them out and complement your protein somewhere else, with a soup or main dish containing dairy products, with tofu or eggs, or with a soufflé or omelet for dessert.

Mint is a traditional ingredient in tabouli, but I've found out over the years that not everybody likes it. So I've made it optional.

If you do things in advance, you can make this salad a day ahead of time. Then you needn't soak the bulgur in boiling water. Just add enough water to the vinaigrette to cover the bulgur by an inch, and soak the bulgur in it overnight. Each grain will become saturated in the pungent flavors of the vinaigrette (to which the cumin gives a unique, marvelous flavor), and the tabouli will be irresistible.

    1 cup (250 ml) garbanzo beans, washed and picked over
    4 cups (950 ml) water
1½ cups (350 ml) raw bulgur or 3 cups (700 ml) cooked
    1 cup (350 ml) boiling water (if using raw bulgur)
      Juice of 1 lemon
  ½ cup (120 ml) vinegar
    1 clove garlic, minced or put through a press
    1 teaspoon (5 ml) prepared mustard
      Salt and freshly ground pepper
  ½ teaspoon (2.5 ml) ground cumin
  ¾ cup (180 ml) olive oil, or use part safflower oil
    1 bunch green onions, sliced (both white part and green)
  ½ cup (120 ml) minced fresh parsley
  ½ cup (120 ml) minced fresh mint (optional)
    2 tomatoes, chopped
    1 cucumber, peeled and diced

Place the garbanzos and 4 cups (950 ml) water in a pressure cooker and bring to a boil. Cover and bring to 15 pounds (7 kg) pressure, then turn to medium heat and cook for 45 minutes. Meanwhile, prepare the rest of the salad.

If using raw bulgur, place in a bowl and pour on the boiling water. In a small bowl or measuring cup, mix together the lemon juice, vinegar, garlic, mustard, salt, pepper, and cumin. Whisk in the oil and pour the dressing over the bulgur.

Prepare the remaining vegetables. By the time the garbanzos are cooked, the bulgur should have absorbed all the liquid; if it has not, pour off some of the excess. Toss the bulgur with the cooked garbanzos and remaining ingredients and serve; or chill and serve.

MENU SUGGESTIONS

Soups: Hot or Iced Tomato Soup (page 72); Pureed Zucchini Soup (page 70)

Vegetable dishes: Any green vegetable, simply steamed; Turnips with Lemon and Honey (page 173)

Desserts: Gingered Fruit (page 312); Figs Poached in Madeira (page 311); Banana Yogurt Freeze (page 315)

♥ Omit salt; substitute 2 tablespoons (30 ml) safflower oil and ⅔ cup (160 ml) water or liquid from the garbanzos for the olive oil.

♥ MIDDLE EASTERN BEET SALAD
SERVES 4 TO 6

PREPARATION TIME: 15 minutes
UNSUPERVISED STEAMING: 20 minutes

Beets are one of those vegetables that you either love or hate. I'm a big fan: I love borscht, beet salads, and simply steamed beets. Until I came across this interesting salad, I'd usually had them with a vinaigrette. But this Middle Eastern version, seasoned with cumin, paprika, and cinnamon, is currently at the top of my list.

    2 pounds (1 kg) beets, trimmed and peeled
    Juice of 1 lemon
    ½ teaspoon (2.5 ml) ground cumin
    ½ teaspoon (2.5 ml) paprika
    ¼ teaspoon (1.25 ml) ground cinnamon
    Salt and freshly ground pepper to taste
    ¼ cup (60 ml) safflower oil
2 to 3 tablespoons (30–45 ml) chopped fresh parsley
    Leaf or romaine lettuce

Cut the beets in half and place in a steamer. Steam 20 minutes, or until crisp-tender. Refresh under cold water and dice.

While the beets are cooking mix together the lemon juice, cumin, paprika, cinnamon, salt, pepper, and safflower oil. Toss with the diced beets and the parsley. If you have the time, cover and chill for an hour or more. Otherwise serve over lettuce leaves.

♥ Omit salt; use only 2 tablespoons (30 ml) safflower oil.

♥ LEEKS VINAIGRETTE
SERVES 4 TO 6

PREPARATION TIME: 15 minutes
UNSUPERVISED MARINATING: 1 hour, if possible

I've had good leeks vinaigrette and bad ones. When they're bad, the leeks are overcooked and are too saturated with oil. I've been served badly prepared leeks even in popular restaurants in Paris, where they are served whole and taste as if they've been sitting in oil all day. I think they're much more appealing sliced.

- 2 pounds (1 kg) leeks
- 1 tablespoon (15 ml) safflower oil
- 2 tablespoons (30 ml) dry vermouth
   Juice of ½ lemon
- 3 tablespoons (45 ml) wine vinegar
- 1 small clove garlic, minced or put through a press
- 1 teaspoon (5 ml) Dijon-style mustard
   Salt and freshly ground pepper to taste
- ¼ teaspoon (1.25 ml) dried marjoram
- 2 teaspoons (10 ml) chopped fresh herbs (such as parsley, basil, dill), alone or in combination
- ¾ cup (180 ml) olive oil, or a combination of olive and safflower oil

FOR GARNISH: Radishes, cucumber slices, and parsley

Cut the leeks in half lengthwise. Run under cold tap water, letting the water wash away the grit caught between the layers. Slice the white part crosswise and discard the tough green part.

Heat the 1 tablespoon (15 ml) safflower oil in a lidded, heavy-bottomed skillet and sauté the leeks over a medium-low flame until they begin to soften, about 3 minutes. Add the vermouth and stir, then cover and cook slowly for another 5 to 10 minutes, stirring occasionally.

Meanwhile, make the dressing. Stir together the lemon juice, vinegar, garlic, mustard, salt, pepper, and herbs. Whisk in the oil and toss with the hot leeks. Chill or let stand at room temperature for an hour or two. Toss again and garnish.

Note: This is good even if you don't have time to marinate the leeks.

♥ Substitute 2 tablespoons (30 ml) safflower oil and ½ cup (120 ml) vegetable stock or water for the olive oil, or use Yogurt Vinaigrette (page 276).

♥ WARM OR CHILLED CAULIFLOWER OR BROCCOLI VINAIGRETTE
SERVES 4 TO 6
PREPARATION TIME: 20 minutes

FOR THE DRESSING:

    Juice of 1 lemon

¼ cup (60 ml) red wine vinegar

1 to 2 cloves garlic, to taste, minced or put through a press

1 teaspoon (5 ml) Dijon-style mustard or ½ teaspoon (2.5 ml) dry mustard

1 green onion, finely minced (both green part and white)

½ teaspoon (2.5 ml) dried tarragon

    Salt and freshly ground pepper to taste

¾ cup (180 ml) olive oil, or a combination of olive and saf-flower oil

FOR THE SALAD:

1 small Bermuda onion, poached (see instructions below)

1 large head cauliflower or large bunch of broccoli (1½ to 2 pounds; 700 gm–1 kg), trimmed and broken into florets

2 tablespoons (30 ml) chopped fresh herbs (such as basil, thyme, dill, rosemary, marjoram), alone or combined

½ cup (120 ml) chopped fresh parsley

2 to 4 tablespoons (30–60 ml) freshly grated Parmesan cheese (optional)

Combine all the ingredients for the dressing except the oil and stir well. Whisk in the oil. Set aside.

Slice the onion and place in a small saucepan. Cover with water, bring to a simmer, and poach 4 to 5 minutes. Drain and refresh under cold water.

Steam the cauliflower or broccoli 5 to 10 minutes, just until crisp-tender. Drain and toss immediately with the herbs and onion. Toss with the dressing and top with the optional Parmesan. Serve hot, warm, or chilled.

This can also be served on a platter over a bed of lettuce leaves.

♥ Substitute 2 tablespoons (30 ml) safflower oil plus ½ cup (120 ml) vegetable stock or water for the olive oil; omit salt. Use ½ teaspoon dry mustard.

♥ WARM POTATO SALAD WITH CARAWAY
SERVES 4 TO 6
PREPARATION TIME: 15 to 20 minutes
UNSUPERVISED COOKING: 10 to 20 minutes, to taste

In Jean Renoir's movie *Rules of the Game* a cook is defending his boss, who he insists is an aristocrat. "He knew to toss the potatoes for the salad in wine right after cooking them. Now *there* is an aristocrat."

I guess you could call this salad aristocratic, then, as you toss the potatoes in wine before you add the vinaigrette. The caraway adds a distinct character—but make sure your guests like caraway; it's one of those tastes some people detest.

FOR THE DRESSING:
Juice of ½ lemon
3 tablespoons (45 ml) wine vinegar
1 to 2 teaspoons (5–10 ml) Dijon-style mustard, or more to taste
2 cloves garlic, minced or put through a press
¼ teaspoon (1.25 ml) dried marjoram
½ teaspoon (2.5 ml) dried tarragon
½ cup minced (120 ml) fresh parsley
Salt and freshly ground pepper to taste
½ cup (120 ml) olive or safflower oil

FOR THE SALAD:
2 pounds (1 kg) new or boiling potatoes
¼ cup (60 ml) dry white wine
½ to 1 teaspoon (2.5–5 ml) caraway seeds, to taste
4 to 6 green onions, minced (both white part and green)
2 tablespoons (30 ml) chopped fresh parsley for garnish

Steam the potatoes for 10 to 20 minutes, until crisp-tender.

Meanwhile, prepare the dressing. Mix together all the ingredients except the oil. Whisk in the oil and blend well.

When the potatoes are done, rinse with cold water, hold with a towel or mitt and slice ½ inch (1.5 cm) thick. If the potatoes are large, cut them in half lengthwise and then slice. Toss the potatoes with the wine, caraway seeds, and green onions, then with the dressing. Sprinkle the chopped parsley over the top and serve. Or chill and serve.

♥ Substitute ¼ cup (60 ml) safflower oil and ¼ cup (60 ml) vegetable stock or water for the oil in the dressing, or use Yogurt Vinaigrette (page 276).

♥ WATERCRESS, MUSHROOM, AND TOFU SALAD
SERVES 4 TO 6
PREPARATION TIME: 15 minutes

You can omit the tofu in this recipe and still have a nice watercress and mushroom salad.

FOR THE DRESSING:
- 3 tablespoons (45 ml) wine or cider vinegar
- 1 teaspoon (5 ml) tamari
- ½ teaspoon (2.5 ml) dry mustard or 1 teaspoon (5 ml) Dijon-style
- 1 small clove garlic, minced or put through a press (optional)
  Salt and freshly ground pepper to taste
- ½ cup (120 ml) olive or safflower oil

FOR THE SALAD:
- 2 cakes (½ pound (225 gm) tofu
- 2 bunches watercress
- ¼ pound (100 gm) mushrooms, wiped and sliced thin
- 2 tablespoons (30 ml) fresh herbs (such as basil, dill, thyme, marjoram; optional), alone or in combination

Mix together all the ingredients for the dressing except the oil. Whisk in the oil and set aside.

Mash the tofu in a salad bowl and toss with the dressing. Add the watercress, mushrooms, and optional herbs and toss again. Serve.

♥ Omit the tamari; substitute 2 tablespoons (30 ml) oil and ¼ cup (60 ml) vegetable stock or water for the oil in the dressing. Add more vinegar to the tofu-dressing mixture if it tastes too bland.

♥ LEFTOVER GRAINS SALAD*
serves 4 to 6
Preparation time: 15 to 20 minutes

I can't think of a better way to use up leftover grains than in a salad. While brown rice salad has always been a favorite of mine, with all the marvelous combinations of flavors and textures, bulgur, couscous, millet, wheat berries, and other grains work just as well. Even a leftover "risotto" (see pages 107–111) would be good in this dish.

2 to 3 cups (475–700 ml) cooked grains (such as brown rice, wheat berries, millet, bulgur, couscous, kasha)
1 sweet green pepper, seeded and diced
1 sweet red pepper, seeded and diced (optional)
4 radishes, trimmed and sliced
½ cucumber, peeled and diced
½ cup (120 ml) sunflower seeds or chopped walnuts
¼ cup (60 ml) Roasted Soybeans (page 60)
1 stalk celery, trimmed and minced
½ cup (180 ml) chopped fresh herbs (such as parsley, basil, thyme, marjoram, tarragon, dill), alone or combined
½ cup (120 ml) freshly grated Parmesan cheese
4 green onions, both white and green parts, chopped
1 head leaf or romaine lettuce, leaves separated, washed and dried
1 recipe Vinaigrette (page 274), Yogurt Vinaigrette (page 276) or Tofu Mayonnaise (page 277)
For Garnish: ½ cup (120 ml) sprouts, tomato wedges or halved cherry tomatoes, hard-boiled egg slices, radish roses, ripe olives, whole green onions, fresh herbs

Toss the leftover cooked grains together with all the ingredients except the lettuce leaves. Toss with the vinaigrette or dressing of your choice.

Line a salad bowl or platter with the lettuce leaves and top with the salad. Decorate with garnishes of your choice.

♥ Omit sunflower seeds or walnuts and Parmesan; use Low-Fat Vinaigrette (page 275) or Yogurt Vinaigrette (page 276); don't use olives or hard-boiled eggs for garnish.

*Auxiliary recipe: requires cooked grains

♥ LEFTOVER BEANS SALAD*
SERVES 4 TO 6
PREPARATION TIME: 15 to 20 minutes

I once lived on this salad for a week after 70 instead of 100 people showed up at a catering job. The vinaigrette acts like a kind of preservative, so the beans last quite a while.

You can use whatever beans you have on hand for this salad, even a combination. You can also serve a warm version, using pressure-cooked beans. If you make a big pot of beans every week, this dish is a perfect way to use up any leftovers. It makes a filling, high-protein meal with whole-grain bread or pasta.

    3 cups (700 ml) cooked beans (such as garbanzos, white beans, kidney beans, lentils, pintos, black beans)
    1 Bermuda onion, sliced thin and poached 4 to 5 minutes, then drained (see instructions, page 290)
    1 sweet green pepper, seeded and chopped
    1 tablespoon (15 ml) chopped fresh herbs (such as dill, basil, marjoram, thyme, rosemary), or more to taste
    2 tablespoons (30 ml) chopped fresh parsley
    2 cups (475 ml) cooked brown rice or other grains such as bulgur, millet, couscous (optional)
    1 clove garlic, minced or put through a press
    3 tablespoons (45 ml) wine vinegar
    1 recipe Vinaigrette (page 274)
      Salt, freshly ground pepper, and dried or prepared Dijon-style mustard to taste, if necessary
    ½ cup (120 ml) freshly grated Parmesan cheese (optional)
    FOR GARNISH: alfalfa sprouts, sliced tomatoes, romaine or leaf lettuce leaves, whole green onions, radish roses

Toss together the beans, onion, green pepper, herbs, and optional grains with the garlic, wine vinegar, and vinaigrette. Season with salt, pepper, and mustard if necessary.

Line a bowl or platter with lettuce leaves and top with the beans. Decorate with garnishes of your choice. Sprinkle with optional Parmesan.

♥ Use Low-Fat Vinaigrette (page 275); omit cheese and salt.

*Auxiliary recipe: requires cooked beans

♥ COLESLAW
SERVES 4 TO 6
PREPARATION TIME: 10 to 15 minutes

> ¼ cup (60 ml) cider vinegar
> 2 tablespoons (30 ml) mild honey
> Salt to taste
> ¾ cup (180 ml) plain low-fat yogurt
> ½ head green cabbage, finely shredded
> 2 carrots, grated
> 2 to 4 tablespoons (30–60 ml) grated onion, to taste

Mix together the vinegar, honey, salt, and yogurt and toss with the cabbage, carrots, and grated onion. Serve immediately, or chill and serve.

♥ Omit salt.

♥ JÍCAMA AND ORANGE SALAD WITH AVOCADOS
SERVES 4 TO 6
PREPARATION TIME: 15 minutes

Jícama is a large, brown, odd-looking root vegetable that somewhat resembles an overgrown turnip. It's white and fleshy on the inside, with a texture much like that of a radish, and is very juicy and sweet. I think it's one of the most refreshing of vegetables. In Mexico fruit vendors sell it in large slices or spears with lemon juice and chili powder sprinkled on it, which is one of the best ways to eat it. I also love it in a salad, like the one below, with oranges and avocados. You could add it to almost any other salad for a nice crunchy variation, and it's welcome on a platter of raw vegetables.

> 1½ pounds (700 gm) jícama, peeled and sliced ¼ to ½ inch
> (0.7–1.5 cm) thick and about 2 inches (5 cm) wide
> 3 oranges, peeled, white membranes removed, sectioned
> 2 avocados, peeled, seeds removed, and sliced (optional)
> 1 recipe Vinaigrette (page 274) or juice of 1 lime
> Chili powder and ground cumin to taste

Arrange the jícama, optional avocados, and orange sections on a platter and either drizzle on the Vinaigrette or douse with the juice of a lime; sprinkle on chili powder and cumin to taste.

♥ Omit avocados; use the lime juice dressing.

COTTAGE CHEESE AND TOMATO SALAD WITH MISO DRESSING
SERVES 4

PREPARATION TIME: 10 minutes

FOR THE SALAD:
- 1½ cups (350 ml) low-fat, small-curd cottage cheese
- 1 large ripe tomato, chopped
- 1 cucumber, peeled and diced or sliced thin
- 2 cups (475 ml) alfalfa, mung, or lentil sprouts
  Romaine or Boston lettuce leaves

FOR THE DRESSING:
- 2 tablespoons (30 ml) cider vinegar or wine vinegar
- 1 clove garlic, minced or put through a press
- 1 tablespoon (15 ml) fresh lemon juice
- 1 to 2 teaspoons (5–10 ml) miso, to taste
- ¼ cup (60 ml) safflower oil

Toss together the cottage cheese, tomato, cucumber, and sprouts. Line a platter with lettuce leaves.

Stir together the vinegar, garlic, lemon juice, and miso until the miso is dissolved; whisk in the safflower oil. Toss with the cottage cheese mixture. Mound the salad on the lettuce leaves and serve.

♥ ORIENTAL SALAD
SERVES 4 TO 6
PREPARATION TIME: 20 to 30 minutes

The inspiration for this recipe came from a salad I ate at, of all places, a French restaurant in New York. What made that salad "Oriental" were shiitake mushrooms (long, thin-stemmed mushrooms with small tops), bamboo shoots, bean sprouts, and snow peas. The dressing was distinctly flavored with sesame oil, and though I have not quite duplicated that dressing, I think I can safely call this an Oriental Salad.

FOR THE DRESSING:
1 tablespoon (15 ml) cider vinegar or wine vinegar
½ teaspoon (2.5 ml) grated or minced fresh gingerroot
2 tablespoons (30 ml) Tamari-Bouillon Broth (page 62) or water
3 tablespoons (45 ml) safflower oil
1 tablespoon (15 ml) tamari
2 tablespoons (30 ml) dry sherry
1 teaspoon (5 ml) sesame tahini
2 tablespoons (30 ml) sesame oil

FOR THE SALAD:
½ pound (225 gm) romaine lettuce, leaves separated and washed
1½ cups (350 ml) mung bean sprouts
1 4-ounce (100 gm) can bamboo shoots, drained
1 cup (250 ml) shiitake mushrooms, if available, or sliced mushrooms
4 radishes, trimmed and sliced
¼ pound (100 gm) snow peas, briefly steamed
½ small cucumber, peeled and sliced thin
2 tablespoons (30 ml) chopped fresh cilantro

Combine all the ingredients for the dressing and mix thoroughly.

Line a platter or large salad bowl with the romaine. Place the sprouts in a mound in the middle and surround with the bamboo shoots. Sprinkle the mushrooms over the top of the sprouts. Place the radish slices, snow peas, and cucumber slices all around the bamboo shoots; sprinkle cilantro over the top.

Bring to the table and pour on the dressing.

♥ Omit the tamari; reduce the safflower oil to 1 tablespoon (15 ml) and the sesame oil to 1 tablespoon (15 ml); increase the water or stock to ¼ cup (60 ml).

♥ SIMPLE CABBAGE AND CARROT SALAD WITH FRESH HERBS

SERVES 4

PREPARATION TIME: 20 minutes

The cabbage here is shredded very thin, and the purple, orange, and the fresh green herb specks are beautiful.

FOR THE DRESSING:
 1 tablespoon (15 ml) fresh lemon juice
 2 tablespoons (30 ml) wine vinegar or cider vinegar
 ½ teaspoon (2.5 ml) Dijon-style mustard
 1 small clove garlic, minced or put through a press
   Salt and freshly ground pepper
 ⅓ cup (80 ml) olive oil

FOR THE SALAD:
 1 pound (450 gm) purple cabbage, cored and shredded fine
 1 medium carrot, scrubbed, grated fine
 1 teaspoon (5 ml) chopped chives
 1 teaspoon (5 ml) chopped fresh dill
 ½ teaspoon (2.5 ml) chopped fresh thyme

Stir together the lemon juice, vinegar, mustard, garlic, and salt and pepper to taste. Whisk in the olive oil. Set aside.

Place the cabbage in a bowl; put the grated carrots in the center, then place the herbs on top of the carrots. Bring the salad to the table, toss with the dressing and serve.

♥ Substitute Low-Fat Vinaigrette (page 275) or Yogurt Vinaigrette (page 276) for the dressing.

♥ HOT AND SOUR BEAN SPROUT SALAD

SERVES 4 TO 6

PREPARATION TIME: 20 to 25 minutes

This salad is bursting with the vital crunch of sprouts and juicy cucumbers. The dressing is hot, but not too hot, with a delicious mixture of either peanuts or sesame (or both), ginger, and hot pepper. You can alter the amount of hot pepper flakes you use in the dressing according to how picante you want the salad to be. There is hardly any oil, and if you leave out the tamari it's quite suitable for a low-fat/low-sodium diet. I have often made a meal of this salad, along with a simple tofu preparation like Tofu Cutlets (page 131) or Chilled Tofu with Dipping Sauces (page 132). If you can't get to an Oriental food market to get the hot red pepper oil, make the salad anyway and add 1 more tablespoon sesame oil.

FOR THE DRESSING:

    2 tablespoons (30 ml) sesame tahini or crunchy peanut butter
1 to 2 tablespoons (15–30 ml) tamari, to taste
    ¼ cup (60 ml) cider vinegar or white wine vinegar
    1 tablespoon (15 ml) hot red pepper oil or hot spiced oil (available in Oriental food markets; optional)
    ½ teaspoon (2.5 ml) red pepper flakes, or ¼ teaspoon (1.25 ml) cayenne (omit for less picante dressing)
    2 tablespoons (30 ml) sesame oil
    1 tablespoon (15 ml) finely minced or grated fresh ginger
    1 clove garlic, minced fine
    1 cup (250 ml) Tamari-Bouillon Broth (page 62)
    Freshly ground pepper to taste

FOR THE SALAD:

    3 cups (700 ml) mung bean sprouts, or a combination of mung, lentil, sunflower, and alfalfa
    1 medium or large cucumber, peeled and shredded or cut in julienne strips
    3 green onions, chopped (both white part and green)
    3 tablespoons (45 ml) chopped fresh cilantro
    1 head leaf or red tip lettuce, leaves separated, washed and dried
1 to 2 tablespoons (15–30 ml) sesame seeds
    2 tomatoes, sliced or cut in wedges, for garnish

Combine all the ingredients for the dressing in a blender and blend until smooth.

Combine the sprouts, cucumber, green onions, and cilantro and toss with 1 cup (250 ml) of the dressing.

Line a salad bowl or platter with the lettuce leaves, top with the sprout mixture, and pour on the remaining dressing. Sprinkle the sesame seeds over the top and garnish with tomatoes.

♥ Omit tamari; use 1 tablespoon (15 ml) each of the nut butter and the sesame oil; omit sesame seeds in the salad.

♥ HOT AND SOUR BUCKWHEAT NOODLE SALAD
SERVES 6
PREPARATION TIME: 20 to 25 minutes

This is one of those unforgettable salads, satisfying and exciting at the same time. I've seen the most conservative eaters come back for seconds. Those unmistakably nutty buckwheat noodles are wonderful against the crunchy cucumbers and sprouts with picante dressing, the same as that used in the preceding Hot and Sour Bean Sprout Salad.

Dressing for Hot and Sour Bean Sprout Salad (page 298); adjust the amount of hot pepper to taste

FOR THE SALAD:
  6 dried mushrooms
  1 tablespoon (15 ml) tamari
  2 teaspoons (10 ml) salt
  2 tablespoons (30 ml) safflower oil
  ½ pound (225 gm) buckwheat noodles (soba)
  2 tablespoons (30 ml) sesame oil
  1 cup (250 ml) mung bean sprouts
  1 cucumber, peeled and shredded or diced
  ⅔ cup (160 ml) chopped walnuts
  3 tablespoons (45 ml) chopped fresh cilantro
  1 head leaf or red tip lettuce, leaves separated, washed and dried
     Tomato wedges or radishes, for garnish

Begin bringing about 4 quarts (4 L) water to a boil in a large pot. Meanwhile, place the dried mushrooms in a small bowl and add boiling water to cover. Add the tamari and stir. Let stand for about 15 minutes, while you prepare the rest of the salad.

When the pot of water comes to a boil, add the salt and safflower oil. Add the noodles and cook al dente, about 5 minutes. Drain, rinse with cold water, and toss with the sesame oil in a bowl.

When the mushrooms are soft, drain, rinse thoroughly to remove grit, cut off the stem and discard, and cut the caps into slivers.

Toss the noodles with the mushroom slivers, the sprouts, cucumber, walnuts, cilantro, and dressing. Line a bowl or platter with the lettuce leaves and top with the noodle mixture. Garnish with tomato wedges or radishes and serve.

♥ Use only 1 tablespoon (15 ml) each nut butter and sesame oil in the dressing; omit tamari in mushroom-soaking liquid; omit salt and use 2 teaspoons (10 ml) safflower oil in the cooking liquid; toss the soba with only 1 tablespoon (15 ml) sesame oil; substitute 3 tablespoons (45 ml) sunflower seeds for the walnuts in the salad.

COLD MARINATED ZUCCHINI, ORIENTAL STYLE
PREPARATION TIME: 10 minutes

Even though this salad has to marinate for a couple of hours I consider it a "fast feast" because it's so easy to put together. It's important to slice the zucchini paper-thin for this recipe, so sharpen your knives. This keeps for several days, refrigerated in a covered container.

½ cup (120 ml) tamari
1 teaspoon (5 ml) freshly grated ginger
¼ cup (60 ml) wine vinegar or cider vinegar
1 small clove garlic, minced or put through a press
1 tablespoon (15 ml) mild honey
¼ cup (60 ml) water
2 tablespoons (30 ml) sesame oil
4 medium zucchini, washed and sliced paper-thin
2 green onions, finely chopped (white part and green)

Mix together the tamari, ginger, vinegar, garlic, honey, and water. Whisk in the sesame oil. Toss with the zucchini and green onions. Cover and refrigerate several hours.

♥ COLD PASTA SALAD

SERVES 4 TO 6

PREPARATION TIME: 20 minutes in all

This high-class macaroni salad is a real weakness of mine. I like it best in the spring, when my garden is full of fresh herbs. You can be as imaginative as you want here, adding whatever vegetables and herbs you might have on hand. It keeps well in the refrigerator as long as your pasta is cooked al dente. You can toss the noodles with either a vinaigrette-type dressing or tofu mayonnaise, or both.

FOR THE DRESSING:

    Juice of 1 lemon
2 tablespoons (30 ml) wine vinegar
1 large clove garlic, minced or put through a press
¼ teaspoon (1.25 ml) dried tarragon
    Salt and freshly ground pepper
½ cup (120 ml) safflower oil

FOR THE SALAD:

¾ pound (350 gm) whole-grain elbow macaroni or spirals (4½ cups cooked; 1 L)
½ cup (120 ml) chopped fresh herbs (such as parsley, basil, rosemary, marjoram, dill, thyme, or a combination)
½ cup (120 ml) freshly grated Parmesan cheese
3 tablespoons (45 ml) Romano cheese, freshly grated, or use ¾ cup (180 ml) Parmesan in all
⅓ cup (80 ml) Roasted Soybeans (page 60) or chopped walnuts
1 small sweet green or red pepper, or 3 mild banana peppers, seeded and thinly sliced or chopped
3 tablespoons (45 ml) chopped chives or minced green onion (green part only)
4 radishes, sliced (optional)
4 mushrooms, sliced (optional)
2 tomatoes, cut in thin wedges (optional)
½ cup (120 ml) Tofu Mayonnaise (page 277)

Begin heating the water for the pasta in a large pot.

Mix together the lemon juice, vinegar, garlic, tarragon, and salt and freshly ground pepper to taste. Whisk in the safflower oil. Set aside.

Cook the pasta al dente. Drain immediately in a colander and rinse for several minutes with ice-cold water. Shake the colander to remove as much water as possible, then place the cooked pasta in a bowl. Toss with the herbs, Parmesan, Romano, soybeans, and the vegetables (including the optional ones). Toss again with the optional Tofu Mayonnaise (this makes a creamy and luscious coating). Chill until ready to serve.

Note: ¾ cup (180 ml) of the mayonnaise may be substituted for the vinaigrette. You may want to add more garlic to the mayonnaise.

MENU SUGGESTIONS

This makes a nice accompaniment to cold soups and light cheese or egg dishes. It's also nice with any of the vegetable dishes that don't include grains (the simpler vegetable dishes, such as Green Beans à la Provençal (page 147), Brussels Sprouts with Lemon-Mustard Butter (page 149), or any simply steamed vegetable).

♥ Use the tofu mayonnaise only; omit the salt and cheeses.

DESSERTS

PUFFED DESSERT OMELETS
PRUNE SOUFFLÉ
APRICOT SOUFFLÉ
PEARS POACHED IN RED WINE
PEACHES POACHED IN RED WINE
STRAWBERRIES IN RED WINE AND PRESERVES SYRUP
FIGS POACHED IN MADEIRA
STRAWBERRIES IN CHAMPAGNE
APPLES WITH LIME JUICE
GINGERED FRUIT
BAKED GRAPEFRUIT WITH TEQUILA OR SHERRY
CANTALOUPE WITH APRICOT PUREE AND ALMONDS
PEACHES WITH MARSALA OR AMARETTO
STRAWBERRIES OR RASPBERRIES WITH RED WINE
BANANA YOGURT FREEZE
PEACH BANANA FREEZE
PINEAPPLE BANANA MINT SHERBET
STRAWBERRY SHERBET
STRAWBERRY FREEZE
ORANGE ICE
NOODLE KUGEL
TOFU NOODLE KUGEL
BREAD PUDDING
RICE OR LEFTOVER GRAINS PUDDING*
FRUIT AND CHEESE PLATTER

*Auxiliary recipe

Dessert is always remembered long afterwards if it's exciting. People never hesitate to request their favorites, and children, especially, always anticipate this course, hoping for the dishes they love. The trouble with many desserts, however, is that their recipes are complicated, not something you can whip up after work. If Bavarian Cream and fancy cakes are what comes to mind when you think of what constitutes a real sweet, then this chapter may disappoint you. But you can't make those desserts in fifteen minutes. You can, however, make light, refreshing sherbets, soothing fruits poached in wine, elegant soufflés, and outstanding, subtle, sweet omelets that will melt in your mouth. You can liven up fruits by dousing them with liqueurs or marinating them in surprising mixtures like lime juice, ginger, and honey.

When I cooked for heart patients, who felt deprived of so many of their favorite foods, the desserts both they and I became most enthusiastic about were my frozen fruit ices—the Banana Yogurt Freeze, Peach Banana Freeze, and Strawberry Freeze on pages 315–317. These are merely fruit that has been frozen solid, then blended in a food processor with a little yogurt until smooth. They become like soft ice cream, as sweet as the fruit itself, and when flavored with either vanilla or liqueur are just amazing. What a wonderful way to allow yourself and your family all the pleasures of ice cream! The patients I served would come back for seconds and sometimes even thirds, and I never worried about how much they ate.

The simplest additions can enhance fruit. Mint, for example, can make plain oranges or pineapple into something altogether different. Lime juice will change the face of apples, and a little champagne poured over strawberries will transform dessert into a celebration.

Some of the recipes here can even provide you with complete protein, specifically the omelets (pages 306–307), soufflés (pages 307–308), and grain, bread, and noodle puddings (pages 318–321). It really doesn't matter where you get your protein in a meal, as long as you get it. These dishes are so substantial that I usually eat the leftovers for breakfast.

Many of the fruit dishes in this chapter call for liqueurs. It certainly isn't necessary for you to run out and spend a hundred dollars stocking your liquor cabinet. All fruit can stand alone, and as such usually serves me well as dessert. But if you want to be a little extravagant, your palate will appreciate the liqueurs, and the recipes make perfect, easy desserts for dinner parties. They are nice, light, but memorable finishes to filling meals.

Most of these dishes are so easy that you can practically make them while the coffee or tea is brewing. Even the soufflés: if your dried fruit is pureed, soufflé dish prepared, eggs separated, and oven preheating, you can just fold everything together, turn it into the dish, slide it in the oven, and in twenty minutes you'll have something grand and ambrosial. Friends have asked me hopefully if my Prune Soufflé (page 307) would be appropriate for this book, and I'm glad I could answer yes.

As you will see by the contents of this chapter, a dessert needn't be one's downfall. For those of you who like something sweet after dinner, any recipe here will allow you to live well—and long.

PUFFED DESSERT OMELETS
SERVES 4
PREPARATION TIME: 5 minutes in all

Ann Clark, who lived in France for six years and now teaches French *cuisine bourgeoise* in Austin, is one of the most brilliant, authentic cooks I know. She taught me the technique for these luscious dessert omelets, and I owe her much gratitude. I couldn't believe it when I began making these. They melt in your mouth almost before you can groan with delight, and they're so light that you could almost eat an entire one by yourself (as I was tempted to do when I tested the recipes). They are not very sweet, but have a subtle flavor. If you wish, you may add a bit more honey or liqueur.

PUFFED AMARETTO OMELET
    3 eggs, separated
1 to 2 tablespoons (15–30 ml) mild honey, to taste
    3 tablespoons (45 ml) Amaretto liqueur
    ⅛ teaspoon (scant 1 ml) freshly grated nutmeg
    1 tablespoon (15 ml) unsalted butter
2 to 3 tablespoons (30–45 ml) slivered almonds, browned in butter, or toasted dry, in the oven for garnish.

Beat the egg whites in a bowl until they form stiff peaks. Beat the egg yolks in another bowl with the honey, Amaretto, and nutmeg. Gently fold into the egg whites.

Heat a 10- or 12-inch (25–30 cm) omelet pan over medium-high heat and add the butter. When the foam subsides and the butter just begins to color, add the omelet mixture. Do not stir. Cook over a medium flame for exactly 1 minute. The top should be soft and the bottom browned. Slide out onto a serving platter, folding the omelet in half as you do. Garnish with the almond slivers and serve at once.

PUFFED GRAND MARNIER OMELET

    3 eggs, separated
1 to 2 tablespoons (15–30 ml) mild honey, to taste
    3 tablespoons (45 ml) Grand Marnier
      Pinch of freshly grated nutmeg
    1 orange, sliced, for garnish

Proceed as in the preceding Puffed Amaretto Omelet.

Note: When you first make these, you might worry that they will taste like raw eggs, because the whites seem almost uncooked. They don't. The whites set, yet remain so light that they melt in your mouth immediately. And the yolks do cook and contribute to the delicious browned surface.

    These, of course, should not accompany an egg-based main dish or soup.

PRUNE SOUFFLÉ
SERVES 4 TO 6

PREPARATION TIME: 15 minutes
UNSUPERVISED SOAKING OF PRUNES: at least 2 hours, up to overnight
UNSUPERVISED COOKING: 20 minutes

Though you have to have enough foresight to soak the prunes in Marsala for this recipe, it's so easy to put together that it really is a "fast feast." I first made it on a whim, when I wanted to get rid of a package of prunes that had been sitting around forever. Some friends were coming for dinner, so I just whipped up this soufflé after we'd finished our salad, and we all never forgot it.

    1 pound (450 gm) pitted prunes
    2 cups (475 ml) Marsala
    4 egg yolks
   ½ cup (120 ml) plain low-fat yogurt
    6 egg whites
      Pinch of cream of tartar
   ½ cup (120 ml) heavy cream, whipped or ½ cup plain low-fat yogurt for topping

Pour boiling water over the prunes. Let stand for 15 minutes and drain.

Soak the prunes for several hours or overnight in the Marsala, adding a little water if the Marsala doesn't cover them.

Preheat the oven to 400 degrees (200°C) and butter a 2-quart (2 L) soufflé dish.

Drain the prunes, retaining the liquid, and puree in a food processor or blender, adding the egg yolks, yogurt and about ¼ cup (60 ml) of the soaking liquid.

Beat the egg whites until they form stiff peaks, adding the cream of tartar when they begin to foam. Stir one fourth of the whites into the prune mixture until just blended. Gently fold in the rest.

Carefully turn into the prepared soufflé dish and bake for 20 minutes, until puffed and browned. Serve with whipped cream or yogurt flavored, if you wish, with some of the soaking liquid.

APRICOT SOUFFLÉ
SERVES 6
PREPARATION TIME: 15 minutes
UNSUPERVISED SOAKING: at least 2 hours, or overnight
UNSUPERVISED COOKING: 20 minutes

Like the Prune Soufflé (page 307), this dessert requires you to be organized enough to soak the apricots, but after that it's a breeze.

    1 pound (450 gm) pitted dried apricots
    ½ teaspoon (2.5 ml) vanilla
    ½ cup (120 ml) milk or plain low-fat yogurt
    2 tablespoons (30 ml) cognac
    1 tablespoon (15 ml) Amaretto (optional)
    4 egg yolks
    6 egg whites
      Pinch of cream of tartar
    ½ cup (120 ml) heavy cream, whipped, or ½ cup plain low-fat yogurt for topping

Place the dried apricots in a bowl and pour on boiling water to cover. Let soak several hours, or overnight. Drain.

Preheat the oven to 400 degrees (200°C) and butter a 2-quart (2 L) soufflé dish.

Puree the apricots in a food processor or blender with the vanilla, the milk or yogurt, Cognac, optional Amaretto, and the egg yolks until smooth.

Begin beating the egg whites. When they start to foam add the cream of tartar and continue to beat until they form stiff peaks. Stir one fourth into the apricot mixture until just blended and gently fold in the rest.

Carefully transfer to the prepared soufflé dish and bake for 20 minutes, or until puffed and browned.

♥ PEARS POACHED IN RED WINE
SERVES 2

PREPARATION TIME: 10 minutes
UNSUPERVISED POACHING: 15 to 20 minutes

I like this dish in the fall, when pears are at their best. The cardamom lingers on your palate, giving the dish a unique touch.

        2 cups (475 ml) red wine
⅓ to ½ cup (80–120 ml) mild honey, to taste
        ½ cup (120 ml) raisins
        1 3-inch (8 cm) stick cinnamon
¼ to ½ teaspoon (1.25–2.5 ml) cardamom, to taste
        3 firm ripe pears, cored and sliced
           Juice of ½ lemon
        ¼ cup (60 ml) slivered almonds (optional)
        ½ cup (120 ml) heavy cream, whipped, or ½ cup (120 ml)
           plain yogurt, for topping

Combine the wine, honey, raisins, and cinnamon and cardamom in a 2-quart saucepan and bring to a simmer. Cover and simmer for 5 minutes. Meanwhile, core and slice the pears. Place them in a bowl of water acidulated with the juice of ½ lemon.

After 5 minutes drain the pears and add to the poaching liquid along with the almonds. Cover and poach for 10 to 15 minutes. Serve warm, topped with whipped cream or yogurt.

♥ See instructions following Peaches Poached in Red Wine, following.

♥ PEACHES POACHED IN RED WINE

Substitute 4 ripe peaches, peeled, pitted, and sliced for the pears and proceed as you would for the pears.

♥ Substitute apple juice for the red wine; omit honey; reduce raisins to ¼ cup (60 ml). Top with yogurt instead of whipped cream.

STRAWBERRIES IN RED WINE AND PRESERVES SYRUP
SERVES 4 TO 5
PREPARATION TIME: 15 minutes

The idea for this recipe comes from my friend Camilla Smith. I'm not sure how Camilla does her version—she told me briefly one day—but I couldn't really remember her directions when I got back to my own kitchen. That's why I haven't taken the liberty to call this "Camilla's Strawberries in Red Wine and Preserves Syrup." This is a sweet, ambrosial combination. If you can find unsweetened preserves or preserves made with honey (Arrowhead Mills makes some), so much the better.

  1 cup (250 ml) red wine
  1 tablespoon (15 ml) mild honey
 ¼ cup (60 ml) red currant or black currant preserves, or grape jam
  2 pints (1 L) ripe strawberries, hulled and cut in half or quarters
     Plain low-fat yogurt or whipped cream for garnish

Combine the wine, honey, and preserves in a saucepan and bring to a rapid boil. Boil down to half the original volume, which should take 5 to 10 minutes. Meanwhile, prepare the strawberries and place in a bowl. Pour the syrup over the strawberries. Stir, then cover and chill until serving time, the longer the better. Serve with plain yogurt or whipped cream on the side.

FIGS POACHED IN MADEIRA
SERVES 4 TO 6

PREPARATION TIME: 10 to 15 minutes
POACHING TIME: 5 minutes for fresh; 15 minutes for dried

Figs are to me the most sensuous fruit. Unfortunately, fresh figs aren't always easy to come by, and their subtlety is a taste sensation completely different from that of dried figs. But dried figs are great too, and go well with Madeira, so you can make this dish with whichever you can get.

  1 pound (450 gm) fresh figs, or ½ pound (200 gm) dried, stemmed and cut in half lengthwise (unless very small)
  2 cups (475 ml) Madeira
  ½ cup (120 ml) heavy cream, whipped, or ½ cup (120 ml) plain low-fat yogurt for topping (optional)

Combine the figs and Madeira in a saucepan and bring to a simmer. Poach fresh figs for 5 minutes, dried for 15, or until tender. Serve hot, warm, or chilled, topped with whipped cream or yogurt if you wish.

STRAWBERRIES IN CHAMPAGNE
SERVES 4 TO 6

PREPARATION TIME: 5 to 10 minutes

This will make a party out of dessert, or give your dinner party a second wind. I've always had a weakness for champagne, at any time of day, and dessert is certainly an appropriate place for it.

  2 pints (1 L) ripe strawberries, hulled, cut in half if large, and chilled
  1 split good champagne, either dry or semi-dry, chilled

Place the strawberries in an attractive bowl (glass is nice) and bring to the table. Uncork the cold champagne, pour over and serve.

♥ APPLES WITH LIME JUICE
SERVES 4 TO 6
PREPARATION TIME: 10 minutes, at most

It's amazing how much more exciting a mere apple is with the addition of lime juice. If Eve had only known . . .

    2 to 3 large sweet apples, such as Delicious or McIntosh
            Juice of 2 limes

Core and slice the apples and toss with the lime juice. Chill until ready to serve.

♥ GINGERED FRUIT
SERVES 6
PREPARATION TIME: 15 minutes

This is one of those magical dishes that may look fairly ordinary on paper, but that having tasted you never forget. Ginger, lime juice, and honey go together beautifully and make an evocative marinade for the fruit. It's nice to be able to come up with a fresh fruit dish in the wintertime, when most of these ingredients are available.

       1 cup (250 ml) dried or fresh figs
      ⅓ cup (80 ml) fresh lime juice
      ¼ cup (60 ml) mild honey
    2 to 3 teaspoons (10–15 ml) minced or grated fresh ginger
       2 pink grapefruit, skins and membranes removed, sectioned
       2 ripe pears, cored and diced
       1 bunch red grapes (about ½ pound; 225 gm) (seedless if available)
      ½ cup (120 ml) shaved coconut

If you are using dried figs, place them in a bowl and pour boiling water over them. Let stand 10 minutes, then drain and cut in half lengthwise. Cut the fresh figs in half lengthwise, unless they are very small.

Mix together the lime juice, honey, and ginger and toss with all the fruit in a glass or ceramic bowl. Sprinkle the coconut on the top. If possible, chill for an hour and toss once before serving.

♥ Reduce honey to 2 tablespoons (30 ml); reduce lime juice to 3 tablespoons and ginger to 2 teaspoons.

♥ BAKED GRAPEFRUIT WITH TEQUILA OR SHERRY
SERVES 4 TO 6
PREPARATION TIME: 10 minutes
UNSUPERVISED COOKING: 13 minutes

You can always omit the liquor here, but it does add a nice touch, and some of the alcohol will evaporate under the broiler. The tequila version is my favorite.

> 2 to 3 grapefruit, cut in half
> ¼ to ⅓ cup (60–80 ml) either tequila or dry sherry
> Ground cinnamon
> 2 tablespoons (30 ml) mild honey (optional)

Preheat the oven to 300 degrees (150°C).

Section the grapefruit. Douse each half with a tablespoon (15 ml) of either tequila or sherry, then sprinkle with cinnamon. If you wish, drizzle a teaspoon (5 ml) of honey over each.

Place in a baking dish and bake for 10 minutes. Turn on the broiler and place the grapefruit underneath it for 3 minutes. Serve at once.

This is also nice for brunch.

♥ Reduce alcohol to 1 teaspoon (5 ml) per grapefruit; omit honey.

♥ CANTALOUPE WITH APRICOT PUREE AND ALMONDS
SERVES 6 TO 8
PREPARATION TIME: 15 to 20 minutes

This was first served to me on an idyllic afternoon in the south of France. Lulu Peyraud, the proprietress of Domaine Tempier, a beautiful vineyard near Bandol, had invited me to lunch. I had been told by another great cook that Lulu was the best, but I was hardly prepared for the extraordinary lunch I was served in that exquisite setting. When I arrived at the vineyard I felt as though I had just walked through the gate at Proust's Combray, and time stopped for the afternoon. Lulu fed us luscious hors d'oeuvres—tomatoes filled with pesto, lettuce leaves filled with cucumber salad, and a fantastic tapenade on croutons. Then we reveled in a traditional bouillabaisse, cooked in a huge cauldron over an open fire. It was my first, and it was better than my wildest dreams. After the bouillabaisse came fresh figs with goat cheese, and then, to top it off, small Cavaillon melons filled with fresh apricot puree, the perfect finish to an incredible

313

meal. The closest we can come to Cavaillon melons here are small ripe cantaloupes, and they work well. Unfortunately, good, sweet apricots are rarely available, but if you can find them, jump at the opportunity and make this dish.

    1 pound (450 gm) fresh ripe apricots
       Juice of 1 lemon
1 or 2 tablespoons (15–30 ml) mild honey (optional)
       Orange juice as necessary
3 or 4 small ripe cantaloupes, cut in half, seeds removed
   ¾ cup (180 ml) blanched almonds

Peel the apricots by blanching them in boiling water for half a minute, then running them under cold water. The skins will come off easily.

  Pit the apricots and puree them with the lemon juice in a blender or food processor, adding the honey if the apricots are not very sweet. If the puree isn't liquid enough (it should be the consistency of a sauce), add a little orange juice.

  If you wish, scallop the edges of the cantaloupes. Place on plates and fill the cavities with the puree.

  Sprinkle the almonds over the puree and serve.

PEACHES WITH MARSALA OR AMARETTO
SERVES 6
PREPARATION TIME: 5 minutes

    3 large ripe peaches
   ½ cup (120 ml) either Marsala or Amaretto
   ¼ cup (60 ml) chopped almonds
       Sliced fresh strawberries for garnish (optional)

Drop the peaches into boiling water to cover for 1 minute, then drain and run under cold water. Peel off the skins. Cut the peaches in half and remove the stones. Place each half on a plate. Spoon a table-spoon (15 ml) or more of Amaretto or Marsala into the cavities. Sprinkle in chopped almonds and serve immediately, or chill and serve. Garnish with strawberries, if you wish.

STRAWBERRIES OR RASPBERRIES WITH RED WINE
SERVES 6
PREPARATION TIME: 10 minutes for strawberries, 3 for raspberries

    2 pints (1 L) strawberries, hulled and cut in half if large, or 2 pints (1 L) raspberries
       Red wine
    ½ cup (120 ml) heavy cream, whipped and sweetened with a little mild honey, or ½ cup (120 ml) plain low-fat yogurt (optional)

Place the berries in wine glasses and cover them with red wine. Serve, passing whipped cream or yogurt, if desired.

♥ BANANA YOGURT FREEZE
SERVES 4
PREPARATION TIME: 5 minutes (after fruit is frozen)

Banana Yogurt Freeze is the best reason I can think of to own a food processor, since it really can't be made in a blender. This has all the sensual attributes of soft ice cream with none of the fat, sugar, or calories. Frozen bananas are just tossed into the food processor with yogurt and vanilla, and the mixture is transformed. It's unbelievable. Whenever you buy bananas, freeze some of them (see directions below) making sure they are ripe. Then you'll always have the makings for this delicious dessert.

    4 large or 8 small ripe bananas
    1 cup (250 ml) plain low-fat yogurt
    2 teaspoons (10 ml) vanilla, or more to taste
       Freshly grated nutmeg to taste

Peel the bananas, cut in chunks, and freeze in plastic bags. They take 24 hours to freeze solid.

    Place the yogurt and vanilla in a food processor and add the banana chunks. Using the pulse action of the food processor, process until almost smooth. Then process for several seconds until the mixture is completely smooth. Add nutmeg to taste, adjust the vanilla, and serve. Or hold in the freezer for up to 2 hours (it will become too hard if frozen any longer).

♥ PEACH BANANA FREEZE
SERVES 4
PREPARATION TIME: 5 minutes (after fruit is frozen)

This is as ambrosial—maybe even more so—as the banana freeze.

    3 peaches
    2 small or medium ripe bananas
    1 cup (250 ml) plain low-fat yogurt
    2 teaspoons (10 ml) vanilla
      Freshly grated nutmeg to taste

Blanch the peaches in boiling water for 20 seconds. Run under cold water and remove the skins. Cut in half and remove the pits, then cut in chunks and freeze in plastic bags.

Peel the bananas, cut in chunks, and freeze in plastic bags.

Place the yogurt and vanilla in a food processor and add the frozen fruit. Process as in the preceding recipe for the Banana Yogurt Freeze, until smooth. Add nutmeg to taste, adjust vanilla, and serve at once, or hold in the freezer for up to 2 hours.

♥ PINEAPPLE BANANA MINT SHERBET
SERVES 6
PREPARATION TIME: 10 minutes at most
UNSUPERVISED FREEZING IN A SORBETTIER: 1 hour

If you have a sorbettier or ice cream freezer, frozen fruit ices are definitely "fast feasts," and they are always popular. The heart patients I cooked for were delighted when we served them these frozen desserts. How could something be as good as ice cream, and healthy too? But they are healthy, as healthy as the fruit from which they're made. Usually there is no need to sweeten them, because the fruits themselves have so much flavor.

    ½ cup (120 ml) orange juice
    2 to 3 tablespoons (30–45 ml) fresh mint leaves, plus additional
        for garnish
    1 large ripe pineapple, peeled, cored, and chunked
    1 tablespoon (15 ml) fresh lime juice
    1 large ripe banana
      Sliced fresh strawberries or oranges for garnish (optional)

Blend the orange juice and mint together in a blender until the mint is liquefied. Blend in the remaining ingredients, except the garnishes, and puree until smooth. Place in a sorbettier in the freezer or in an electric ice cream freezer and freeze until set. Hold in the freezer in a covered container. If it freezes solid, let soften in the refrigerator for an hour before serving. Garnish, if desired, with strawberry or orange slices.

Note: If you don't have a sorbettier or ice cream freezer, the sherbet may be frozen in ice trays or a baking pan. Place the puree in the freezer until just beginning to set, about 1 hour. Remove from the freezer and beat with an electric mixer, a whisk or in a food processor to break up the ice crystals. Place in the freezer again and repeat once more when just beginning to set. Pack into a container and freeze.

♥ STRAWBERRY SHERBET
SERVES 6
PREPARATION TIME: 10 minutes
UNSUPERVISED FREEZING IN A SORBETTIER OR ICE CREAM FREEZER: 1 hour

    3 pints (1.5 L) strawberries, hulled
3 to 4 tablespoons (45–60 ml) crème de cassis liqueur or black cherry concentrate (available in whole-foods stores)
3 to 4 tablespoons (45–60 ml) fresh lemon juice
    1 cup (250 ml) sliced fresh strawberries, and fresh mint, for garnish

Puree all the ingredients except the garnishes and follow the freezing procedure for Pineapple Banana Mint Sherbet (page 316).

♥ STRAWBERRY FREEZE
SERVES 4
PREPARATION TIME: 5 minutes after fruit is frozen

    2 pints (1 L) strawberries, hulled and frozen
    ½ cup (120 ml) crème de cassis liqueur or black cherry concentrate (available in whole-foods stores)
    ½ cup (120 ml) plain low-fat yogurt

Place the frozen strawberries in a food processor with the liqueur and yogurt. Pulse on and off until the berries are mashed, then puree until you have a smooth ice. Serve at once, or store in the freezer. If frozen solid, let soften in the refrigerator for 30 minutes.

♥ ORANGE ICE
SERVES 4
PREPARATION TIME: 3 minutes

This always reminds me of Good Humor creamsicles, even though it isn't creamy (in fact it's probably more like a popsicle). It's one of those healthy, easy ices like the preceding strawberry and pineapple banana mint sherbets.

1 can frozen orange juice concentrate (small)
Mint for garnish

Make the orange juice according to the directions on the can. Freeze in a sorbettier or ice cream freezer. Serve when it reaches "snow-cone" consistency.

NOODLE KUGEL
SERVES 6 TO 8
PREPARATION TIME: 15 minutes
UNSUPERVISED BAKING: 35 to 45 minutes

This noodle pudding is one of those high-protein desserts that also serves well as a breakfast, as I discovered the week I was testing the recipe. You can assemble it before you begin the rest of your dinner, and it can bake while you prepare that and eat.

3 eggs
1 cup (250 ml) plain low-fat yogurt
½ cup (120 ml) low-fat cottage cheese (small curd)
3 tablespoons (45 ml) mild honey
1 tablespoon (15 ml) lemon juice, or more to taste
½ to 1 teaspoon (2.5–5 ml) ground cinnamon, to taste
¼ to ½ teaspoon (1.25–2.5 ml) freshly grated nutmeg, to taste
1 teaspoon (5 ml) vanilla
¼ cup (60 ml) currants or raisins
1 medium apple, pear, or peach, cored or pitted and chopped
¼ pound (100 gm) flat noodles or 1 cup (250 ml) macaroni, preferably whole-wheat

Preheat the oven to 325 degrees (165°C) and butter a 1½- or 2-quart (1.5–2 L) baking dish or casserole.

Begin heating a large pot of water for the noodles. In a large bowl, beat the eggs together with the yogurt, cottage cheese, honey, lemon juice, cinnamon, nutmeg, and vanilla. Stir in the raisins and fruit.

Cook the pasta al dente and drain. Rinse with cold water in a strainer and shake out excess water. Add to the egg mixture and mix well. Turn into the buttered casserole and cover with foil or a lid.

Bake for 35 to 45 minutes, until firm and a crust has begun to form around the outside. Remove from the oven and allow to stand for 15 minutes before serving.

♥ TOFU NOODLE KUGEL
SERVES 6 TO 8

PREPARATION TIME: 15 minutes
UNSUPERVISED BAKING: 35 to 45 minutes

This is as delightful as the traditional kugel and perfect for those who are trying to avoid eggs and dairy products. It too is good for breakfast.

       2 cakes (½ pound; 225 gm) tofu
       ½ cup (120 ml) plain low-fat yogurt
       ¼ cup (60 ml) mild honey
       1 tablespoon (15 ml) sesame tahini
  2 to 3 tablespoons (30–45 ml) fresh lemon juice, to taste
  ½ to 1 teaspoon (2.5–5 ml) ground cinnamon, to taste
       ½ teaspoon (2.5 ml) freshly grated nutmeg
       1 teaspoon (5 ml) vanilla
       ¼ pound (100 gm) flat noodles or 1 cup (250 ml) macaroni, preferably whole-wheat
       ¼ cup (60 ml) currants or raisins
       1 apple, pear, or peach, cored or pitted and chopped

Preheat the oven to 325 degrees (165°C) and butter a 1½- to 2-quart (1.5–2 L) baking dish or casserole.

Bring a large pot of water to a boil. Meanwhile blend together the tofu, yogurt, honey, tahini, lemon juice, spices, and vanilla in a blender or food processor until completely smooth.

Cook the pasta al dente and drain. Rinse with cold water, then drain well and place in a bowl. Mix with the tofu mixture, currants, and fruit. Turn into the prepared baking dish, cover, and bake for 45 minutes, until set. Let stand 15 minutes before serving.

BREAD PUDDING
SERVES 6 TO 8

PREPARATION TIME: 10 minutes
UNSUPERVISED BAKING: 45 minutes

My earliest cooking jobs were not glamorous. My first one was at a bowling alley; I lasted five days. Later I took a job in a dark basement bar, where I mostly sliced a lot of pastrami and "turkey roll" and made vast amounts of potato salad. But I did get to make the specials there, which is probably why I took the job. For most of these I was limited to leftover ingredients, but in the restaurant business that's what often determines what the soup du jour will be, and I didn't really mind.

We never threw away bread ends at this bar, and every other day I made a big bread pudding. I grew quite fond of these; they're tasty and nutritious, a good way to "sneak" protein into the meal, and a good way to use up bread that is drying out. I like it for breakfast as well as dessert.

3 to 5 cups (700 ml–1.2 L) diced whole-grain bread
2 cups (475 ml) warm milk
1 cup (250 ml) orange juice
3 eggs, separated
⅓ cup (80 ml) mild honey
1 teaspoon (5 ml) vanilla
½ teaspoon (2.5 ml) freshly grated nutmeg
   Grated rind and juice of ½ to 1 lemon, to taste
½ cup (120 ml) raisins
¼ cup sunflower seeds
   Vanilla-flavored milk or whipped cream for topping (optional)

Preheat the oven to 350 degrees (180°C) and butter a 2-quart (2 L) baking dish or soufflé dish.

Place the bread in a bowl and pour in the warm milk and the juice.

Beat the egg yolks together with the honey, vanilla, and nutmeg. Add the lemon rind and juice and pour over the bread. Add the raisins and optional sunflower seeds, and stir together lightly.

Beat the egg whites until stiff but not dry and fold into the bread mixture. Pour into the prepared baking dish, then place in a pan of hot water and bake for 45 minutes, or until beginning to brown on the top.

Remove from the oven and cool, or serve hot. Top, if you wish, with milk or whipped cream flavored with vanilla.

RICE OR LEFTOVER GRAINS PUDDING*
SERVES 6

PREPARATION TIME: 10 minutes
UNSUPERVISED BAKING: 50 minutes

Here is another one of those high-protein desserts. It's a great way to use up leftover grains. This, like the noodle kugels (pages 318 and 319) and the Bread Pudding (page 320), can be assembled before dinner and baked while you eat. They all can also be baked before dinner and reheated.

> 3 eggs
> 1⅓ cups (330 ml) milk
> Pinch of salt
> ⅓ cup (80 ml) mild honey
> 1 teaspoon (5 ml) vanilla
> 1 teaspoon (5 ml) grated lemon peel
> 1 tablespoon (15 ml) fresh lemon juice, or more to taste
> ¼ to ½ teaspoon (1.25–2.5 ml) ground cinnamon
> ¼ teaspoon (1.25 ml) freshly grated nutmeg
> ½ cup (120 ml) currants or raisins
> 2 cups (475 ml) cooked brown rice or other grain, such as millet or bulgur
> 1 pint (0.5 L) fresh strawberries, blueberries, or raspberries, pureed with ¼ cup (60 ml) orange juice, for topping (optional)

Preheat the oven to 325 degrees (165°C) and butter a 1½- or 2½-quart baking dish or soufflé dish.

Beat the eggs together with the milk, salt, and honey. Stir in the vanilla, lemon peel, lemon juice, cinnamon, nutmeg, currants, and the rice or grains.

Pour into the prepared baking dish and bake for 50 minutes, until set. Serve warm or cold, topped with the optional pureed berries.

*Auxiliary recipe: requires cooked grains

♥ FRUIT AND CHEESE PLATTER
Preparation time: 10 minutes

One of the most spectacular desserts I've ever eaten was a platter of fresh figs and goat cheese, fragrant with rosemary, served after an extravagant meal in the south of France. Another was a ripe "Poire William" with a rather dry goat cheese that had been generously seasoned with black pepper. Black pepper isn't a seasoning we normally associate with dessert, but the combination was delicious.

Fruit and cheese seems a very ordinary conclusion to a meal, yet there are an incredible number of interesting variations on this theme. Goat cheese is just one kind of cheese to consider, and even there you can choose between strong, creamy ones like Bûcheron or more subtle, sweeter ones like Philou or Sainte Maure, considered the king of goat cheeses. You can serve a selection of soft cheeses and hard, strong and mild. You shouldn't, however, serve cheeses which are too strong, like limburger, with fruit, because the cheese will overwhelm the delicacy of the fruit.

Choose fruits in season: apples and pears in the fall and winter; melon and strawberries in the spring; peaches, plums, and fresh figs in the summer. Exotica like imported mid-winter strawberries are not only expensive, but usually taste disappointing. Exceptions are imported Hawaiian pineapple, Moroccan clementines, mangoes, and kiwi fruit—all at their best whenever available. You can choose between cantaloupe, Crenshaw, and honeydew, white peaches and yellow, green figs or black, red grapes or green, or Concord grapes in the fall. Even if you only have the more common fruits available, there are always different kinds to choose from, and different ways to present them.

Though always marvelous by itself, fruit can be embellished in a number of ways. Fresh mint will turn pineapple and oranges into something very special; a hint of cardamom is marvelous with strawberries; dried or crystallized ginger can transform cantaloupe; and cinnamon goes nicely with apples and oranges. Liqueurs and spirits, too, can add a new dimension to fruits. Apples with calvados, bananas with rum, cantaloupe with port, pineapple with kirsch—all very festive dishes, and they can all be flamed, which makes them even more impressive. Just warm the liqueur gently, set it aflame, and pour it over the fruit. Not long ago I ended a meal with great fanfare just by pouring flaming whiskey over some fresh Georgia Belle peaches.

Use the list below as a guide, and experiment with different combinations.

FRUITS	GARNISHES AND OTHER ADDITIONS

Fall and Winter:

apples (McIntosh, Northern Spies, Ida Reds, Granny Smith, golden delicious, winesaps, pippins, and more, depending on where you live)	calvados, cinnamon, lime or lemon juice, ginger, allspice, nutmeg, red wine
pears (Comice, Bartlett, Seckel, Anjou, William)	red wine, kirsch, lemon juice, white wine
pomegranate	red wine, crème de cassis
oranges	mint, Grand Marnier, ginger, cinnamon, cumin
grapefruit	tequila, sherry, Grand Marnier, ginger, honey
pineapple	mint, tequila, kirsch, lime juice
persimmons	
black and red grapes (also seedless red grapes)	champagne
Concord grapes	red wine
kumquats	
tangerines	mint, white wine
clementines	
bananas	rum, white wine, cinnamon, vanilla, nutmeg

Spring and Summer:

William pears	red wine, kirsch, lemon juice, white wine
peaches	red or white wine, Amaretto, champagne, crème de cassis, cinnamon, cardamom, whiskey
apricots	red or white wine, Amaretto, champagne, crème de cassis, cinnamon, cardamom, whiskey

Spring and Summer, cont'd.

nectarines — red or white wine, Amaretto, champagne, crème de cassis, cinnamon, cardamom, whiskey

strawberries, raspberries, blueberries, blackberries — champagne, red wine, crème fraîche, cardamom, mint, honey, yogurt, cream

cantaloupe and Crenshaw melon — port, crystallized ginger, dried or fresh ginger, lime juice and pepper

honeydew — mint, lime juice

papaya — lime juice, mint

cherries — kirsch, red wine

watermelon (red or yellow) — mint, vodka, Grand Marnier

loquats

fresh figs — mint, cream

plums (red, purple, green) — red wine, white wine, vanilla

green and red grapes — mint

mangoes — lime juice, mint

CHEESES

Hard, nutty-tasting varieties:
Gruyère
Jarlsberg
Appenzeller
Emmenthaler
Comté
Raclette
Cheddar (mild, sharp, New York, Vermont, raw milk, Wisconsin)
Cantal
Mimolette
Gouda (also with caraway seeds or cumin seeds)
Edam

Rich, semisoft varieties:
Danbo (also with caraway)
Morbier
Port Salut
Bonbel
Havarti
Pyrhennes
Saint Paulin

Soft, buttery varieties and soft, crumbly cheeses:
Chevre (Bûcheron, Sainte Maure, Philou, Poitou)
Camembert
Brie de Meaux
Boursin
Gourmandise (various flavors such as kirsch and walnut)
Brillat Savarin
Saint André
Caprice des Dieux
Toma
Montrachet

Blue-type cheeses: (especially good with apples and pears)
Stilton
Blue
Roquefort
Belle Bressane

APPENDIX:

ADDITIONAL MENUS FOR SPRING

VERY QUICK CREAM OF PEA SOUP (page 85)
TURNIPS GRUYÈRE (page 199)
SLICED TOMATOES
TOSSED GREEN SALAD (page 280)
FRESH PEARS

ORIENTAL SALAD (page 297)
TOFU CUTLETS (page 131)
SIMPLE SOBA WITH SESAME OIL (page 254)
STEAMED BEETS AND BEET GREENS (page 148)
GINGERED FRUIT (page 312)

MUSHROOM TACOS (page 269)
SIMPLE PICANTE ZUCCHINI (page 168)
CUCUMBER YOGURT SALAD (page 282)
STRAWBERRY SHERBET (page 317)

PUREED ZUCCHINI SOUP (page 70)
WHOLE-GRAIN PASTA WITH BUTTER AND HERBS (page 214)
TOSSED GREEN SALAD (page 280)
ORANGE ICE (page 318)

PUFFED ASPARAGUS OMELET (page 183)
POTATOES WITH WHITE WINE AND HERBS (page 161)
FATTOUSH (page 285)
APPLES WITH LIME JUICE (page 312)

SIMPLE CHEESE, BREAD, AND MUSHROOM CASSEROLE (page 186)
TOSSED GREEN SALAD (page 280)
FRESH STRAWBERRIES

———

PATTYPAN SQUASH STUFFED WITH SAVORY ALMOND FILLING
(page 166)
RICE WITH MISO TOPPINGS** (page 134)
CHILLED TOFU WITH DIPPING SAUCES (page 132)
WATERCRESS AND MUSHROOM SALAD (page 292; omit tofu)
PEACHES WITH MARSALA (page 314)

———

PICANTE GARBANZOS (page 105)
LEFTOVER GRAINS SALAD* (page 293; use brown rice)
STEAMED ZUCCHINI
BANANA YOGURT FREEZE (page 315)

———

ASPARAGUS TIMBALE (page 193)
BAKED CELERY POTATO PUREE (page 154)
TOMATO SALAD (page 284)
STRAWBERRIES IN RED WINE AND PRESERVES SYRUP (page 314)

———

ROSEMARY'S CHILLED LETTUCE AND POTATO SOUP (page 81)
GRUYÈRE PUFFS (page 188)
MIDDLE EASTERN BEET SALAD (page 288)
SLICED MELON

———

BROCCOLI OR CAULIFLOWER "GRATIN" WITH TOFU CREAM SAUCE
(page 143)
TABOULI (with or without pressure-cooked garbanzos) (page 286)
FRESH PEARS

———

HOT AND SOUR SOUP (page 67)
STEAMED VEGETABLES OF YOUR CHOICE
BROWN RICE** (page 96)
ORANGE ICE (page 318)

———

GAZPACHO (page 87)
SPINACH AND RICE GRATIN* (page 197)
TOSSED GREEN SALAD (page 280)
SLICED PEACHES

———

*Auxiliary recipe
**Cook additional or save leftovers for auxiliary recipe.

CHEESE, STRING BEAN, AND SESAME CASSEROLE (page 194)
TURNIPS WITH LEMON AND HONEY (page 173)
MILLET OR COUSCOUS
TOSSED GREEN SALAD (page 280)
FIGS POACHED IN MADEIRA (page 311)

———

HOT AND SOUR BUCKWHEAT NOODLE SALAD (page 300)
MUSHROOMS WITH WHITE WINE AND HERBS (page 158)
SLICED TOMATOES
PINEAPPLE BANANA MINT SHERBET (page 316)

———

SIMPLE CHEESE, BREAD, AND MUSHROOM CASSEROLE (page 186)
STEAMED STRING BEANS
TOSSED GREEN SALAD (page 280)
STRAWBERRIES IN RED WINE AND PRESERVES SYRUP (page 310)

———

TOFU CUTLETS (page 131)
THIN-SLICED CAULIFLOWER WITH SESAME SEEDS AND GINGER
(page 151)
BROWN RICE (page 96)**
ORIENTAL SALAD (page 297)
BANANA YOGURT FREEZE (page 315)

———

AVOCADO TACOS (page 263)
CARROTS WITH DILL (page 150)
LETTUCE SALAD WITH ORANGES (page 281)
RICE OR LEFTOVER GRAINS PUDDING* (page 321)

———

PIPÉRADE (page 184)
BAKED CELERY POTATO PUREE (page 154)
TOSSED GREEN SALAD (page 280)
PEACHES WITH MARSALA (page 314)

———

SIMPLE GARLIC SOUP PROVENÇAL (page 64)
PASTA WITH COTTAGE CHEESE OR RICOTTA AND TOMATO SAUCE
(page 208)
TOSSED GREEN SALAD (page 280)
ORANGE ICE (page 318)

———

A BIG POT OF BEANS (page 98)
RICH JALAPEÑO CORNBREAD (page 53)
STEAMED BROCCOLI
CURRIED CARROT SALAD (page 284)
APPLES WITH LIME JUICE (page 312)

*Auxiliary recipe
**Cook additional or save leftovers for auxiliary recipe.

ADDITIONAL MENUS FOR SUMMER

Braised Stuffed Artichokes in Wine (page 116)
Mushrooms with White Wine and Herbs (page 158)
Fattoush (page 285)
Pineapple Banana Mint Sherbet (page 316)

Leftover Grains Salad* (page 293)
Zucchini with Rosemary or other herbs (page 167)
Tomato Salad (page 284)
Puffed Grand Marnier Omelet (page 307)

Tomato and Mozzarella Salad (page 282)
Pasta with Broccoli, Calabrian Style (page 213)
Orange Ice (page 318)

Chilled Tofu With Dipping Sauces (page 132)
Chinese-Style Vegetables, with Couscous (or bulgur)
(page 137)
Cucumber Yogurt Salad (page 282)
Fresh peaches

Chilled Buttermilk Soup (page 86)
Pattypan Squash Stuffed with Savory Almond Filling
(page 166)
Tossed Green Salad (page 280)
Banana Yogurt Freeze (page 315)

Chilled Pureed Zucchini Soup (page 70)
Curried Cauliflower Puree (page 79)
Watercress, Mushroom, and Tofu Salad (page 292)
Melon

Tofu and Poblano Tacos (page 268)
Jícama and Orange Salad with Avocados (page 295)
Minted Fresh Peas (page 160)
Figs Poached in Madeira (page 311)

Rosemary's Chilled Lettuce and Potato Soup (page 81)
Tomato Salad (page 284)
Steamed asparagus
Bread Pudding (page 320)

*Auxiliary recipe

FAST VEGETARIAN FEASTS

WHOLE-WHEAT PITA OR BREAD
TABOULI WITH PRESSURE-COOKED GARBANZOS (page 286)
MIDDLE EASTERN BEET SALAD (page 288)
WHITE BEAN PÂTÉ (page 55)
STRAWBERRY SHERBET (page 317)
FRUIT AND CHEESE PLATTER (page 322)

———

FLORENTINE TOMATOES (page 171)
WARM POTATO SALAD WITH CARAWAY (page 291)
STEAMED SUMMER SQUASH
PUFFED AMARETTO OMELET (page 306)

———

UPAMA (page 126)
COOKED CURRIED CUCUMBERS (page 156)
CURRIED CARROT SALAD (page 284)
WATERMELON

———

RISI E BISI** (page 108)
TOMATO SALAD (page 284)
TOSSED GREEN SALAD (page 280)
SLICED MELON (with any of the accompaniments on page 313)

———

TOMATOES STUFFED WITH RICE AND LENTILS* (page 113)
TOSSED GREEN SALAD (page 280)
STEAMED CAULIFLOWER
SLICED PEACHES

———

CORN PUDDING (page 196)
GREEN BEANS À LA PROVENÇAL (page 147)
FATTOUSH (page 285)
PEACH BANANA FREEZE (page 316)

———

HOT AND SOUR BUCKWHEAT NOODLE SALAD (page 300)
CHILLED TOFU WITH DIPPING SAUCES (page 132)
SZECHUAN-STYLE SWEET AND SOUR CHINESE CABBAGE (page 145)
ORANGE ICE (page 318)

———

ICED TOMATO SOUP (page 72)
ASPARAGI ALLA PARMIGIANA WITH POACHED EGGS (page 191)
TOSSED GREEN SALAD (page 280)
CANTALOUPE WITH APRICOT PUREE AND ALMONDS (page 313)

———

*Auxiliary recipes
**Cook additional or save leftovers for auxiliary recipe.

PRESSURE-COOKED BEANS** (page 98)
RICH JALAPEÑO CORNBREAD (page 53)
OKRA AND TOMATOES (page 159)
COLESLAW (page 295)
BANANA YOGURT FREEZE (page 315)

LEFTOVER BEANS SALAD* (page 294)
TOMATO SALAD (page 284)
CORN ON THE COB
WATERMELON

MIGAS (page 185)
GUACAMOLE (page 283)
STEAMED ZUCCHINI
STRAWBERRY FREEZE (page 317)

FETTUCCINE WITH PESTO (page 215)
TOMATO AND MOZZARELLA SALAD (page 282)
STEAMED ASPARAGUS
STRAWBERRIES IN RED WINE AND PRESERVES SYRUP (page 310)

*Auxiliary recipe
**Cook additional or save leftovers for auxiliary recipe.

ADDITIONAL MENUS FOR FALL

MISO SOUP WITH BUCKWHEAT NOODLES (page 70)
BAKED YAMS OR SWEET POTATOES WITH LIME (page 169)
HOT AND SOUR BEAN SPROUT SALAD (page 298)
ORANGE ICE (page 318)

SPICY EGGPLANT MISO SAUTÉ WITH BULGUR (page 122)
TOSSED GREEN SALAD (page 280)
PUFFED AMARETTO OMELET (page 306)

CHINESE-STYLE TOFU AND VEGETABLES (page 138)
BROWN RICE** (page 96)
ORIENTAL SALAD (page 301)
APPLES WITH LIME JUICE (page 312)

OMELET OF YOUR CHOICE (pages 176–183)
BAKED SWEET POTATO AND RUM CASSEROLE (page 169)
TOSSED GREEN SALAD (page 280)
RICE OR LEFTOVER GRAINS PUDDING* (page 321)

CREAMY CELERY AND GARLIC SOUP (page 76)
CAULIFLOWER BAKED WITH TOMATOES, CHEESE, AND SESAME
(page 195)
WATERCRESS AND MUSHROOM SALAD WITHOUT THE TOFU
(page 292)
TOFU NOODLE KUGEL (page 319)

BROWN RICE AND LENTILS** (page 112)
PEPPERS, TOMATOES, AND HERBS (page 161)
COLD MARINATED ZUCCHINI, ORIENTAL STYLE (page 301)
SLICED ORANGES WITH MINT

TOMATOES STUFFED WITH RICE AND LENTILS* (page 113)
SOUFFLÉED RUTABAGA PUREE (page 165)
TOSSED GREEN SALAD (page 280)
FRESH PEARS

EGGPLANT, POTATOES, AND MUSHROOMS BRAISED IN WHITE WINE
(page 157)
TOFU CUTLETS (page 131)
LETTUCE SALAD WITH ORANGES (page 281)
BANANA YOGURT FREEZE (page 315)

---

*Auxiliary recipe
**Cook additional or save leftovers for auxiliary recipe.

APPENDIX

A BIG POT OF BEANS (page 98)
DELICATE CORN FRITTERS, OR "CORN OYSTERS" (page 155)
TOSSED GREEN SALAD (page 280)
ORANGE ICE (page 318)

CREAM OF SPINACH AND POTATO SOUP (page 80)
TURNIPS WITH APPLES AND PORT (page 172)
LEFTOVER BEANS SALAD* (page 294)
GINGERED FRUIT (page 312)

CHEDDAR CHEESE SOUP WITH VEGETABLES (page 66)
TOSSED GREEN SALAD (page 280)
CARROTS COOKED IN VODKA (page 150)
PRUNE SOUFFLÉ (page 307)

TOMATO AND MOZZARELLA SALAD (page 282)
FETTUCINE WITH SPINACH PESTO (page 215)
SIMPLE STEAMED ZUCCHINI
PEARS POACHED IN RED WINE (page 309)

RISI E BISI** (page 108)
BROILED TOMATOES (page 170)
WATERCRESS, MUSHROOM, AND TOFU SALAD (page 292)
APPLES WITH LIME JUICE (page 312)

PICANTE GARBANZOS (page 105)
BROWN RICE (page 96)
TOSSED GREEN SALAD (page 280)
ORANGE ICE (page 318)

CELERY TOMATO SOUP WITH RICE (page 77)
SIMPLE CHEESE, BREAD, AND MUSHROOM CASSEROLE (page 186)
TOSSED GREEN SALAD (page 280)
BANANA YOGURT FREEZE (page 315)

POTATOES GRUYÈRE (page 198)
FLORENTINE TOMATOES (page 171)
WARM OR CHILLED CAULIFLOWER OR BROCCOLI VINAIGRETTE
(page 290)
STRAWBERRY SHERBET (page 317)

CREAM OF SPINACH AND KASHA SOUP (page 78)
SLICED TOMATOES
TOSSED GREEN SALAD (page 280)
FIGS POACHED IN MADEIRA (page 311)

---

*Auxiliary recipe
**Cook additional or save leftovers for auxiliary recipe.

Fast Vegetarian Feasts

Steamed Beets and Beet Greens (page 148)
Coleslaw (page 295)
Noodle Kugel (page 318)
Black-Eyed Peas (page 104) with Rich Jalapeño Cornbread
(page 53)

Red Wine "Risotto" With Cauliflower (page 111)
Zucchini with Rosemary or Other Herbs (page 167)
Tossed Green Salad (page 280)
Puffed Amaretto Omelet (page 306)

Chilled Tofu with Dipping Sauces (page 132)
Chinese-Style Snow Peas and Water Chestnuts (page 140)
Couscous
Fruit and Cheese Platter (page 322)

ADDITIONAL MENUS FOR WINTER

Hot Tomato Soup (page 72)
Kasha with Mushrooms, Water Chestnuts, and Celery**
(page 128)
Steamed broccoli
Curried Carrot Salad (page 284)
Fresh pears

Cabbage Leaves Stuffed with Kasha, with Creamy Tofu
Sauce* (page 130)
Steamed or Pressure-Cooked Beets and Beet Greens
(page 148)
Coleslaw (page 295)
Apricot Soufflé (page 308)

Avocado Tacos (page 263) with Salsa Fresca (page 261)
Steamed green vegetable of your choice
Watercress, Mushroom, and Tofu Salad (page 292)
Gingered Fruit (page 312)

Bulgur** and Purple Cabbage with Apples and Onions
(page 124)
Baked Potatoes (page 164)
Tossed Green Salad (page 280)
Prune Soufflé (page 307)

Simple Garlic Soup Provençal (page 64)
Tabouli with Pressure-Cooked Garbanzos (page 286)
Fruit and Cheese Platter (page 322)

Rosemary's Lettuce and Potato Soup (page 81)
Thin-Sliced Cauliflower with Sesame Seeds and Ginger
(page 151)
Grains (optional)
Tomato Salad (page 284)
Pears Poached in Red Wine (page 309)

Delicate Corn Fritters, or "Corn Oysters" (page 155)
Baked Yams or Sweet Potatoes with Lime (page 169)
Tossed Green Salad (page 280)
Noodle Kugel (page 318) or Tofu Noodle Kugel (page 319)

---

*Auxiliary recipe
**Cook additional or save leftovers for auxiliary recipe.

FAST VEGETARIAN FEASTS

A BIG POT OF BEANS** (page 98)
RICH JALAPEÑO CORNBREAD (page 53)
STEAMED BROCCOLI
LETTUCE SALAD WITH ORANGES (page 281)
STRAWBERRY FREEZE (page 317)

POTATO AND REFRIED BEAN TACOS* (page 264)
JÍCAMA AND ORANGE SALAD WITH AVOCADOS (page 295)
SIMPLY STEAMED CAULIFLOWER
GINGERED FRUIT (page 312)

CHEDDAR CHEESE SOUP WITH VEGETABLES (page 66)
MIXED GRAINS BREAD (page 45) OR HERBED TRITICALE BREAD
(page 51)
TOSSED GREEN SALAD (page 280)
APPLES WITH LIME JUICE (page 312)

PASTA AND TOMATO SAUCE WITH SOY GRITS (page 205)
MUSHROOMS WITH WHITE WINE AND HERBS (page 158)
TOSSED GREEN SALAD (page 280)
STRAWBERRY SHERBET (page 317) OR FRESH FRUIT

SWEET AND SOUR CABBAGE (page 141)
MILLET
CUCUMBER YOGURT SALAD (page 282)
FRESH FRUIT

BARLEY MUSHROOM PILAFF (page 127)
WARM BROCCOLI SALAD (page 290)
SLICED TOMATOES
FRUIT AND CHEESE PLATTER (page 322)

SPINACH AND MUSHROOM OMELET (page 176)
HOT AND SOUR BUCKWHEAT NOODLE SALAD (page 300)
BANANA YOGURT FREEZE (page 315)

HOT AND SOUR SOUP (page 67)
CHINESE CABBAGE WITH SESAME AND GINGER (page 144)
BROWN RICE AND SOY GRITS** (page 96)
TOSSED GREEN SALAD (page 280)
BREAD PUDDING (page 320)

---

*Auxiliary recipe
**Cook additional or save leftovers for auxiliary recipe.

FRIED RICE AND SOY GRITS WITH VEGETABLES* (page 114)
CURRIED CARROT SALAD (page 284)
PEARS POACHED IN WINE (page 309)

———

SIMPLE MISO SOUP (page 68)
CELERY POTATO "GRATIN" (page 142)
MIDDLE EASTERN BEET SALAD (page 288)
APPLES WITH LIME JUICE (page 312)

———

TOFU VEGETABLE CURRY (page 136)
MILLET**
COLESLAW (page 295)
ORANGE ICE (page 318)

———

ELEGANT PRESSURE-COOKED WHITE BEAN SOUP (page 74)
ZUCCHINI WITH ROSEMARY OR OTHER HERBS (page 167)
TOSSED GREEN SALAD (page 280)
RICE OR LEFTOVER GRAINS PUDDING (Millet)* (page 321)

———

BROCCOLI TIMBALE (page 192)
BAKED POTATOES (page 164)
TOMATO SALAD (page 284) OR TOSSED GREEN SALAD (page 280)
FRESH PEARS

———

LENTIL AND TOMATO SOUP WITH PASTA (page 84)
LETTUCE SALAD WITH ORANGES (page 281)
APRICOT SOUFFLÉ (page 308)

*Auxiliary recipe
**Cook additional or save leftovers for auxiliary recipe.

INDEX

Salad
  Cabbage and, 298
  Curried, 284–85
Cauliflower
  "Gratin," 143
  in Red Wine, 152
  Red Wine "Risotto" with, 111–12
  with Sesame Seeds and Ginger, 151
  Soup
    Cheese, 80
    Pureed Curry of, 79–80
  with Tomatoes, Cheese, and Sesame, Baked, 195
  Vinaigrette, Warm or Chilled, 290
Celery
  Kasha with Mushrooms, Water Chestnuts, and, 128–29
  and Potato
    "Gratin," 142–43
    Puree, Baked, 154
  Soup
    Creamy Garlic, 76–77
    Tomato, with Rice, 77–78
Ceviche, 255–56
Chalupas, 260
  Garnishes for, 261
Champagne, Strawberries in, 311
Cheese, 175
  Bread, and Mushroom Casserole, 186–87
  Cauliflower Baked with Tomatoes, Sesame, and, 195
  and Fruit, for Dessert, 322–25
  Gruyère
    Potatoes, 198
    Puffs, 188
    Turnips, 199
  Omelet Filling, 178
    Apple and, 179
    Strawberry and Brie, 179
  Parmesan
    Asparagus with, 190–91
    Asparagus with Poached Eggs and, 191–92

food processor for grating, 22
with Pasta. See Pasta Salad
  Mozzarella and Tomato, 282
  Tomato and, with Miso Dressing, 296
Soup
  Cauliflower, 80
  with Vegetables, 66–67
Spinach and Rice Gratin, 197
String Bean, and Sesame Casserole, 194
Tacos, Potato and, 266
Cherries, Garnishes for, 324
Chick-peas. See Garbanzos
Chilies. See Peppers, Hot
Chinese Cabbage
  with Sesame and Ginger, 144–45
  Sweet and Sour, Szechuan-Style, 145–46
Clementines, Garnishes for, 323
Cod, 228
  Broiled, with Coriander Sauce, 244–45
  Ceviche, 255–56
  Fillets with Tomato-Mint Sauce, 234–35
  Poached, with Baby Artichokes, 249–50
Coleslaw, 255
Complementary Proteins, 5–6
Concord Grapes, Garnishes for, 323
Coriander
  Grilled or Broiled Mackerel or Bluefish with Cumin and, 250–51
  Sauce, Broiled Fish with, 244–45
Corn
  Fritters, Delicate ("Corn Oysters"), 155
  Green Tomato, and Tofu Tacos, 270–71
  Pudding, 196
  and Rye Muffins, with Bran, 54
Cornbread
  Jalapeño, 53